Journal for the
Academic Study of
Magic

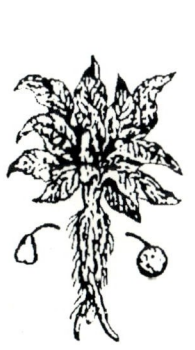

ISSN 1479-0750

ISBN 1869928 725

Published by Mandrake of Oxford, PO Box 250, Oxford, OX1 1AP, UK. http://www.mandrake.uk.net

In association with the Society for the Academic Study of Magic, c/o Dep't of Historical Studies, University of Bristol,
13 Woodland Road, Bristol, BS8 1TB, UK
http://www.sasm.co.uk/index.html

Bibliographic conventions: please cite as: David Evans (Ed.), *The Journal for the Academic Study of Magic,* 2, (Mandrake, Oxford, 2004)

Copyright of individual articles remains with the author(s), while editorial, style, layout etc of the Journal is © SASM, JSM and Mandrake of Oxford 2004.

All rights reserved. No part of this Journal may be reproduced or utilized in any form or by any means, electronic or mechanical including photocopying, recording or by any information storage and/or retrieval system, without express prior permission in writing from the Publishers.

Short extracts may be reproduced for review purposes. A copy of the review, and notification of where and when it appeared would be appreciated, sent to SASM please.

Journal for the Academic Study of Magic, Issue 2.
Editorial Note

It is with very great pleasure that I welcome you to Issue 2 of the JSM. This issue is considerable bigger in terms of page count than the first issue, and we intend to remain at this size and format in the future. We have received some very encouraging feedback from readers, for which we thank you, and trust that this volume will not disappoint. The scope and quality of submissions this time around was certainly most exciting and encouraging, and the range of academic disciplines from which people are studying magic seems to be ever-growing. The editorial board of the JSM has grown considerably since Issue 1 and we can now, justifiably, boast a versatile and skilled panel that mixes years of experience and academic respect with newer up-and-coming academics across many disciplines and spanning the world.

The Spring of 2004 sees the 100th anniversary of Aleister Crowley's *Book of the Law*, and it is to be hoped that the academic study of such matters is encouraged by the various events being organised around the world to coincide with the centenary of this hugely influential and still hotly-debated book in modern occultism. If the scope of academics in this field and the continued marvellous support of our publisher, Mandrake of Oxford, is any measure of the good health of the academic approach to the study of magic, then students of this area should be most heartened.

I look forward to writing the editorial for issue 3, to appear sometime in spring 2005

Dave Evans

General Editor

Spring 2004

Further details about the JSM, and extensive links and resources pages can be found on our website

www.sasm.co.uk/index.html and we can be contacted *via* email at **socacademicstudymagic@btopenworld.com**

We also maintain a mailing list for updates on the Journal (calls for papers, notification of publishing date etc) and a separate academic e-forum where researchers from any background can exchange ideas and generally 'network'.

Conference Report 2003: Magical Practice and Belief, 1800-2003

April 2003 saw our conference at Bristol University, organised by Alison Butler, which was a tremendous event with a captivating variety of speakers from both the academic and practical magic spheres. There was very lively debate, much enjoyed and appreciated, judging by the feedback we have received, from a very eclectic audience, who in many cases travelled a considerable distance to attend. The 'short format' talks provided a challenge to the speakers and allowed considerably more topics to be covered in a day than would other wise have been possible. It was most encouraging that we were being asked, "when's the next one?" by people before the lunch break. There <u>will</u> be another similar event held at some point, most likely in the Bristol area again, but it will be in 2005 at the very earliest due to various work commitments, since for such an event to run smoothly there is considerable effort required to arrange everything, including booking speakers well in advance.

The initial intent to produce a *Proceedings of….* volume was complicated by the fact that many speakers were presenting abridged versions of their current research which was already 'In Press' with other publishers, so we look forward instead to reviewing their books when they are published. One or two other pieces have already appeared on the internet, please see our website at http://www.sasm.co.uk/conf.html for more details. The conference would not have, been possible without the generous financial and practical support of University of Bristol Historical Studies Department, University of Bristol Alumni Foundation and the Royal Historical Society for which we are profoundly grateful.

Book Review Policy:

Following debate within the editorial panel about exactly what kind of books we should be reviewing (inspired by an unsolicited review copy of a very good practical magic book that we were sent by a publisher, and which is reviewed herein) we have reached the view that we would not be doing our job properly if we ignored what occultists are writing - this would be akin to producing a Journal about French culture yet reading nothing written in French or by a French person. This does not mean that we will be reviewing every last 'how to do spells' book, occult novel or collection of magical verse that is published, but we shall endeavour to cover some of the more significant books by practitioners in this and future issues, in a proportion of perhaps 1 practitioner titles to 4-5 academic titles. Would publishers and authors who wish to submit practical occultism books for review please contact us *first*, to discuss their potential review copies and whether we are able to review them. Thankyou.

Responses:

We welcome responses to articles, written in a reasoned, academic style and of less than 1000 words. If suitable these will be included in a future edition of the JSM, with a reply from the author of the original article. Responses of a longer nature will possibly warrant the respondent writing a full article for us.

A Technical Note for Prospective Authors:

As a multidisciplinary journal receiving articles from disparate scholars trained in multitudinous methods of citation we have decided that from JSM 3 onwards we will be moving to the somewhat more straightforward *Harvard* academic referencing system; since this seems to suit the majority of our submitting authors. Please see the website **www.sasm.co.uk/index.html** for further details on the implementation of this process. Full details of how to submit an article to the JSM can also be found there.

Contents

Conference Report 2003: Magical Practice and Belief, 1800-2003 4
Book Review Policy: 5
Responses: 5
A Technical Note for Prospective Authors: 5
JSM2 Contributors list, in Alphabetical Order: 10

Alien Selves: Modernity and the Social Diagnostics of the Demonic in 'Lovecraftian Magick'
Justin Woodman 13

Wishful Thinking? Notes towards a psychoanalytic sociology of Pagan magic
Dave Green 48

A Shell with my Name on it: The Reliance on the Supernatural During the First World War
Vanessa Chambers 79

The Metaphysical Relationship between Magic and Miracles
Morgan Luck 103

'I will not go to the Devil for a Cure' : Witchcraft, Demonic Possession, and Spiritual Healing in Nineteenth-Century Devon
Jason Semmens 132

The Human Body in Southern Slavic Folk Sorcery
Andrija Filipovic and Anne M. Rader 155

Four Glasses Of Water:
Lionel Snell 177

The Land Near the Dark Cornish Sea: The Development of Tintagel as a Celtic Pilgrimage Site
Amy Hale 206

Trafficking with an 'onslaught of compulsive weirdness':
Kenneth Grant and the Magickal revival
Dave Evans 226

Magic through the Linguistic Lenses of Greek mágos, Indo-European
*mag(h)-, Sanskrit *māyā* and Pharaonic Egyptian *Ḥeka*.
Aaron Cheak 260

Research Notes: The symbolism of the pierced heart
Joyce Froome 287

Shamanic Motifs in Fin-de-Siècle Russian Art: The Case of Nicholas
Roerich
John McCannon 300

Feature Book Review Section: Shamanism

Book Reviews 362

Obituaries 385

Editorial Board

General and Administrative Editor:
Dave Evans, University of Bristol

Peer Review Panel:
Dr. Jenny Blain (University of Sheffield, UK)
Alison Butler (recently completed PhD at University of Bristol, UK)
Dr. Owen Davies (University of Hertfordshire, UK)
Dr. Doug Ezzy (University of Tasmania, Australia)
Dr, Susan Johnston Graf (University of Pennsylvania, USA)
Dr. Dave Green (University of West of England, UK)
Matt Lee (recently completed PhD at University of Sussex, UK)
Prof. Sabina Magliocco (California State University, USA)
Prof. Sarah Pike (University of California, USA)
William Redwood (recently completed PhD at University College, London, UK)
Prof. Geoffrey Samuel (University of Newcastle, New South Wales, Australia)
Dr. Robert J Wallis (University of Southampton/American International University, London, UK)
Justin Woodman (recently completed PhD at Goldsmith's, London, UK)

In addition to the peer reviewers we have two dedicated book review panellists:
Neil L Inglis, a freelance writer who divides his time between the USA and UK, and
Bradley A. Skeen, a freelance researcher in Neoplatonism and Magic in St. Louis Missouri, USA.

JSM2 Contributors list, in Alphabetical Order:

Vanessa Chambers is a postgraduate student at the Institute of Historical Research, London.

Aaron Cheak is researching a PhD at the Religious Studies Dept, University of Queensland, Australia, and is an editor on the new Religious Studies Journal *Khthonios*.

Dr. Owen Davies lectures in History at the University of Hertfordshire and is a Peer Review editor for this journal.

Dave Evans is a PhD student in the history of 20th Century British Occultism at University of Bristol, and General-Admin Editor for this Journal.

Andrija Filipovic is a student at the University of Philosophy in Serbia.

Joyce Froome is a freelance author and an assistant curator at the Museum of Witchcraft, Boscastle, Cornwall, UK.

Dr. Dave Green lectures in sociology at the University of the West of England and is a Peer Review editor for this journal.

Dr. Amy Hale is Adjunct Professor in Humanities and Anthropology at the E-Campus of St. Petersburg College, St. Petersburg, Florida, USA.

Neil L Inglis is a freelance writer who divides his time between the USA and the UK, and a book reviewer for this journal.

Matt Lee has recently completed his PhD in Philosophy at University of Sussex, is a film-maker, editor of the Chaos Magick journal *Razor Smile* (www.indifference.demon.co.uk/) and is a Peer Review editor for this journal

Morgan Luck is researching a PhD in philosophy at the University of Nottingham, UK, concerning the metaphysics of miracles.

Sabina Magliocco is Associate Professor in Anthropology at California State University and is a Peer Review editor for this journal.

John McCannon is Assistant Professor of History at the University of Saskatchewan, Canada.

Anne M Rader is pursuing a graduate degree in Waldorf education at Mount Mary College, USA and is preparing a book for educators on 'story as a teaching tool'. She is the moderator of an egroup for discussion of Sabbatic Craft: http://groups.yahoo.com/group/The_Witches_Sabbath/

William Redwood has recently completed a PhD in Anthropology at University College, London and is a Peer Review editor for this journal.

Jason Semmens is a post-graduate researcher and a Museums Documentation Officer in South Wales. He is currently researching witchcraft beliefs and practices in Cornwall and Devon, and has contributed papers to local history and peer-reviewed academic journals.

Bradley A. Skeen is a freelance researcher in Neoplatonism and Magic in St. Louis Missouri, USA. Other publications include a piece on Graeco-Egyptian magic in *Die Zeitschrift für Papyrolgie und Epigraphik*, and he is a book reviewer for this journal.

Lionel Snell (*a.k.a.* **Ramsey Dukes**) is a magician, occult philosopher, long-standing author of numerous books, and is based in London. See www.occultebooks.com

Dr. Robert J Wallis is an Archaeologist and Art Historian, based at the American International University in London, and Southampton University, and he is a Peer Review editor for this journal.

Justin Woodman has recently completed a PhD in Anthropology at Goldsmiths in London and is a Peer Review editor for this journal.

Alien Selves: Modernity and the Social Diagnostics of the Demonic in 'Lovecraftian Magick'.

Justin Woodman

Introduction

This article examines the significance of the category of the 'demonic' as applied within the theory and practice of 'Lovecraftian' magick [1]: a 'style' of magical practice inspired by the fictional universe of the 'Cthulhu mythos' created by the author H. P. Lovecraft, and popularised within certain sectors of the contemporary Euro-American magical subculture. For these contemporary 'Lovecraftian' magicians, the demonic is mobilised as a potent 'apocalyptic' weapon in contesting the alienating consequences of modernity, and forms an ambivalent moral category distinct from Christianised conceptions of supernatural evil. An equivalent moral ambivalence has also been noted in a number of recent anthropological accounts of postcolonial African modernities [2] - modernities partly characterised by an emerging (and global) tendency 'to interpret modern processes of change in terms of 'witchcraft" [3]. These accounts recognise that the idiom of the demonic - both in African contexts and more widely - encompasses a simultaneous fascination with and desire to be 'modern', and a deep anxiety about where society is heading. The demonic, in this understanding, is not a barrier or resistance to change...Rather, the proliferation of images of excess or evil might actually be seen as part and parcel of that 'modernity'...This signals a moral indeterminacy or ambivalence that rails against the prevailing dualistic assumptions that have characterized the study of morality.[4]

Within this reading, indigenous conceptions of witchcraft, the supernatural powers of evil, and other 'occult' forces have come to be treated as

> a form of historical consciousness, a sort of social diagnostics...that try to explain why the world is the way it is, why it is changing and moving in a particular manner at the moment.[5]

Valuable though they are, by placing African witchcraft at the centre of their analyses [6] many of these accounts unwittingly reproduce problematic representations of the non-Western Other: as 'primitive' and otherwise unable to grasp the complexity of modernising processes in 'rational' socio-economic terms [7]. The alternative - followed here - is to retain the usefulness of these recent theoretical formulations by further demonstrating that the transglobal processes of modernisation (and the forms of subjectification they generate) are equally intangible to everyday Euro-American thought, and that contemporary Western magical conceptions of the demonic constitute a comparable idiom for understanding these occluded processes. Specifically, I locate my discussion around a group of 'Lovecraftian' magicians' calling themselves the 'Haunters of the Dark' (hereafter referred to as the HOD), who formed the focus of anthropological fieldwork conducted in London between 1999 and 2001. The ambivalent character of the demonic was powerfully evident in the HOD's spirit possession practices: within the group's loosely ritualised encounters with otherworldly forces, the demonic did not represent a source of absolute evil, but constituted a form of 'alien otherness' disruptive of the rationalising aspects of modernity. While such practices critiqued a conception of modernity-as-instrumental rationality[8], they nonetheless gave voice - via the ambivalent character of the demonic - to a perception of modernity as both problematic *and* desirable. As a consequence, Lovecraftian magick not only resists but celebrates modernity in its various, multiple guises[9]: whether conceived of as a postmodernity in which the universalising Enlightenment metanarrative of rational progress is reduced to a localised, situated discourse; or as late / reflexive modernity, which does not so much reject the progressive trajectory of Enlightenment epistemology as recognise that the radical doubt which 'was always at the origin of the Enlightenment's claims to certainty, becomes thoroughly exposed to view.[10] Whilst the disparate theoretical articulations of both late- and post-modernities mark out incommensurable conceptual terrains, they nonetheless share a central concern with uncertainty [11]. In either case, the HOD's engagement with a 'demonic alter' was indented in the processual and contingent production of selfhood via the interiorisation and transformation of uncertainty[12], and practitioners' viewed their own sense of self as emergent from and creatively aligned with the indeterminacy said to characterise the social matrix of modernity.

Lovecraftian magick is, then, not so much marginal to the perceived hegemonic centres of modernity, but exists in a juxtaposed relationship with those (increasingly contingent) centres [13]. The analyses presented here is, therefore, one which seeks to overcome those oppositional metanarratives (i.e. centre-periphery / marginal-mainstream / accommodation - resistance) which have largely circumscribed the theorising of 'subcultures' within the social sciences [14].

The Cthulhu Mythos: An Overview

Originating in a series of loosely-connected stories written by the American writer of supernatural fiction Howard Philips Lovecraft (1890 - 1937), and developed by other genre writers[15], the Cthulhu mythos constitutes a nebulous fictional myth-cycle concerning the 'Great Old Ones' or 'Old Ones' - described by the Lovecraftian magician Zebulon as 'transdimensional entities...who, 'when the stars are right', can enter into our world via psychic or physical gateways'.[16] The eponymous Cthulhu (a mountainous squid-like extraterrestrial entombed in the city of R'lyeh beneath the Pacific Ocean) is perhaps the best known of Lovecraft's Old Ones; others include Yog Sothoth, Nyarlathotep, Shub Niggurath, and Azathoth. These entities are typically depicted as vastly ancient, amoral, cosmic monstrosities, which inhabit chaotic, liminal spaces beyond the rational and ordered universe of human perception. Whilst there is said to exist a global but secretive cabal of cults seeking to facilitate the return of these monstrous beings, those humans unfortunate enough to encounter the Old Ones are invariably sent insane, or otherwise meet some horrible (and usually unspeakable) doom.

More importantly for Lovecraft - a self-styled 'mechanistic materialist'[17] - the Old Ones gave voice to the writer's own 'cosmic' brand of philosophical pessimism: therein, the human subject becomes alienated and decentred by the knowledge of its own insignificance in a blind and ultimately purposeless cosmos.[18] In the opening paragraph of *The Call of Cthulhu* - the narrative of which concerns the irrevocable eventuality of Cthulhu's apocalyptic awakening from an aeon-long slumber - Lovecraft thus writes:

We live on a placid island of ignorance in the midst of black seas of infinity, and it was not meant that we should voyage far. The sciences, each straining in its own direction, have hitherto harmed us little; but some day the piecing together of dissociated knowledge will open up such terrifying vistas of reality, and of our frightful position therein, that we shall either go mad from the revelation or flee from the deadly light into the peace and safety of a new dark age'.[19]

Such knowledge - a canon of 'forbidden' or 'blasphemous' lore detailing the monstrous antediluvian world of the Old Ones - forms a thematic cornerstone of the Cthulhu mythos: one which undermines anthropocentric assumptions that 'man is either the oldest of the last or earth's masters, or that the common bulk of life and substance walks alone'.[20] Although usually of pre-human provenance, this lore is nonetheless contained within archaic tomes, 'black books', and 'nameless' grimoires written by the Old Ones' human and less-than-human worshippers. Foremost of these tomes is the (wholly fictional) *Necronomicon*, supposedly written by the (equally fictive) 'Mad Arab' Abdul Alhazred in Damascus during the 8th Century C.E., and later translated into English by the very real Elizabethan magus, John Dee[21]. This blurring of fact and fiction - a key feature of the Lovecraft's literary methodology - has led some occultists to assume, erroneously, that the atheist Lovecraft actually believed in the veracity of the Cthulhu mythos. Exacerbated by a number of scholarly essays contained in one published version of the *Necronomicon*[22], a new mythology has emerged linking

Lovecraft to the ceremonial magician Aleister Crowley [23], and claiming that Lovecraft was in fact inspired by an authentic body of esoteric lore. As a further testament to the power of Lovecraft's fictive milieu, over twenty other versions of Lovecraft's fabled *Necronomicon* have been published since the 1950s.[24] No longer a literary device but a manifest social reality, one edition of the *Necronomicon* has even been cited in an unsubstantiated case of 'Satanic' crime.[25]

The Cthulhu Mythos and the Left-Hand Path

As a consequence of the Old Ones' eventual return to our world, Lovecraft tell us that

> mankind would...become as the Great Old Ones; free and wild and beyond good and evil, with laws and morals thrown aside and all men shouting and killing and revelling in joy. Then the liberated Old Ones would teach them new ways to shout and kill and revel and enjoy themselves, and all the earth would flame with a holocaust of ecstasy and freedom.[26]

Perhaps as a result of these powerfully transgressive and antinomian sentiments, the Cthulhu mythos has found favour amongst those interested in the 'darkside' of the Western occult tradition - otherwise denoted by the popular misnomer 'black magic' - and problematically defined by Richard Cavendish as a morally reprehensible attempt at self-deification through association with the powers of evil[27]. Richard Sutcliffe has rightly criticised this view as an 'outmoded and value-laden'[28] misperception of the 'Left-Hand Path': a term derived from Eastern Tantric traditions.[29] For Sutcliffe, the Left-Hand Path variously encompasses Western forms of Tantra, Aleister Crowley's magical philosophy of Thelema, and Chaos magick - groupings which are not concerned with the celebration of evil, but with an (often transgressive)

> attempt to engage in magical praxis which does not accept externally imposed limitations, but rather tries to celebrate the totality of human experience in all of its folly and grandeur.[30]

The ultimate aim of such praxis is 'to unite the microcosmic human with the macrocosmic Universe'[31], sharing with neo-paganism and the New Age a focus on the 'spiritualised' or non-egoic self. However, in this respect Sutcliffe's definition does require some qualification: while many Thelemic magicians identify themselves as followers of the Left-Hand Path, others equate the term with the selfish and egoistic pursuit of power - contemporary Satanism being a case in point. Satanists often refer to themselves as followers of the Left-Hand Path, but - insofar as their ideology often values egoic self-deification over spiritual transcendence - form an exception to Sutcliffe's definition.

Lovecraftian magick places a marked emphasis on self-knowledge and self-transformation by transgressing the perceived limitations of human and social norms, and as such constitutes a form of Left Hand Path praxis. However, this is a somewhat arbitrary categorisation, as Lovecraftian magick does not inhabit a discrete subcultural niche; the term is thus applied here as a broad and permeable category, denoting the often eclectic use of the Cthulhu mythos by diverse groups and individuals as an unfixed and nebulous mytho-fictional resource. As such, Lovecraftian magick is constituted within a complex and overlapping set of genealogical relations, a summarised version of which is presented in the following section.

A Genealogy of 'Lovecraftian Magick'

One of the key figures responsible for bringing Lovecraft's work to the centre of contemporary magical theory and practice is Kenneth Grant - an associate of the ceremonial magician Aleister Crowley, and also a one-time member of the Crowley-led Ordo Templi Orientis (OTO). During the 1950's, Grant claimed to be in contact with extraterrestrial forces which he came to identify with Lovecraft's Old Ones;[32] his subsequent exegesis of Crowley's writings led Grant to suppose that they contained a system for communing with these very same forces - a reading of Crowley's magical philosophy which may have been instrumental in Grant's expulsion from the OTO (now known as the Caliphate OTO). Grant later founded the Typhonian OTO, a group that has since explored connections between Lovecraft's fiction and the occult systems of both Crowley and the magician and visionary artist

Austin Osman Spare (sometimes referred to as the 'grandfather' of Chaos magick)[33].

Lovecraft's fiction gained widespread recognition in North America during the 1970s [34] - particularly within the then burgeoning counterculture.[35] This period also saw the rise of Anton LaVey's San Francisco-based Church of Satan, which incorporated elements of the Cthulhu mythos in its ritual practices[36] - as did the Temple of Set, a later schismatic offshoot led by ex-Church of Satan member Michael Aquino[37]. During this time Grant had also begun to collate his findings in a series of influential publications (collectively known as the 'Typhonian Trilogies')[38]. In these books, Grant has suggested that, by allowing the Old Ones ingress into the human consciousness, humanity can reclaim its extraterrestrial evolutionary heritage and attain cosmic consciousness in doing so.[39]

The 'extraterrestrialist' project visible in Grant's work has also been coupled with that found in the countercultural writings of Timothy Leary, Robert Anton Wilson and William Burroughs. These sources have also informed the "stellar" magicks currently being developed by Left-Hand Path magicians, largely in response to the perceived biological imperative of making an evolutionary leap off planet.

The work of both Grant and LaVey also exerted a formative influence on the ideas of later Lovecraftian groups including the Esoteric Order of Dagon (EOD): a North American magical order styling itself as 'an occult Order descended from the Sirius-mystery cults of ancient Egypt, Babylon and Sumeria'.[40] The EOD emerged in the late 1980s as one of the first organisation (with members spread across North America and the United Kingdom)[41] dedicated solely to an occult exegesis of Lovecraft's fictional myth cycle.

More recent magical elaborations of the Cthulhu mythos are found in the practice of 'Chaos magick', which appeared in the United Kingdom during the late 1970s. The tenets of Chaos magick are partly derived from popular exegeses of quantum theory and the science of 'chaos' or 'non-linear dynamics' - ideas which have been used to promote and legitimise the

'Chaoist' view that observable reality is founded upon indeterministic, acausal, and non-teleological bases. In the face of this ontological uncertainty - and underpinned by the desire to achieve liberation from the alienating effects of social indoctrination - Chaos magicians advocate a radical epistemological and moral relativism (encapsulated in the motto 'Nothing is True, Everything is Permitted'). This relativism underpins the Chaos magical practice of *paradigm shifting,* by which practitioners attempt to switch between belief systems (sometimes arbitrarily) in order to unmask the contingency and socially-valorised nature of supposedly monolithic worldviews. Although Chaos magicians regularly appropriate recognised cultural systems as part of this practice, they also 'invest belief' in self-invented or fictional cosmologies - Lovecraft's Cthulhu mythos being a case in point - in order to undermine those culturally-indented categorical distinctions which separate the 'real' from the 'unreal'. The popularity of the Cthulhu mythos amongst Chaos magicians is also a consequence of its promotion as a workable magical 'paradigm' by the influential magician Phil Hine[42] (whose website[43] also forms an important on-line repository of Lovecraftian magical material).

This briefly-sketched cultural and historical framework constitutes the foundation upon which the Haunters of the Dark formulated their own explorations of the Cthulhu mythos - explorations which, I suggest, can be taken as an index of wider anxieties produced by the experience of modernity, where indeterminacy (like Lovecraft's fictive deity, the 'blind idiot god' Azathoth) reigns supreme.

The Haunters of the Dark: Making the Old Ones Manifest

The Haunters of the Dark[44] - who I first met at a pagan moot in central London during September 1999 - was comprised of eight male members (myself included), most of who identified themselves as Chaos magicians[45]: Jason, a twenty-seven year old art student; Guy, another student in his late twenties; Alan, a civil servant in his late forties; Rob, an internet researcher in his late twenties; Stuart, an administrative assistant in his late-thirties (who only remained with the group for a short time); Damien, a psychology graduate in his mid-twenties who worked in an occult bookshop; and Dane, a freelance writer and internet researcher in his early thirties. From October 1999, the HOD met on a twice-monthly basis in various London pubs; these meetings comprised largely of preparatory discussions, which enabled the group not only to determine aims and objectives, but also to evolve itself - along broadly Chaos magical lines - as a largely informal body without a visible hierarchy or structure.

In 2000, the HOD began conducting a series of spirit possession rituals - performed at roughly one-month intervals - by which they hoped to communicate with the Old Ones. The first ritual was held during February 2000 in a room above the bookshop where Dane worked. Rob had previously noted that the entity known as Nyarlathotep - a darkly satanic entity described by Lovecraft as the ' 'Black Man' of the witch-cult'[46] - was often depicted as an anthropomorphic intermediary between humanity and the Old Ones[47]; it was thus decided that for this first ritual, a preliminary encounter with Nyarlathotep would best prepare the group for later experiences involving the wholly-other Old Ones.

On the occasion of the group's fourth possession ritual (which occurred in July 2000), the HOD met at an area of urban woodland area in north London - by which time the group had evolved a style of practice which became stereotypical of later rituals. On this occasion, the Old One Shub Niggurath - a perverse alien fertility deity sometimes depicted as an amorphous, protoplasmic cloud and known as the 'Black Goat of the Woods with a Thousand Young' - was to be invoked, with Damien acting as the receptacle for the entity's incarnation.

The ritual took place under the cover of darkness in a clearing in the woodland. After each of the participants had donned black robes and gathered in a circle, Alan - who led the ritual proceedings on this occasion - asked Damien to kneel in the centre of the group; using a ritual liturgy he had prepared some days earlier, Alan proceeded to invoke Shub Niggurath whilst the rest of the group repeatedly chanted 'Ia Shub Niggurath'. As we raised the chant, Damien began hyperventilating - a method commonly used by the group to facilitate entrance into the requisite trance state. When

Alan had judged that Shub Niggurath had taken possession of Damien, he gestured to us to stop chanting. Damien arose unsteadily from the floor, head bowed, and began wandering aimlessly around the perimeter of the circle. Alan then addressed the possessing entity:

> Alan: Who are you?
> Damien/Shub Niggurath: Dirt and leaves and soil.
> A: Shub Niggurath, Black Goat of the Woods with a Thousand Young, will you answer the questions of those who call you forth?
> D/SN: Ask.
> Dane: Tell us your secret word.
> D/SN: What are you to me? I am my will. What is it to you? I have nothing to share with you.
> A: Will you answer our questions? Give to us your power?
> D/SN: Give me your questions.
> A: What word shall we use to summon you?
> D/SN: By my name am I called. No word is needed.
> Dane: I have a question, Black Goat of the Woods. Which direction will our workings take next?
> D/SN: Your...your workings are not me. You are [pause] you are products. You are not me.
> Rob: Shub Niggurath, how should we serve you?
> D/SN: To do, to act, to serve my will, my [pause] not my will.
> R: Not your will?
> D/SN: My will is the sound of the trees, of the rivers, of the grass, the sound of the soil is my will. My will is not you. Give me your questions.
> [...]
> R: Shub Niggurath, how may we serve you?
> D/SN: You may serve me by being what is truest to you, by doing you truest nature, your truest will. Finding that for yourself, you may serve me.
> [...]
> A: Black Goat of the Woods with a Thousand Young, be again at the centre of us, we thank you for your presence, we thank you

for your power. We ask you now that you return to your preferred place in the Dark of The Woods, and leave the mind and body of this our brother Damien. We bid you hail and farewell.

The HOD's possession rituals were founded upon a habitual core of trance-facilitating techniques, but beyond this basic question-and-answer format, ritual formed a volatile, unstructured and negotiable space. By the following year group members also began referring to themselves as being part of a 'post-Lovecraftian' group, as entities and forces (variously known as 'Uranakai', 'Lazul' and 'Orzaz') - hitherto unknown within the 'canon' of the Cthulhu mythos - began to spontaneously manifest via possession.

Alan believed that while the Old Ones haunted a perceptual strata 'below and beyond normal human consciousness', they nevertheless formed an intrinsic component of the human psyche. The HOD's practices were thus founded upon a holistic framework which recognised an ontological unity between the Old Ones and human beings - a fact which was often confirmed via dialogue with the Old Ones. The first example is taken from the group's very first possession, involving Nyarlathotep:

> Jason: Nyarlathotep, how do we evolve humanity into something else?
> Nyarlathotep: *Seek for me within* and go beyond the form before you into
> Chaos (my emphasis).

The following exchange occurred during a ritual possession by the Old One Hastur:

> Rob: Are we of the Old Ones?
> Hastur: Yes, and the Old Ones are of you.

Also significant is Shub Niggurath's reply to Rob's repeated question 'How may we serve you?': 'You may serve me by being what is truest to you, by doing you truest nature, your truest will. Finding that for yourself, you may serve me'. This suggests, indirectly, an ontological permeability between human consciousness and that of the Old Ones.

Ultimately, the HOD saw themselves as preparing a psychic conduit through which the Old Ones could enter our world. According to Jason, this would precipitate 'an apocalypse of consciousness', or the awareness of reality divested of the veneer of socialisation and moral conditioning. In contrast to Lovecraft's bleak nihilism, the group held that such an 'apocalypse' would force the human species to abandon its petty moral, ethnic, religious and national differences, and make the evolutionary quantum leap into an 'extraterrestrial' mode of existence,

During the early stages of the HOD's formation, Jason suggested that if they hoped to attain an awareness of the Old Ones as aspects of human consciousness, the group should not conclude their possession rites by attempting to exorcise the Old Ones' presence. As a consequence, participants sometimes reported that the Old Ones continued to interpenetrate their everyday awareness days or even weeks after possession rituals. This often resulted in feelings of paranoia, personal dissolution, and even physical illness. However frightening, such experiences were seen to precipitate the 'apocalypse of consciousness', shunting participants - sometimes unwillingly - into a 'new mode of being'.

Alien Selves: Becoming Hybrid

The HOD did not, therefore, seek to worship the Old Ones; rather, they sought *identification* with them as avatars of a 'post-human' metamorphosis; similarly, the Satanist Anton LaVey refers to the Old Ones as 'the spectres of a future human mentality'[48] - a view echoed by Rob, who suggested that 'the Old Ones are our future selves who only appear as monstrous because we lack the language to directly perceive them'. Accordingly, Rob felt that the Old Ones represented

> our evolutionary heritage. They are memories of dinosaurs, the silence of space, and the primordial chaos of the big bang. In order for the human species to evolve beyond it current status of clever talking chimp, we must somehow find a way to awaken

these long forgotten elements that shaped the development of our consciousness.

He also added that Lovecraftian magick was fundamentally concerned with

> waking up the Great Old Ones that lie sleeping...the primeval consciousness of the universe which has been lying dormant in humanity but is now slowly waking up...becoming the monsters ourselves.

Dane similarly noted that possession by the Old Ones constituted a method of 'trying to approach the unthinkable through the monstrous'. Rob referred this identification-with-monstrous-otherness as 'interspecies symbiosis'[49], noting that Lovecraft commonly used the themes of human-alien hybridity and miscegenation to evoke horror and disgust in his tales; for example, in the story 'The Shadow Over Innsmouth' Lovecraft introduces the 'Deep Ones': a race of batrachian, sea-dwelling humanoids who worship Cthulhu and mate with humans to produce monstrous but immortal offspring[50].

A month or so prior to the Shub Niggurath possession, the group conducted a 'shapeshifting' ritual by which they sought to encompassing the transformative effects of hybridity by assuming the mantle of Deep One consciousness and identity[51]. On this occasion I was asked to lead the ritual, which took the form of a 'pathworking' or guided-imagery exercise designed to facilitate the participants' ideational transformation into Deep Ones:

> Imagine floating in deep, green waters; those waters begin to churn in a gentle whirlpool pattern around you, drawing you deeper and deeper, ever downwards. Down past the rough hulking shapes of early human consciousness, the instinctual drives of flight or fight of your mammalian ancestors, down past the sleek alien ripples of reptilian consciousness, returning to the warm womb of the sea where you float at the brink of the blackest, atavistic depths of amphibian consciousness, the ancient dream-time of Cthulhu...your limbs become fluid and undulating;

> fins sprout from your back and your skin takes on the sheen of
> **beautiful iridescent scales that shimmer in the darkness**...you sense
> in the distance other presences writhing in the dark waters, and
> you cry out to them with a profound sense of kinship, a guttural,
> inarticulate, prehuman croaking - the primal tongue of the Deep
> Ones. Your joyful cry reaches out to touch those swimmers in
> darkness, your brothers and sisters the Deep Ones, drawing them
> toward you. Within that darkness the inhuman sound of your call
> coalesces to take form and substance as a symbol of
> power...your cry dissipates across time and space drawing you
> back to your human form in the here and now.

As the ritual progressed, the participants' movements became more sluggish as they adopted hunched or awkward poses whilst making low, inhuman-sounding noises. Afterwards, members of the HOD reported that they had felt themselves changing, returning to the primeval roots of consciousness, where human selfhood and alien Deep One fused.

'Not in the Spaces We Know, But Between Them'

This concern with identification with a monstrous other is an ideational manifestation of Left Hand Path magick's transgressive sensibility, derived from Aleister Crowley's millenarian notion of the 'Aeon of Horus': a new spiritual *zeitgeist* heralding a self-liberating time of 'Force and Fire'[52] (and mirrored in the Nietzschean strains of Lovecraft's own apocalypticism).

Thus, the practice of Lovecraftian magick was, according to Dane, all about 'calling on the Old Ones to liberate us from society'. Likewise, Phil Hine claims that encounters with such forces of unreason are fundamental to the emancipatory project of magic: to stand in the presence of the Old Ones is, Hine suggests, to embrace madness as a radical metamorphosis of awareness and become transformed by the experience. Hine also describes this as 'becoming 'alien'', an 'evolution into a new mode of being'[53] which confers total autonomy from the values and judgements of society of large.

To embrace the alien, to become monstrous or hybrid, is also to step into the margins between boundaries. Drawing on Mary Douglas'[54] symbolic analysis of anomaly and marginality, Martin Bridgestock[55] argues that a concern with the marginal, the anomalous, and the interstitial is characteristic of horror fiction: it is the incursion of chaos - the violation of established cultural codes and categories - which generates the experience of horror. Lovecraft's Old Ones evoke such feelings because they exist '[n]ot in the spaces we know, but *between* them'[56]: inhabiting 'the borderland between mental categories', such entities threaten 'our entire system of thought and, by implication, the society which generates it'.[57] Chaos threatens to disrupt socially-inscribed conceptual categories but is also the source from which the initial categories of thought are drawn.[58] As James Kneale notes, 'while we might inevitably locate the place of horror on the threshold...we do not have to value these thresholds in the entirely negative way that Lovecraft did'[59]; in seeking the erosion of socially-normative, differentiating boundaries through contact with marginal, 'demonic' beings, Lovecraftian magicians are also seeking an experience of undifferentiated completeness. As a case in point, members of the HOD did, indeed, view the evocation of horror as inducing an experience of the sacred[60].

This concern with the marginal was often mapped onto the social spaces utilised by the HOD. According to Levy, Mageo and Howard, '[t]he poorly-lighted night and the socially uncolonized spaces (bush, forest, wilderness) around communities are perfect settings for uncanny experiences'.[61] These notions are congruent with the urban context in which Chaos magick is often practised, where the uncanny is located in socially uncolonized or liminal spaces: deserted churches, cellars, squats, subway tunnels, urban woodlands, sewers, and areas of pronounced urban decay. Although such spaces are no longer associated with the irruptions of the uncanny, in the cultural imagination they have become populated with other peripheral and dangerous figures: rapists, child-murderers and drug addicts.[62] For a time, the HOD transferred their site of operations to a derelict hospital in South London: members of the group reported that the palpable sense of fear experienced while winding their way through the vast and unlit building (which was occasionally patrolled by security guards) facilitated states of trance and possession.

For Lovecraftian magicians, these sites provide a physical manifestation of what Kenneth Grant calls 'the Portals of Inbetweeness'[63] : magical gateways leading to 'the zones of Non-Being'.[64] Grant also refers to these 'zones' as the Tunnels of Set (named after Set or Seth, the Egyptian deity of evil and confusion[65]), conduits to a chaotic, non-linear, and intrinsically alien universe.[66] The Tunnels of Set comprise the averse side of the kabballistic Tree of Life - a key symbols of the Western magical tradition - and are inhabited by the *qlippoth*: a Hebraic word meaning 'shells' or 'harlots'[67], and which commonly denotes 'demonic' entities which are also conceived of as disruptive unconscious forces lurking within the human psyche. The chaotic non-linearity of the Tunnels of Set constitutes an alternative to the neo-Platonic spatialised hierarchy which otherwise dominates Western ceremonial magic; they represent liminal spaces where the socially-ordained prism of everyday perception and cognition is rendered ineffective, where linear narratives of spiritual progress collapse allowing magicians to attain a brief but pristine glimpse of an 'authentic' reality.

For the HOD, explorations of these spaces often generated experiences which were beyond the power of language to describe. Nonetheless, the group would attempt to refract the fragmentary consciousness indicative of inbetweeness via an often jumbled and impressionistic discourse. This is evident in the following example, which marks an encounter (via possession) with a monstrous cosmic entity named Orzaz: a hitherto unknown Old One inhabiting the Lovecraftian 'inbetween' space which the HOD referred to as 'the Ghooric Zone':

> Dane: Are we in the presence of Orzaz, or someone else?
> Damien / Orzaz: Yes...Orzaz.
> Dane: Have you got anything to say to us?
> D/O: Do not look to the stars, look between the stars. Listen to the stars. The sounds open the portal which is the stars...Do not call Orzaz, Orzaz is. See Orzaz, do not call Orzaz. The call of Orzaz is Orzaz.
> Dane: The blackbirds of which you have spoken
> before [these were mentioned in an earlier possession ritual] ...
> D/O: They are not birds, they are black, but they are not black -

they are only black to you because you cannot see the colour that they are...
Dane: In which way does their nature impact with ours?
D/O: They move between you and as they move you can move with them and by moving with them you move through the portal which is the sound of Orzaz. The sound of Orzaz and the portal is the same...the vault is the sound of Orzaz. Opening the vault opens Orzaz. It is the sound...of the wings, of birds, as you call them...The beatings of their wings is the sound of Orzaz.......although they are not wings. You see them as wings in the same way you see the colour, and therefore they are your wings. You make them wings and you make them black.

The mental zones in which such encounters took place were described by Dane as 'pre-conceptual' and 'beyond language', and formed within the magical imagination an heterotopia: 'an impossible space, a realm of difference as Derrida would have it...an endless deferral of meaning...a space that has no knowable ontological ground'.[68] Such a deferral is evident in Orzaz derision at the HOD's attempts to clarify and categorise the inhabitants of the 'inbetween' spaces according to this-worldly referents (i.e. 'blackbirds').

The magician Michael Staley (a member of the Typhonian OTO) also suggested that the Old Ones emerge 'from a common background, a continuum, and that continuum is consciousness' of which 'our awareness registers only a limited subset or waveband'[69]. Accordingly, it is from this limited perceptual waveband that everyday cognitive categories are drawn; and it is the intrusion into consciousness by the 'undimensioned' Old Ones that disrupts the categorical boundaries and socially-circumscribed modes of thought, causing them to dissolve within the undifferentiated wholeness, continuum or 'primal chaos' of consciousness. After becoming possessed by the Old One Yog Sothoth, Alan thus felt the boundaries between his own sense of self and the intruding entity dissolve; he also experienced the entity as existing simultaneously at all points in the space where the possession occurred, undermining his normative conceptions of space and causality.

To the extent that such encounters appear to mystify rather than reveal reality, the claim that the Old Ones form a type of social diagnostics would appear questionable. However, for members of the HOD the conceptual disruptions emergent from such experiences served to highlight the differentiated, contingent and constructed nature of human social relations. In contrast, Lovecraft's own use of the Cthulhu mythos represents a continuation of modernity's rationalising concern with delimiting 'the horror of indetermination'[70] evoked by the socially-anomalous Other. Peter Geschiere notes some 'intriguing convergences' between the indeterminate, non-localised nature of occult powers and

> 'new forms of global mobility that, according to some, spell the end of the territorial nation-state as the main organizing principle of global society...Seen in this light, it is clear that the association of witchcraft and modernity is...about converging visions of open space, both frightening and enticing.'[71]

For Geschiere, such 'intermediary spaces' become filled by a variety of religious, ethnic and nationalistic discourses which structure uncertainty through the creation of fixed identities[72], inversely demonising those who fall outside the perimeters of stabilised identities. This is evident in Lovecraft's own racist demonisation of 'polluting' ethnic groups within the Cthulhu mythos, where the 'degenerate' worshippers of the Old Ones are depicted as ethnic stereotypes of the worst sort[73].

In their more fearful aspects, Geschiere's 'intermediary spaces' bring to mind the paranoia, fear and anxiety which the Old Ones' dissolution of structured, bounded space evoked for members of the HOD. Underlining the social diagnostics inherent in the group's conception of the Old Ones, Geschiere's analysis was perceptively echoed in the following e-mail sent by Rob:

> The negative fear and paranoia...[experienced] when humans step outside of their consensus reality. When we encounter something as alien as the Lovecraftian gnosis, our knee jerk reaction is one of fear, it automatically presses our fight or flight buttons. But this

doesn't necessarily mean that the Lovecraftian entities are inherently 'evil'. The negative emotional responses seem to occur because of our own conditioned fear of stepping beyond the construct we mistake for empirical 'reality'

Conversely, the HOD attempted to disembed themselves from the constructed categories of race and ethnicity, subsequently treating their practices as antithetical and resistant to Lovecraft's racism. Thus, Alan (himself of Anglo-Asian descent) claimed that by nominally identifying themselves as 'worshippers' of the Cthulhu mythos, members of the HOD had effectively constructed affiliations with the same ethnic groups which Lovecraft demonised. Rob also noted that

> The process of working creatively with non- human entities forces us to take responsibility for these fear complexes by putting us in a situation where we must adapt to a radically alien concept of the universe in order to operate effectively'.

Or as Jason claimed, magical experience 'enables you to be a little less dogmatic about other people'. In this respect, the HOD's use of science-fictional idioms is significant: not only does science fiction literature utilise techniques of 'defamiliarisation and estrangement'[74] - enabling readers to re-envision their world from radically new perspectives - but, as Marion Adler also observes,

> science-fiction and fantasy probably come closer than any other literature to systematically exploring the central concerns of Neo-Pagans and Witches...writers of science fiction and fantasy are bound less than any others by the political, sexual, and racial mores of their society...Science fiction has been the literature of the visionary; it has been able to challenge preconceived notions about almost everything, while at the same time attending to fundamental questions of the age.[75]

Union with the alien Old Ones, notions of transmutation and hybridity, aim to bring about a transformation of the socially-experienced self in a manner suggestive of Donna Haraway's 'blasphemous' cyborg, which holds 'incompatible things together'.[76] Like the cyborg, the Old Ones do not hold an expectation of a finished whole, but of a holism that is processual, changing, dynamic and fundamentally chaotic, offering a model for rethinking socially-defined notions of difference and otherness which have otherwise circumscribed exclusionist national, ethnic, religious and political identities[77]. As a type of social diagnostics, union and identification with the 'alien within' makes visible the socialised bifurcation of self and other: thus, ritualised encounters with the "demonic" Old Ones enabled members of the HOD to unpack some of the moral problematics surrounding ambivalence.

Selfhood and Uncertainty

Towards the end of my research Alan, Damien, Garth and Rob discussed the fact that they had increasingly come to feel 'comfortable' working with forces that other pagans viewed as intrinsically dangerous and 'demonic'. The normalisation and integration of the Old Ones became points of reference from which these magicians began 'evolving' the self. However, this evolution was not viewed in strictly orthogenic or teleological terms, but as a process of increasing diversity and complexity - a notion embodied in the Chaos magick motto 'Mutate to Survive'.[78]

Lovecraft imbues quantum mechanics with a magical quality, so that mathematical formulae open doorways to dimensions beyond the space-time continuum[79]. Lovecraftian magicians sometimes refer to these paradoxical sites as 'hyperspace' - a concept derived from popular exegeses of post-Newtonian physics[80]. Dane thus suggested that within these 'hyperspatial' and 'hyper-real' sites, the Old Ones falter indeterminately between states of existence and non-existence:

> 'Surely in the hyper-reality [of the Old Ones]...terms like 'existence' and 'non-existence' are pretty much a meaningless bunch of wank...that which doesn't live cannot die and exists as a nightmare or dream 'exists' ".

According to Erik Davis - and evident in the HOD's encounter with Orzaz - the 'hyperspatiality' explored by Lovecraft's is idiomatic of a Derridian 'crisis of representation'[81]; inasmuch as the Cthulhu mythos 'marks the limits of language, limits which paradoxically point to the Beyond'[82], the reality of the Old Ones is articulated through imaginary and incomprehensible prehuman languages: '*N'gai, n'gha'ghaa, bugg-shoggog, y'hah; Yog-Sothoth, Yog-Sothoth*'[83], for example. In practice, the HOD attempted to 'move beyond language' by evoking the Old Ones through the schizoid 'word salad' of dissociated language, glossolalia and 'barbarous words of evocation'.[84] Similarly, the names 'Nyarlathotep', 'Azathoth', etc., did not, according to Damien (and implied by Alan's experience of Yog Sothoth), signify discrete entities with definable characteristics and personalities[85]: they were simply labels which gave conceptual form to the inconceivable. Rob thus asked rhetorically whether 'the Great Old Ones can be used as a language for accessing the higher extraterrestrial circuits of consciousness?'. For the magician Stephen Sennitt, it is chaos and ontological indeterminacy which lies behind the 'language' or phenomenological masks of the Old Ones, who 'are ultimately random, but only in the same sense that we ourselves are ultimately random'.[86]

The social diagnostics inherent in this resonates with (and is indeed inspired by) recent trends in social theory, which hold that the overarching cultural determinants which defined 'traditional' identities have been displaced; a range of possible metacriteria have instead emerged, from which the individual has to chose or alternate between.[87] Thus 'the content and form of prevalent anxieties...have become altered'[88] by a globalised and relativised social milieu, resulting in identity problems as 'traditional' cultural conceptions of order and categorisation are disrupted. Similarly, Richard Sennett[89] suggests that such problems arise as a consequence of the increasing pressures brought to bear upon our decision-making capabilities within this milieu. Drawing upon the work of Fromm and Marcuse, Sennett however argues that attempts to maintain fixed and stable metacriteria ultimately inhibit the possibilities for human freedom. For Sennett, disorder and diversity become a necessary condition of that freedom: static environments and social structures lead to static, unfulfilled personalities, 'self-slavery'[90], and alignment to an ahistorical and imagined preconceived order. As already noted, this order may generate 'the desire for purity'[91], or that specific (but by no means monolithic) rendering of modernity which seeks to subordinate the inchoate and ambivalent elements of reality to an overarching notion of rational order.[92] Through identification with the Old Ones, Lovecraftian magicians are not, therefore, seeking refuge from the late-modern condition of 'ontological insecurity'[93] in transcendental absolutes; rather, they claim to embrace a type of 'ontological anarchism' where the self is a shifting site of multiple selves and subjectivities.

The HOD's exploration of inbetweeness thus enunciates a space which is disruptive of the rational, hierarchical distinctions emergent from *Enlightenment formations of modernity* - for practitioners, such shifting otherworldly sites form the ontologically indeterminate basis of an alternative conception of modernity, one uncoupled from Enlightenment ascriptions. The dissonant experience of this late- or post- modern milieu - of fragmentary selves and the erosion of a coherent locus of identity - was sometimes expressed (albeit obliquely) by members of the HOD during trance and possession. The following transcript is taken from an occasion in 2001 when Dane and Damien both undertook a trance-induced exploration of the Ghooric Zone, where the Old Ones lie 'dead but dreaming':

Dane: They [i.e. the Old Ones] give us our selves.
Damien: They give us our mortality, our selves are our mortality.
Dane They free us from the lie of self.
Damien: The lie of self is the lie of non-mortality.
Dane: Mortality and non-mortality pertain to the self, the words mean nothing to the dead gods who do not live and therefore cannot die...because they do not live or die, these words mean nothing.
Damien: That does not make the self dead, and cannot die. That does not make the self that which eternal dreams and is dead but does not die.
Dane: Because of the waves crashing.
Damien: The waves that crash are not the self. The waves that crash are the echoes of dead gods.
Dane: And we are the sounds?
Damien: We are the ripple, we are the scum that washes ashore.

> We are the foam, the sputum.
> Dane: We are dead gods?
> Damien: We are the remains of dead gods. We are made from the carbon of dead gods. The dead gods that fossilised. We are of their bodies, we are of their forms but we are not them.
> Dane: The dead gods were the dead gods are the dead gods shall be.
> Damien: Shall they be dead gods or shall they be new gods?
> Dane: This is the question.
> Damien: And what is the answer?
> Dane: What is an answer to a dead god?

Here, the experience of the self is attributed to the detritus of the Old Ones, or the 'dead gods' which Dane defined as those habitual beliefs, roles and behaviours commonly mistaken as the core self or identity. Within the discourses of Chaos magick, these 'dead gods' are also conceived of as Socratic 'daemons'[94], or as 'psychodenizens': taking the form of quasi-autonomous and self-replicating mental virii,[95] these daemons are 'transmitted' through the media and various social and cultural institutions; in thus coming to 'possess' human beings, they create the desires, neuroses, and habitual patterns of behaviour which give shape to modern forms of subjectification. Such daemons constitute the socially-determined self, and as a conglomerate are mistaken for an essential, core identity. For Dane, it was only through a total awareness of the dead gods or Old Ones - beyond the concerns of personal identity - that one could overcome the

> limitations of human thought...We need to become serpent-like to overcome these, we need to regularly shed the skins of our ideas and our limitations or physicality, shedding these and our attachments to them. The ... [Old Ones] reflect a route out of the prison we now inhabit, (a conceptual prison, I assume rather than a physical one)...Essentially then...we shouldn't let ourselves be fooled into thinking that any sort of concept we hold is capable of containing the reality of that which is unnameable. These projected interpretations and names being but skins that we

should shed. Along with perhaps, the skin which identifies our sense of self with our singular bodies and minds.

The HOD's identification with the Old Ones essentially reframes the resurgence of these entities as an 'apocalypse of consciousness' - an experience emergent from what James Aho calls 'the apocalypse of modernity'[96], wherein the Enlightenment project of anthrocentric humanism and 'the human centre of modernity has destabilised and collapsed. Its fragmentation has opened a space for new revelations'.[97]

For the HOD, the Old Ones formed a type of social diagnostics by which the ambivalence, disorderliness, ruptures, and uncertainties of late modern 'risk society' were made transparent to experience and strategically managed. The 'new revelations' presented by the Lovecraftian oeuvre mark the limits of rational progress and offer a counter-narrative or 'alternate ordering'[98] to Enlightenment modernity's teleological certainties - but one that is nonetheless derived from the epistemological centres of that same modernity (i.e. scientific discourse). Part of the attraction of the Cthulhu mythos thus lies in a compatibility between practitioners' use of 'postmodern science'[99] - with its attendant indeterminacies and 'quantum voids' - and Lovecraft's own 'twisted materialism in which scientific 'progress' returns us to the atavistic abyss'[100].

Marc Auge observes that 'mythologies speak of origins but these are cited, used, explored and re-imagined in order to answer the questions asked by the present'.[101] The adoption of Lovecraft's mythology as a system of belief indicates a substantively new and emerging magico-religious response to a crisis of meaning and identity instigated by processes of rationalisation, secularisation, and globalisation. Here, Lovecraftian magick responds to this crisis in a manner critical of Peter Beyer's supposition that, despite globalisation's relativising thrust, religious thought universalises the transcendent as 'a *structured* reality' (my emphasis)[102]:

Lovecraftian magicians do in fact attempt to articulate an alternative conception of the transcendent - as unstructured hyperspace, the abysmal chaos of the Great Old Ones - mirroring practitioners' perception of the social landscape as divested of 'ultimate sacred postulates'[103] and lacking any clear, structural or meaningful locus. It is, as Geschiere suggests, the very non-localised - indeed globalised - character of occult discourses which makes them so durable as metaphors of modern, globalising processes of change[104].

Ultimately, this conception of the sacred entails a recasting of the groundlessness of being, and the decentralisation of the self (with uncertainty as its consequence), as sources of potential self-emancipation and creativity rather than the cause of cynicism or existential angst. Lovecraftian magicians utilise a category of 'fictive' demonic spirits or entities as 'local takes on experience and the world'[105]. Lovecraftian magick emerges as a method of imaginally and metaphorically exploring (and consuming) the multiple, fragmenting and transforming categories of the self in the increasingly complex and uncertain socio-cultural context of postmodernity or late modern 'risk society'; it is the very fact that the semantic economy of the demonic is one of ambivalent and 'indeterminate' meanings that allows it to accommodate and integrate the enticing and unsettling experience of transglobal modernity's open-ended dynamism[106].

Lovecraftian Magick and Late/Post Modernity

Through the mimesis of possession, encounters with Old Ones enabled members of the HOD to internalise the anomic uncertainties promulgated by modernity in its various guises: if not making the contingencies of spectacular consumer culture appear more predictable, at least making them manageable through instances of 'controlled' possession by the indeterminate ontological roots (i.e. the Old Ones) of that cultural *zeitgeist*. For the HOD, this process entailed immersion in, and the consumption of, signs and images of exotic otherness. In this respect, the ambivalent nature of demonic 'psychodenizens' sheds light on the enticements of modernity - insofar as magicians may choose not to exorcise these 'demons', but enter instead into a 'Faustian' pact: what the Chaos magician Ramsey Dukes refers to as working in a positive sense *with* 'evil' (or those internalised sources of human alienation) rather than *for* it.[107]

In their discussion of spirit possession, Levy, Mageo and Howard note that '[t]wo conditions are necessary for full possession to flourish: people who are psychologically disposed to dissociation, and a cultural environment that makes conventional use of possession episodes'.[108] The assumption that trance necessarily involves dissociation is questionable: anthropologists have applied the category in ways which often do not reflect the semantic variability of equivalent terms found in the cultures studied; thus, possession metaphors may be used in different cultural milieux to describe a variety of emotions and behaviours which do not necessarily entail dissociation.[109] While trance states *are* widely pathologised within Euro-American culture, trance-induced explorations of Lovecraft's fictive universe have, arguably, become conventionalised - particularly within postmodern formulations which characterise the current social milieu as

> a melange of fiction and strange values, intense affect-charged experiences, the collapse of boundaries between art and everyday life, an emphasis upon images over words, *the playful immersion in unconscious processes as opposed to detached conscious appreciation*, the loss of a sense of reality, of history and tradition; the decentring of the subject"(my emphasis).[110]

Furthermore, some of the magicians I worked with viewed such 'peripheral' trance states as maintaining concrete links to 'mainstream' culture, being controlled extensions of non-dissociative and culturally-normative altered states of consciousness. Dane, for example, told me that:

What people fail to see is that possession is like going to the cinema. When you watch a film or read a book, it's the same as possession: you become totally overshadowed by the experience and lose sense of yourself and you enter another reality.

Contemporary Western magical practice is often formulated via a bricolage-like sampling of any number of magico-religious traditions[111]; such practices are indicative of the detraditionalised utilitarian self of late- or post- modern consumer culture, wherein practitioners seek spiritual fulfilment through the consumption of experiential trips into mystical realms[112]:

> The 'whole experience' of revelation, ecstasy, breaking the boundaries of the self and total transcendence...has been put by postmodern culture within every individual's reach, recast as a realistic target and plausible prospect of each individual's self-training, and relocated as the product of a life devoted to the art of consumer self-indulgence.[113]

As such, contemporary magical beliefs form a type of 'self-spirituality'[114] which may also be considered as the narcissistic outcropping[115] of globalising consumer culture. For Cohen, Ben-Yehuda and Aviad, the formation of science fiction and occult subcultures are thus indicative of a personal decentralisation which

> reflects radical secularization in an extreme form: all ends become equally valuable, or better, relative and ultimately valueless. The individual hence turns upon himself, and the immediate here and now: the new narcissism...and the hedonistic desire for instant gratification, frequently manifested by late modern youth, are ultimately an adaptive stance, reflecting the nature of the radically secularized universe into which it has been born.[116]

In this respect, Lovecraftian magick is not so much a 'marginal' practice, but the formalisation of an 'elective centre' which embraces and is adaptive to uncertainty, ephemerality, and postmodernity's multitudinous array of beliefs, ideologies, styles and lifestyle options. As Peter Geschiere notes, witchcraft movements and spirit cults may appear not only as a consequence of social and economic deprivation[117], but also during periods of economic boom 'when people have to deal with potentialities that appear highly promising but...impossible to control and, moreover, highly mysterious in their unpredictability' - the profusion of lifestyle choices perhaps being a case in point.

The emergence of elective centres which take science fiction and the occult as their locus is also indicative of a shift in the way that 'otherness' is conceptualised within global modernity: '[d]ifference ceases to threaten, or to signify power relations. Otherness is sought after for its exchange value, its exoticism and pleasures, thrills and adventures it can offer'.[118] This is also apparent in the manner by which the Old Ones no longer came to signify an alien other for the HOD, but formed the springboard for an arguably narcissistic celebration of an unbounded 'postmodern' self. In other words, 'otherness' has - to a degree - also become commoditised within the Lovecraftian magical milieu[119]. This is not to say that Lovecraftian magicians are little more than 'consumers': the HOD's embracing of the disorderly 'otherness' of the Old Ones caused the following question to be posed during Dane and Damien's dialogic exploration of the Ghooric Zone: 'shall they be dead gods or shall they be new gods?'. Ultimately, it is through continual shedding and restructuring of 'dead gods' - those components which constitute the shifting, multiple sites of 'postmodern' selfhood - by which Lovecraftian magick attempts to answer this question; in doing so, it also constitutes itself as an adaptation to the disorienting consequences of modernity as much as it articulates a possible mode of resistance.

Notes

1 This archaic spelling is commonly used by Left-Hand Path magicians for a variety of practical and symbolic reasons. See for example John Symonds, & Kenneth Grant, 'Editors' Introduction' in Aleister Crowley, *Magick* (London: Guild, 1986, 1973), xvi.

2 See for example Jean Comaroff & John Comaroff, *Modernity and its Malcontents* (Chicago: University of Chicago Press, 1993); Peter Geschiere, *The Modernity of Witchcraft: Politics and the Occult in Postcolonial Africa* (USA: University Press of Virginia, 1997); and H. Moore & T. Sanders, T. (eds.), *Magical Interpretations, Material Realities* (London: Routledge, 2001).

3 Peter Geschiere, 'Globalisation and the Powers of Indeterminate Meaning: Witchcraft and Spirit Cults in Africa and East Asia", in *Globalization and Identity* ed. by B. Meyer & P. Geschiere (Oxford: Berg, 1999), 211.

4 John Mitchell, 'Introduction' in *Powers of Good and Evil: Social Transformation and Popular Belief* ed. by P. Clough & J. Mitchell (Oxford: Berghahn. 2001), 5-6.

5 Moore & Sanders, *Magical Interpretations* (London: Routledge, 2001), 20.

6 But see Clough & Mitchell, *Powers of Good and Evil* (Oxford: Berghahn. 2001) as a recent corrective to this overdetermined contextual focus.

7 It should be noted that many of the theorists in question are cognisant of this problem. See for example Geschiere, 'Globalisation and the Powers of Indeterminate Meanings' (1999), 212.

8 It is this modernity which is often cited as the originary point of New Religious Movements - see Robert Bellah, 'New Religious Consciousness and the Crisis in Modernity' in *The New Religious Consciousness* ed. by C. Glock & R. Bellah (Berkeley: University of California Press, 1976), 180-202. The "modernisation" of witchcraft in Africa represents an "alternative" rendering of modernity which is not explicitly tied to the instrumental rationality view.

9 See for example Paul Heelas, *The New Age Movement: The Sacralization of the Self and the Celebration of Modernity* (Oxford: Blackwell, 1996)

10 Anthony Giddens, 'Living in a Post-Traditional Society' in *Reflexive Modernization* ed. by U. Beck, A. Giddens, & S. Lash (Cambridge: Polity Press, 1994), 58.

11 In this respect, I treat late modernity and postmodernity not so much as epochal breaks from, but constituent elements of "modernity". See Barry Smart, *Postmodernity* (London: Routledge, 1993).

12 See Dave Green, 'Opposites Attract: magical identity and social uncertainty' in *Journal for the Academic Study of Magic* 1 (2003), 73-101.

13 See for example Kevin Hetherington, *The Badlands of Modernity* (London: Routledge, 1997)

14 See for example: Hetherington, ibid., 20-24; and Sophie Day, Evthymios Papataxiarchis & Michael Stewart (eds.), *Lilies of the Field* (Oxford: Westview Press, 1999).

15 For an indication of the vast number of authors - both "fans" and professionals - who have contributed to the Cthulhu mythos, see Chris Jarocha-Ernst, *A Cthulhu Mythos Bibliography and Concordance* (Seattle: Armitage House, 1999).

16 Zebulon, 'Dark Entries: An Introduction to the Magick of the Cthulhu Mythos' (http://www.phine.ndirect.co.uk/ktulmyth/darkent.htm. N.d.a), 1.

17 See for example: H. P. Lovecraft, *Miscellaneous Writings* (Wisconsin: Arkham House, 1995), 133 - 198; and S. T. Joshi, *A Dreamer and A Visionary: H. P. Lovecraft in His Time* (Liverpool: Liverpool University Press, 2001), 131.

18 Joshi, ibid., 244-246.

19 H. P. Lovecraft, 'The Call of Cthulhu' in H. P. Lovecraft, *Dagon and Other Macabre Tales* (Wisconsin: Arkham House, 1987, 1926), 125.

20 H. P. Lovecraft, 'The Dunwich Horror' in H. P. Lovecraft, *The Dunwich Horror and Others* (Wisconsin: Arkham House, 1984, 1928), 170.

21 H. P. Lovecraft, 'History of the Necronomicon' in H. P. Lovecraft, *Miscellaneous Writings* (Wisconsin: Arkham House, 1995. 1927), 52-53.

22 George Hay (ed.) 1978 (1992). *The Necronomicon: The Book of Dead Names* (London: Skoob Books, 1992).

23 Lovecraft knew of Crowley - see H. P. Lovecraft, *Selected Letters Volume V* (Wisconsin: Arkham House, 1976), 120) - but there is no evidence to suggest that Crowley had read Lovecraft's work.

24 See Daniel Harms & John Gonce, *The Necronomicon Files: The Truth Behind the Legend* (California: Night Shade Books, 1998), 51-76.

25 B. Ellis, 'Legend-Trips and Satanism: Adolescents' Ostensive Traditions as 'Cult' Activity' in (eds.), *The Satanism Scare* ed. by J. Richardson, J. Best, & D. Bromley (New York: Aldine de Gruyter, 1991), 289.

26 Lovecraft, 'Cthulhu'(1987), 141.

27 See for example Richard Cavendish, *The Powers of Evil: in Western Religion, Magic and Folk Belief* (London: Routledge & Kegan Paul, 1975)

28 Richard Sutcliffe, 'Left-Hand Path Ritual Magick: An Historical and Philosophical Overview' in *Paganism Today* ed. by Graham Harvey & Charlotte Hardman (London: Thorsons, 1995), 110. See also Katon Shual, *Sexual Magick* (Oxford: Mandrake, 1995), vi.

29 See for example Kenneth Grant, *The Magical Revival* (London: Skoob Books, 1991, 1972), 39; and *Cults of the Shadow* (London: Skoob Books, 1994, 1975), 2.

30 Sutcliffe 'Left Hand Path'(1995), 131; see also Graham Harvey, *Listening People, Speaking Earth: Contemporary Paganism.* (London: Hurst & Co, 1997), 97.

31 Sutcliffe, ibid., 124.

32 See for example: Gerald Suster, *The Legacy of the Beast* (London: W.H. Allen, 1988), 215; Francis King, *Modern Ritual Magic: The Rise of Western Occultism* (Dorset: Prism Press, 1989), 166; and Peter Koenig, 'Kenneth Grant and the Typhonian O.T.O.'(http://www.cyberlink.ch/~koenig/k_grant.htm.).

33 The Typhonian OTO's irregular journal *Starfire* often contains articles dealing with Lovecraftian themes.

34 Over a million paperback editions of Lovecraft's work had apparently been sold in the USA by June 1973 - see S. T. Joshi, 'Introduction' in H. P. Lovecraft & W. Conover, *Lovecraft at Last* (New York: Copper Square Press, 2002), xiii.

35 Gary Lachman, *Turn Off Your Mind: The Mystic Sixties and the Dark Side of the Age of Aquarius* (London: Sidgewick & Jackson, 2001), 39-58.

36 Anton LaVey, *The Satanic Rituals*, (New York: Avon, 1972).

37 Harms & Gonce, *Necronomicon Files* (1998), 111.

38 Grant, *Magical Revival* (1991); *Aleister Crowley and The Hidden God* (London: Skoob Books, 1992, 1973); *Cults of the Shadow* (London: Skoob Books, 1994, 1975); *Nightside of Eden* (London: Skoob Books, 1994, 1977); *Outside the Circles of Time* (London: Fredrick Muller, 1980); *Hecate's Fountain* (London: Skoob Books, 1992); *Outer Gateways* (London: Skoob Books, 1994); *Beyond The Mauve Zone* (London: Starfire Publishing, 1999); and *The Ninth Arch* (London: Starfire Publishing, 2002).

39 See for example Grant, ibid. (1992), 37.

40 The Esoteric Order of Dagon, *Starry Wisdom* 1 / 1 (1987), 1.

41 The Esoteric Order of Dagon, *Starry Wisdom: Dunwich Lodge.* (USA: Starry Wisdom Press, 1995); *The Esoteric Order of Dagon: An Introduction* (USA: Miskatonick University Press, 1992); and *The Directory of the Esoteric Order of Dagon* (USA: Miskatonick University Press, n.d.a.); and John Day, 'Shadow over Philistia: A review of the Dagon Cult' in *Journal for the Academic Study of Magic* 1 (2003), 39-41.

42 Phil Hine, *The Pseudonomicon* (Irvine: Dagon Productions, 1994).

43 Phil Hine, 'Fifth Aeon Egregore' (http://www.phhine.ndirect.co.uk); see also Phil Hine, *Prime Chaos* (London: Chaos International, 1993), 94 - 106.

44 This is a pseudonym.

45 Women were not, however, excluded from the group, and female partners of some of the group's members occasionally participated in ritual activities. Without meaning to reduce my analysis to generalised gendered stereotypes, men were more attracted to the sometimes aggressive and confrontational approach of this "style" of magick.

46 Lovecraft, ibid., 286.

47 See for example H. P. Lovecraft, 'The Dreams in the Witch House' in H. P. Lovecraft in H. P. Lovecraft, *At the Mountains of Madness* (Wisconsin: Arkham House, 1985, 1932), 262-298.

48 LaVey, *Satanic Rituals* (1972), 178.

49 An idea also contemporaneous with the human-extraterrestrial hybridisations which form a core element of recent alien abduction narratives.

50 See H. P. Lovecraft, 'The Shadow Over Innsmouth' in Lovecraft (1984), 303 - 367. Robert Temple, in his popular work of "alternative archaeology" *The Sirius Mystery* (London: Arrow, 1999, 1976), argues that amphibian extraterrestrials from the Sirius star system - similar to Lovecraft's Deep Ones - have intervened in humanity's evolution in the distant past, and may be preparing to return to the earth in the near future. The Sirius / Deep One connection also plays a significant

role in some Thelemic magical recensions of Lovecraft - see for example Stefan Dziklewicz, 'Dagon Rising' in *Starfire* 1/4 (1991), 63-78.

51 See also Hine *Prime Chaos* (1993), 100; and *Pseudonomicon* (1994), 39.

52 Aleister Crowley, *The Confessions of Aleister Crowley* (London: Arkana, 1989, 1969), 404.

53 Hine, *Pseudonomicon* (1994): 9.

54 Mary Douglas, *Purity and Danger* (London: Routledge 1994).

55 Martin Bridgestock, 'The Twilit Fringe - Anthropology and Modern Horror Fiction' in *Journal of Popular Culture* 23/3 (1989),115-123.

56 Lovecraft, *Dunwich Horror* (1984), 155-198.

57 Bridgestock, 'Twilit Fringe'(1989), 115.

58 Douglas, *Purity and Danger* (1994), 95.

59 James Kneale, 'From Beyond: H. P. Lovecraft and the Place of Horror', paper delivered as part of the "Placing Horror' seminar series (University of London, 11th March 2003).

60 See Jack Morgan, quoted in Kneale, ibid.

61 R. Levy, J. Mageo, & A. Howard, 'Gods, Spirits, and History' in *Spirits in Culture, History, and Mind* ed. by J. Mageo & A. Howard (London: Routledge, 1996), 20.

62 Charles Stewart, *Demons and the Devil: Moral Imagination in Modern Greek Culture* (New Jersey: Princeton University Press, 1991), 132, 189.

63 Grant, *Nightside*, (1994), 126. The concept of 'inbetweeness' as used by Grant was initially developed by Austin Spare: see Austin Osman Spare, 'The Book of Pleasure (Self-Love): The Psychology of Ecstasy', facsimile in A. Spare, *From the Inferno to Zos: The Writings and Images of Austin Osman Spare* (Seattle: First Impressions, 1993); Grant, *Magical Revival* (1991), 180; and *Cults of Shadow* (1994), 197-198.

64 Grant, *Nightside* (1994), 129.

65 See for example Norman Cohn, *Cosmos, Chaos and the World to Come: The Ancient Roots of Apocalyptic Faith* (London: Yale University Press, 1993), 12.

66 See for example Kenneth Grant, *Images and Oracles of Austin Osman Spare* (London: Fredrick Muller, 1975), 12.

67 For a further elaboration of the "demonic" and "interstitial" associations of this term, see William Gray, *The Tree of Evil* (Gloucestershire: Helios, 1974), 17.

68 Hetherington, *Badlands* (1997), 67.

69 Personal communication.

70 Zygmunt Bauman, *Modernity and Ambivalence.* (Cambridge: Polity Press, 1991), 51.

71 Geschiere, 'Globalisation and the Powers of Indeterminate Meanings' (1999), 234.

72 Ibid., 233; see also Mattias Gardell, *Gods of the Blood* (London: Dukes University Press, 2003), 1 - 18.

73 Lovecraft's racist Othering is also made quite explicit in his naming of the Old Ones (i.e. Yog Sothoth and Shub Niggurath).

74 Robert Scholes quoted in Marion Adler, *Drawing Down the Moon* (New York: Penguin, 1986), 286.

75 Ibid. (1986), 285.

76 Donna Haraway, *Simians, Cyborgs, and Women* (New York: Routledge, 1991), 149.

77 A small number of neo-Nazi Satanist groups - including the Order of the Nine Angles - do, however, appear to have embraced the racist elements of Lovecraft's mythology. See for example A. Long & D. Myatt 1998 'The Order of the Nine Angles' in *Nox, The Black Book Volume 1: Infernal Texts* ed. by S. Sennitt (Logos Press: Mexborough, 1998), 6 - 22; and Nicholas Goodrick-Clarke, *Black Sun: Aryan Cults, Esoteric Nazism and the Politics of Identity* (New York: New York University Press, 2002), 215 - 223.

78 Hine, *Prime Chaos* (1993), 120.

79 See for example Lovecraft, *Mountains of Madness* (Wisconsin: Arkham House, 1985), 262 - 298.

80 See for example Michio Kaku *Hyperspace* (Oxford: Oxford University Press, 1995).

81 Erik Davis, 'Calling Cthulhu: H. P. Lovecraft's Magick Realism' (http://www.levity.com/figments/lovecraft.html, 1995), 5.

82 Ibid., 6.

83 Lovecraft, *Dunwich Horror* (1984), 175.

84 Grant, *Magical Revival* (1991), 100-118; see also Hine, *Pseudonomicon* (1994), 16.

85 See also Hine, ibid., 19.

86 Stephen Sennitt, *Liber Koth* (Logos Press: Mexborough, 1997), 7.

87 See R. Baumeister, *Identity, Cultural Change and the Struggle for Self* (Oxford: Oxford University Press, 1986), 247.

88 Giddens, *Modernity* (1991), 32.

89 Richard Sennett, *The Uses of Disorder* (London: Faber & Faber, 1996 [1970])

90 Ibid., xviii.

91 Ibid., 22.

92 Bauman, *Modernity and Ambivalence* (1991), 15.

93 Anthony Giddens, *Modernity and Self Identity* (Cambridge: Polity Press, 1991), 53.

94 See for example Frater Equilibrium. 2001. *The Neonomicon: Personal Daemonkeeping and Chaos Magic* (United Kingdom: Privately Published, 2001).

95 This is a recasting of William Burroughs' claim that language is a psychic "virus" which acts as an instrument of social control. See for example - 1985. William Burroughs, *The Adding Machine: Collected Essays* (London: John Calder, 1985), 48-52, 88-96. This concept of the "demonic" also follows Richard Dawkins' concept of the "meme": see Richard Dawkins, *The Selfish Gene* (Oxford: Oxford University Press, 1989), 192; and *The Blind Watchmaker* (Harmondsworth: Penguin 1986), 158; see also Dan Sperber, 'Anthropology and Psychology: Towards and Epidemiology of Representations' in *Man* 20 (1985), 73-89; and *Explaining Culture: A Naturalistic Approach* (Oxford: Blackwell 1996), 56, 100-106.

96 James Aho, 'The Apocalypse of Modernity' in *Millennium, Messiahs, and Mayhem: Contemporary Apocalyptic Movements* ed. by T. Robbins & S. J. Palmer (London: Routledge, 1997), 61-72; see also Giddens, *Modernity*, (1991), 4.

97 Aho, 'Apocalypse of Modernity' (1997), 62. See also Douglas Kellner, 'Popular culture and the construction of postmodern identities' in S. Lash & J. Friedman (eds.), *Modernity and Identity*, (Oxford: Basil Blackwell, 1992), 142.

98 Hetherington, *Badlands* (1997), vii.

99 Jean-Francois Lyotard, *The Postmodern Condition: A Report on Knowledge* (Manchester: Manchester University Press, 1979).

100 Davis, 'Calling Cthulhu' (1995), 5. It has also been suggested that Lovecraft's apocalyptic vision resonates with contemporary fears concerning environmental collapse (as a consequence of scientific materialism and mass consumption) - see for example George Hay, 'Preface' in G. Hay & R. Turner, *The R'lyeh Text: Hidden Leaves from the Necronomicon* (London: Skoob Books, 1995), 9-10; and Barry Walker, 'The Call of Cthulhu: A Modern Magickal Mythos' in *White Dragon* 25 (1999), 12-15.

101 Marc Auge, *The War of Dreams: Studies in Ethno Fiction* (London: Pluto Press, 1999), 19.

102 Peter Beyer, *Religion and Globalization* (London: Sage, 1994), 6.

103 Roy Rappaport, *Ecology, Meaning, and Religion* (Berkeley: North Atlantic Books, 1979), 117.

104 Geschiere, 'Globalization and the Power of Indeterminate Meanings' (1999), 233-234.

105 Michael Lambek, 'Afterword: Spirits and Their Histories' in J. Mageo & A. Howard (1996), 238.

106 See Geschiere, 'Globalization and the Powers of Indeterminate Meanings' (Oxford: Berg, 1999).

107 Ramsey Dukes, *What I Did in My Holidays: Essays on black magic, Satanism, and other nicities.* Oxford: Mandrake/The Mouse That Spins, 1998), 22.

108 Levy, Mageo & Howard, 'Gods, Spirits, and History'(London: Routledge, 1996), 19.

109 Vincent Crapanzano, 'Introduction' in *Case Studies in Spirit Possession* ed. by V. Crapanzano & V. Garrison (New York: John Wiley & Sons, 1977), 10.

110 Mike Featherstone, 'Postmodernism and the Quest for Meaning' in *The Search for Fundamentals: The Process of Modernisation and the Quest for Meaning* ed. by L. van Vucht Tijssen, J. Berling & F. Lechner (Dordecht: Kluwer Academic Publishers, 1995), 222.

111 Sabrina Magliocco, 'Ritual is My Chose Art Form: The Creation of Ritual as Folk Art Among Contemporary Pagans' in *Magical Religion and Modern Witchcraft* ed. by James Lewis (Albany: SUNY Press, 1996), 121-140.

112 See for example Paul Heelas, 'The limits of consumption and the postmodern 'religion' of the New Age' in *The Authority of the Consumer* ed. by R. Keat, N.Whiteley & N. Abercrombie (London: Routledge, 1994), 102-115; and 'The New Age: Values and Modern Times' in *The Search for Fundamentals: The Process of Modernisation and the Quest for Meaning* ed. by L. van Vucht Tijssen, J. Berting & F. Lechner (Dordecht: Kluwer Academic Publishers, 1995), 143-170.

113 Zygmunt Bauman, 'Postmodern Religion?' in *Religion, Modernity, and Postmodernity* ed. by Paul Heelas (Oxford: Blackwell, 1998), 70.

114 See for example Heelas, *New Age Movement* (1996).

115 See for example Christopher Lasch, C. 1978. *The Culture of Narcissism* (New York: W.W. Norton, 1978). However, see also Dave Green, this edition.

116 E. Cohen, N. Ben-Yehuda, N., & J. Aviad, 1987. 'Recentering the world: the quest for 'elective' centers in a secularized universe' in *The Sociological Review* 35 / 2 (1987), 323.

117 See for example I. M. Lewis, *Ecstatic Religion: A Study of Shamanism and Spirit Possession* (London: Penguin, 1971).

118 Jonathan Rutherford, *Identity: Community, Culture, Difference.* (London: Lawrence & Wishart, 1990), 11.

119 See for example: Paul Heelas, 'Introduction: On Differentiation and Dedifferentiation" in *Religion, Modernity, and Postmodernity* ed. by Paul Heelas (Oxford: Blackwell, 1998), 5-6; and Adam Possamai, 'Alternative Spiritualities and the Cultural Logic of Late Capitalism' in *Culture and Religion* 4 / 1 (2003), 31-45.

Wishful Thinking? Notes towards a psychoanalytic sociology of Pagan magic

Dave Green

> Magic is wishful thinking that dodges blocks in this furrowed world.[1]

This article focuses on a number of issues that have largely remained unarticulated in current academic discourses about contemporary Paganisms – the relationships between Freudian psychoanalysis, and societal and magical transformation. In particular, the article begins to *imagine* – and it is a huge task - both what a post-Freudian psychoanalytic sociology of magic might look like, and what it could contribute to the academic study of magic. Whilst critical re-readings of Freud's work can provide academics with numerous avenues of esoteric exploration, this article necessarily has to concentrate on a single topic – the relationships between narcissism and magic in comprehensively commodified contemporary cultures. A psychoanalytic sociology is developed around the claim that whilst the commodified ego and magical processes of ego loss might appear opposed, the narcissism of consumer culture active not only structures the Pagan revolt against consumerism, but, counter-intuitively, also structures its practices. Before detailing these arguments there is a need to sketch out briefly how an emergent psychoanalytic sociology might take shape:

Why a *psychoanalytic* sociology of magic?
Magic has been unjustly neglected by contemporary sociology. Whilst classical sociological theorists such as Weber and Durkheim placed magico-religious phenomena at the heart of psycho-social explanations of the rise of modernity,[2] their observations have remained underdeveloped by sociologists of magic. Where they have been developed, they have been mainly applied to pre-modern and non-modern forms of magical practices, intimating that contemporary magic is little more than a culturally marginal Romantic reaction to the exigencies of (late) modern living.

A related problem, which faces any sociologist of magic, is that sociology is a discipline moulded by Enlightenment reason, and as such is founded upon the cornerstone of the application of rationality to social phenomena. Even though there has been a vehement rejection of positivistic methodology within contemporary sociological hermeneutics, over a century after its birth sociology is only just coming to terms with the non-rational, embodied and affective nature of social actors and phenomena. The postmodern theoretical turn, in particular, has not only overseen the 'death' of the author, but is pervaded with an anti-humanism, which theorises the symbolic 'death' of the individual subject. That is, man is not a free agent, but a discursively made and unmade construct.

As a remedy to this perceived theoretical cul-de-sac, a number of social theorists have begun to apply psychoanalytic theory as an essential corrective to this view of humanity as passive, incorporeal, and devoid of emotion. Indeed, a return to Freud has become a central component in contemporary social theory from firstly, the socialization theory of Talcott Parsons; through, secondly, the civilization theories of the Freudo-Marxist (and Reichian) *Institut für Sozialforschung*[3] of, for example, Adorno, Marcuse,[4] Horkheimer, Benjamin and Fromm; Lasch's 'culture of narcissism'; and, Deleuze and Guattari's post-structural schizo-analysis;[5] to, thirdly, to the post-Oedipalism of Lacan and the Freudo-feminists – notably, Kristeva, Cixous and Irigaray.

Adherents of such psychoanalytic sociologies recognise the many problems with Freud's theory of psycho-sexual development, particularly his centrality of Oedipus, the delicate issues surrounding sex and seduction, and the universality of his theories. Thus, psychoanalytic sociologies have, for example, tended to reject the rigidity of Freud's psycho-sexual theory in favour of neo-Kleinian notions of developmental positions; have abandoned Freud's evolutionary schema which links psycho-sexual development to societal development, and hence, reinforces the link between magical practices and primitivism;[6] and, have dismissed Oedipus for a post-Oedipalism which views the Oedipus Complex as both (literally) paternalistic and a function of patriarchy. These reconceptualizations of Freud recast him as an important social theorist – a pioneer in the attempt to understand the unconscious and affective motivations of social beings. Likewise, any psychoanalytic sociology of magic must reject Freudian metanarrative for more nuanced and situated readings of his theories which curb their monolithic sexualised excesses and emphasise the personal and socio-cultural effects of unconscious processes. Indeed, scratch the surface and Freud the social theorist is revealed.

One excellent example of the social in Freud's thought is represented by his concept of the super-ego; that part of the self which introjects social prohibitions, instilling in the process self-criticism and self-control.[7] Furthermore, in my own sociology department at the University of the West of England, for example, a post-Kleinian psychoanalytic sociology is being developed to examine, amongst others, racism and racial hatred, cyber-space, and celebrity.[8] Such a psychoanalytic sociology is a sociology not only of the psychic relatedness of self and *other*, but of self and *otherness*. As such it can be successfully applied to contemporary magic.

Freudianism and magic

In order to develop such a perspective one widespread preconception has to be explored further - are not Freud and magic uneasy bedfellows? The received wisdom is undoubtedly yes. Freud's evolutionary scheme, primarily based upon Frazer's accounts of rebirth and myths of the 'Vegetation God', views magic as a primitive and pre-scientific form of human cognition and practice akin to the misrecognitions, irrationality and omnipotence of childhood thought. When considering totemism in particular, magico-religious practices are said by Freud to be riddled with Oedipal sexual angst, with deities being mere projections of the Oedipal triangle. One sees such ideas as a central plank of both Geza Roheim's scholarly *Magic and Schizophrenia*, and M. D. Faber's ill-informed *Modern Witchcraft and Psychoanalysis*:

Roheim, in a sense, outdoes Freud himself by placing various types of premodern magics within Freud's theory of psycho-sexual development. So, for example, the Masai's often ritualistic uses of spitting to express either contempt and astonishment are linked to orality. The traditional Serbian cure for female sterility is for the woman to put 'the excrement of a pig, or of a black hen hatched before St. George's Day, into her shoes. In labour pains, a woman swallows excrement in order to facilitate delivery.'[9] Roheim connects these with the anal psycho-sexual phase. And so on. Whilst most of these connections stretch lay credulity, Roheim is at least consistent when attempting to produce a socio-cultural development of classical Freudian theory.

Whereas Roheim's study is a scholarly psychopathological development of Freud's ideas on premodern forms of indigenous magic grounded within a meta-analysis of anthropological data, Faber's critique of contemporary witchcraft heavily relies on hearsay. It reduces the praxis of Goddess Spiritualities to a cathartic and pseudo-therapeutic re-enactment of Oedipus. Faber, for example, both points to the omnipotence of thought inherent to witchcraft,[10] then views merely this as a cathartic *cri du coeur* of female witches he deems powerless against the weight of Patriarchy.[11] Indeed, Faber even intimates that patriarchy is an imaginary construction made real through the power of the fears and phantasies of the witches themselves!

Freud's reputation amongst academics of magic has not only been dented by the uncritical application of his theories by others. Importantly, Freud has suffered through his uneasy relationship with Jung. Occultists have tended to contrast the archetypal atheistic scientist Freud, with the spiritual shaman that is Jung. Thus, whilst as Jung has rightly been influential in occult studies through his researches, for example, into pagan myths, the Tarot, the I Ching, alchemy, and Gnosticism - and the applicability of ideas to, for example, Wiccan initiation ritual[12] – Freud has, in every sense, remained a bogeyman. This is unfair to Freud. A more balanced view, one must note two major caveats: Firstly, the occult influences that underpin Freud's work;[13] and, secondly, the applicability of a post-Freudian sociology to the study of magic.

Freud as occult theorist?
The dispute between Freud and Jung has passed into the history of ideas not only as falling out between friends, but as symbolic of the incommensurability of science and mysticism. Indeed, it is this perceived incompatibility between the two that has prevented the majority of scholars and magical practitioners from formulating an accurate assessment of the potential of Freudian theory for the study of contemporary magic.

The portrayal of Freud as a scientist, contra Jung, is particularly misguided. The edifice of Freud's theories as scientific is built upon shaky ground indeed, particularly if one takes into account the occult underpinnings of Freud's theory of the self. It is extremely possible that the Freudian oeuvre may have their roots in Jewish Cabalism, of which he appears to have had a working knowledge.[14] Indeed, there are parallels in the methodology of Freud's clinical work in recognising and overcome neuroses and in the way the 'Tree of Life' glyph is used to promote a union with the divine and a psychic holism, notably through the importance of the interpretation of dreams, the employment of free association, and the centrality of sexuality. It is also interesting that one of Freud's closest early associates, Wilhelm Fliess, had strong esoteric leanings, even producing an occult thesis that menstruation was numerically linked to the operations of the turbinate scrolls of the nose and biorhythmically linked to people's fates.[15] Freud even attempted to apply Fliess' numerological theories to the study of neuroses.[16] Furthermore, one of Freud's closest associates, Friedrich Eckstein, was a devotee of Blavatsky and noted the Neo-Platonic influences upon his friend's theories of the unconscious.[17] Then came his relationship with Jung, confirming both the rise of esoteric psychology and Freud's infallible - one might say unconscious - sense for becoming involved with occultists.

James Webb's *Occult Establishment*, charts this 'shared journey' between psychoanalysis and the occult.[18] He notes how Freud's concepts of healing being based on the restoration of lost equilibrium and harmony has a basis in Paracelsianism, and the development of such occult healing in the work of the theosophist Franz Hartmann.[19] Similarly, despite Freud's disavowal of an alliance between occultists and psychoanalysts, the antipathies that both occult science and the early psychoanalysts faced by the established natural science establishment links both groups to the Romantic revolt of Goethean *Naturphilosophie*.[20]

Thus, one should re-cast Freud as an important anti-establishment figure,[21] rather than merely the sceptical adversary of Jung. Given this, one should engage with Freud with the imaginative approach that one reserves for the work of Jung, and for other theorists informed by occultism.[22] Indeed Webb concludes that it is erroneous to disentangle psychoanalysis, psychical research and the fin-de-siècle Occult revival. Indeed, the occult legacy of Freudian ideas can be seen in the magico-aesthetic manifestos of the Surrealists; more generally in Crowley's psychologization of magic; and potently in Spare's sigilizations, where he consciously inverts Freud's concept of neurotic repression in order to suppress magical desires within the unconscious.

Let us now examine the second caveat: Freud's ideas on cultural evolution, Oedipus, and psycho-sexual development have harmed the applicability of his ideas to the academic study of magic. Freud's attitude to the occult phenomena, however, as Cavendish states, 'swung between attraction and repulsion.'[23] Freud's attraction to the occult produced a significant, albeit less well known, body of work on occult and psi-phenomena, with his mapping of the unconscious opening whole new vistas of psychoanalytically informed para-psychological and psychical research. He is surprisingly uncritical - sometimes even accepting - about occult phenomena. Freud, for example, published on premonitory dreams, synchronicity, and telepathy.[24] These pioneering writings influenced other early psychoanalysts to study the occult, for example, Hitschmann, Deutsch, Roheim, and Zulliger.[25] Freud's ideas were also to catch the attention of a certain C.G. Jung.

Given this, a psychoanalytic sociology of magic can begin to open up new avenues of academic inquiry. Examples are numerous, but include: Freud's concept of the uncanny[26] can be successfully employed in both the hermeneutics of magical texts and on fictional texts that have exerted an influence on magical practices; for instance the works of H.P. Lovecraft,[27] or even Terry Pratchett.[28] The inter- and intra-psychic conflicts of the witch-hunts, and even contemporary discrimination and *bitchcraft*, are open to such analyses. The adoption of alterity and alternative identities by magicians can also be scrutinised under a similar theoretical rubric. Much of the remainder of this article, however, concentrates on the importance of Freudian narcissism in understanding how magical selves develop. This is based, in part, upon a critical re-reading of Ian Parker's psycho-social analysis of the New Age:

Freud emphasises the importance of the ego in mediating between our inner demands for immediate satisfaction, and the demands of normative cultural values. Magical and mystical enlightenment – Buddhism and Spare's *Sorceries of Zos* are important heuristics in this respect - on the other hand, emphasises ego loss as a pre-requisite of illumination. However, in this magical overcoming of the self, the ego must be built, developed and only then identified as limiting, before it can be neutralized or lost. In contemporary Western capitalist cultures, selves and processes of identity construction – that is, of ego building - are increasingly tied to commodification, consumption and branding.[29] Indeed, sociology has long recognised that the aesthetics of *consumption* have replaced *production* as primary signifiers of social identity. Whilst such commodification in spiritual milieux is most apparent in New Age practices, the psycho-social effects of consumer culture are important starting points for any psychoanalytic sociology of Pagan magic:

The commodification of magic
The commodification of magico-religious phenomena has spawned the notion of the *spiritual supermarket*. This an ideational realm where religious consumers can pick between competing forms of religiosity, or, as common in New Age practices, take personally meaningful elements from a number of spiritual traditions and then reinsert them in one's own spiritual *bricolage*.[30] Even a cursory examination of The New Age movement reveals this

fundamental relationship between spirituality and consumption.[31] Importantly for this article, many Pagans – and indeed scholars of Paganisms - make commodification a prime distinction between the New Age and Paganism. For example this Druid contended:

> The main difference between Paganism and The New Age is the decimal point. You would spend £500 on a New Age rebirthing workshop, but only fifty quid on the pagan equivalent.

This unaligned female pagan was extremely critical of commodification:

> I'll be controversial: Paganism is more discerning, and contains less bollocks ... The best example is an advert I saw for instructions on making a Feng Shui soap holder to improve your money flow!

Many differentiate between the two by arguing that whilst the New Age is thoroughly commodified, Paganisms are relatively free of commodification. This is only partially correct. An analysis of Pagan practices and discourses reveals a fundamental relationship between Paganisms and commodification.

Bowman, for example, discusses the ways in which Celtic Paganism is increasingly commodified.[32] Attend large-scale Pagan conferences, such as the national Pagan Federation conference, and one will see the roaring trade that the stalls are doing selling Pagan accoutrements – robes, altar cloths, tarot pack, etc. Pagan magazines are full of advertisements for similar cottage industries.[33] In all of these ways Pagan identities are subjects of, and subject to, commodification.[34]

Doug Ezzy's excellent analysis of commodified witchcraft internet sites reveals a significant trend towards commodification within popular Paganisms.[35] Furthermore, Ezzy makes two important distinctions between what he terms *commodified* and *non-commodified* forms of witchcraft. Firstly, he argues that non-commodified forms of witchcraft are based around gift-giving, rather than consumption. That is, magical initiation, for example, is a gift to be passed on rather than bought and sold.[36] Secondly, he tends to see Wicca as free of commodification in comparison to other forms of witchcraft, particularly teen witchcraft. Certainly knowledge tends to be given, rather than consumed, within Pagan circles, but – as noted above - Paganisms are clearly not free of the insidious influences of consumer culture. Rather, Pagans attempt to resist the worst features of consumer culture, but their practices are still structured in some senses by the psycho-social effects of commodification - particularly its attendant narcissism. Indeed, consumer culture and magic are both underpinned by (opposing) forms of narcissistic wish fulfilment – the consumer's desire to buy more and better, and the magician's desire to transform self and other(ness).

Narcissism and the New Age

The work of Ian Parker on narcissism in the New Age is an important heuristic when attempting to understand the psycho-social influence that processes of commodification have on Paganisms.[37] By developing his work, this article demonstrates the ways in which Pagans seek to identify with forms of *otherness*.[38] In particular, Parker uses Christopher Lasch's neo-Freudian sociological reading of the Narcissus myth and Baudrillard's ontological play of signs in his analysis of New Age discourses and identities.[39]

Narcissism: From the individual to the cultural

For Holmes, narcissism exists, and is used, in three overlapping contexts – lay, psychoanalytic, and sociological contexts:[40]

In the lay sense it merely refers to a vain, solipsistic self-preoccupation, sometimes referred to as egoism. Psychoanalytic ideas about narcissism tend fall under three distinct headings: libidinal narcissism, destructive narcissism, and healthy narcissism. Freud's classical brand of libidinal narcissism distinguished between primary narcissism - a normal developmental stage in which the infant displays egocentricity- and, secondary narcissism - a pathological state in which the libido is withdrawn from the external world to be re-invested in oneself, often in an attempt to regain, and a regression to, a fantasized point of fusion with the mother figure.[41] By contrast, clinicians such as Abraham, and the neo-Kleinians

Rosenfeld and Kernberg,[42] all emphasise the destructive elements of narcissism in which self-love leads one to destroy all forms of otherness.[43] Finally, healthy narcissism, as demonstrated in the ego psychology of Kohut,[44] stresses phenomena 'such as parental adoration of their children, the child's excitement in itself and its world, and 'normal' hopes, aspirations, ambitions and ideals as all belonging to the sphere of positive narcissism'.[45] In contra-distinction to negative consumerist forms of commodification, magical practices are structured by this latter healthy narcissism.[46]

In the sociological sense – which I align to a contemporary psychoanalytic sociological perspective - narcissism is obsessive in its attention to the self at the expense of relationships and despairing in its sense that nothing of worth lies within as a source of strength and values.[47] In this sense, narcissism has come to be seen as a part of the late modern malaise of individualism and ontological insecurity. In particular, the irrationality and inhumanity of the Second World War – especially the holocaust - and the post-war rise of 'mass culture' were seen to facilitate sociological narcissism.[48] Such contemporaneous concerns particularly troubled the Freudo-Marxists of The Frankfurt School. Adorno and Horkheimer,[49] for example, indicted manufactured mass culture – including popularist forms of occultism such as tabloid astrology[50] - as the ideological site for the post-war smoothing over of conflict. For Adorno and Horkheimer, this *dumbing down* of the art of critique corresponded to a global desire to wish away conflict 'magically'.[51]

For the Frankfurt theorists, societal forms of narcissism was said to be catalyzed by the break-up of wartime families in Nazi Germany, with children suffering because of absent father figures and reverting to narcissistic states, stuck at a pre-Oedipal phase, with fascist leaders representing the ego-ideal coming to act as patriarchal surrogates.[52] One sees this logic in the work of Christopher Lasch.[53] Lasch indicts modern consumer culture for breaking down any secure site for the formation of identity and 'provoking individuals to seize upon commodities as idealized introjects to form the self.'[54] The modern consumer creates a coherent narrative of identity through the consumption of products, fulfilling the dictates of narcissistic consumer culture that equates happiness with the consumption of status symbols.

However, this hides a hollowness beneath the surface – an *absence*[55] – which, according to Kernberg, is caused by the inability of the narcissistic consumer to form relationships with others of any significant depth.[56] Narcissistic culture therefore is, for Lasch, shallow and self-absorbed.

Although Lasch's condemnation of the superficiality of consumer culture is meretricious, his solution – a return to the secure patriarchal structures that dominated the pre-fascist nuclear family[57] - is not. Kovel rightly criticizes Lasch by reminding him of the positive aspects of Freudian narcissism,[58] and, following Kohut,[59] that a resolution of the narcissistic *crisis* leads to the development of reciprocal moral personal relationships.[60] In a related way, this article contends that it is the resolution of the same crisis that fuels the transformative processes of magic. Furthermore, any reaction against narcissism, for Kovel, must not re-embed individuals within patriarchal familial structures, but rather lead to the development of human communities which are not based around consumption but *pure relationships*,[61] shared beliefs and morality. Indeed, these are the sorts of characteristics that underpin many Pagan collectivities, such as covens and the *Temporary Autonomous Zones* of festival culture. Likewise, For Parker, the New Age movement - rather like Carpenter's characterization of the dynamics of Paganisms[62] - is one of the contradictory responses to the postmodern condition, carrying traces of this cultural turn whilst simultaneously challenging some of the more cynical, superficial aspects of it. Whilst Parker's characterization of the New Age practitioner as someone who revokes individualism for a sense of community is both inaccurate and over simplistic,[63] his sentiments when arguing that New Age 'practices celebrate the turn away from some of the excesses of modernity ... at the same time as they retrieve some human values from the postmodern world'[64] do have an analogue with Paganisms. That is, Paganisms are not consciously narcissistic, but rather adapt the mechanisms of narcissism as transformative magical methodology.

Narcissism, nature and Paganism

Having outlined these approaches to narcissism these will now be applied to the question of Pagan magic, via Parker's heuristic of the New Age. Parker argues that the postmodernization of certain sectors of society does not mean that 'the possibility of social and personal enlightenment is

...over.'[65] He does, however, argue that the postmodernization of culture has affected the way that one views nature, with New Agers, in particular, seeking a close identification with the alterity of *nature* which now completely lies outside *culture*. In this respect, Parker defines the New Age movement in terms that are startlingly close to academic definitions of Paganisms, citing an identification with nature coupled with an almost postmodern spiritual bricolage as ways of coping with contemporary existential crises.[66] For Parker, New Age networks attempt to get back to the real - the *authentic* - through Romantic identifications with cultures that seem closer to nature than our own, 'fixing upon a Baudrillardian simulacrum for which no original seems to exist.'[67]

Given this, Parker sees psychoanalytic discourse - through the lens of narcissistic culture - as impacting on New Age identity and selfhood in three main ways;[68] firstly, through the allure and *seduction* of new age practices and discourses; secondly, through the *fetishism* of new age bodies; and, thirdly, via the *narcissism* of New Age desire. Parker's arguments will now be considered in some depth, explaining the terms and explicating their relevance to a psychoanalytic sociology of Paganisms:

The seductions of Paganism and the New Age

The concept of seduction is central to Freudian psychoanalysis. Indeed, psychoanalysis was only founded after Freud made the conceptual 'double' into the realms of the unconscious and infantile sexuality, and then linked the two by a symbolic, rather than literal, notion of seduction.[69] For Parker, such ideas of seduction and repression lie at the heart of New Age discourses on self and identity:[70]

> New age networks have followed through the idea that unconscious, preconscious or subconscious forces affect our awareness of the world and can be blocked in some way. In the new age networks, these unconscious energies are also located (and sometimes with explicit reference to Jungian ideas) in collective unconscious forces, and they are then extended beyond humankind to all forms of life or planetary being...At the same time as the new age movement holds to the idea that there is

something underneath, there is a concern, however, with the interconnection of experience and the idea that such interconnection can be evoked in fantasy through the play of signs. Like Baudrillard, then, the seduction is through the work of signs which evoke sensuality rather than the sensuality itself which is striking through to the surface.[71]

In particular, he gives the example of the romanticization of animals by New Agers, especially the way in which certain species – particularly Dolphins - come to represent nature as a whole. Parker contends that the celebration of the connection between humans and dolphins is, 'at times, something that is politicized as a struggle to resist more traditional definitions of perversity'.[72] He cites the example of a case between an owner of a dolphinarium and a protester seeking the release of his captive dolphins, which became a *cause celebre* in the tabloid press. The owner of the dolphinarium accused the protester of committing lewd acts with one particular dolphin while swimming with him in the open sea.[73] Indeed, Parker notes the various ways in which popular culture sees dolphins in anthropomorphic terms; either as purveyors of an Atlantean wisdom, as in the film *Cocoon*, or as playful and protective playmates for youngsters, as in *Flipper*.[74] Such an anthropomorphization of dolphins led the dolphin sexual abuse case to be reported in the context of a moral panic in the press concerning child sexual abuse, with tabloid journalists infantilizing the dolphin in their reportage.[75]

The fact that this 'rape of nature' was observed by the public is crucial both to the court case and to theoretical concerns outlined here. This connection between the visible and the obscene is made forcibly in Baudrillard's work on consumption, but is particularly marked in his discussions of pornography.[76] Developing Baudrillard's opposition between seduction and obscenity, New Agers – for Parker - live in the realm of seduction with their uses of music, colour and smell to evoke a connection with nature, whilst moderns, with their exposure to a directly visible *porno culture* are 'all the more horrified by what is visible.'[77] It is this visibility, rather than the specific representation, which horrifies Baudrillard:[78]

> The body is a symbolic veil, and is nothing but that; it is seduction that is to be found in this play of veils, where strictly speaking the body is abolished 'as such'. This is where seduction plays, and never where the veil is torn away in order to reveal a desire or truth.[79]

This tearing of the veil, for Baudrillard, leads to madness and modern malaise – 'too great a proximity of everything.'[80] In contrast, the New Age involves a process of spiritual *re-veiling*.[81] These processes of re-veiling become all the more difficult - yet all the more urgent - within modern rationalized, secular society.[82] As Baudrillard states, 'The loss of public space occurs contemporaneously with the loss of private space. The one is no longer a spectacle, the other no longer a secret'.[83] Thus, Parker concludes that the new age is one powerful response to the loss of natural space during times of ecological crisis – *Risk Society* is one such example[84] – and it is structured by the psychodynamic seductions articulated by Baudrillard.

Such a response is probably even more marked within Paganism and related magical movements with their attendant constructions of sacred nature. Witches have been traditionally associated with animal familiars[85] – the stereotypical black cat or owl - and this tradition of empathy and romanticization of animals continues with contemporary practitioners of forms of the craft and can be found in the neo-shamanic notions of shapeshifting and the power animal.[86]

Seductions are, however, not confined to the relationships of magicians with animal others; indeed, seduction lies at the heart of most magical practices particularly in ceremonial magic where elaborate preparations are made to ensure that the ambiance is perfect in an attempt to maximise the efficacy of the rite.[87] Ritual uses of correspondences, for example, act as elaborate psycho-social props, subtly altering the consciousness of the magician. In other words, correspondences seduce both the senses and the magical will in a manner congruent to the Baudrillardian play of veils.[88]

Similarly, the wearing of a veil – the magical robe – is part of the role play of magic.[89] Wearing garb which is 'other' in relation to everyday street wear is a modernist and pragmatic way of *interiorising otherness*.[90] This is also true, however, of *skyclad* ritual. Ostensibly, this is a symbolic attempt by Wiccans to strip away modern profane trappings and revert to a presocial – *Dionysian* - state of nature.[91] In the Wiccan context it is believed that nudity facilitates communion with the sacred by this opening up the self to otherworldly experience. This intuitively might appear to be at odds with the wearing of magical robes, but it is part of this process of adopting the mantle of otherness. Disrobing, albeit secretly, in a society where public nudity is still a rare occurrence, is an act of wilful alterity on a par with dressing in anachronistic robes.[92] As Baudrillard argues, the body is a symbolic veil, and although sex, playful inversions of traditional sex roles, and sexual polarities play significant parts in Pagan ritual, most Pagan rituals do not tend to be erotic in a conventional sense; at least not in the commodified sense of Baudrillard's *porno culture*. Being part of a skyclad ritual is strangely untitillating after the initial (sub)culture shock and voyeurism. Although the rites often employ sexual imagery, the atmosphere engendered can become strangely desexualized.[93]

These examples illustrate the symbolic abolition of the body - in the Baudrillardian sense. - replaced by the simultaneous seductions and veiling of magic and mystery. Therefore the visible, rather than being *horrific*, becomes the transformative ground that gives mystery its efficacy in such rites. As processes of scientization, secularization, and, losses and infiltrations of public and private space continue to threaten to strip away mystery, Pagan magical practices constitute a symbolic re-veiling of both magical selves and spaces.[94] As long as the mysteries of the otherworld are always in some sense *other* and hidden – *occult* - then this seduction can continue to be pursued. The magician, seemingly paradoxically, believes that these seductions will reveal the true nature of what lies beneath the visible, particularly the perceived obscenities of modernity - *gnosis*. Thus, ritual spaces not only deliberately play upon the tensions between self and other, this world and otherworld, but upon the tensions between seduction and obscenity. In doing so they emulate the liminality of Turner and Bakhtin's *carnivalesque*.[95] In an attempt to arrest the loss of ecologically important public spaces and existentially vital private spaces, the spaces of magical ritual become conscious inversions of Baudrillard's spaces of consumption - *secretive*.[96]

Fetishism, The New Age and magical bodies

In psychoanalysis, an erotic attention to a particular part of the body or specific category of object – a fetish - generally is derived from a refusal to acknowledge an absence. For Freud, it is the disavowal of reality, particularly the absence of the phallus – the primary Freudian signifier of power - and the consequent quest to locate the phallus somewhere else.[97] Baudrillard's discussions of the role and play of signs within the production of commodity fetishism sociologically transforms this classic psychoanalytic reading of sexual fetishism. For Baudrillard, fetishism becomes a consumerist and pathological obsession with adornment – by extension with the signs of consumption.[98] Thus, fetishism becomes a cultural politics played out and inscribed upon the canvas of the body:

> [A]nything will serve to rewrite the cultural order on the body; and it is this that takes the effect of beauty. The erotic is thus the reinscription of the erogenous in a homogeneous system of signs (gestures, movements, emblems, body heraldry) whose goal is closure and logical perfection – to be sufficient unto itself.[99]

Parker, echoing Baudrillard's sentiments, argues that fetishism within New Age movements becomes a literal and ubiquitous mark of identity which is worn on the body - body piercing.[100] Thus, in the fetishism of piercing there is a disavowal of absence and a consequent valorization of a part that stands for that which is missing. For Parker, the absence in New Age movements is the exotic *other* of non-modern cultures:

> Body piercing not only guarantees a part of the body as a reference point but it also connects the pierced body of the Western devotee with the pierced bodies of fetishized 'others' in cultures where the practice is a defining characteristic of membership.[101]

Parker goes on to argue, however, that these practices are not about the conservation of cultures threatened by globalization,[102] but rather as a way of transforming modernity through a shift towards exoticism and retraditionalization.[103]

An interesting example of the relationship between fetishism and tradition within Paganism is tattooing or *sacred skin art*. Sacred skin art is ubiquitous in Pagans of all ages and traditions.[104] Like piercing, it marks both a rejection of, and absorption in, the narcissistic fashions of modernity. A recent article in *Pagan Dawn* asks, 'Is there a more profound relevance for us as spiritual beings in permanently marking our temporary flesh than the desire to be different, rebellious or fashionable?'[105] Palin describes how, as a tattoo artist, Pagans began to approach her, asking her to use the painful and ecstatic experience of tattooing — as a sacred, as well as aesthetic, experience. Thus the process of tattooing sacred symbols onto the body – marking out the skin upon which these symbols rest for special attention – becomes ritualistic rather than mechanical. That is, the very process of tattooing has become fetishized, the ritualism involved in sacred skin art marking it out in contra-distinction to the Fordist mechanics of secular tattooing.[106]

Palin notes many examples of ritualised skin art in non-modern cultures, paralleling the non-Western identifications of new age piercing.[107] The ritualization of skin art coupled with the sacred symbols used becomes part of the simultaneous Pagan desires for spiritual individualism, and for community and tradition as existential anchors: [108]

> We can begin to re-introduce a sense of sacred mark-making and ceremony into our lives, into the community at large by ridding the tattoo of its negative and restricting imagery and showing it as a personal celebration of the body and of life itself. We can welcome diversity with a new respect for individual choice and freedom of expression, this can be part of our Pagan practice, rejoicing in life's myriad facets.[109]

Thus, for Palin, 'community' does not just equate with the Pagan 'community', but the wider human community, paralleling the non-Western identifications of Parker's new age piercers:

> The tattoo is a tool for transformation, both of our own lives and of society as a whole. We can reclaim our own sense of time and place, remembering the body paint and stunning engraved personal adornments of the ancestors, reflecting our own rich heritage and creating meaningful visual language for this age. Subtle changes to our own energy matrix will radiate outwards. How better to affect change than by permanently making an aesthetically pleasing statement upon the body as part of our sacred journey?[110]

Skin art is not only a disavowal of absence, but a catalyst of spiritual transformations seen as missing from modern secular life.[111]

Narcissism, The New Age and Pagan desire

The narcissistic redirection of libidinal interest upon one's own self – 'the recathexis of the ego'[112] – is likened by Freud to that of a single-celled organism whose retractable limbs reach out for pleasurable morsels and then are invisibly reabsorbed into its body.[113] Importantly for Freudians, this pleasure must be mediated, otherwise it is merely auto-eroticism, not narcissism.[114] Therefore, narcissistic practices 'require an other for whom the display is intended.'[115] For Baudrillard, such mediation is conducted through the play of signs and, by extension, becomes an integral element of contemporary subjectivities. Such mediation is paralleled in the New Age movement:

As Parker notes, 'In the new age networks there is always a sense of mediation, either through energies flowing through chakras, ley lines ... or through rituals in like-minded spiritual communities.'[116] In order to illustrate this mediated desire, Parker uses the fringe New Age practice of self-trepanation. Dr Bart Huges, a Dutch physician, was the pioneer of self-trepanation, arguing that the skull – and by extension the self – could be returned to an infantile state by cutting a small disk of bone out of the skull with a special surgical drill called a *trephine*.[117] That is, the artificial fontanelle thus created mediates energy between the self and the outer world. Amanda Feilding,[118] another advocate — used an electric drill for her procedure and describes the subsequent trepanized state as 'an internal economy pleasantly floating above the poverty barrier.'[119] In addition to this ecstatic state, Feilding discusses a post-trepanation loss of ego, interpreting this as a heightened, infantile, state of awareness and consciousness.[120]

Returning to Baudrillard, Parker argues that narcissism is not only played out on such a localised stage as the cranium, but that New Age networks 'also attempt to work through the narcissistic paradoxes on a wider world stage where the postcolonial 'other' returns to fuse with the excolonial centre, working through and with, for example, the idealization and defence of 'indigenous peoples".[121] This literal physical opening up of the self and ego through self-trepanation has become replaced, by many New Agers, by a symbolic opening up through, for example, 'shamanist ritual, world music or political activity around issues of development.'[122] Ritual - whether collective or individual, ceremonial or instinctual - arguably forms the main avenue of spiritual transformation within Pagan magic. Importantly, rituals mediate between the ritual actors and the forces with which they wish to commune and connect. One sees this in two main senses:

Firstly, Faivre's characterisation of esotericism emphasises mediation, particularly the relationships between esoteric correspondences, mediation processes and the imagination.[123] For Faivre, correspondences act as esoteric mediators which are activated by the *active* magical *imagination*:

> It is the imagination that allows the use of these intermediaries, symbols and images to develop a gnosis, to penetrate the hieroglyphs of Nature, to put the theory of correspondences into active practice and to uncover, to see, and to know the mediating entities between Nature and the divine world.[124]

Secondly, communion with the Otherworld is a mediational reality for Pagan magicians. That is, the Otherworld is an ontological realm which simultaneously mediates between ordinary reality and otherwordly reality, and is co-extensive with both this worldly and otherworldly forces and entities. In other words, the Otherworld is a sacred milieu which is both of quotidian, material reality, but also transcendent in relation to it.[125] Given this, the mediational aspect of the Otherworld parallels wider pagan processes of identification with Otherness. One sees this, for example, in Pagan identifications with other cultures and indigenous spiritual traditions - as outlined above in the case of the New Age; in Pagan identifications with the divine, Nature, and the non-human *Other* through ritual practice; in the artistic mediation and motivation provided by the Druidic *Awen*; in the mediations of spirit provided by the Chakra system on the body, and of geomantic chakras at locations such as Glastonbury and Sedona;[126] and even in the alchemic *rubedo* stage.[127] In addition, the modernist tendency of the post-Crowleyan systematisation of magic has meant that the Cabalistic tree of life - yet another mediating magical matrix - is often subtly interwoven with the chakra system and/or the tarot, developing yet further layers of mediated spiritual practice.[128]

Escaping Baudrillard's mirrors: Towards a conclusion

Clearly destructive narcissistic culture and selves sit uncomfortably with such notions of ego loss and transformation within Paganisms.[129] Pagan spiritual transformation, therefore, is not just about the overcoming of the self, but also about overcoming the narcissism of consumer culture wherein one is in danger of being seduced by the allure of a product, fetishizing its symbolic *capital*, and becoming absorbed into the realm of signifiers which denote its cultural use and value. Pagans, although outspoken critics of consumer culture, are not however unaffected by its seductions. Rather, Pagan discourses and practices are simultaneously structured by narcissism yet seek to distance practitioners from its worst excesses.

This happens in two main ways: Firstly, as outlined in this article, the destructive narcissism of consumer culture is sublimated into the healthy narcissism of magical practices. Its material seductions inverted – and subverted - to become spiritual seductions. Secondly, in a more general sense, practitioners employ the existential strategies or modalities of tradition, the ritualization of otherness, and complex science as a means of both legitimating their practices and grounding their identities, discourses and practices in frameworks removed from modern consumption processes.[130] That is, Paganisms are both rooted in modernity, but form a critical reaction to it.

In conclusion, an emergent psychoanalytic sociological framework opens up *new lines of academic flight* for the study of magic. Far from grounding magical practices in classical Freudianism, this perspective seeks to transcend its strictures; firstly by attempting to uncover the unconscious mechanisms which mutually structure magician and society; and, secondly by forging new theoretical connections between seemingly disparate Pagan practices.

Notes

1 Daniel O'Keefe, *Stolen Lightning* (New York: Vintage Books, 1983), 31.

2 Particularly in their characterisations of the disenchantments of modern Capitalism. Durkheim's modernity is characterised by *anomic* social relations, that is by a normlessness and forms of increasing differentiation between social roles and individuals. Weber is even more pessimistic, speaking of societies beset by bureaucracy and a joylessness born out of the decline of magic and increasing rationalization and rational governance of the self.

3 Otherwise known as The Frankfurt School.

4 Whilst Adorno was critical of popular occultism and saw it - developing Marx - as a form of fatalistic false consciousness, Marcuse's notions of spiritual and perceptual revolution are akin to many magical ideas of personal and social liberation. See, for example, James Webb, *The Occult Establishment* (La Salle, Ill.: Open Court, 1976), 474-5.

5 It has to be noted that whilst using looting his conceptual toolbox, Deleuze and Guattari are also openly hostile to many of Freud's theoretical excesses.

6 Indeed, for 'primitive' one might more properly read 'primal', restoring magic to its place at the centrality of human and personal development.

7 Effectively, the super-ego is the policeman that lies within. It is an internal mode of surveillance. Also see Michel Foucault, *Discipline and Punish* (New York: Vintage Books, 1979).

8 Other important developments of psychoanalytic sociologies are present in departments at the University of Essex, and of East London. Zygmunt Bauman postmodern sociology of the other is another key touchstone.

9 Geza Roheim, *Magic and Schizophrenia* (Bloomington, Ind.: Indiana University Press, 1955), 25.

10 Akin to Starhawk's notion of the *younger self*. See Starhawk, *The Spiral Dance* (San Francisco, CA: HarperSanFrancisco, 1989), 35-6.

11 Indeed classic Freudianism in differing forms, has become an increasing part of witchcraft historiography. For example, Lyndal Roper, *Oedipus and the Devil* (London: Routledge, 1994). This despite the extensive critical literature which advocates the socio-historica specificity of Freud's ideas to advanced Capitalist countries. Heinemann's is an interesting post-Kleinian recasting of these ideas. See Evelyn Heinemann, *Witches* (London: Free Association Books, 2000).

12 Vivianne Crowley, *Wicca. The Old Religion in the New Age* (London: The Aquarian Press, 1989).

13 See James Webb, 345-416. Also B.J. Gibbons, *Spirituality and the Occult* (London: Routledge, 2001), 103-11.

14 See note 13.

15 Indeed James Webb, 358, notes how the theories of Fliess became tangled with those of Berdyaev, Hartmann, Levi, Papus, Kemmerich, Wirth, Steiner, von Liebenfels, and Horbiger.

16 James Webb, 359.

17 Interestingly, Joseph Breuer, Freud's teacher and collaborator, was also a regular visitor to a Viennese family where Rudolf Steiner was employed as a tutor.

18 See Susan Greenwood, *Magic, Witchcraft and the Otherworld* (Oxford: Berg, 2000), 125-8.

19 Susan Greenwood, 125

20 This is evidenced by Freud's statement:

It is by no means self-evident that the strengthening of the interest in occultism represents a danger for psychoanalysis. On the contrary, one might expect a mutual sympathy between the two. Both have been subjected by official science to the same unfair and arrogant treatment. (Cited in James Webb, 371).

21 Indeed, superficially at least, Freud has some commonalities with Crowley if one thinks of their blending of scientific and occult theories and the way in which their oeuvres was illuminated or otherwise by their drug habits.

22 It is inevitable that Freud's copious cocaine habit meant that his personal phantasies and demons, mediated by altered states, affected his theories – almost magically one might say. Freud's theories could be said to pertain to the Jungian *imaginal*, which we should then read creatively through the lens of the imagination. Certainly much of the impact of Freud upon popular culture has been through imaginative uses of Freudian theory by creative writers.

23 Richard Cavendish, *A History of Magic* (London: Arkana, 1987), 161.

24 See George Devereux (ed.) *Psychoanalysis and the Occult* (London: Souvenir Press, 1974), 49-109.

25 See George Devereux (ed.).

26 The *unheimlich*.

27 See Justin Woodman, this edition.

[28] See Graham Harvey (2000) **Error! Reference source not found.** diskus/harvey_2.html

29 For example, Peter Grey 'The Nike Conspiracy' in *Razor Smile* (Issue 1, Samhain 2002), 36-7.

30 See, for example, Paul Heelas, 'The limits of consumption and the post-modern 'religion' of the New Age, in R. Keat, N. Whiteley, and N. Abercrombie (eds.) *The Authority of the Consumer* (London: Routledge, 1994), 102-15; and, *The New Age Movement: the Celebration of the Self and the Sacralization of Modernity* (Oxford: Blackwell, 1996).

31 See note 30; also Kevin Hetherington, K. 'Stonehenge and Its Festival: Spaces of Consumption', in R. Shields (ed.) *Lifestyle Shopping*. (London: Routledge, 1992), 83-98.

32 Marion Bowman, 'The Commodification of the Celt', in *Folklore in Use* (1994, 2), 143-52.

33 When I think back to my early days of magical practice it was marked by a profound desire to do things 'the right way'; that is by purchasing the correct colour candles, the correct blend of incense, a carefully crafted athame, etc. Indeed I wanted to do things 'by the book' thus, a vast range of 'magical' tomes were purchased as I sought occult knowledge, and – more naively - occult truth.

34 As this Thelemite, one of my research respondents, notes:

Magic may be spreading around the world, but as it does it comes over to people in nice, neat packages. It's so commercial these days ... it makes me laugh. Even serious magicians are more commercial now…There are lots of soundbites and precious few oaths sworn these days.

Such commodification, however, is universal within magical milieux prompting discussion of a *McDonaldization* of occulture See König, P. (2001) 'The McDonaldization of Occulture', paper delivered to *The Spiritual Supermarket* conference, INFORM, London School of Economics, April, 18th-22nd April, 2001.

35 Doug Ezzy, 'The Commodification of Witchcraft', in *Australian Religion Studies Review* (2001, 14, 1), 31-44. Of particular interest is the Australian witch Fiona Horne who now has a soft-core show on satellite television in the UK promoting sacred sex and the use of ritual in combating sexual problems.

36 This has an analogue in the esoteric notion of *transmission*.

37 Ian Parker, *Psychoanalytic Culture* (London: Sage, 1997), 172-184. As explained below Parker's characterisation of the New Age is so non-specific that it certainly holds for Paganisms.

38 See Dave Green, 'Opposites Attract: Magical Identity and Social Uncertainty' in *The Journal for the Academic Study of Magic* (Issue 1, 2003).

39 As Ian Parker states

it is possible to see reflections of these kinds of change in Western self-experience in some recent responses to modern technology in the 'new age' movement. We will also see here how Enlightenment technological reason analysed by the Frankfurt School provokes rather romantic fantasies about the nature of 'nature', and these fantasies now underpin a growing and potent sub-cultural milieu in the West. (Ian Parker, 163)

40 See Jeremy Holmes, *Narcissism*. (Cambridge: Icon Books, 2001). Its genesis, however, is rooted in Classical myth and literature, for example in Ovid, Shakespeare's 62nd sonnet, and even in Oscar Wilde's *The Picture of Dorian Gray*.

41 See Sigmund Freud, 'On Narcissism', in A. Richards (ed.) *On Metapsychology*. (Harmondsworth: Penguin, 1984); that is, in narcissism, 'the ego-ideal (the heir of narcissism) is regulated by the development of the super-ego (the heir of the Oedipus complex), but we cannot help loving those who replace our earliest love objects, and we resent those who threaten to disrupt that first most intense love.' See Ian Parker, 36. The rise of Goddess spirituality, for example, might be seen by some Freudians as symptomatic of these narcissistic processes.

42 For example, K. Abraham, *Selected Papers* (London: Hogarth Press, 1973); H. Rosenfeld, *Psychotic States: A Psycho Analytic Approach* (New York: International Universities Press, 1965); Otto Kernberg, *Borderline Connections and Pathological Narcissism* (New York: Jason Aronson, 1975).

43 This destructive narcissism stands in marked contrast to Pagan identification with otherness; for example in Dave Green (2003).

44 See H. Kohut, *The Analysis of the Self* (New York: International Universities Press, 1971).

45 Holmes, 8; This certainly lies in marked contrast to destructive, negative forms of narcissism which Kohut sees as stemming from abuse.

46 This idea will be developed below.

47 As Parker argues:

There is a price to be paid for enlightenment, and each individual loses connection with other people, and from their own desire at the same time as they gain the ability to reflect critically upon themselves and rationally appraise different courses of action. (Ian Parker, 23)

48 As Parker argues:

After the Second World War the hopes of the Enlightenment seemed to have collapsed into a kind of culture in which all the contradiction was erased, and no critical distance or potential for change remained. (Ian Parker, 163-4)

49 Theodor Adorno and Max Horkheimer, *Dialectic of Enlightenment* (London: Verso, 1993).

50 Theodor Adorno, *The Stars Down to Earth* (London: Routledge, 2001). For Adorno, popular Occultism in general, and tabloid astrology in particular, is just another part of a hegemonic culture industry. That is the Occult is merely the wishful thinking of would-be escapists. Whilst disagreeing with this – and indeed seeing much contemporary occultism as counter-hegemonic - I believe that the desire to change oneself and one's world magically is linked intrinsically to (positive or healthy) narcissism.

51 As Parker states about the work of the Frankfurt School on mass culture:

'Mass culture stimulates and structures narcissistic kinds of experience, and it dissolves the struggle for personal or social enlightenment into a collective illusion that things can get better if you simply *wish* hard enough.' (Ian Parker, 165)

One can also see an overlap here with Baudrillard's notions of hyperreality and simulation.

52 See, for example, Theodor Adorno, 'Freudian Theory and the pattern of fascist propaganda', in A. Arato and E. Gebhardt (eds.) *The Essential Frankfurt School Reader.* (Oxford: Blackwell, 1978); J. Benjamin, 'The End of Internalization: Adorno's Social Psychology', in *Telos* (1977, 32), 42-64.

53 See Christopher Lasch, *The Culture of Narcissism: American Life in an Age of Diminishing Expectations.* (New York: Norton, 1978). Janine Chasseguet-Smirgel also pursued this Lasch's logic, but here arguments are less relevant here due to its oversimplification of societal narcissism: Her work draws upon classical Freudian narcissism and Otto Kernberg's clinical work on narcissistic personality types. See Janine Chasseguet-Smirgel, *The Ego Ideal: A Psychoanalytic Essay on the Malady of the Ideal.* (London: Free Association Books, 1985a); *Creativity and Perversion.* (London: Free Association Books, 1985b); also J. Alt and F. Hearn 'Symposium on Narcissism: the Cortland conference on narcissism' in *Telos* (1980, 44), 49-58. Chasseguet-Smirgel's work is controversial, for example, arguing that homosexuals are more likely than heterosexuals to be 'perverts' (Chasseguet-Smirgel, 1985b); and, that ideology is 'illusory' (Chasseguet-Smirgel, 1985a). Hence, any challengers to the status-quo are little more than narcissistic fantasists who wish to mould society to their own ends; see for example, Janine Chasseguet-Smirgel, and Grunberger, B. (1976) *Freud or Reich? Psychoanalysis and Illusion* (London: Free Association Books, 1976).

54 Ian Parker, 168.

55 Such a 'hollowness beneath the surface' of society and relatedness has resonance with the absence of Baudrillard's postmodern consumer culture. Baudrillard is useful in describing post-Enlightenment phenomena, such as the New Age, and indeed Paganism, because his theoretical descriptions and uses of seduction, fetishism and narcissism correspond so closely to the way those notions structure the phenomena.

56 See Otto Kernberg (1975). It has to be noted here that such an absence is a consequence of negative or destructive forms of narcissism. I believe that whilst the quest of some ceremonial magicians, for example Thelemites, is towards a spiritual absence – i.e., nothingness, the void, etc. – that this quest is the result of positive or healthy forms of narcissism.

57 See, for example, M. Wangh, 'Some unconscious factors in the psychogenesis of recent student uprisings', in *Psychoanalytic Quarterly* (1972, 41), 207-23; C. Badcock, *Madness and Modernity*. (Oxford: Blackwell, 1983).

58 See J. Kovel, *The Radical Spirit* (London: Free Association Books, 1988).

59 See H. Kohut (1971); also *How does Analysis Cure?* (Chicago: University of Chicago Press, 1984).

60 However, as Parker notes about critics such as Kovel:

Although such critics argue that there are positive aspects of narcissism, however, they are still not necessarily overjoyed by trends in contemporary culture. (Ian Parker, 168)

61 For example, Anthony Giddens, *Modernity and Self-Identity* (Cambridge: Polity Press, 1991).

62 See Dennis Carpenter, 'Emergent Nature Spirituality: An examination of the Major Spiritual Contours of the Contemporary Pagan Worldview', in James Lewis (ed.) *Magical Religion and Modern Witchcraft*. (Albany, NY: State University of New York Press, 1996), 35-72.

63 Note Paul Heelas (1996).

64 Ian Parker, 171-2.

65 Ian Parker, 172; see also Dave Green (2003).

66 Hence my justification of appropriating many of the spiritual dynamics of what Parker terms 'New Age' and re-labelling them 'Pagan' .For Parker, 'the new age movement is on response to that crisis which finds different ways of coping with the seductiveness of contemporary consumer culture, the fetishizing of bits of the body, and with narcissistic forms of self-identity.' (Ian Parker, 172).

67 Ian Parker, 172. He cites, for example, the Bialystock Indians, group of New Age Poles who live in tepees and wear clothing resembling the Native Americans of the Hollywood *Western*. See M. Wiernikowska, 'Tipis and totem poles', in *The*

Guardian, (24th November 1992), 12. In this sense New Age reality becomes fictive.

68 Ian Parker, 172-183.

69 That is, Freud performed a *volte-face* from his previous work, which argued that many neuroses were the result of the actual physical abuse and seduction of children, to a theory of sexual fantasy in which the child became a source of desire and a *tabula rasa* for the projection of the sexual desires of others.

70 It must be made explicit here that Parker's uses of psychoanalytic - mostly Neo-Freudian – concepts in order to understand the New Age movement are qualitatively different from the New Age (and Pagan) applications of psychodynamic – mostly Jungian – theory in their attempts to understand the divine.

71 Ian Parker, 174-5.

72 Ian Parker, 175.

73 Whilst the press printed lurid details of the alleged act – the entangling of the dolphin's penis around the leg of the protester – the ensuing court case focused more upon the extent to which the committal of such an act was carried out in a manner in which would offend the public. Indeed representatives of the public were taken out in the dolphinarium owner's boat to observe whether such behaviour was a danger to public morals. The protester was eventually acquitted.

74 Ian Parker, 175-6.

75 As Parker continues, 'The lurid details of the activist's encounter with the dolphin and prurient interest in what unthinkable things might be going on underwater seemed to touch a fear that some last area of innocence was being despoiled.' (Ian Parker, 176)

76 Jean Baudrillard, 'Fetishism and Ideology: The semiological reduction', in Jean Baudrillard *For a Critique of the Political Economy of the Sign* (St. Louis: Telos Press, 1981), 150-1.

77 Ian Parker, 176.

78 That is, as Parker states, 'seduction is symbolic exchange for Baudrillard, the attempt to get beneath that exchange is an end to the erotic.' (Ian Parker, 176)

79 Jean Baudrillard, 'The ecliptic of sex', in P. Foss and J. Pefanis (eds.) *Jean Baudrillard, Revenge of the Crystal* (London: Pluto Press, 1990), 150. In brief, Baudrillard argues that eroticism is linked to seduction, in that the erotic is a process of selective veiling and unveiling of the body, as, for example, in the come-hither sexuality of striptease. Despite the fact that flesh is revealed in such an art-form, it is this selective exposure of flesh which remystifies the body, abolishing it as a pornographic entity, that is an entity which is totally visible and

totally without mystery. The mystical revealing of skyclad bodies, for example, prevents them from being, in Baudrillard's terms, pornographic

80 Jean Baudrillard, 'The ecstasy of communication', in H. Foster (ed.) *Postmodern Culture*. (London: Pluto Press, 1983), 132.

81 As Parker observes:

Technology invades and destroys the sea as a mysterious invisible place and animals living there, and the new age movement invests again these areas with a numinous quality. This is the romantic veiling work that the new age performs on dolphins. As things which were distant become close, the new age produces them again as new mysteries. The new age participates, then, in postmodern *fantasies* of nature rather than attempting to go straight back to the real, but it also tries to find in these dreams some *meaning*. [emphases in the original] (Ian Parker, 176)

82 As Parker states, 'The possibilities for seduction, for the sense of things desired being hidden and desired all the more for that, are under threat as the urban centres simultaneously spread and collapse.' (Ian Parker, 176-7)

83 Jean Baudrillard (1983), 130.

84 Ulrich Beck, *Risk Society* (London: Sage, 1992).

85 See, for example, Diane Purkiss, *The Witch in History*. (London: Routledge, 1996), 134-9.

86 See, for example, Michael Harner, *The Way of the Shaman* (San Francisco: HarperSanFrancisco, 1990). Shapeshifting is particularly emphasised in the various works of Castaneda.

87 It is important to note here that efficacy, as opposed to performance – *enacting* rather than mere *acting* – is an important feature of ritual activity. See, for example, R. Schechner, *Performance Theory*. (London: Routledge, 1994).

88 As this research participant, a self-defined ceremonial magician, argues:

Props put me in the mood for workings. I wouldn't feel half as magical if I called myself Fred Smith, wore jeans, and performed the ritual under a strip light.

89 See Dave Green (2003).

90 Note Howard Eilberg-Schwartz, 'Witches of the West: Neopaganism and Goddess Worship as Enlightenment Religions', in *Journal of Feminist Studies in Religion* (1989, 5, 1), 77-95.

91 Indeed Gardner was a naturist himself.

92 As this Gardnerian Wiccan research participant observes:

Being skyclad helps be to connect with the forces of nature, but it's also a magic prop. Robes work in a similar way. It's strange that being naked becomes a bit like a uniform that I might wear for work ... mmm, I've not thought of this before, but being naked is a bit like wearing a uniform for ritual ... magic work, I suppose. It's a bit odd to be openly nude in the South of England.

93 As this research participant states:

Part of looking forward to my first skyclad ritual was...well, you know, the...the titillation. It's a let down as far as that goes and you soon get used to being naked...The more natural it becomes the better the ritual seemed to work for me. (A Druid, who used to be a practising Wiccan)

Indeed a similar phenomenon is often reported in anthropological fieldwork in non-modern societies where the Western anthropologist is in closely confined to (mostly) naked bodies of the opposite sex for long periods of time. See, for example, Alan Tormaid Campbell, *Getting to Know Wai-Wai: An Amazonian Ethnography.* (London: Routledge, 1995). Campbell states of his time with the Wayapi of North-Eastern Brazil, 'sexual urges simply did not arise when living in Indian settlements' (Campbell, 230).

94 In some ways akin to Berger's concept of a sacred canopy. See Peter Berger, *The Sacred Canopy: Elements of a Sociological Theory of Religion.* (New York: Doubleday, 1967).

95 See Dave Green (2003).

96 Furthermore, mystery is necessarily bound with secrecy. Although the veil of secrecy surrounding Pagan practices has been steadily lifted since Gardner's time, secrecy still persists as a partial psycho-social remnant of premodern heretical practices, but mostly endures out of real fears of anti-pagan prejudice and discrimination.

97 Sigmund Freud 'Fetishism', in A. Richards (ed.) *On Sexuality* (Harmondsworth: Penguin, 1977). Again, there is this idea of absence. As Parker succinctly puts it, 'What has been refused at one point is marked at another. The repudiation of the loss of the object fails as this lost object returns in the form of a fetish'. (Ian Parker, 178)

98 In particular, Baudrillard extends the notion to postmodern readings of popular cultural icons such as Andy Warhol and Velvet Underground associate Nico, who 'only seemed more beautiful because her femininity was purely an act. Something more than beauty, almost sublime emanated from her, a different seduction. The deception to be uncovered was that she was a false drag, a real woman playing at drag' (Jean Baudrillard, 1990, 134).

99 Jean Baudrillard (1981), 94.

100 For Parker,

The insertion of pieces of metal marks the pierced parts of the body out for particular attention, and holds it there. These parts of the body may stand, in classic psychoanalytic vision, for the absent phallus, in the ear, tongue, eyelid or nipple, or lower lip (where the metal is called a labret). The parts of the body may be marked as the location of what is absent, piercing of the inner labia or clitoral hood, or, in an increasingly popular practice in the UK, in the marking of the phallus itself, a fetishistic guarantee against absence. (Ian Parker, 179)

101 Ian Parker, 179

102 That is, 'an attempt to retrieve what has been lost or to keep to keep present what may disappear.' (Ian Parker, 179)

103 See Paul Heelas, Scott Lash, and Paul Morris (eds.) *Detraditionalization*. (Oxford: Blackwell, 1996).

104 Indeed, a female Pagan acquaintance lives by the dictum 'Give Blood – get a tattoo!'

105 Poppy Palin, 'Sacred Skin Art' in *Pagan Dawn* (2000, Issue 136), 18.

106 Indeed, one of my research participants confided that he enjoyed the ritualistic element involved in obtaining his tattoos and piercings. He observed that pain was a part of initiation in many premodern cultures and how these experiences lead to a better understanding of both one's body and the transformative nature of ecstatic experience.

107 Poppy Palin, 18-19.

108 The symbols used are often pentagrams, symbols depicting gender or solar/lunar polarities or Celtic designs

109 Poppy Palin, 19.

110 Poppy Palin, 19.

111 This point was demonstrated in my research in discussion with the late Thelemite Gerald Suster. He stated that the large pentagram tattoo on his shoulder was seen as emblematic of his own spiritual journey.

112 Ian Parker, 181.

113 See Freud (1984). As Parker states this recathexis

is like an amoeba sending out parts of itself, the pseudopodia, for the material in these limbs will always return and be absorbed again into the body of the creature. Narcissism, which revolves around a visual metaphor of Narcissus gazing into the pool at his own image, is also, then, to do with the sucking inward of energy. (Ian Parker, 181)

114 Having said this acts of auto-eroticism are bound up with the mediations of magical use, for example, the use of sigilization in Spare's sorceries of Zos - for a brief introduction see Nevill Drury, *The History of Magic in the Modern Age: A quest for personal transformation*. (New York: Carroll & Graf, 2000), 127-34 – specifically within contemporary chaos magic. See, for example, Justin Woodman, 'A Means to an End? The Role of Altered States of Consciousness in Chaos Magic', paper delivered to *Shamanism in Contemporary Society* conference at

the Department of Religious Studies, University of Newcastle-Upon-Tyne, 24th June, 1998.

115 Ian Parker, 181.

116 Ian Parker, 182. I will return to these examples later in the article.

117 Such a trepanised state has parallels with Starhawk's *younger self*. See Note 10.

118 She twice ran unsuccessfully as a UK parliamentary candidate on a 'Free Trepanation on the NHS' ticket

119 Amanda Feilding, 'Interview with Amanda Feilding', in *Fortean Times* (1991, 58), 44.

120 Thus, trepanation parallels Pagan notions of ego loss, self-mastery, and spiritual transformation. Furthermore, New Age practices such as cranial osteopathy and Indian head massage function as narcissistic, but less extreme, forms of trepanantion.

121 Ian Parker, 182-3.

122 Ian Parker, 183.

123 Antoine Faivre, *Access to Western Esotericism* (Albany, NY: SUNY Press, 1994), 10-5.

124 Antoine Faivre, 12.

125 As this unaligned respondent states:

I am a pantheist, but within this the Otherworld is, well...other. It's implied in the name. I can journey to this Otherworld, but am also always part of it.

Also note H. Van Hove, 'Higher Realities and the Inner Self: One Quest? Transcendence and the Significance of the Body in the New Age Circuit', in *The Journal of Contemporary Religion* (1996, 11, 2), 185-194.

126 See, for example, Adrian Ivakhiv *Claiming Sacred Ground* (Bloomington, IND: Indiana University Press, 2001).

127 See, for example, Vivienne Crowley, *Jungian Spirituality*. (London: Thorsons, 1998), 64-70.

128 See, for example, Aleister Crowley, *777* (London: Neptune Press, 1955); Ted Andrews, *More Simplified Magic* (Jackson, TN.: Dragonhawk Publishing, 1998).

129 As this shaman, a research respondent, argues:

We are part of an increasingly consumer society and magic is therefore part of that...Consumption is magical for some people. We need to recognise these things and modern life has also brought with it great advances...Let's not throw out the baby with the bathwater...We can't escape consumption in the modern world but we can do our best to resist its...its excesses.

130 See Dave Green (2003).

A Shell with my Name on it: The Reliance on the Supernatural During the First World War

Vanessa Chambers

> Stephen took a pack of cards from the wooden shelf by the door, some stubs of candle and some sand. He made the shape of a pentangle on the table, placing several cards face down and linking them with trails of sand. He lit the candles and placed them at five equidistant points...
>
> He inserted the tip of the knife under the card nearest him and flipped it over. It was an eight. 'Good,' he said. The next card was the four of hearts...Stephen levered the next card slowly up. It was the two of clubs...The fourth card was the ace of hearts. 'Peace,' said Stephen.[1]

In *Birdsong*, Sebastian Faulks' harrowing account of First World War trench warfare, the protagonist relies on magic and fortune-telling to help him survive the horror around him. Albeit a work of fiction, *Birdsong* is factually accurate and well researched.[2] Evidence shows that soldiers did rely upon a multitude of supernatural props to help sustain and support them during those harrowing times: these ranged from individual charms to mass supernatural sightings. At home, too, people visited fortune-tellers and spiritualists as the conflict continued and mourning became almost a national pastime. Indeed, as Historian Jay Winter explains: 'The Great War, the most 'modern' of wars, triggered an avalanche of the 'unmodern".[3] By considering the reliance placed on the supernatural both in the trenches and at the home front, I hope to highlight a relatively unexplored aspect of the conflict that had a significant impact on the lives of both soldiers and civilians. Moreover, I have identified an important gender change in the dissemination of these beliefs from the traditional female culture to the all-male culture of the trenches. There is also a possibility that the authorities made use of these beliefs for propaganda purposes.

The term 'supernatural' relates to forces above and outside the laws of nature[4] and has been used here to synergistically combine belief in magic, charms, amulets, mascots, talisman, rituals, fortune-telling and apparitions. The term 'superstition' has also been used although this term is somewhat problematic. At the time, its use was often derogatory, linking superstitions to 'old wives tales' and 'nonsense' that had no place in modern warfare. As one army chaplain wrote disparagingly at the time, the superstitious soldier is either 'a polytheist or a devil-worshipper, or, more probably, just a fool'.[5] Nevertheless, there was a widespread belief, both at home and at the front, that the outcome of events could be influenced by certain rituals, objects or actions. It is in this sense that the term 'superstition' has been used throughout this article. Surprisingly, because these beliefs are essentially hidden, there are many good primary sources available including journals, diaries, photographs, novels, letters, reminiscences, newspaper and journal articles, online collections, paintings, and transcribed oral testimony.[6]

Taking Luck to the Front
There is much evidence to show that soldiers going off to fight in the Great War took with them a wide variety of "lucky" charms, amulets, mascots, and other "protective" objects. Indeed, Paul Fussell, in his authoritative work on the making of modern memory, asserts that 'no front-line soldier or officer was without his amulet...no talisman was too absurd'. He lists amongst the paraphernalia found in soldiers' tunic pockets -

> Lucky coins, buttons, dried flowers, hair cuttings, New Testaments, pebbles from home, medals of St. Christopher and St. George, childhood dolls and teddy bears, poems or Scripture verses written out and worn in a small bag around the neck[7]

A close search through the photographic archives of the Imperial War Museum reveals evidence to support this: soldiers wearing amulets, holed medallions or charm bracelets can be seen. Moreover, the recent exhibition held at the Imperial War Museum of the BBC television series 'The Trench', displayed a case containing some of the objects that soldiers took with them to the trenches for luck.[8]

Of course, this faith in mascots and charms was not new. It had its basis in the oral tradition, myth and folklore of the past and this gave these beliefs authority. A whole range of beliefs (throwing salt, touching wood, etc.) had passed from generation to generation, from neighbour to neighbour, promulgated mainly, though not entirely, by women.[9] Moreover, and importantly, these did not occur only in the countryside as has been assumed, but were prevalent in the urban environment too.[10] Edward Lovett's research into magic in early twentieth-century London validates this.[11] Furthermore, a tendency by soldiers to carry charms and mascots was noticed in earlier wars. In 1900, a journal article discussed battleground "superstitions" and concluded that 'numbers of men even among the volunteers do not depart for the front without a charm of some kind'.[12]

Clearly, as historian Owen Davies explains, 'soldiers about to go to the front...must have been burdened with a terrible fear of the unknown, of the knowledge that only sheer luck might prevent them being the next victim'.[13] It seems reasonable, therefore, that they would clutch at anything purporting to increase their chances of survival. This, some historians have suggested, demonstrates the diminishing influence of traditional religion and the need to find explanations and answers that the churches were simply unable to give.[14] Certainly, references to lucky objects are found within many primary documents. Edwin Vaughan writes in 1917 of 'an ever-increasing bunch [of charms]'.[15] Furthermore, he made certain that both his rosary and a lucky sovereign were sewn into his tunic.[16] Lovett mentions the farthing that many soldiers had sown into their left brace 'just over the position of the heart'. The farthing represented the Monarch, who represented God, so Lovett asserts that the soldier was indirectly seeking God's protection by positioning this over his heart. Moreover, Lovett traced this practice back to at least the Crimean war.[17] Ellen Ettlinger, writing for *Folklore* in 1939, lists other objects carried by soldiers during the war:

A holed "Lucky Stone"…
A "Holed Devon Stone"…
A large seed from Africa…
A Mandrake Root, carried as an Amulet…
'Four-Leaf Clover Amulets', and 'Merry-Thoughts'
Coin-amulets and religious medal-amulets[18]

Lovett's list includes: 'left-handed whelks', 'little wool figures – called Golliwogs', a 'carved amber bead', and 'an old farthing with a hole through it'.[19] The range of objects considered lucky by soldiers was clearly quite diverse, but tended to be items traditionally thought to be lucky. It is, however, interesting to note the changing use of some of these such as holed stones, traditionally used as protection against witches.[20] The 'Golliwog' may have had its precedent as a traditional votive offering.[21] Owen Davies records the changing use of objects like horseshoes over time,[22] and it is interesting to note that items traditionally used to ward off harm from an individual, e.g. a suspected witch, were now being used against harm of a more general and wide-ranging nature. Lovett records oral testimony in which the storytellers attribute their survival to the carrying of these "lucky" items. It is worth considering an example of Lovett's findings here, since this provides good evidence of growing belief in lucky objects during the war. Moreover, it confirms that women were primarily responsible for initiating these beliefs. The following records Lovett's conversation with a mother whose son was at the front (spelling as original):

> Lovett: "Did you give him anything for luck when he went out?"
> Mother: "Why, of course I did! Everybody does that."
> Lovett: "Do you mind telling me what you gave him?"
> Mother: "Oh, it don't matter what you give 'em. I gave 'im a very old metal button, and I ses 'Jack, my boy, there's a mascot for you, and I hope God'll take care of you.'"

The son held the mascot before each attack and firmly believed it would help take care of him. He returned safe and sound.[23]

Examples of new uses for religious objects are often found. Bibles, New Testaments, prayer books, and prayer itself were used as talismans, alongside other lucky objects, rather than in the traditional Christian religious sense. One historian confirms: 'those who never took Holy Communion elsewhere did so at the front – in the belief…it would stop them being hit – to make extra sure they might carry a Bible as a talisman'.[24] Another writes: 'this grasping for supernatural help implied no acceptance of the regime of moral discipline and formal religious observances encouraged by their chaplains'.[25] Lieutenant Bass embarking for the front in 1916 remarks that an old soldier distributed New Testaments at the dockside, noting how popular they were with the departing soldiers.[26] Similarly, Edmund Blunden's commanding officer gave him a pocket Testament which he kept with him always.[27]

Some beliefs were more ordinary. Soldiers like Frank Richards thought that a pack of cards was as important as a Bible to a soldier.[28] Others like Mark Plowman, however, praised rum for providing succour and a feeling of protection, equating its serving to 'a moment of religious worship'.[29] As one contemporary commented sardonically, 'the British soldier has certainly got religion; I am not so sure, however, that he has got Christianity'.[30]

Religious or otherwise, soldiers often visited shelled foreign churches: amongst the scattered debris, they sought small relics. For example, Lieutenant Bass pocketed a piece of stained glass from the shattered church window at Meaulte. There is no proof that this was for luck, nevertheless he returned later for another piece.[31] Gunner Smedley, too, noted a piece of marble he picked up from the ruined cathedral at Ypres.[32] Robert Graves tells of a piece of stained glass he presented to another soldier, Jenkins, despite a warning from a Catholic soldier that it would bring him bad luck. Graves notes 'Jenkins got killed not long after'.[33] It is interesting that the local Catholic churches amazed both Bass and Smedley: presumably as Protestants, they would have been unaccustomed to Catholic splendour. Bass writes of an almost spiritual encounter he had at a church at Noeux les Mins where he thought he saw a statue of the Virgin Mary move: 'Never seen anything better in my life', he enthuses.[34] The novelty of these scenes and the impact of the ritualised landscape are discussed again later.

Many soldiers believed in the power of positive thought and the importance of loyalty to one's friends and relied upon these for their continuing survival.[35] Others placed great emphasis on particular actions becoming portents of bad luck, or shields of good luck, which kept them safe. Being lucky at cards, for example, might mean bad luck would follow, as if one's quota of good luck could run out: 'Duffy told me…I would get killed during the next action I was in, and that all men who were lucky at gambling very soon had their lights put out', narrates Richards.[36] For Robert Graves, it was the deliberate preservation of his virginity that he believed kept him safe. In later reminiscences, he confessed: 'I held a strong superstition that its loss [his virginity] would prejudice the magical power of survival that had so far taken me through five months of trench warfare – the average life of a wart [lieutenant] was six weeks at that time'.[37]

The variety in the range of lucky mascots and beliefs is very apparent. It is worth considering here where these were actually obtained, but as already noted, they originated from a range of older beliefs and practices. They did not begin with the war, but the war furthered their continued and often changed usage. Some practices, like the coins sewn into braces, were apparent in earlier conflicts. Mascots were often pressed on soldiers by loved ones. Some were sold in shops that, presumably, took advantage of the growing demand like the shop near Long Acre, which sold lucky beads and charms.[38] One historian, Turner, confirms that the trade in various lucky items, such as talismans and amulets, was stimulated by the war. He mentions one, which apparently sold by the 'millions': 'Touchwood was a tiny, sparkling-eyed imp surrounded by a khaki cap, with his legs crossed…he was presented by the actress Delysia to 1,200 officers and men'.[39] Pocket Testaments and Bibles were either already carried by soldiers or were widely distributed at docksides and overseas and, as shown above, were often used outside their original religious purpose.

Docksides and ports were also likely places to trade in cauls: some babies are born with a membrane (caul) covering their face which has to be removed to allow the baby to breathe. Belief in the magical and lucky properties of cauls, specifically against drowning at sea, has been dated back to at least 1547[40] and instances of this belief are still found today.[41] Moreover, this luck is supposedly transferable to whoever is in possession of the caul and prices reached as much as 30 guineas at the end of the eighteenth century, dropping to just a few pence before the First World War.[42] Clearly, these beliefs were strong during the First World War as cauls rose in value to as much as five pounds during the conflict.[43] Other lucky items were already traditional good luck symbols due to scarceness, such as the four-leaf clover, which was the subject of a popular postcard sent home from the front. Others evolved and took on a new significance during wartime conditions, such as the holed-stone.

It was a belief in the lucky properties of certain objects, like those discussed above, that soldiers tapped into when they deliberately brought mascots and other objects with them. As already discussed, they tended to be variations of older beliefs, but a particularly interesting phenomenon occurred during wartime: instead of being disseminated only through the customary route of "old wives tales" and female culture, they became part of the all-male world of trench warfare. This is discussed in more detail in relation to fortune-telling.

Trench "Superstitions" and tales of the Supernatural

Soldiers in the trenches were haunted by their dreadful surroundings and the constant fear of death, as evinced in the incredibly descriptive language used in their writings. There are numerous references in the literature to magic, enchantment, supernatural experiences, and a general analogy of life in the trenches to a living hell. Plowman wrote of 'a land of foreboding, even of horror, where blind Death keeps groping hideously'.[44] Sleep deprivation and constant fear caused soldiers in the trenches to sometimes misinterpret events and to be more susceptible to superstitious fears, as in Vaughan's description:

> I saw the blanket slowly lifted and a head appeared in the dim light of the candle. I hardly repressed a scream of horror, and an icy numbness gripped me as I scanned – a blackened face, thick lips and aquiline nose, big eyes that stared at me…it was the face of the dead man that I had buried.[45]

Robert Graves believed he really saw a ghost: 'at Béthune, I saw the ghost of a man named Private Challoner', he writes.[46]

Not all supernatural-type beliefs were dark and mysterious though. The following extract from Bass' diary is a sardonic list of superstitions:

- It is considered very unlucky to be killed on a Friday
- It is unlucky for 13 to sit down to a meal when rations have been issued for only 7
- If the sun rises in the East, it is a sure sign that there will be stew for dinner[47]

Like all jokes, however, it only works if it has a basis in reality and although the quote is tongue-in-cheek and derogatory, it does indicate that other soldiers took superstitions very seriously, otherwise why would Bass bother to be so derisory.

Other trench beliefs had more functional foundations, such as unlucky third light. This is thought to be the time a sniper needed to locate and fire on a target. An early reference to this is a letter published in *N&Q* in 1916,[48] but it appears to also have had significance for soldiers during earlier conflicts such as the Boar War (1899-1902) and the Crimean War (1853-6).[49] The number three anyway has associations with good and bad luck, such as 'third time lucky' and common folklore holds that deaths come in threes.[50] One soldier told Blunden 'It's the third time. They've sent me over, this is the third time. They'll get me this time'.[51] Fatalism like this is seen often, for example the belief that a shell had someone's name on it. Cairns' Army and Religion survey found many instances of this, for example 'if there is one for you [a shell] you'll get it if your number is on it' and 'I'm not for it until one comes for me…If I've got to go, I've got to go'.[52] Others had premonitions of death such as 'by the way, sergeant, I'm going to get killed tomorrow. I know that. And I know that you're going to be all right'.[53] Fatalism served a functional purpose, helping to steady nerves under stress. As one private wrote on Christmas Day 1916: 'after the manner of fatalists, we come to regard being alive and well as merely luck'.[54]

Some trench beliefs grew from the physical conditions the soldiers had to endure in the trenches such as the mud and exposure to the elements. There was even a view that the Germans could somehow supernaturally control the weather. Blunden writes: 'Another storm…was now creeping on miserably with grey vapour of rain over the whole field. It was one of the many which caused the legend…that the Germans could make it rain when they wanted to'.[55] Other natural phenomena were considered portents of disaster as again Blunden describes:

> One evening a wisp of vapour was seen by my working party to glide over the whole sky from west to east, preserving all the time a strange luminous whiteness and an obvious shape, as some said, that of a cross, as others antipathetically held, of a sword…My batman…told me that he read coming disaster in this sword.[56]

Clearly, anything out of the ordinary could be construed by tired, battle-weary soldiers as signs of forthcoming disaster or omens of hope.

Sometimes, the apparent invulnerability of religious objects was considered portentous. Crucifixes were deemed very powerful and the many that remained undamaged surrounded by devastation, gave credence to the belief that they possessed supernatural protection. Many photographs show unharmed crucifixes and religious statues surrounded by devastation and debris such as a picture of the statue of the Madonna in Montauban. All around is flattened and ruined by shellfire, but the statue remains entirely unharmed as a working party digs out an unexploded shell directly beneath it. Whether this is evidence of divine protection, luck or merely a set-up for the camera, it is impossible to tell. Moreover, crucifixes were significant because of the proliferation of roadside calvaries that formed part of the battlefield landscape. These, like the aforementioned churches, were remarkable to the average British soldier.

The army's use of Field Punishment No. 1 for public shaming of minor misdemeanours reinforced these scenes. Offenders were tied to a fence, wheel or other immobile object, in the manner of a crucifixion, for several hours a day.[57] One soldier's account is as follows:

> You're spread-eagled with the hub of the wheel in your back, and your legs and wrists handcuffed to the wheel. You'd do two hours up and four hours down for seven days, day and night…And the only reason I was there was because I missed a roll-call.[58]

Early in 1917, the War Office circulated a letter and diagram explaining the punishment's proper procedure. The need to officially standardise this suggests a more haphazard and inhumane practice had prevailed. Such constant reminders of Christ on the cross made some believe they too were being sacrificed just like Christ.[59] As Plowman commented sardonically, 'Wouldn't the army do well to avoid punishments which remind men of the Crucifixion'.[60]

Nevertheless, in a Catholic country like France, reminders of Christ and religious objects naturally abounded. One of the most renowned at the time was the leaning statue of the Virgin and Child at Albert. Numerous accounts mention the statue after it was badly damaged, but continued somehow to remain precariously leaning atop the basilica at Albert as if, Plowman wrote, 'it is bowed as by the last extremity of grief'.[61] Some said that when the statue finally fell, the war would end. Graham describes it poetically as 'the leaning Virgin who… yearned o'er the city'.[62] To Manning it was an 'avenging wrath'.[63] The belief by both sides that the statue's fall would herald the end of the war was discussed in *Folklore* in 1929 and speculation was raised as to whether propaganda had been involved when the British finally toppled it in 1918:

> I have wondered whether it was entirely an accident that the statue came down under the first few rounds of British shell fire. In any case, this fact had a definite psychological effect. The sign, as many believed, had been given, and, when the allies pushed forward in this sector, they did so with great heart.[64]

Angels at Mons

The most famous story of all, which gained credence right at the war's beginning, is that of the Angels of Mons. Various confused versions were produced, and even today, the story retains its fascination. Recent research is the latest of many attempts over the past eighty-eight years to separate fact from fiction.[65] Indeed, nowadays the tale has gained legendary status, but the truth remains elusive. A brief synopsis of the most repeated explanation follows.[66]

After the British defeat at Mons in August 1914, a journalist for the *London Evening News*, Arthur Machen, wrote a fictional story entitled *The Bowmen*, printed on 29th September 1914. In this, the British are losing against the Germans when a soldier invokes a call to St. George, '*Adsit Anglis Sanctus Georgius* – May St. George be a present help to the English'. This brings forth a host of ghostly Agincourt bowmen who fire a 'cloud' of arrows at the advancing Germans who fall in their thousands, allowing the British to retreat. 'Angels' are not mentioned, but Machen describes 'a long line of shapes, with a *shining* about them'.[67] This 'shining' is thought to have transformed bowmen to angels in the promulgation of the tale. Fussell explains: 'It was the *shining* that did it: within a week Machen's fictional bowmen had been transformed into real angels, and…credited as fact'.[68] Machen, a noted writer of occult fantasy, always vehemently denied his story was true, but it grabbed the public imagination and would not be denied. He queried how 'a nation plunged in materialism of the grossest kind has accepted idle rumours and gossip of the supernatural as certain truth?'[69] Recent investigation answers this, calling it 'a timely piece of patriotic wish-fulfilment that caught the mood of the nation'.[70]

Certainly, contemporary interest in the Angels of Mons was high and a large number of pamphlets, books, sermons and newspaper articles on the subject were produced. Explanations for the phenomenon abounded. One contemporary, Ralph Shirley the Editor of the *Occult Review*, saw precedence in alleged tales of ghostly aid during the Civil War and claimed that wars somehow developed people's innate psychic abilities. Shirley argued against the view that the strain and stress, lack of nourishment and long forced marches caused hallucinations: it simply made soldiers more receptive to psychic influences, he asserted.[71] There are three main theories concerning the Angel of Mons story. Firstly, Machen's story was separate and coincidental. Secondly, it caused the rumours, which, in a sort of

"Chinese-whisper" way, then transformed Bowmen to Angels. Lastly, there really had been some kind of supernatural event or mass hysteria causing hallucinations. Even historian A.J. Taylor appears to subscribe to this: 'it was the first British battle; and also the only one where supernatural intervention was observed, more or less reliably...Indeed, the 'angels of Mons' were the only recognition of the war vouchsafed by the Higher Powers', he wrote in 1963.[72] There is, possibly, another explanation: that it suited the authorities to allow this story to grow and circulate for propaganda purposes. This is, however, speculative. Certainly, the propagation of this inspirational tale was useful at a time when public confidence had been dealt a blow with the early defeat at Mons. Recent research has shown that the rumours were repeated in churches across the land 'as a method of boosting morale on the Home Front and to foster belief in the rightness of the British cause'.[73]

Although there was so much contemporary interest, there is no corroborative evidence. All accounts were second or third-hand and witnesses were anonymous with any subsequent sworn statements easily shown as false or hoaxes. The closest to true testimony is that given by a nurse, Phyllis Campbell, who repeated stories from wounded soldiers. This, however, has also been discredited: Campbell, the daughter of a novelist, apparently had a tradition of telling ghostly and supernatural tales. Although the diary of Brigadier-General Charteris does actually mention the rumour three weeks before Machen's story was printed, Charteris' diary was not published until 1931. Furthermore, it appears that some of the dates in the diary had later been altered, which unfortunately tends to discredit this source.[74] Clearly, the Angel of Mons is not going to be easily dismissed or laid to rest and not for nothing has it been called 'one of the most astonishing legends not only of this century [20th] but of all time'.[75]

The above shows categorically that there was widespread belief in the supernatural in the trench culture of the Great War. Soldiers were under immense levels of stress and duress, combined with lack of sleep and constant terror of death. They were bound to believe that any event slightly out of the ordinary had some kind of portentous meaning and superstitions easily would have gained ground. Even the battle landscape contributed, with its incorporation of roadside calvaries and the reinforcement of this landscape with such sights as soldiers undergoing field punishments. It is interesting to speculate on the impact that such a ritualised landscape had on mainly Protestant soldiers in a Catholic country where such sights were entirely new. Certainly, the churches, roadside calvaries and religious symbols were noticed and remarked upon in the soldiers' writings. Some of the beliefs that grew out of those dark days remained firmly in the trenches and have no bearing today. Yet others affected not only the soldiers at the time, but filtered back and had a widespread impact on people and morale at home: they have became enduring legends which still have the power to fascinate today.

The Home Front
It is clear, then, that Angel of Mons type stories had a major effect back home. Possibly this was encouraged and utilised for propaganda purposes or to help boost morale. Certainly, once news of the Mons retreat began to filter back home, recruiting soared.[76] It is quite probable, therefore, that the Angel story, with God on the side of the British, aided this recruiting spur, hence its dissemination and that of similar stories. This, however, is speculative. Similarly, German-atrocity stories were not officially verified, neither were they definitely refuted. The government commissioned report, chaired by Bryce, and the resulting appendix contained shocking stories of supposed atrocities. It was in this atmosphere of suspicion, fear and uncertainty, that fortune-tellers proliferated. Women seeking reassurance about their loved ones visited fortune-tellers, but so did soldiers at home on leave, taking their premonitions back to the front with them. Others paid money in prayer shops or visited mediums.

Fortune-tellers and mediums had, according to one historian, 'flourished like weeds in the back streets of the industrial towns where they fattened on the insecurity of the working class in a period of great poverty and unemployment'.[77] This has been heralded as evidence of the growing secularism in nineteenth-century Britain, related to social conditions and class. A detailed history of fortune-telling is not possible here.[78] Suffice to say that traditionally it was often local 'wise' women who would read tea-leaves or palms and were an integral part of the local female culture. Various official moves strove to drive them out and legislation in 1824 made them prosecutable under section four of the Vagrancy Act (5 Geo.IV. c. 83,s.4), along with the almost obsolete Witchcraft Act (1736). Under the new act 'persons pretending or professing to tell fortunes, or using any subtle craft, means, or device, by palmistry or otherwise, to deceive and impose' were to be considered as 'rogues and vagabonds', punishable with three months' hard labour, or by a fine of £25'.[79]

Nevertheless, during the First World War, fortune-telling burgeoned and for some became very lucrative. When Almira Brockway was charged with pretending to tell fortunes in January 1917, the detective in charge reported that her account books showed an income of £115 in 34 days.[80] The *Daily Mail* exclaimed, 'since the war began the country has been overrun with charlatans, spiritualists, and fortune tellers'.[81] Analysis of prosecutions during the war period reveals interesting evidence of this growth: At the trial of Beatrice Emma Smith in 1917, the prosecutor stated that fortune-telling was rife with 53 practising in one metropolitan district alone and during the trial of Madame Jacques, the prosecutor reported that 30 or more had set up business in the Edgware Road district.[82]

The authorities attempted to deal with this increase, as the contemporary article entitled 'Fortune-telling and the War' in *The Justice of the Peace* shows: 'The war has greatly stimulated the age-old desire of the human race to peer behind the veil', it states. Furthermore, the article pointed out that 'the charlatans…who trade on the fears and folly of mankind', could still be prosecuted under the almost forgotten section four of the Witchcraft Act. This carried a much harsher penalty (up to one year's imprisonment with or without hard labour) than the Vagrancy Act. Moreover, not only was the length of punishment greater, the stigma of being prosecuted under the Witchcraft Act might alert the public to the fraudulent and opportunist nature of this trade.[83] Magistrates were, however, generally reluctant and embarrassed to invoke a law that mentioned witchcraft and magic.[84]

The following table shows the number of fortune-telling prosecutions reported in *The Times* from 1911-1921. Despite the above discussion, prosecutions were most likely to be for 'pretending to tell fortunes' under the Vagrancy Act:[85]

Figure 1: Frequency of Prosecutions Under the Vagrancy Act 1911-1921

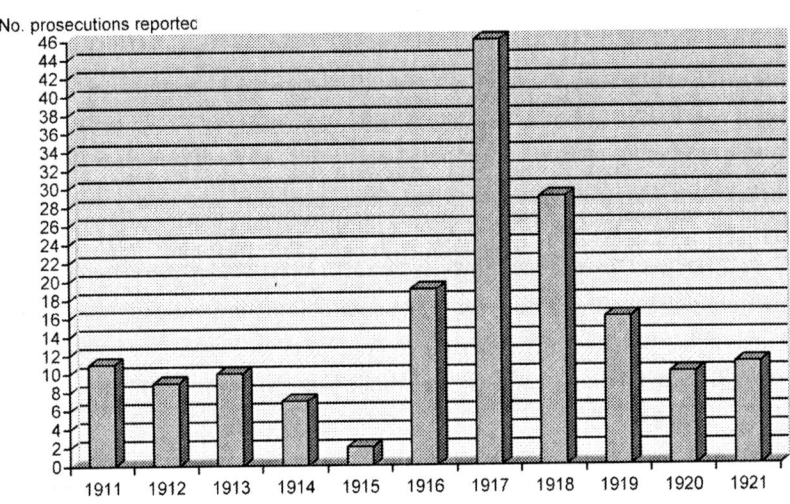

Clearly, the period 1916-18 produced the most reports of prosecutions, with a huge increase in 1917, which more than doubles that of 1916. One interpretation is that events in 1917, such as the collapse of Russia, may have caused more uncertainty on the Home Front: therefore, more people visited fortune-tellers, which led to more notice by the authorities and higher prosecutions. Certainly, the graph does prove that there was considerable interest in the activities of fortune-tellers and the reporting of their prosecutions. Of course, the graph might simply show that the authorities were keener to prosecute at that time, or that *The Times* chose to report prosecutions more often. Periodic police sweeps had taken place before the war[86] and the 1917 figure may just represent another of these. Further research of police records would reveal whether this was the case. The figures do, however, appear to endorse the view that fortune-telling increased during the war years, as opportunists seized the chance to earn money from people's uncertainty.

It has already been noted earlier that certain traditional female beliefs became part of the all-male world of trench warfare. Evidence also points to the changing gender of those who frequented fortune-tellers during wartime. Previously resort to fortune-telling tended to be frowned upon by men, not necessarily because of disbelief, but more a general concern that it was wrong.[87] During the war, however, instead of servant girls seeking information on future husbands, or local women having their fortunes told, soldiers too began to use these services. Davies concludes that 'fortune-telling entered the popular consciousness to an extent that it had never done in peacetime'.[88] There is evidence of soldiers at home on leave consulting fortune-tellers in an attempt to bolster courage to return to the conflict. Moreover, it was not just privates who visited fortune-tellers, but officers were also found consulting them. Following a police raid on Madame Vox in 1917, the detective in charge gave the following evidence: 'In the studio sitting opposite to her at a bamboo table was a wounded officer, with his hand lying on a cushion. The prisoner was examining his hands'.[89]

Certainly, troops were accustomed to the activities of fortune-tellers. Blunden's description below of a parody from a troops' stage entertainment of 1917 clearly shows this.

> The "wench" was listening earnestly. The wizard read "her" hand, scratching it. "Ah, there's a bit of luck for you. I can see it. There's the firing line. We don't 'ave no breastworks in this part. Ah, there's that bit of luck again. You're going to 'ave a letter. Your sweetheart's on the road to Poperinghe. He's gone in for a glass of stout. He's come out again – they don't give credit. He's in the street outside. He's coming into this 'all. He's———" (commotion at the back, shouting and blundering over forms; a red-nosed gruesome figure…comes hurrying up the middle passage…"he's coming on to this platform! !"[90]

Again, like the aforementioned sardonic list of superstitions in Lieutenant Bass' diary, the joke only works if the soldiers are seeing something familiar to them.

In an environment where even the First Lord of the Admiralty (Balfour) was caught 'touching wood' in the House of Commons,[91] it is evident that unscrupulous people were quick to take advantage of the situation. In a series of investigative exposés,[92] the *Daily Mail* revealed one opportunist, F.L. Rawson, who set up a 'psychic bucket shop' where worried relatives paid on a sliding scale to have a prayer said for an absent loved one. Charges ranged from 7 guineas for Rawson's services to 1 guinea for an ordinary 'supplicant' to say a 'long distance prayer'. Rawson told *Daily Mail* undercover reporter, Harold Ashton, 'if you had adopted my system…you could have gone to the front and walked slap up to the German lines — and not a bullet or a shell would have touched you…you would have been immune'. Ashton revealed a large clientele of well-dressed, wealthy women, including members of the peerage, who were all taken in by Rawson's claims to 'allay by his magic, the sufferings of the wounded, the perils of the missing, and the pain of the starving soldiers held prisoner in Germany'. Naturally, prayer was available free from any religious minister, but the presumption is that paying for something gives it more potency, similar to crossing a fortune-teller's palm with silver. One historian's explanation is that as people became more disillusioned with traditional religion, they 'sought mystical shelter elsewhere, in the arms of upstart sciences, old delusions and…charlatanry'.[93]

The unprincipled entrepreneur, Rawson, had previously promulgated a notion that soldiers would have indemnity if they carried a copy of and repeated Psalm 91:[94]

> I will say of the Lord, He is my refuge and my fortress…(91:2)
> Thou shalt not be afraid for the terror by night;
> nor for the arrow that flieth by day…
> A thousand shall fall by thy side, and ten thousand at
> thy right hand; but it shall not come nigh thee…(91:7)

Presumably, Rawson was only too happy to provide copies of these verses - for a fee. A similar belief was widespread amongst German soldiers who carried with them "Schutzbriefe" ("protective" letters purported to be written by Jesus, the Virgin Mary or the Saints). New research reveals these were extremely popular with German soldiers during the First World War.[95] This is a new use of an older tradition, which held that the possession of an apocryphal letter, said to have been written to or by Christ, gave the owner protection from harm. Certainly, these were peddled during the eighteenth and nineteenth centuries as protective charms.[96]

It is evident, then, that in the wartime conditions of intense uncertainty and worry, some people were susceptible to those who claimed to be able to tell fortunes, or to use some form of supernatural power or magic to aid those serving at The Front. Clearly, some were practitioners of long-standing in the local community who truly believed they had a 'gift' and who genuinely wanted to help ease people's fears and worries. Others were mere opportunists, quick to jump on the bandwagon and make money out of the situation. The authorities attempted to control fortune-tellers by prosecuting them and newspapers tried to warn people of the dangers by exposing frauds. Nevertheless, some people continued to seek reassurance from those purporting to see into the future or to have some supernatural ability to control events. Sometimes, the reassurance that people were seeking was not forthcoming because whilst most soothsayers gave optimistic readings, others predicted death for those serving at The Front. Marie Charles, prosecuted in 1916, told a worried wife whose husband was about to depart for the front that he would not return. The prosecutor could not imagine 'anything more shocking and distressing' and he continued, 'pretences to foretell were doing much more harm now than in other days'.[97]

Conclusion
As this article has elucidated, for many it was not enough to trust in pure chance alone, or to place one's faith solely in God or religion, or even in the ideal of righteousness – belief in the age old adage that good defeats evil. In an attempt to increase their chances of survival, many people placed some reliance upon various forms of supernatural support, either alongside traditional beliefs or independently. Theologist, Dr. Clifford Marrs, states:

'in England the religious response to the First World War...seems to have been not the return to the churches that some had predicted – but...a mixture of fatalism and magic at the front'.[98] This reliance took many forms

from soldiers taking or wearing a supposed lucky charm or amulets, to belief in the significance of certain actions. It played a major role in the lives of many soldiers and civilians. Bronislaw Malinowski, the pioneering anthropologist of the early twentieth-century, put it succinctly:

> The function of magic is to ritualise man's optimism,
> to enhance his faith in the victory of hope over fear.
> Magic expresses the greater value for man of confidence
> over doubt, of steadfastness over vacillation, of optimism
> over pessimism.[99]

This certainly seems to be the case with the reliance upon the supernatural during the First World War.

A pattern has emerged of both social and cultural continuity and change. Clearly, those supernatural props and experiences that the war triggered were older beliefs adapted in the light of uncertainty and wartime anxiety, rather than new practices. Moreover, these became part of the male trench culture and were adopted and disseminated by solders, rather than by women. This gender change is significant.

There is also some speculation and evidence that certain beliefs were encouraged and used by the authorities for propaganda purposes. The authorities did, however, attempt to control some areas such as fortune-telling and to protect the public. Certainly, worried and anxious people were prey to entrepreneurs who seized the opportunity to make money, whilst other practitioners truly believed they were gifted with foresight and had more altruistic motives.

The above findings tap into the historiography and ongoing debates concerning the impact of the First World War on British society, as well as those concerning popular religion in Britain and its interaction with traditional religion. Further research, therefore, would augment the scholarship already undertaken by historians like Davies, Hazelgrove and Winter. Other historical debates would be informed by further research into the prosecutions of fortune-tellers and mediums, not least the impact of war on crime in society. An analysis of police records would verify the reasons for the increases in the reporting of prosecutions noted in Figure 1. Finally, it is hoped that this article has shown that for some people, both soldiers and civilians, reliance upon the supernatural during the First World War had a significant impact on their lives. These beliefs helped them to feel safe in times of anxiety, danger and adversity, and they provided succour in times of loss, death and bereavement.

Notes

1 S. Faulks, *Birdsong,* (London: Vantage, 1994), 292-3

2 Wheeler, *Sebastian Faulks's Birdsong* (London: Continuum, May 2002)

3 J. Winter, *Sites of Memory, Sites of Mourning – The Great War in European Cultural History,* (Cambridge: Cambridge University Press, 2000), 54

4 *OED,* (Oxford: Oxford University Press, 1996)

5 T.W. Pym and G. Gordon, *Papers from Picardy by two chaplains,* (London: 1917), 188, 201, 202 quoted in Winter, *Sites,* 65

6 I would like to thank the helpful staff at the Imperial War Museum, and the librarian of the Folklore Society, Dr. Caroline Oates, for sharing some of her vast store of knowledge, and in particular, I would like to thank Dr. Owen Davies of the University of Hertfordshire for his constant support, advice and encouragement.

7 Fussell, *The Great War and Modern Memory,* (Oxford: Oxford University Press, 2000 edition), 124 – Henceforth *GWMM*

8 Imperial War Museum, Photographic Archives, (examples Q.6682, 28th May 1918 and Q.777, 7th July 1916) and Imperial War Museum, *The Trench* exhibition March 2003

9 S.C. Williams, *Religious Belief and Popular Culture in Southwark c.1880-1939,* (Oxford: Oxford University Press, 1999), 56 – Henceforth *Religious Belief*

10 *Ibid.,* 54-86

11 Edward Lovett, *Magic in Modern London,* (Croydon: 1925) – Henceforth *MML*

12 *Cassell's Saturday Journal,* 4 Apr. 1900, 620, quoted in Williams, *Religious Belief,* 67

13 O. Davies, *Witchcraft, Magic and Culture 1736-1951*, (Manchester: Manchester University Press, 1999), 267 – Henceforth *Witchcraft*

14 See for example Williams, *Religious Belief,* 169-70 and J.Bourke, *Dismembering the Male: Men's Bodies Britain and the Great War,* (London: Reaktion, 1999), 231

15 E. Campion-Vaughan, *Some Desperate Glory: The Diary of a Young Officer, 1917,* (Frederick Warne, 1981), 3

16 *Ibid.*, 193

17 Lovett, *MML,* 70-1

18 E. Ettlinger, 'British Amulets in London Museums', *Folk-Lore,* vol. L (1939), 149-171

19 Lovett, *MML,* 10-14

20 Davies, *Witchcraft,* 267

21 Lovett, *MML,* 27

22 Davies, *Witchcraft,* 273

23 Lovett, *MML,* 34

24 H. McLeod, *Religion and the People of Western Europe 1787-1989,* (Oxford: Oxford University Press, 1997), 94f

25 A Wilkinson, *The Church of England and the First World War,* (London: SMC Press, 1996), ch. 7-8

26 Bass, 'Diary', Begins Sept. 14, 1916, IWM 77/94/1

27 E. Blunden, *Undertones of War,* (Glasgow: Collins, 1978, 1928), 22

28 F. Richards, *Old Soldiers Never Die,* (London: Faber & Faber, 1933), 29

29 Mark VII, (pseud. Plowman), *A Subaltern on the Somme in 1916,* (London: J.M. Dent, 1927), 174-5

30 B. Matthews (ed.), *Christ: and the world at war,* (London: James Clarke, 1917), 42

31 Bass 'Diary', Oct 1st, 4th 1916

32 G. Smedley, 'Diary', 27 Sept. 1916, IWM 01/58/1

33 R. Graves, *Goodbye To All That,* (London: Cassell,1977, 1929), 104

34 Bass 'Diary', Dec. 21st 1916

35 F. Manning, *The Middle Parts of Fortune,* (London: Penguin,1990) first published as Anonymous, *Her Privates, We,* (1929), Introduction by Paul Fussell (1990), xii

36 Richards, *Old Soldiers Never Die,* 29

37 R. Graves, 'My First Amorous Adventure', *Playboy,* January 1972, 247

38 Lovett, *MML,* 42

39 E.S.Turner, *Dear Old Blighty*, (London: Michael Joseph, 1980), 138

40 T. Forbes, *The Midwife and the Witch*, (New Haven: Yale University Press, 1966), 95

41 *Daily Mail*, Letters, 26 August 1996, quoted in J. Simpson & S. Roud, *A Dictionary of English Folklore*, (Oxford: Oxford University Press, 2000), 51

42 *Ibid.*

43 Turner, *Dear Old Blighty*, 107

44 Plowman, *A Subaltern on the Somme*, 129

45 *Ibid.*, 43

46 Graves, *Goodbye To All That*, 106

47 Bass, 'Diary', Begins Sept. 14 1916

48 Simpson & Roud, *A Dictionary of English Folklore*, 69

49 H.W. Howes, 'Functional Aspects of European Folklore', *Folklore*, V.41 (1929), 255-257 and Simpson & Roud, *A Dictionary of English Folklore*, 69

50 Simpson & Roud, *A Dictionary of English Folklore*, 356

51 Blunden, *Undertones of War*, 107

52 D.S. Cairns (Ed.), *The Army and Religion, An Enquiry and its Bearing upon the Religious Life of the Nation*, (London: Hodder & Stoughton, 1919), 159

53 Graves, *Goodbye to all That*, 105

54 Private L. Hart, Letter home, 25 December 1916 in L. Macdonald, *1914-1918 Voices and Images of the Great War*, (London: Penguin, 1991), 186

55 Blunden, *Undertones of War*, 173

56 *Ibid.*, 37

57 http://www.firstworldwar.com/atoz/fieldpunishment.htm

58 Private W. Underwood, in M. Arthur, *Forgotten Voices of the Great War*, (London: Ebury Press, 2002), 69

59 Fussell, *GWMM*, 118

60 Plowman, *A Subaltern on the Somme*, 30

61 *Ibid.*, 41

62 Graham, *The Challenge of the Dead*, 92

63 Manning, *The Middle Parts of Fortune*, 19

64 Howes, 'Functional Aspects of European Folklore', 256

65 D. Clarke, 'Rumours of Angels: A legend of the First World War', *Folklore*, Vol. 113, No. 2, October 2002, 151-173

66 For two investigative articles see D. Clarke, 'Rumours of Angels...' and

K. McClure, 'Angels to the Rescue', *Fortean Times*, No. 68, (April/May 1993), 34-37

67 A. Machen, 'The Bowmen', *London Evening News*, (29th September 1914):3

68 Fussell, *GWMM*, 116

69 *Ibid.*

70 Clarke, 'Rumours of Angels', 154

71 R. Shirley, *The Angel Warriors at Mons: including numerous confirmatory testimonies, evidence of the wounded and certain curious historical parallels – An Authentic Record*, (London: 1915)

72 A.J. Taylor, *The First World War: An Illustrated History*, (London: George Rainbird, 1963), 26

73 Clarke, 'Rumours of Angels', 160-1

74 *Ibid.*, 161-4

75 A. John, 'Arthur Machen and "The Angels of Mons"', *The Anglo-Welsh Review*, 1964-5, 14,10-14

76 H. Costello, 'Powers of Persuasion', *BBC History Magazine*, Vol. 4, No. 2, February 2003,12-15

77 G. Nelson, *Spiritualism and Society*, (London: 1969), 160-1

78 For more details on the history of fortune-telling see:

Davies, *Witchcraft*, in particular 246-270 and

Williams, *Religious Belief*, 75-80

79 Davies, *Witchcraft*, 54

80 *The Times*, 1st January 1917

81 *Daily Mail*, 13th January, 1917

82 *The Times*, 19th February 1917

83 *The Justice of the Peace*, 20th January 1917, 28

84 O. Davies, *Cunning Folk: Popular Magic in English History*, (London: Hambledon, 2003), 23-4

85 *The Times*, 1911-1921 from

The British Library Newspaper Library, *Official Index to the Times 1906-1980*

86 Davies, *Witchcraft*, 266

87 Williams, *Religious Belief*, 78

88 Davies, *Witchcraft*, 268

89 *The Times*, 19th February 1917

90 Blunden, *Undertones of War*, 157

91 *T.P.'s Weekly*, 4th December 1915 in

I. Opie and M. Tatem (Eds.), *A Dictionary of Superstitions*, (Oxford: Oxford University Press, 1990), 450

92 Harold Ashton, 'Prayer Shop', *Daily Mail,* Jan. 6, 8, 9, 10-13, 17, 1917

93 Turner, *Dear Old Blighty,* 139

94 *Ibid.*

95 N. Freytag, 'Witchcraft, Witch doctors and the Fight against Superstition in 19th Century Germany' in W. de Blécourt and O. Davies (eds), *Popular Magic in Modern Europe* (Manchester: Manchester University Press, forthcoming). I am grateful to Owen Davies for this reference.

96 Davies, *Witchcraft,* 126

97 *The Times,* 9th December 1916

98 Dr. C. J. Marrs, *Changing Scenes: Church & Society 1900-1945,* on http://www.woodlandsproject.com/Papers_on_Mission/1900-1945/1900-1945.html

99 B. Malinowski, *Magic, Science and Religion,* in J. Needham (Ed.), *Science, Religion and Reality,* (London: Sheldon, 1925), 83

The Metaphysical Relationship between Magic and Miracles

Morgan Luck

The terms 'magic' and 'miracle' are notoriously difficult to define. Considered in relation, this difficulty is magnified. In this paper I attempt to overcome this hardship by establishing a metaphysical framework, based solely upon the substance and causal relata of the events involved, within which these terms can be defined and their relationship determined. As the notion of magic has, in relation to miracles, been largely neglected within contemporary philosophy, rival definitions of magic shall be contrasted to a single fixed definition of a miracle. To ascertain which definition of magic is superior, each will be evaluated in reference to set criteria. By this method I will argue that reciprocal interactionist magic is the superior account of magic.

Criteria for the Evaluation of Magic.

To determine which definition of magic is superior, I will evaluate each in relation to four criteria. The first criterion supposes that magic involves a sense of causation. The second, that there is a clear distinction between magical and non-magical events. The third, that there is a distinction between miracles and magic. And the forth, that it is logically possible for magic to occur. I shall now detail the first criterion..

Criterion One: Magical Causes and Magical Effects.

I propose that magic generally concerns both cause and effect. Middleton concurs with this proposition.

> Magic is usually defined subjectively rather than by any agreed-upon content. But there is a wide consensus as to what this content is. Most peoples in the world perform acts by which they intend to bring about certain events or conditions, whether in nature or among people, that they hold to be the consequences of those acts. If we use Western terms and assumptions, the cause and effect relationship between the act and the consequence is mystical, not scientifically validated.[1]

This proposition is also evident within Cunningham's characterisation of magic as 'the projection of natural energies to produce needed effects.'[2] The proposition, that magic concerns both cause and effect, is not only reflected by our intuitions regarding how magic occurs, but also by our assessment of where and when magic does not occur.

The decline of magic during the sixteenth and seventeenth centuries, notes Thomas, 'coincided with a marked improvement in the extent to which this environment became amenable to control.'[3] A similar point was made by Malinowski, who stated that when the Trobriander fishermen of North-West Melanesia fish in the local lagoon they never resort to fishing magic. However, when they venture out into open seas they do employ magic as protection from the dangers of wind and rain. Malinowski asserts that this is because the lagoon waters are calm, therefore as the fishermen are able to 'completely rely on their knowledge and skill, magic does not exist.'[4] Thomas and Malinowski's observations marry well with this first criterion. This is because the absence, or decline, of magic can be accounted for by reference to the presence, or incline, of non-magical means to cause similar, or identical, effects.

With this emphasis on causation outlined, we can begin to recognise two senses of magic - *magical causes* and *magical effects*. I define a magical cause as the first cause within a magical sequence, and a magical effect as the last effect within a magical sequence, where this sequence is recognized in terms of a causal chain of events. To illustrate this notion further, consider a rain dance that magically, according to some account of magic, causes rain to fall. The rain dance is an example of a magical cause, and the subsequent rainfall an example of a magical effect. Therefore, in order for a definition of magic to satisfy the first criterion regarding magic, it must be able to identify both a magical cause and a magical effect. The second criterion concerns the distinction between magical and non-magical events.

Criterion Two: Magical and Non-Magical Events.

If a definition of magic were unable to distinguish between magical and non-magical events, such a definition would be of limited explanatory strength. Likewise, if a definition rendered all events magical then the term itself would becomes surplus to requirements, being now synonymous with a 'normal' event. Consequently, the second criterion regarding the definition of magic is that it must be able to distinguish between, and allow for, both magical and non-magical events. The third criterion concerns a definition's ability to distinguish between magic and miracles.

Criterion Three: Magic and Miracles.

In order to define and relate miracles and magic within the same metaphysical framework we must able to distinguish between them. Many previous distinctions between these terms can be reduced to the generalisation 'magic bad - miracles good'. For example, a Catholic definition of magic is 'the art of performing actions beyond the power of man with the aid of powers other than the Divine.'[5] Whilst Aquinas defines miracles as those things 'which are done by Divine agency beyond the order commonly observed in nature.' Both definitions concern events that are caused by something outside of nature. Likewise, they agree that these events are beyond the power of other natural causes. The only difference between these two definitions is that one cause is 'divine' and the other is not. I reject such distinctions, as I am committed to a religiously neutral and purely metaphysical account of the terms. In which case the religious or political allegiance of divine or demonic agents has little bearing. The only distinction between miracles and magic I am willing to acknowledge are those based upon the substance and causal relata of the events involved. To make such a neutral distinction however, we must first establish a suitable definition of the term miracle.

To establish the definition of a miracle, I will reduce the following six accounts to their most basic form; considering only the substance and causal relata of the events involved.

1. A miracle is a natural event with a supernatural cause.[6]
2. A miracle is an intended outcome of an intervention in the natural world by a supernatural agent.[7]
3. A miracle is…that of an event (immediately) resulting from God's direct intervention in nature.[8]
4. A miracle is…a violation of a law of Nature by a god, that is, a very powerful rational being who is not a material object.[9]
5. Those things are properly called miracles which are done by divine agency beyond the order commonly observed in nature[10]
6. A miracle may accurately be defined, a transgression of a law of nature by a particular volition of the deity, or by the interposition of some invisible agent[11]

From these definitions we can discern two common attributes. The first concerns substance dualism. Miracles require both natural and anatural events. By natural events I mean events that are reducible to, or constituted by, some account of the substance of nature. I do not mean normal events. Likewise by anatural events I mean events that are *not* reducible to, or constituted by, some account of the substance of nature. This dualism is explicit within definitions one, two, three and four, and implicit, given the transcendent property of 'divine agents', within definitions five and six.

The second attribute concerns substance interaction. Miracles require the possibility of natural events being anaturally caused. Although definitions four, five and six refer to these natural events in terms of a violation or transgression of a law of nature, I do not regard this stipulation as necessary. This is based upon the recent scholarship of Mumford, Clarke, Hughes and Adams,[12] who all promote the possibility of a law-abiding miracle. With these two attributes identified I shall now provide the fixed definition of the term miracle.

Based upon the notion of substance interactionism I hold the most basic definition of a miracle to be as follows.

> Miracle: An event of type x with a cause of type y. Where x and y are different substances.

This definition advances the notion that the metaphysical significance of substance interaction alone is of such calibre, that no further stipulations are warranted to guarantee its miraculousness. So provisos such as: Miracles only refer to natural events with anatural causes; Miraculous causes must be divine rather than demonic; And miraculous effects must be signs,[13] wonders or marvels, are dismissed.

This definition of a miracle can be further subdivided into two distinct types: natural miracles and anatural miracles.

> Natural Miracle: A natural event with an anatural cause.
> Anatural Miracle: An anatural event with a natural cause.

The traditional sense of a miracle is indicative of a natural miracle, an example of which would be God parting the Sea of Reeds.[14] Whilst the untraditional sense of a miracle, I wish to here establish, is indicative of an anatural miracle, an example of which would be a person's prayer causing a Saint to petition God on their behalf. With the fixed definition of a miracle established, we are now in a position to implement the third criterion, being that there must be a religiously neutral and purely metaphysical distinction between magic and miracles. The forth criterion concerns logical possibility of magic.

Criterion Four: Magic and Logical Possibility.

I hold that any definition of magic that does not allow for the logical possibility of its occurrence is of limited value. The only reason to define magic in such a 'straw man' manner is to undermine the validity of its possibility. Spinoza employed such a strategy when he argued against the possibility of miracles.

By defining a miracle in terms of a violation of a law of nature, he was able to assert that they could not occur. As nothing,

> ...comes to pass in nature in contravention to her universal laws, nay, nothing does not agree with them and follow from them, for... she keeps a fixed and immutable order.[15]

Since it not my aim here to disprove the possibility of magic outright, the forth criterion is that the occurrence of magic must be logically possible. With these four criteria detailed, I shall now proceed to introduce the rival accounts of magic.[16]

Magic

The history of the term magic reveals a fragmented past.[17] Without a single definition to anchor the term, it has outgrown its Asyro-Babylonian roots and branched out in accordance with numerous influences. For example, due to the political and religious powers responsible for the Great Witch-Hunt of the Middle Ages, the term magic became synonymous with witchcraft, which in turn became synonymous with Satan worship.[18] Whilst in New England in the nineteenth-century, the founders of Mormonism practised magic within the context of Christianity.[19] In order to avoid such variance, I will reduce rival accounts of the term magic to the substance and causal relata of the events involved. With these basic components identified, I will then proceed to evaluate each account of magic in relation to the given criteria.

I shall be considering three basic groups of magic, natural magic, anatural magic and interactionist magic. Within the natural magic group I shall detail paranormal natural magic, paralucky natural magic and synchronous natural magic. Within the anatural magic group I shall detail paranormal anatural magic, paralucky anatural magic and synchronous anatural magic. And within the interactionist magic group I shall detail natural interactionist magic, anatural interactionist magic, and reciprocal interactionist magic.

Natural Magic

The essential characteristic of natural magic is that it only involves natural events. Agrippa introduces natural magic well by the following statement, 'those who believe the operations of magic to be above or against nature are mistaken... they are only derived from nature and in harmony with it.'[20] Ficino, another well-known proponent of natural magic,[21] also took great pains to distance natural magic from the idea that it concerned forces outside of nature.[22] Giordano referred to this group as 'natural magic in the proper sense,'[23] and MacGregor Mathers as the type of magic that exercised 'control of the secret forces of nature.'[24] I shall now introduce three different types of natural magic: paranormal natural magic, paralucky natural magic and synchronicitious natural magic.

Paranormal Natural Magic

Giordano characterises this type of magic as a natural force, similar to magnetism. However, unlike magnetism, he suggests that this force cannot be explained in terms of normal physical processes. Rather it is paranormal, for in order to understand it we must assume 'a spirit or soul in things.'[25] These spirits or souls should not be confused with anatural entities; rather they are better comprehended, as Hall suggests, as 'the unseen forces of nature.'[26] A similar expression can be found with Barrett who held that,

> Natural magic is, as we have said, a comprehensive knowledge of all Nature, by which we search out her secret and occult operations throughout her vast and spacious laboratory.[27]

The underlying notion behind paranormal natural magic therefore, is that it concerns some secret, unseen or occult connection between natural events. I shall now proceed to give this type of magic more rigid a definition.

I assert that paranormal natural magic refers to a causal connection between natural events that is beyond normal explanation. To better comprehend this type of magic, consider the following illustration. A magician, angry with a king, speaks a curse, where this curse directly causes the king to die. This should be regarded as natural magic because it concerns only natural events, and paranormal because the causal connection between the curse and the death of the king is beyond normal explanation. We can therefore, define paranormal natural magic as:

> Paranormal Natural Magic: A natural event with a direct paranormal natural cause.

If instead of cursing the king, the magician decided to use poison, this would not be considered magical. As although the act of poisoning, like all natural magic, concerns only natural events, being poisoned is not a paranormal cause of death.

Paranormal natural magic satisfies the first, second and third criteria established to evaluate rival definitions. The first criterion is satisfied by the first natural event being identified as the magical cause and the last natural event the magical effect. The second is satisfied by magical events possessing a paranormal causal connection, whilst non-magical events either do not, or are anatural in substance. And the third is satisfied by this definition of magic being distinct from a miracle. The forth criteria however, being that the occurrence of magic must be logically possible, is not wholly satisfied. To understand why this is the case we must establish what constitutes a paranormal causal connection. I assert that the only means by which a causal connection can be determined to be 'beyond normal' derives from our approach to the laws of nature.

If we assume that a causal connection between natural events that conforms to the laws of nature is normal, how then would a paranormal causal connection be best defined? The answer, as employed by Aquinas,[28] Hume[29] and Swinburne[30] in their definition of a miracle, is as a violation of a law of nature. To illustrate this point, consider the following example. If a law of nature stated that the heating water to 100 degrees Celsius causes it to boil, no one would consider the causal connection between water heated to this temperature and its subsequent boiling as paranormal. Therefore, the only means by which a causal connection can be considered paranormal is if it did not correspond with the laws of nature. In this case, only if this heating caused the water not to boil would it be considered paranormal.

Paranormal natural magic requires a violation of a law of nature. Cunningham mirrors this view, defining magic as 'the practice of causing change through the use of powers as yet not defined or accepted by science.'[31] This sentiment is also shared by LaVey and Middleton, who state that magic is never 'totally scientifically explainable'[32] or 'scientifically validated.'[33] With this relation between paranormal causal connections and the laws of nature outlined, the only remaining question is can such a violation occur? In order address this question I will outline two opposing approaches to the laws of nature: Anti-Humeanism and Humeanism. Within the Anti-Humean section I will detail Necessity Theory and Scientific Essentialism. Within the Humean section I will detail Naive Regularity Theory, Systematic Theory and Probabilism. The first account I will detail is Necessity theory.

Necessity theory holds that necessity is a property of the laws of nature. Proponents of this approach include Kneale,[34] Armstrong,[35] Tooley[36] and Dretske.[37] According to this theory the reason why heating water to 100 degree Celsius causes it to boil is because there is a law of nature stating that this must be the case. This law prescribes upon nature, making it necessary that water boil at this temperature. If water did not boil at this temperature, necessitarians would not accept that a law has been violated. Instead they would argue that we were wrong to recognise water boiling at this temperature as a law. This is because, as laws dictate what must occur, counter-instances to laws of nature cannot occur. This argument can be expressed as follows.

1. A law of nature is a necessary relation.
2. A violation of a law of nature is violation of a necessary relation.
3. A necessary relation cannot be violated.
4. A violation of a law of nature cannot occur

In other words, if a law is actual it cannot be violated, and if a law can be violated it is not actual. Consequently, a violation of a law of nature according to Necessity theory cannot occur. The next Anti-Humean account of the laws of nature I will consider is Scientific Essentialism

This emphasis on necessary relations is also stressed by Ellis' Scientific Essentialism. In this case the laws of nature are necessary not because they are primitive or plutonic, but because they supervene on the essential nature of things. Ellis describes his theory as,

> The view that explanations in the physical and biological sciences typically involves postulates concerning the essential natures of the fundamental natural kinds of objects and processes occurring in the world. On this view, the causal laws that apply in these areas describe the operation of the essential properties of these natural kinds, and are metaphysically necessary.[38]

Scientific Essentialism therefore, holds that laws of nature do not reflect universal rules that govern the relation of events, but instead concern the essential properties of particulars.

For example, if a law of nature stated that water boils at 100 degree Celsius, we would assume that it is essential to the identity of water that it boil at this temperature. If on one occasion water were not to boil when so heated, this would mean that we were wrong to consider this a law, as it seems boiling at this temperature is not an essential property of water. Inversely if this law was true, and something did not boil at 100 degrees Celsius, then this something could not be water. Once again the laws of nature refuse to be violated.

1. Laws of nature correspond to the essential properties of things.
2. Every thing that occurs has an essential property.
3. A violation of a law of nature does not correspond to the essential properties of things.
---
4. A violation of a law of nature cannot occur.

Scientific essentialism makes a violation of the law of nature tantamount to a logical contradiction, which it is generally considered not even an omnipotent power, let alone a magical one, is able to cause. With these two

Anti-Humean accounts detailed I shall now outline three contrasting Humean accounts of the laws of nature, the first being Naïve Regularity theory.

According to Naïve Regularity theory, laws of nature are general truths that describe the regular pattern of events.

> Regularity exponents analyse laws as true, contingent, universal generalisations which are omni-spatially and omni-temporally unrestricted in scope. Purported necessary connections between the antecedent and consequent events described in the law are regarded as gratuitous.[39]

Under such a theory it is impossible for a violation to occur. This argument can be expressed as follows.

1. Laws of nature are generalisations based on the occurrence of events
2. Every event that occurs can be accounted for by these generalisations
3. A violation of a law of nature cannot be accounted for by these generalisations

---

4. A violation of a law of nature cannot occur.

For example, if a law of nature stated heating water to 100 degree Celsius causes it to boil, and yet we were come across a counter-instance, such as heating water to this temperature causing it to freeze, this would not represent a violation, but instead a new law of nature. In this case the law would become, heating water to 100 degree Celsius causes it to boil or freeze. According to Naïve Regularity Theory therefore, a violation of a law of nature cannot occur. I shall now detail Probabilism's approach to the laws of nature.

One of the most common approaches to the laws of nature within the scientific community is probabilism. Proponents of probabilism, such as Suppes[40] and Eells,[41] approach laws of nature as statistical generalisations. Laws expressed in this fashion lose all sense of necessity. Instead laws are acknowledged as statistical generalisations based on the regular patterns of events.

> There is ...a rhythm and a pattern behind the phenomena of nature which is not apparent to the eye, but only to the eye of analysis; and it is these rhythms and patterns which we call Physical Laws...[42]

According to Probabilism it is impossible for a violation to occur. This is because there are no strict laws to violate. For example, consider that heating water to 100 degree Celsius causes it to boil 99 times in the omni-temporal history of the universe, and this heating has never caused anything but this boiling. Accordingly we could form the law - heating water to 100 degree Celsius causes it to boil 100 % of the time. However, had this heating caused water, to boil 99 times, and not to boil once, this single instance of not boiling would not represent a violation of a law. Rather it would be a positive instantiation of the following law - heating water to 100 degree Celsius causes it to boil 99 % of the time. A violation consequently can never occur.

1. Laws of nature are generalisations based on the probable occurrence of natural events.
2. Every natural event that occurs can be accounted for by these generalisations.
3. A violation of a law of nature cannot be accounted for by these generalisations.

---

4. A violation of a law of nature cannot occur.

Consequently Probabilism also does not allow for the occurrence of a violation of a law of nature. I shall now introduce the final account of the laws of nature, Systematic theory.

One of the most successful Humean approaches is Lewis's systematic theory.[43] Lewis, based upon the work of Ramsey [44] and Mill,[45] defines a law of nature as a contingent generalisation 'if and only if it appears as a theorem (or axiom) in each of the true deductive systems that achieves a best combination of simplicity and strength.'[46] According to such a definition a violation of a law of nature is possible. To understand this possibility some elaboration must given to what exactly constitutes the 'best combination of simplicity and strength.'

Suppose that we were able to account for 99 % of all natural events by appealing to only 3 laws of nature. This would be an example of a very strong and simple set of axioms. Now imagine that the 1 percent of the natural events these laws cannot accommodate constitute violations. In order to contain these anomalous natural events, and so avoid violations, the laws of nature might have to be complicated by adopting a great number of additional laws. According to Lewis this sacrifice of simplicity may not be worth the small gain in strength. If this were the case therefore, we should accept that these natural events constitute violations of the laws of nature.

> Laws are very important, but great masses of particular fact count for something too; and a localised violation is not the most serious difference of law.[47]

This possibility can be expressed as follows.

1. Laws of nature are axioms with the best combination of simplicity and strength.
2. It is possible that these laws may be substantially simpler and insubstantially weaker by not accounting for the occurrence of certain natural events.
3. It is possible these unaccounted natural events could be in violation of the axioms with the best combination of simplicity and strength.
4. A violation of a law of nature can occur.

It is possible under Lewis's systematic theory therefore, for a violation of the laws of nature to occur. One potential problem however, that proponents of magic may have operating under this theory, is the relationship magical events have with the frequency of their occurrence.

Although the simplicity of the laws is important, Lewis also states this should not overshadow the importance of a large body of events. Consider possible worlds P and Q. In possible world P natural event X occurs *n* times. In possible world Q natural event X occurs *n* + 1 times. In possible world P natural event X cannot be accounted for within the laws of nature without sacrificing considerable simplicity, so, as previously discussed, it is accepted as a violation of the laws of nature, and deemed magical. In possible world Q however, event X has occurred to such an extent that if it is not accounted for by the laws of nature too much strength will be lost. Therefore, in possible world G, the laws of nature do account for event X, and consequently this event is not deemed magical. Therefore, which events are or are not magical depends partly on the frequency of their occurrence.

I have asserted that the only means by which paranormal natural magic can satisfy the forth criteria, is by a violation of a law of nature being logically possible. I have also demonstrated that such a violation is impossible under all but one of the given accounts of the laws of nature. This was Lewis's systematic theory. Paranormal natural magic therefore, is only available to those who are willingly to accept (a) that magic must violate a law of nature, (b) that Lewis' systematic approach to the laws of nature is correct, and (c) whether an event is magical or not depends partly on the frequency of its occurrence. I shall now proceed to detail the second type of natural magic, paralucky natural magic.

Paralucky Natural Magic

Malinowski suggested that 'magic is used as something which over and above man's equipment and his force helps him to master accident and to ensnare luck.'[48] The essential characteristic of this type of magic therefore, is that it influences 'the elements of chance and luck.'[49] Weibel also referred to this type of magic when she asserted that the act of pilgrimage might have a magical quality, where pilgrims sought to generate 'events where the outcome is determined by luck as a way of obtaining spiritual reassurance.'[50] Gmelch similarly indicated that the superstitious manner that American baseball players attempt to control the elements of chance is akin to magic.[51] With this relationship between luck and magic introduced, I shall now define paralucky natural magic.

Paralucky natural magic, like paranormal natural magic, refers to a causal connection between natural events. In this case however, the connection is paralucky, being beyond normal luck.[52] To better comprehend this type of magic, consider the following illustration. Shamus, upon finding a four-leafed clover, picks it and holds it up to the sunlight in order to take a closer look. This causes him to notice a rainbow in the sky, which in turn causes him to walk towards its apparent end. Along the way he trips, falls into a bush, and discovers a chest full of treasure. Such as case might be regarded as magical because the causal connection between the finding of the clover and the finding of the treasure is seemly beyond normal luck. We can therefore, define paralucky natural magic as:

> Paralucky Natural Magic: A natural event with a paralucky natural cause.

Note that this type of magic can involve direct or transitive causation. The only stipulation is that causal connection between the magical cause and the magical effect is beyond normal luck.

Paralucky natural magic satisfies the first, third, and forth criteria established to evaluate magic. The first criterion is satisfied by the first natural event constituting a magical cause and the last natural event a magical effect. The third is satisfied by this definition of magic being distinct from the fixed definition of a miracle. And the forth is satisfied due to the logically possibility of a causal connection between natural events being beyond normal luck. The second criterion however, is not satisfied. This is because paralucky causal connections do not provide a clear distinction between magical and non-magical events. To understand why, reconsider this paralucky causal connection in relation to probabilism.

Consider the causal connection between events A and B. If the probability of A causing B is within the value of p, where p is a suitably low probability, let us consider this a paralucky causal connection. Where if the probability of A causing B was $p + 1$, there would be more of a chance of A causing B, and so this connection would be less than paralucky. However, should we really hold all causal connections within this probability value to be magical?

I believe not. For example, on the microscopic scale the chances of a particular radioactive isotope decaying at a particular time can be considerably low, and yet if and when this event occurs we do not generally consider this magical. Likewise on the macroscopic scale, long causal chains of low probability are also not generally considered as magical. Such as those causal chains highlighted by Chaos theory, the best known of which being the 'Butterfly Effect'.[53] Consequently, there is no means to distinguish between highly improbably causal connections and paralucky causal connections.

Not only does paralucky natural magic make magical those events we intuitively regard as non-magical, but given the inherent low probabilities on both the microscopic and macroscopic scale; there could also be an oversaturation of magical events. This definition therefore, fails to conform to the second criterion regarding magic, as it does not provide a clear distinction between magical and non-magical events. We must therefore, either reject this type of magic or accept that all causal connections within the value of p are magical.

Synchronicitious Natural Magic

Synchronicity, as North suggests, 'is like magic happening',[54] and has been closely linked with activities as divination and tarot.[55] Jung coined the term synchronicity to describe what he referred to as an 'acausal connecting principle.'[56] This principle was laid out in order to explain the 'the simultaneous occurrence of two or more meaningfully but not causally connected events.' Jung claimed that this acausal connection between events should be regarded as 'equal in rank to causality as a principle of explanation.' Analogies have been drawn between synchronicity and the notion of magic,[57] some even by Jung himself.[58] Hence the term has become the focal point for a whole new approach to magic.

To better understand this type of magic, consider the following illustration. A husband lies in a coma in hospital while his wife prays for his health at the local church. As soon as she finishes her prayer she returns to the ward only to find her husband conscious and well. The prayer and the recovery are not causally connected, but they do represent a meaningful co-incidence. We can define synchronicitious natural magic as,

> Synchronicitious Natural Magic: One natural event in synchronicity with another.
> Where synchronicity is defined as a meaningful coincidence between events.

Synchronicitious natural magic satisfies the second, third and forth criteria. The second criterion is satisfied by magical events being in synchronicity with each other, whilst non-magical events either are not, or are anatural in substance. The third is satisfied by this definition of magic being distinct from a miracle. And the forth is satisfied due to the logically possibility of a meaningful coincidence between events. This account of magic however, does not satisfy the second criterion regarding magic, as it does not contain a causal connection.

Consider a counterfactual analysis of the previous case. Had the wife chosen not to pray for her husband's health, she would have still returned to the ward to find him recovered. The prayer therefore, is not the cause of her husband's recovery. As the second criterion states that magic must contain a magical cause and a magical effect, synchronous natural magic does not satisfy this criterion. On this point Von Franz concurs, stating that,

> Ascribing the arrangement of synchronistic events to the observer's unconscious would thus be nothing other than a regression to primitive-magical thinking, in accordance with which it was earlier supposed that, for example, an eclipse could be "caused" by the malevolence of a sorcerer. Jung even explicitly warned against taking the archetypes (of the collective unconscious) or psi-powers to be the *causal agency* of synchronistic events.[59]

This definition of magic therefore, is only available to those who are willing to acknowledge that magic does not involve a magical cause or effect. I shall now introduce the second magical group, anatural magic.

Anatural Magic

Anatural magic solely involves anatural events. This type of magic is usually evident within polytheistic religions, where Gods are able to affect other Gods magically.[60] For example, according to Greek mythology, Hera once borrowed Aphrodite's magic girdle to rekindle Zeus's desire for her.[61] Similar stories are also evident within Hinduism. For example, on one occasion the Goddess Mahâdevî exerted magical power over the God Brahma, causing him to nearly rape Anasûyâ.[62] This type of magic can also be read into monotheistic religions. As mentioned previously, within Catholicism magic sometimes defined as 'the art of performing actions beyond the power of man with the aid of powers other than the Divine.'[63] If we assume that the devil is able to interact with other fallen angels in a manner humans cannot, according to this definition such an interaction would be magical. In addition, assuming that both the Devil and other fallen angels are anatural, this magical interaction would solely involve anatural events. I shall now proceed to define this type of magic.

With the exception of the type of substance involved, anatural magic is identical in form to natural magic. Anatural magic can therefore be similarly divided into the following subgroups: paranormal anatural magic, paralucky anatural magic and synchronicitious anatural magic.

> Paranormal Anatural Magic: An anatural event with a direct paranormal anatural cause.
> Paralucky Anatural Magic: An anatural event with a paralucky anatural cause.
> Synchronicitious Anatural Magic: An anatural event in synchronicity with another.

Since these definitions are identical in form to those previously discussed under natural magic, they are similarly prone to the same criticisms.

These criticisms include paranormal anatural magic being unable to occur under all but one account of the laws of anature, paralucky anatural magic failing provide a clear distinction between a magical and non-magical anatural events, and synchronicitious anatural magic containing no magical cause or effect. In lieu of repetition, I shall proceed by introducing a forth criticism. Anatural magic is unable to contain natural events. The overwhelming majority of traditional cases of magic make reference to a magical cause or effect that is natural in substance, such as a rain dance causing rain to fall. Without reference to natural events, anatural magic may prove to be far too exclusive. I shall now introduce the third and final magical group, interactionist magic.

Interactionist Magic

Interactionist magic centres on the notion that magical events are causally connected to events of a different substance. This opinion is mirrored by Godwin's description of occultism.

> It is of the very essence of the occult worldview that earthly events are not the result of material cause and effect alone, but that they are influenced by other levels of being.[64]

Clarke also shares this sentiment, characterising magic as a particular type of 'interaction between the natural and the supernatural.'[65] It is this possibility, the possibility of events being caused by what Blamires refers to as 'Otherworld powers, forces, and dynamics,'[66] that is the essence of this notion of magic. I shall now detail three different types of interactionist magic: natural interactionist magic, anatural interactionist magic and reciprocal interactionist magic.

Natural Interactionist Magic

Consider the following illustration of natural interactionist magic. A demon, angry with a human, wills him to die, where this willing causes him to die. This sequence is regarded as magical because the natural event of the human's death has an anatural cause. In this context natural interactionist magic can be defined as,

> Natural Interactionist Magic: A natural event with a direct anatural cause

Note that this type of magic is direct. This is to guard against the possibility of losing the distinction between a magical event and a non-magical event.

For if we allow transitive causation and assumed the natural universe had an anatural cause, every natural event would consequently become magical.

Natural interactionist magic satisfies the first, second, and forth criteria. The first criterion is satisfied by the anatural event being identified as the magical cause, and the natural event the magical effect. The second is satisfied, as magical events are distinguishable from non-magical events, as magical events will always have causal relata of a different substance to themselves. And the forth is satisfied due to the logically possibility of a natural event having an anatural cause. The third criterion however, is not satisfied. This is because this definition is indistinguishable from the definition of a natural miracle. An additional criticism is that this definition is unable to incorporate natural magical causes. It is common within the tradition of magic to refer to certain natural objects, sounds and symbols as magical. This is because they are believed to be able to cause certain magical effects, such as a rain dance causing rain. Evans-Pritchard concurs with this point.

> It is this material substance which is the occult and essential element in the rite, for in the substance lies the mystical power which produces the desired end.[67]

These first natural events cannot be contained within natural interactionist magic. Consequently, this definition is only available to those who are willing to accept that (a) magic and miracles are identical and (b) that magical causes are not natural in substance.

Anatural Interactionist Magic

Anatural interactionist magic is identical to natural interactionist magic; save only for the inversion of substances.

> Anatural Interactionist Magic: An anatural event with a natural cause

An example of this type of magic would be a human speaking a blasphemy that causes a God to become angry. This type of magic also satisfies the first, second, and forth criteria. The first criterion is satisfied by the natural event being identified as the magical cause, and the anatural event the magical effect. The second is satisfied, as magical events are distinguishable from non-magical events, as magical events will always have causal relata of a different substance to themselves. And the forth is satisfied due to the logically possibility of an anatural event having a natural cause. The third criterion however, is again not satisfied. This is because this definition is indistinguishable from the definition of an anatural miracle. An additional criticism is that this definition is unable to incorporate natural magical effects. So whilst a rain dance may be considered a magical cause, any subsequent natural effects of this dance, such as rain, cannot be contained by this definition. Consequently, this definition is only available to those who are willing to accept that (a) magic and miracles are identical and (b) that magical effects are not natural in substance.

Reciprocal Interactionist Magic

Reciprocal interactionist magic also involves causal interaction between events of different substances, only in this case the magical cause and the magical effect are of the same substance. Malinowski hints at this type of magic when he supposed that magic can be understood as something which 'does not reside in nature, that is, outside man, but in the relation between man and nature.'[68] Malinowski is suggesting that whilst the magical cause and the magical effect are natural, the relationship between these two events is not.

I have previously stated that I believe the term magic to refer to the art by which the anatural is utilised by the natural to influence the natural.[69] I wish to here expand upon this conception of magic.

> Reciprocal Interactionist Magic: An event of type x, caused by an event of type y, caused by an event of type x. Where x and y are different substances.

Assuming all events must be either natural or anatural we can subdivide magic into two further categories: natural reciprocal interactionist magic and anatural reciprocal interactionist magic.

Natural Reciprocal Interactionist Magic: A natural event, caused by an anatural event, caused by a natural event.

Anatural Reciprocal Interactionist Magic: An anatural event, caused by a natural event, caused by an anatural event.

I allow for both types of magic as I regard this pattern of substance interaction to be more important than the traditional view that only natural agents can initiate and/or respond to magic. This position is strengthened by the cases outlined earlier under anatural magic, where Gods magically affect other Gods. However, due to its familiarity I will from here on refer to natural reciprocal interactionist magic in order to better illustrate the character of this type of magic.

Consider the following example of natural reciprocal interactionist magic. Let us refer to the natural event of a rain dance as N1, where the letter denotes the event's substance and the number its place in the causal chain. N1 might be considered a magical cause if it is able to cause a rain spirit to command the rain to fall (A2), where this command causes rain to fall (N3).

$$N1 \rightarrow A2 \rightarrow N3$$

Note that the magical cause (N1) and the magical effect (N2) must be direct, rather than transitive, causal relata of the intermediary event (A2). To explain why I hold this to be the case, consider the following scenario. A farmer, whose crops are dying, begs a witch doctor to perform a rain dance (N1). The farmer's begging causes the witch doctor to perform a rain dance (N2). This rain dance causes a rain spirit to command the rain to fall (A3), which causes rain to fall (N4). Consequently, and much to the farmer's delight, this rainfall causes his crops to grow again (N5).

$$N1 \rightarrow N2 \rightarrow A3 \rightarrow N4 \rightarrow N5$$

Because N1 and N5 are not the direct causal relata of A3 I hold them not to be magical.

If we were to claim N1 was magical then we would have to accept that the farmer's begging was magical. This interpretation however, has little intuitive strength since a common sense distinction can be drawn between that of begging a witchdoctor to perform magic and performing of magic. This intuition can be further strengthened by a counterfactual analysis, whereby if the farmer begged but the witchdoctor did not perform the rain dance, the rain presumably would not fall, inversely had the farmer not begged but the witchdoctor did perform the rain dance, the rain would have still fallen. Likewise, if we were to claim N5 was magical then we would have to accept that there was something magical about rain helping crops grow. This interpretation also posses little intuitive strength, since again a common sense distinction can again be drawn between rain helping crops to grow and crops magically growing despite helpful conditions.

Although I hold that both the magical cause and magical effect must be direct causal relata of the intermediary event, I do allow this intermediary event to be comprised of a causal chain of events of the same substance. For example, a rain dance (N1) would still be considered a magical cause if it caused a dance spirit to request a rain spirit to make it rain (A2), where this request caused rain spirit to command the rain to fall (A3), which in turn caused rain to fall (N4).

$$N1 \to A2 \to A3 \to N4$$

Although this sequence involves two intermediary anatural events I still hold this to be a case of magic. I allow this plurality of intermediary events because it seems highly unconvincing to argue that N4 is not magical simply because its sequence contained more than one anatural intermediary event. One may argue that there is nothing magical about one anatural event causing another, however the witch doctor's rain dance and the subsequent rainfall still satisfy our general intuitions regarding magic.

Reciprocal interactionist magic satisfies all four of the criteria I established to evaluate rival definitions. The first criterion is satisfied by the first event being identified as the magical cause and the last event the magical effect. The second criterion is satisfied by magical events being distinguishable from non-magical events, as magical events will always have causal relata of a different substance to themselves. The third criterion is satisfied by this definition of magic being distinct from a miracle. And the forth criterion is satisfied by the logical possibility of this event sequence. One potential criticism of this type of magic however, may stem from its relationship with miracles.

Although miracles and magic are distinct, magic does entail the miraculous. Reconsider the definitions of natural and anatural miracles.

> Natural Miracle: A natural event with an anatural cause.
> Anatural Miracle: An anatural event with a natural cause.

In relation to these definitions, this form of magic could be defined as:

> A miracle of one type caused by a miracle of the other.

Criticism of this definition may ensue from those who wish to distance miracles from magic. However, unless such a distance can be accomplished without recourse to the type of religious bias I outlined earlier, I do not assume its necessity. So whilst we retain separate notions of magic and miracle, the traditional divide, between for example Moses the miracle worker and Moses the magician, is blurred.

One may attempt to recapture this divide between the magician and miracle worker, is by reference to both the intentional states of anatural agents and Mackie's account of the INUS condition. For example, magical effects are often regarded as,

> ...guaranteed if the controlling rituals are performed accurately, i.e., the ritual compels God. Religious miracles, in contrast, usually result from moral behaviour without guaranteed results despite correct performance of the ritual, emphasise the moral long-range intent of God, and are contained within a religious philosophy.[70]

In light of this distinction a magician could be regarded as a natural agent responsible for an instance of natural reciprocal interactionist magic, where the magical cause is sufficient and necessary for the magical effect, because the anatural agent is compelled to cause the magical effect. Whereas, following Mackie, a miracle worker could be regarded as a natural agent responsible for an instance of natural reciprocal interactionist magic, where the magical cause is an insufficient but necessary part of a condition which is itself unnecessary but sufficient for the magical effect.[71] As the anatural agent is free not to cause the magical effect if they so intend. Such a distinction however, is far from evident.

> The cliché, that the religious man petitions the gods while the magician tries to compel them, is simply false.[72]

So, whether or not there exists a clear division between the miracle worker and the magician remains, for now, a moot point.

Within this paper I provided a metaphysical framework within which the terms miracle and magic were defined and their relationship established. I demonstrated that the only definition of magic that was able to satisfy the given criteria completely, was natural paranormal magic and reciprocal interactionist magic. However, natural paranormal magic is only successful if we accept that (a) magic must violate a law of nature, (b) Lewis' systematic approach to the laws of nature is correct, and (c) whether an event is magical or not depends partly on the frequency of its occurrence. Reciprocal interactionist magic conversely does not depend on any of these factors. In addition it also allows for both natural and anatural magical causes and effects. It is for these stated reasons that I hold reciprocal interactionist magic to be the superior metaphysical account of magic.

Notes

1 Middleton, J. 'Theories of Magic' In *The Encyclopaedia of Religion,* Eliade, M (Ed) 9 (New York: Macmillan, 1987) 82.

2 Cunningham, S. *Wicca: A Guide for the Solitary Practitioner* (St. Paul: Llewellyn Publications, 1990) 19.

3 Thomas, K. *Religion and the Decline of Magic* (New York Charles Scribner's Sons, 1971) 650.

4 Malinowski, B. *Magic, Science and Religion and Other Essays* (New York: Doubleday Anchor Books, 1948) 31.

5 Arendzen J.P. 'Occult Art, Occultism' In *The Catholic Encyclopaedia,* 11 (New York: Robert Appleton Company, 1911)

6 Mumford, S. 'Miracles: Metaphysics and Modality' In *Religious Studies*, 37 (2001) 192.

7 Clarke, S. 'Hume's definition of miracles revisited' In *American Philosophical Quarterly*, 36 (1999) 54.

8 Hughes, C. 'Miracles, Laws of Nature and Causation' In *Proceedings of the Aristotelian Society,* Supplementary Volume 66 (1993) 201.

9 Swinburne, R. 'For the Possibility of Miracles' In *Philosophy of Religion: An Anthology*, 4. Pojman, L. (ed.) (Belmont, CA: Wadsworth Publishing Company, 2003) 269.

10 Aquinas, T. *Summa Contra Gentiles III* (Paris: University of Notre Dame Press, 1955) Ch 98-103.

11 Hume, D. 'Of Miracles', In *Enquiry Concerning Human Understanding*, Selby-Bigge, L.A. (Ed) (Oxford: Oxford University Press, 1748:1975) 115.

12 Adams, R. M. 'Miracles, Laws of Nature and Causation – II' In *The Aristotelian Society*, Supplementary Volume, 60 (1992) 207-224.

13 Adams.

14 Often mistranslated as the Red Sea. See: Crim, K, Furnish, V. & Bailey, L. (Eds) *The Interpreters Dictionary of the Bible*, 4 (Nashville: Abingdon Press, 1962) 21.

15 Spinoza, B. 'Tracatus Theologico-Politicus', In *The Chief Works of Benedict de Spinoza*, Elwes, R.H.M (Trans) (London: George Bell and Sons, 1883) 83.

16 In order to illustrate these rival accounts I will draw upon various strands of magic, such as pre-modern forms of indigenous magic, Paganism, Renaissance Magia Naturalis and Satanism. I acknowledge that such strands differ in numerous respects and do not usually serve to illustrate like magical groups. I stress that these groups are based solely upon the reduction of magic to it most basic metaphysical form, and this conflation of heterogeneous magical strands is not designed to reflect anything other than the explanatory power of my taxonomy.

17 For such a history consider: Seligmann, K. *The History of Magic and the Occult* (New York: Random House, 1997) & Levi, E. *History of Magic*. (New York: Samuel Weiser, 1984).

18 Kors, A.C. & Edward, P. *Witchcraft in Europe* (Philadelphia: University of Pennsylvania Press, 1972)

19 Quinn, D.M. *Early Mormonism and the Magic World View* (Salt Lake City: Signature Books, 1998)

20 Henry, J. 'Magic and Science in the Sixteenth and Seventeenth Centuries' In *Companion to the History of Modern Science* Olby, R.C., Cantor, G.N., Christie, J.R.R. & Hodge, M.J.S. (Eds.) (London: Routledge, 1990) 589.

21 Ficino, M. 'The Apology of Marsilio Ficino' In *Marsilio Ficino's Book of Life*, C. Boer (Trans.) (Spring Publications 1980) 186-187.

22 Walker, D.P. 'Spiritual and Demonic Magic from Ficino to Campanella' In *Studies of the Warburg Institute* 22 (1958) 53.

23 Giordano, B. 'On Magic' In *Cause, Principle and Unity: And Essays on Magic*, Blackwell, R & Lucca, R (Eds & Trans) (Cambridge: Cambridge University Press, 1999) Ch 1.

24 MacGregor Mathers, S.L. *Ritual Magic of the Golden Dawn* (Vermont: Destiny Books 1997)

25 Giordano, Ch 1.

26 Hall,M.P. Magic: A Treatise on Esoteric Ethics (Los Angeles: Philosophical Research Society, 1999) 15

27 Barret, F. *Magus Book One: A Complete System of Occult Philosophy* (London: The Book Tree, 1801: 1999) Ch 1.

28 Aquinas, T. *Summa Contra Gentiles III*, (Paris: University of Notre Dame Press, 1955) 98-103.

29 Hume, D. *Enquiries Concerning Human Understanding*. Selby-Bigge, L.A. (Ed), (Oxford: Oxford University Press, 1975) s.10, pt.1.

30 Swinburne, 11.

31 Cunningham, S. *Encyclopaedia of Magical Herbs* (St. Paul: Llewellyn Publications, 1985) 3.

32 LaVey, A. 'Book of Belial' In *The Satanic Bible* (London: Avon: 1989)110.

33 Middleton, J. 'Theories of Magic' In *The Encyclopaedia of Religion*, Eliade, M (Ed) 9 (New York: Macmillan, 1987) 82.

34 Kneale, W. 'Universality and Necessity', In *British Journal of the Philosophical Society* 12 (1961) 89-102.

35 Armstrong, D. *What is a Law of Nature?* (Cambridge: Cambridge University Press, 1983).

36 Tooley, M. 'The Nature of Laws', In *Canadian Journal of Philosophy*, VIII/4 (1977) 667-698.

37 Dretske, F.I. 'Laws of Nature' In *Philosophy of Science*, 44 (1977) 248-268.

38 Ellis, B. *Scientific Essentialism* (Cambridge: Cambridge University Press, 2001) 57.

39 Beauchamp, T. L. (Ed). *Philosophical Problems of Causation*. (Encino: Dickinson Publishers, 1974) 36.

40 Suppes, P. *A Probabilistic Theory of Causality*. (Amsterdam: North-Holland Publishing Company, 1970).

41 Eells, E. *Probabilistic Causality* (Cambridge: Cambridge University Press, 1991).

42 Feyman, R. *The Character of Physical Law* (Mass.: MIT Press, 1967) 13.

43 Lewis, D. 'Causation', In *Journal of Philosophy*. 70 (1973a), 556-567.

44 Ramsey, F.P. 'Universals of Law and of Fact' In *Philosophical Papers*, Mellor, D. (Ed) (Cambridge: Cambridge University Press, 1990) ch.7.

45 Mill, J.S. *A System of Logic* (London: Longmans, Green and Co, 1843:1965), b.3, ch.4, sc.1.

46 Lewis, D. *Counterfactuals* (Oxford: Basil Blackwell, 1973b) p.73.

47 Ibid, 75.

48 Malinowski, 104.

49 Ibid. 31.

50 Weibel, D. 'Controlling Chance, Creating Chance: Magical Thinking in Religious Pilgrimage' In *Journal for the Academic Study of Magic* 1 (2003)176.

51 Gmelch, G. *Inside Pitch: Life in Professional Baseball* (Washington: Smithsonian Institution Press, 2002)

52 Although I acknowledge not all accounts of this notion of magic require anything more than normal luck, I assert the need for a paralucky causal connection in order to differentiate magical events from non-magical lucky events.

53 E. Lorenz, 'Predictability: Does the Flap of a Butterfly's Wings in Brazil Set off a Tornado in Texas?' In *AAAS Convention of the Global Atmospheric Research Program* (Massachusetts: MIT Press, 1972).

54 North, C. *Synchronicity: The Anatomy of Coincidence* (Brighton: Regent Press, 1997)

55 von Franz M. *On Divination and Synchronicity: The Psychology of Meaningful Chance*. (Toronto: Inner City Books: 1980)

56 Jung, C. *Synchronicity: An Acausal Connecting Principle*. Hull R.F.C (Trans) (Princeton: Princeton University Press, 1973:1988)

57 Aziz, R. *C.G. Jung's Psychology of Religion and Synchronicity* (New York: State University of New York Press, 1990)

58 Jung, C. *Jung on Synchronicity and the Paranormal,* Roderick, M. (Ed) (Princeton: University of Press, 1998)

59 von Franz, M. *Psyche and Matter.* (Boston: Shambhala.1992) 231

60 I acknowledge that the distinction between the natural and anatural is not prominent within all religions. However, the following examples still illustrate the possibility that magic is could be used by anatural agents for anatural ends.

61 Sara Maitland 'The First Family of Olympus' In *Titans and Olympians: Greek and Roman Myth* (London: Duncan Baird Publishers) 63.

62 O'Flaherty, W (Trans) 'Bhavis.ya Purâna' In *Hindu Myths (London:* Penguin Books, 1975)

63 Arendzen.

64 Godwin, J. *The Theosophical Enlightenment* (New York: State University of New York Press, 1994)

65 Clarke, S. 'Hume's definition of miracles revisited' In *American Philosophical Quarterly*, 36 (1999) 56.

66 Blamires, S. *Glamoury: Magic of the Celtic Green World* (St. Paul: Llewellyn Publications, 1995)

67 Evans-Pritchard, E.E. *Witchcraft, oracles and magic among the Azande* (Oxford: Clarendon Press, 1937: 1958), 441.

68 Malinowski, B. 'The Role of Magic and Religion' In *Reader in Comparative Religion: An Anthropological Approach*, William, A. L. & Evon Z.V. (Eds) (New York: Harper & Row, 1965) 108.

69 Luck, M. 'In Defense of Mumford's Definition of a Miracle' In *Religious Studies*, 39/4 (2003) 465 – 469.

70 Anderson, R.D. Inside the Mind of Joseph Smith: Psychobiography and the Book of Mormon (Salt Lake City: Signature Books, 1999) 57.

71 Mackie, J. L. 'Causes and Conditionals' In *American Philosophical Quarterly* 2 (1965) 245-65.

72 Smith, M. *Jesus the Magician: Charlatan or Son of God* (Berkeley: Ulysses Press, 1998) 92.

'I will not go to the Devil for a Cure' : Witchcraft, Demonic Possession, and Spiritual Healing in Nineteenth-Century Devon

Jason Semmens

Cases of demonic possession and witchcraft-inspired obsession are familiar enough themes from the period of the witch-trials, yet their continued occurrence throughout the eighteenth century and into the nineteenth poses questions concerning their nature and function at a time when belief in witchcraft was in decline according to Enlightenment sceptics. The roots of these later cases are embedded in the late seventeenth century, in the discourse of spirits that raged between the sadducees on the one hand, such as John Webster and Francis Hutchinson, and the upholders of the supernatural world - such as Joseph Glanvil, Henry More and Richard Baxter, on the other. Several works appeared during the 1660s through until the early eighteenth century containing stories of witchcraft and demonic possession to underpin belief in the existence of the spirit world and refute the beliefs of the sadducees, whose denial of the involvement of the spirit world in the affairs of men ultimately undermined the actions of God in determining man's fate.[1] The debate continued, although the religious and secular framework within which the later cases occurred were much altered.

The repeal of the 1604 witchcraft act in 1736 and Enlightenment scepticism marginalised belief in possession and removed from it any possibility of recourse to law, so that it became the almost exclusive preserve of Evangelical communities, members of which produced accounts of the affliction and dispossession of individuals to bolster confessional claims. In its early years, Methodism involved itself in possession cases, following the example of John Wesley, and its success at the expense of competing confessions supported Methodism's claims to a purer Christianity. Owen Davies has noted that 'Bristol had been a key focus of the Methodist awakening during the late 1730s and 1740s,' and the city and its hinterland saw two high profile possession cases during the mid-eighteenth century: the Lamb Inn affair of the early 1760s, and that of George Lukins during the 1780s. In both cases Methodist ministers were involved, and in the latter possession provided an effective resolution to the affair.[2]

The case that is the subject of this paper occurred at Plymouth Dock in Devon, during 1820, a period when Wesleyan Methodism had, officially, distanced itself from the early revivalism of its past and had embraced a more sober, temperate approach towards the supernatural. Wesleyan Methodist minister James Heaton (1782 – 1862) became involved with the case and was able to impose his interpretation and structure upon it, thereby determining the outcome of the affair. The affliction of 10 year old John Evens was first brought to Heaton's attention by John Lose, Evens' stepfather, on Tuesday 29 February 1820.[3] Lose approached Heaton in the Ker Street Methodist Chapel after service had concluded and requested his assistance, claiming that the affliction of the boy resembled that of a Biblical demoniac. Heaton could not have resisted the parallel with the despairing father approaching Christ,[4] and went with Lose to his house, next door to his own, to find the behaviour of John Evens of such a singular nature that Heaton attended upon him on an almost daily basis thereafter, making notes on the boy's behaviour as time progressed and of the competing opinions of the causes of the boy's malady as the affliction developed. Evens' fits started a month or two prior to Heaton's attendance and surgeons from the local Dispensary had attended Evens, bleeding and blistering the boy, with little apparent success. The affair continued until 22 March 1820 when the first exorcism was performed, and was successful. The following week, on 28 March, Mrs. Lose, Evens' mother, advised Heaton that Evens was again taken ill, with the same symptoms as before. The death of Heaton's eldest son prevented his immediate attention, but on 19 April a second exorcism was performed, which closed the affair. The case therefore fell into two distinct phases of activity. Heaton produced the only detailed account of the possession to have been published, and is the only person known to have undertaken to write about it – either for public consumption or in private.

James Heaton (1782 - 1862). From The Wesleyan Methodist Magazine 55 (1832), 609 facing, Courtesy of the Cornwall Studies Library.

The Possession Narrative

The first edition of Heaton's description of the possession appeared in the latter half of 1820 under the title *The Demon Expelled: Or, the Influence of Satan, and the Power of Christ, Displayed in the Extraordinary*

Affliction, and Gracious Relief, of a Boy about Ten Years of Age, at Plymouth-Dock, and was printed and sold locally. The book attracted sufficient attention to warrant a further edition, not least because of the 'few objections' that had 'been stated to the writer's view of the subject.' The second edition appeared in 1822, with additions and enlargements, so that 'some parts of the work that were thought obscure, are more fully explained, and much new matter ... added.' The narrative itself was left untouched, the additions consisted of a new preface to supplement the old and an enlargement of the discourse touching on possession in biblical times and what Heaton perceived as the superstitions in his own. To counter any accusation concerning the verity of his account, Heaton also appended a list of people who could testify the truth of his narrative. The overtly evangelical title of the first edition was replaced by the anodyne *The Extraordinary Affliction and Gracious Relief of a Little Boy: Supposed to be the Effects of Spiritual Agency. Carefully Examined, and Faithfully Narrated; with Observations on Demoniac Possession, and Animadversions on Superstition*. Here Heaton bowed to criticism, recognising that 'some expressions in the title of the former edition were thought so bold as to startle some readers, and prevent deliberate examination of their propriety.'[5] The second edition stood at 156 pages, as opposed to the 100 pages of its predecessor, and now carried the note that it was sold by Thomas Blanshard of Paternoster Row, London, (*fl.* 1809 – 1823) the principal bookseller at this time dedicated to producing Methodist tracts and pamphlets, who had some of the earliest editions of John and Charles Wesley's complete works printed and expanded his catalogue to include other Methodist writers. The second edition was bound with Heaton's *Farther Observations*, a short tract exploring the distinguishing marks of demoniac possession, its miseries, the various modes of relief, the scripture mode of expelling demons, its corruption by papal superstitions, astrological practice of physic, and the sinfulness of charms.

Heaton took as his model the earlier pamphlet by Henry Durbin detailing a case of alleged witchcraft that occurred at Bristol in 1761/62, published as *A Narrative of Some Extraordinary Things that Happened to Mr. Richard Giles's Children, at The Lamb, Without Lawford's Gate, Bristol;*

Supposed to be the Effect of Witchcraft (Bristol, 1800). Following Durbin, Heaton adopted an empirical approach and noted events as they occurred throughout the days that he visited the Lose household, seeking to relate concrete physical events that took place within a recognisable environment. The near daily entries followed the same format. As Heaton could not be present throughout every day, he relied upon the testimony of others present for the minutiae described. Consequently, while under the authorship of Heaton, the text has been fashioned by several witnesses: the events filtered through the preconceptions and biases of Heaton and his witnesses. Heaton took pains to ensure that he reproduced the accounts in a manner that he considered to be fair and accurate, and acceptable for assent by all who might investigate the phenomena of spirit possession impartially and objectively. He repeatedly emphasised the results of tests that he performed on the boy to detect fraud, as also those of others who daily came to see the demoniac and sought to test him themselves. Where Heaton differed

from Durbin however was in his animadversions or explanatory remarks that occur throughout the narrative, clarifying certain events and ascribing motives to decisions that were made. Therefore as the printed narrative progresses, a pattern and structure develops that the reader is lead to believe reflected the course of events. This method was later felt to detract from the narrative, as a reviewer in the *Imperial Magazine*, itself an evangelical publication, noted:

> By adopting this mode of proceeding, we cannot but think that he has injured the cause he intended to serve. If Mr. H. had simply given his narrative of the incidents occurring at Plymouth Dock, furnishing evidence and facts, and leaving every reader to draw his own conclusions, he would have appeared more in the character of a disinterested historian, than that of a special pleader, and, as such, his observations would have had more weight.[6]

James Heaton

Heaton was born at Birmingham in 1782[7] and appears to have had the bare rudiments of an education until the age of 15, when his conversion to God convinced him of the necessity of study. His parents had become Methodists themselves some years previously, and it was through his father's influence that Heaton converted, indeed the testament of his friend Titus Close in this regard might equally have been echoed by Heaton himself: 'To be born of religious parents is a great privilege; and those who have been favoured with it have abundant reason to bless the Giver of all good. With such parents I was blessed. For years their prayers ascended to the throne of grace for me; and at length they are answered.'[8] From 1797 onwards Heaton 'sought by diligent study to make up for a defective education,' he also spent a few years engaged in 'active usefulness' at West Bromwich before entering the Methodist ministry in 1806, at the age of 24, and began an itinerant life that lasted until 1849 when he became a Supernumerary and settled once more at Birmingham, where he later died, on 21 August 1862.

Heaton spent his ministry as a home-missionary, taking John Wesley as his example and setting up Societies in previously neglected areas, such as Redditch, 'often suffering severely from the hostility of brutal people.' Several of the Societies he founded endured and were still in existence more than 50 years later. His preaching was described as 'clear, vigorous, spiritual; often marked by a quaintness and originality which gained the attention of his audiences.' Heaton preached with the enthusiasm of a convert. He had a particular fondness for and appeal to children, many of whom were his 'crown of rejoicing.' The habit of study that he acquired after his conversion remained with him throughout his active life, combining this with his ministry to combat 'heresies and errors.' In his early years as a minister, Heaton was especially known for the number of conversions he effected as a result of revivals, the particular experience associated with a fervour of preaching and an inward soul-searching and feeling of guilt for past sins and a dramatic emotive response to the notion that these sins had been forgiven. Wesley himself presided over such revivals and likened the experience to exorcism, with the Devil being driven out by God's grace.

The ministry brought Heaton to the South West in the early 1810s when he went into Cornwall and became a preacher on the Truro circuit, attending several congregations in an area that extended as far geographically as Gwennap and St. Agnes. Here his preaching became noted, and he was prevailed upon by Society members to publish one of his sermons so that the faithful might have a permanent reminder of its content. Heaton demurred, 'being unaccustomed to write for the public,' but finally agreed. The sermon was printed as *A Sermon on Perfect Love* in 1816, and reflected Heaton's belief in an unconditional love of God and his creation, and was reflected in his adoption of the Biblical motto, 'Peace to the Brethren, and love with Faith, from God the Father, and the Lord Jesus Christ' (Ephesians 4: 23), which Heaton claimed was the utterance of his heart. The success of this volume convinced Heaton of his own abilities as an author, and he later came to realise that he might use the press as a corrective to erroneous accounts and doctrines that had spread orally among the Societies, using his pen in tandem with his preaching. In 1818 Heaton was moved to Plymouth Dock and attached to the Ker Street chapel.

The 1821 census described Dock as the most populous urban centre in Devon and Cornwall at the time, having more than a third larger population than nearby Plymouth (33578 persons in Dock as opposed to 21591 persons resident in Plymouth).[9] The chapel was one of several dissenting chapels at Dock, the others being of the Wesleyan and Calvinist Methodist persuasion, and of the 'Old Dissent,' the Baptists, Presbyterians, Quakers and Independents.[10] The Chapel stood on the corner of the junction between Ker Street and Monument Street, and was popularly known as the 'Windmill-Hill Chapel' due to the remains of a windmill that formerly stood behind the site of the chapel on the rise (roughly where the Monument now stands). It was during his ministry there that Heaton was called to attend John Evens, the episode resulting in the two further publishing ventures here under consideration: *The Demon Expelled* of 1820 and two years later his *Farther Observations*. Heaton had already moved from Dock by 1822, spending time at Bradford on Avon in Wiltshire, and later in the decade spent several years in Nottingham, where he was one of 5 preachers on that circuit.[11] While at Nottingham his exposition, *The Christian Faith,*

Considered in its General Nature: Gracious Provision, Duteous Exercise, and Saving Power was published, and was sold in London by John Mason. The book was reviewed in the *Wesleyan Magazine*, the first of his works to be so. The 1830s saw his final publications, two exercises in biography: the *Memoir of Mr. John Dungett, of Newcastle-Upon-Tyne* (London, 1833), and the *Memoir of Titus Close, Wesleyan-Methodist Minister, and for some time Missionary in India*, published in 1836 about the time Heaton was at Bolton. The common experience of both men, which Heaton himself shared, was an early life spent amidst the pleasures of this world, followed by a conversion and subsequent commitment to God, in all three cases to the ministry. The two biographies that Heaton wrote were additions to an already substantial corpus of similar texts, designed to edify the faithful and instruct those who faith might be weak by example.

The Methodist Background

The relationship between Wesleyan Methodism and popular superstition in the latter part of the eighteenth century and the early part of the nineteenth is one that has been commented upon since Wesley made public his positive belief in the matter.[12] Many of his (largely Anglican) contemporaries, for whom the supposed power of witches and their concourse with devils was a relic of a more credulous age, ridiculed and satirised his beliefs and members of his movement who openly professed to have had dealings with spirits. It was also suspected that as Enlightenment discourses concerning science, rationalism and progress had failed to erode popular beliefs in the supernatural to any significant degree, Wesley's Enthusiasm and credulity must have artificially bolstered these beliefs, prolonging their survival beyond what sceptics thought reasonable. Moreover, to the Anglican establishment, the 'paganism' of such beliefs were relics of Catholicism, and as Methodism became more widespread and established, increasingly bitter attacks from Anglican ministers specifically equated Methodist credulity with Popish superstition. More than six hundred printed attacks on the Methodists appeared between 1738 and 1800, and this onslaught continued into the nineteenth century.[13] For example, writing in 1817, the Anglican vicar of Little Petherick in north Cornwall could note in connexion with charms and other popular superstitions that 'in the various ways of worship set afoot in the country by the separatists from the National Church of Christ here, do we not see verified how such charms and other observances as God has not so commanded.' Lyne went on to call Methodism a 'Cunning Craftiness' or 'misrepresentation of religion,' and warned that the Holy Ghost had predicted such a movement.[14]

This question of the perceived enthusiasm and credulity of Methodists is one that the movement began to address in the years following Wesley's death in 1791, as it began to establish itself as a dissenting denomination separate from the Anglican church with its own hierarchy and to court a degree of respectability. As the church hierarchy sought to distance itself from the supernatural beliefs of its founder, it began to berate activists who continued to expound publicly beliefs in the intervention of spirits. As a consequence the Wesleyan Methodist movement split in 1812, when a group of more evangelically minded ministers seceded to form the Primitive Methodists, part of whose early success may have resulted from their refusal to limit the power of Satan in the world, claiming that witchcraft must still exist as the Author of the Bible had plainly indicated so with the prohibitions against magical practitioners in Deuteronomy and the visit of Saul to the Witch of Endor. Furthermore they could cite the beliefs and laws of the previous two centuries.[15]

More recently historians have concerned themselves with explaining the rise and decline of witchcraft beliefs during the early modern period through to the twentieth century, examining the possible divergence between public and private responses to these beliefs. It is within this context that the study of the influence of the Methodist movement on popular culture and pastimes has assumed a new importance. Taking an explanation that echoed those of critics from the eighteenth century, in 1948 R. Trevor Davies believed it 'probable that the Methodist movement gave an impetus to mob violence against witches in the latter part of the eighteenth century and helped witch-beliefs to survive so late into the following century.'[16] It would be logical therefore to expect that witch-beliefs were most prevalent by the nineteenth century in those areas where Methodism had its strongest support, such as Cornwall. Yet as Owen Davies has shown, witch-beliefs were also widespread in those areas not normally accounted Methodist strongholds, furthermore the influence that Wesley and his followers were able to exert over popular culture in the eighteenth century was small, for it was not until later in the nineteenth century that Society membership grew to represent a significant influence. Research has suggested that the opposite of R. Trevor Davies' thesis is correct, that it was the continuance of witch-beliefs and participation in the supernatural in the century or more after 1736 that assisted the growth of Methodism, by the latter's acceptance of those beliefs and the emotive appeal to them. Henry Rack noted that 'One of the factors which enabled Wesley to control his people so far as he did was that he not only tolerated but to a certain extent himself inhabited the same supernatural world.'[17] The later success of the Primitive Methodists lay in their continued stress on the actions of spirits in the world while the Wesleyan Methodists fell largely silent on the matter.

The Loddeswell Precedent

The demoniac adhered to a set of defined, accepted modes of behaviour, displaying their possession by reference to other texts learned orally or through the written word that had their roots in seventeenth-century religious thought. The immediate inspiration for the John Evens case was a family of possessed sisters from the village of Loddeswell in South Devon. During 1819 the four daughters of John Kennard, aged between 7 and 16, at various intervals throughout that year displayed epileptic fits and other signs of possession. Most remarkable was the account of the 11 year-old daughter who was described as having ran up the side of a wall 'to the ceiling, impossible as it may seem, where she remained immovable on her feet for several minutes, her clothes being unaltered in their usual position, as if, by some supernatural law, she had the power of changing the centre of gravity.' Other feats mentioned included superhuman strength and the curious ability to 'whirl around in their chairs ... like tops set in rapid motion.' Medical advice was sought, but proved ineffective. Heaton was able to garner further details of the affair from John Kennard after the latter's visit to Dock in early March 1820. From him Heaton learned that an old woman in the neighbourhood had persecuted one of the children after some altercation between them and it was this woman who came to be suspected of ill-wishing the children. Further evidence of witchcraft was provided by the vomiting of pins by one of the children, and Heaton saw the one that had been given to Kennard's relation at Dock. Heaton could lament that in this case no 'sceptical philosopher ... could prove these effects were produced by another cause,'[18] for the local conjuror was sought out for a cure to the afflictions and was able to provide one. The Kennard case was reported in the *Plymouth and Dock Telegraph* newspaper on 26 February 1820[19] and as far as the details allow, the Kennard possession case would seem to follow the standard possession pattern and was one of village maleficium, where medical assistance had failed in the face of an illness, opening those concerned to possibilities of folk-illness and healing.

Heaton noted that John Kennard was a Baptist, and a Lay-preacher of the gospel. After speaking to Kennard, Heaton thought that 'he therefore has not only the common motives of religion not to deceive his neighbours, but his public character lays an additional obligation upon him, to speak the Truth, and nothing but the Truth.' Heaton went on to note that, 'As to his knowledge, or ability to distinguish the real nature of his family affliction, I apprehend he knows very little of those Philosophical Theories with which learned men have contradicted each other ... but long and painful *experience has made him wise.*'[20] Several themes have been developed here, most prominently the incontestability of the preternatural events that took place and Heaton's own absolution of Kennard's resort to a conjuror to resolve the situation, putting his own humanity and sympathy for the afflicted before religious purity, and excusing him for his ignorance of the literature surrounding possession cases, also his lack of discrimination in discovering what Heaton believed was the true cause of the disturbances despite Biblical condemnation of magical practitioners. It is also possible to detect something of Heaton's own anti-intellectualism, placing experience above learned discourse, in spite of his own reading and participation in that discourse.

An Exercise in Natural Philosophy
The Kennard case reached its conclusion during the opening two months of 1820, culminating in the *Dock Telegraph* article at the end of February. The *Dock Telegraph* had raised concerns about how to deal with the case, and the John Evens affair then unfolding provided a timely opportunity to investigate such a case along the lines of natural philosophy, also to consider

the appropriate Christian response to the phenomena. Heaton described his mission thus: 'The truth of such a case was an important object of enquiry; and, if it lay within the grasp of my ability, I was fully determined to search it out. "Socrates is a friend, and Plato is a friend, but Truth is more a friend." The classical references pointed towards the importance of the use of reason for the acceptance of the account, rather than outright enthusiasm which Heaton realised would damage his credibility. Furthermore he believed that 'the exercise of charity is as important as the investigation of Truth,' in that, while engaged in empirical observation, the primary aim of those investigations should be the relief of suffering, rather than pure scientific or philosophic enquiry.'[20]

It was on 7 March that the first suggestions of witchcraft were voiced, by some of the curious, and by John Kennard, then on a visit to Dock. Kennard heard of the Evens case and came to see the boy for himself. Heaton particularly noted that 'in his (John Evens) hearing, [Kennard] gave the family, and the company present, an account of several things which his own children did and suffered. *He asserted, that 'This boy's affliction was of the same kind as that which troubled his four children: that it was not a natural disorder, but the effect of an evil spirit.*' (Heaton's italics). Kennard's description of witchcraft moved the possession on to its next stage, with Evens leaping onto Kennard's back, regaining his power of speech, and declared that, 'It is no use the Doctor's giving me physic; they can do me no good: I tell you it is the devil that troubles me – I am overlooked.'[21] Evens went on to describe the woman he now claimed had bewitched him, and 'in several things, he imitated her exactly.' More than a century before, the child's testimony as to the identity of his invisible assailant would have been sufficient by law to warrant the apprehension of the suspect for examination. After 1736 however, the crime of witchcraft had been reduced to pretended fortune-telling and imposture, and the public discourse of witchcraft itself had moved to such a degree that Heaton could note, '*His* asserting that he was bewitched, is not sufficient proof of the fact: and it would be cruel to criminate a poor old woman without substantial evidence of guilt.' Heaton went on, 'if it were true, that a wicked human being had employed evil arts to afflict him, that injury could not have been inflicted but by the agency of an evil spirit; therefore, to this great cause of the mischief our attention should be chiefly directed.' Offering a respite from the constant stream of visitors, Heaton had the boy removed to his own house for the rest of the day, where he continued to display distress at the 'sight' of an invisible tormentor, crying out 'Oh! She's pricking me! She's pricking me!' and enquiring 'What do you beat me for? I have done nothing to you?'[22] Loss of speech the following morning brought an end to this behaviour, attempting to incriminate another for his affliction, but by now Heaton had decisively altered the nature of the possession, moving it away from notions of folk-illness and maleficium, towards a more theologically-based malady.

Popular Responses

In surveying the variety of competing explanations offered for Evens' affliction, the lack of written or published alternative accounts is in some degree ameliorated by Heaton's at times extensive recounting of various opinions that were in circulation around the locality, that included 'An old woman, little boys, ingenuity and stupidity, health and disease, religion and wickedness, God Almighty, the boy himself, and an evil spirit.'[23] His enumeration and elaboration of these reflected his aim of a thorough investigation into the causes, citing and then disproving the explanations so as to refine the narrative towards its eventual conclusion, at the same time justifying the course and beliefs that he took. Heaton's care was vital given the extensive incidence of fraud discovered in earlier cases of possession, moreover consideration of his own reputation. A reviewer of his Narrative commented that:

> The writer ... who presumes to intimate, that witchcraft, apparitions, or demoniac possessions, are even possible, does it at the risk of his literary reputation, and forfeits all claim to philosophical acquirement, and to a sound understanding. There are, however, to be found, even in this unbelieving age, numerous individuals, who conceive that public opinion ought not to triumph over evidence; and that truth can sustain no injury from a rigorous investigation of fact.[24]

Early modern episodes of possession were interpreted as signs of God's providence, either as a test, to strengthen the resolve of the godly, or as a punishment – for misdemeanours and transgressions against God's law, and certain of his neighbours believed that Evens was now afflicted for wickedness that he had committed.[25] Heaton made enquiries concerning the boy's character, and found nothing that might distinguish him from any other boy of his age. He later criticised those 'miserable comforters,' for their lack of charity, believing that 'they themselves have been more righteous, because they have been less afflicted than *John Evens*.'[26] By others, the charge of lunacy was levelled, leading to observations of the moon to discover any link with the fits, though none were found.

The most obvious explanation proffered was the sceptical one of fraud, either to merely attract attention or for money. Of the latter Heaton noted that Evens 'wanted for nothing,' and therefore could not have been doing it for any material gain. The Loses were 'not rich; but they are honest: and their daily labour supplies their daily wants,' and as a consequence 'are not such parents more worthy of sympathy and imitation, than of slander and reproach?' During the early days of the affliction various people gave money to Evens during his more lucid moments, more by way of compensation to the parents for the inconvenience caused by the constant visitors. When it came to the parents' attention that it had been intimated that the show was for gain they insisted that no further money should be given to Evens, thereby bringing to a close any further accusations of that kind.[27] During his fits, or when performing feats that were believed to be preternatural others examined him for any evidence of tricks but could find none. Furthermore it was known that the great strength displayed during his convulsions was a sign of his possession and several men tried to grapple with and overcome Evens during these episodes. Apparently it took 'four persons to hold him conveniently, so as to prevent him from injuring himself or others,' while the fits were in progress. On 8 March a test was carried out by one man, who was successful in overcoming Evens, despite his kicking. When Evens fell to the floor and cried 'O my face,' the man declared 'I see now it is all wickedness; - I am quite satisfied, it is nothing but wickedness.' Evens though resumed his fit and the man proved unable this time to restrain him, and required the assistance of three others, after which he retracted his former statement – 'I see now, the boy is really ill.'[28] The repeated tests of human versus preternatural strength challenged the sceptics' stance and reinforced that of believers in a preternatural origin.

The physician and the surgeon from the Dispensary represented the trained medical view of the episode and were in attendance before the case became public. Their initial conclusion was one of epilepsy,[29] though Evens' symptoms frequently contradicted those of epilepsy, and continued unabated in spite of the copious bleeding that Evens was subjected to. They tested Evens for any evidence of insanity or brain disorder but were unable to discover any cause. Heaton turned to medical texts himself, at one point to refute the charge that Evens must be suffering from madness, as he consulted Dr. William Battie's *A Treatise on Madness* (London, 1758) to show that while Battie characterised madness as a case of false perception on the sufferer's part, Evens only displayed these symptoms during his fits. At other times he appeared perfected sensible. Furthermore, Heaton had access to a medical encyclopaedia from which he was able to cite the ideas of the French physician Francois Boissier de Sauvages de la Croix, and the *Works* of Dr. John Cullen. Heaton took particular interest in Dr. Sauvages' admission that a species of disease might exist that he termed 'demonomania,' the madness produced by demons, taken from Sauvages' classification of illnesses: *Nosologia Methodica, Sistens Morborum Classes, juxta Sydenhami Mentem et Botanicorum Ordinem* (Amsterdam, 1768). Heaton also quoted Dr. Cullen's remarks on Sauvages' classification, as Cullen denied the possibility of demonomania, attributing it to a 'species of melancholy or mania; ... some disease, by the spectators falsely ascribed to the influence of an evil spirit; ... of a disease entirely feigned; or ... of a disease partly true, partly feigned.' Heaton attacked Cullen's apparent vindication of the 'wicked one' by removing spiritual influence from the illness altogether, noting that 'wherever even a learned man opposes what is truth, he must involve himself in absurdity.'[30]

Heaton's exploration of medical texts reflected Wesley's own interests in the subject of spiritual healing and should not be seen as being incompatible with his ministry. Methodists viewed spiritual and somatic healing as synonymous, and the discovery of God's forgiveness during revivals was in part physical. What is noticeable in Heaton's reference to medicine however was his appeal to texts that by 1820 were around 60 years old, with the exception of Cullen's *Works* that had been published some 16 years earlier and disagreed with the older works on the subject of spiritual affliction. The disagreement of his medical authorities reflected the inability of the Plymouth physicians to restore Evens to health. Heaton asked 'Who shall decide, when Doctors disagree?'

Sometime around 12 March 1820 the surgeon came once more to Dock, and this time informed the mother of the failure of medicine to relieve Evens, telling her, 'I am sorry to inform you, that we can do no more for your Boy: his appears to be a case which medical treatment cannot possibly relieve.' With this admission of resignation, the medical establishment withdrew from the case.[31]

The retreat of the surgeons left the Loses prey to advice and opinions that reflect the types of alternative medicinal options and magical cures that were available in the early nineteenth century. The spectrum ranged from licensed medical practitioners on the one hand to the home-based herbalists on the other, with a gamut of quacks, pedlars, conjurors and astrologers in between. With the failure of medical cures and the absence of any physiological explanation as to the boy's malady, the case entered its next stage, that of seeking the assistance of a magical practitioner for healing. Heaton recorded the advice received: 'Some advised, "go to the Astrologer; he has cured many as bad as your boy."'[32] Heaton notes that 'there was certain evidence of this fact, that an Astrological Doctor had cured such cases.' Alongside the astrologer, the local 'white witch' or cunningman was mentioned as a likely candidate to effect a cure, and in this there was a strong precedent, as the Kennard children had been cured following a consultation with their local conjuror.

Heaton's source of information concerning conjurors was *Blagrave's Astrological Practice of Physic* by Joseph Blagrave, first published in 1671. The main interest of the book for Heaton was in its treatment and cures for witchcraft and its account of Blagrave's exorcism of a dumb devil from a maid at Basingstoke. The maid's possession mirrored that of Evens in that she suffered fits, was stuck dumb, would leap about like a frog, banged her head against the wall and would try to throw herself down the stairs. Blagrave advised of the would-be exorcist that 'whosoever doth, or shall undertake this business, his faith and belief must be strong without doubting, otherwise he may fail in the performance, for although some ceremonies may be used herein as I have related, yet without God's especial blessing upon the words, wayes, and means used, together with strength of Faith, believing, no man can prevail herein.'[33] Heaton was perceptive enough to distinguish between the various types of magical practitioner around him, classifying them as conjurors, white-witches, astrological or philosophical doctors, and fortune tellers, but they were, nevertheless, he believed, agents of devils. He looked for Biblical precedents for these characters and found them in the accounts of Simon Magus and the exorcists of Ephesus, and quoted St. Paul, Dr. Adam Clarke's Commentary on Acts, Porphyry, and Plutarch as his authorities. Again, in all examples from the Bible, these magical practitioners stood condemned and practised 'curious arts' that were against God's ordinance.

Throughout Heaton's account, the impression that comes across of the parents is one of acquiescence and passive acceptance, relying on authority to discover some means of healing their son for them. That their faith was a strong comfort to them would seem evident and their trust in Heaton implicit. At this stage, when the case again threatened to follow a popular course, Heaton's influence was felt, for although the parents were concerned for the health of their son, they resisted the advice of their neighbours and were guided by Heaton, since he had by now come to a conclusion. In consequence, according to Heaton, 'the answer was, the parents are Methodists, and they will not take any steps, or employ any means for relief, which are inconsistent with Christianity,' and when the local conjuror was suggested to Mrs. Lose, 'The mother replied, "I will not go to the Devil for a cure."'[34]

The Demoniac

As 'physical principles failed entirely to solve the phenomenon,' Heaton turned for his explanation to one 'who ... exercised his profession in a place where, and at a time when, demoniacs were very numerous; and who, in addition to all this, was commissioned, qualified, and employed by our Lord himself, not only to write on such cases, but also to restore lunatics to their right mind, to heal diseases, and to cast out devils; I mean the beloved physician, the Evangelist St. Luke.' Heaton's enquiries had failed to produce a natural explanation of Evens' affliction, and so he turned to the one source that described the kind of symptoms shown and offered remedy to them. Heaton thought that 'It seemed to be reasonable, in spite of prejudice ... to be guided by the Bible, and to consider whether this might not be a case of diabolical possession ... On the principle of demonianism there was some probability that, by studying the records of such cases in the holy scriptures, we might be instructed in the nature of his case, and be directed to the mode of his cure.'[35]

John Evens' body therefore became the site of a battle of good and evil, between the grace of God on the one hand, represented by Heaton, the parents and the godly, and the destructive tendencies exhibited by the boy on the other. James Sharpe has emphasised that the symptoms and events involved in possession cases were not 'a series of random events ... beliefs about witchcraft fall within culturally determined parameters and, while making all due allowance for unique events and individual variations, tended to reproduce a number of recurring cultural motifs.'[36] That these motifs are repeatedly found in these cases points to the fact that they had a specific social function, which we must now consider.

Witchcraft possession cases formed the nexus of a range of beliefs, relationships, hierarchies and concerns and result where there was an imbalance of power, and thus could temporarily invert the normal social structure. That in England these cases should almost exclusively involve the young and therefore most powerless portion of society should come as little surprise. Sharpe highlighted the estimate that throughout the early modern period roughly 40 per cent of the population was under the age of 16, and by 1820 this percentage had barely changed. In a society that was more public than our own, it was an adult concern that youths and children should behave in a due and deferential manner to adults. The demoniac inverted those ideals, placing the convulsed child at the centre of attention and provided the opportunity, albeit short-lived, for the child to dictate the routines of the household, and to gain the ascendancy over the adults present to whom he or she was normally subject. This inversion was also their permission to break the rules of conduct around the home and to indulge in bad behaviour; Evens frequently spat at members of the family, kicked them, punched them, on at least one occasion 'he addressed some of the company in language not fit to be repeated.'[37]

There was also the concern that parents should provide a Christian upbringing for their children. Heaton noted the 'sacred importance and eternal consequence' of 'schools for youth, where useful knowledge and vital piety are planted and cultivated. Such institutions are not only training youthful immortals for heaven, but preparing labourers for the service of Christ.'[38] The home was where the rudiments of faith were learned, and that antipathy and ridicule of religion should have been displayed by the demoniac in the home was especially disturbing. For families of evangelical religions like those of the Kennards and Loses, the church stood at the centre of their religious lives, offering salvation in return for a regime of self-abrogation and sacrifice, a yoke that the children may have found hard to bear. The authority in the home was the father, who enforced discipline and led the family in its religious observances. It comes as no surprise therefore that the only conversation that was attempted with the demon was an openly defiant one between Evens and John Lose, the authority within the family and step-father to Evens.

On Sunday 16 April, John Lose picked up a hymnal to read, which provoked a furious and particularly violent attack from Evens upon him, after which Evens fell to the floor motionless. Lose addressed the prone figure of Evens, the demon voice responded through Evens' noise, as if speaking from his belly, viz:

Lose:	'Thou shalt not reign here, to the annoyance of all the family.'
Demon:	'I will.' (repeatedly)
Lose:	'Thou shalt not.'
Demon:	'But I will.'
Lose:	'God shall drive thee out.'
Demon:	'He can't.'
Lose:	'God is almighty.'
Demon:	'So am I.'
Lose:	'God can do all things.'
Demon:	'So can I.'
Lose:	'There is one thing thou canst not do, thou canst not save sinners.'
Demon:	'Don't want to.'

Evens later repeatedly cried out 'Here's the Great Devil' in a number of different voices.[39]

In a symbolic sense the conversation was between the forces of good and evil, of order and disorder, of social structure and chaos, but also in a very real sense reflected the power relationship between Evens and Lose, and of the temporarily reversed disparity between them. Of the explanations open to him, that of abuse within the family was one that Heaton did not apparently consider.

Heaton's comparison of the Biblical demoniacs with Evens' case convinced him and others that what they were witnessing was one and the same phenomena, 'on the principle of an evil spirit possessing him, the whole of his perplexing case was easily solved. As no other cause was so probable as this, we resolved to meet together, and lay him and his afflicted case before the Lord, intending, ... in the fear of God, according to the ancient divinely authorised christian usage, - to adjure the evil spirit.'[40] The form of exorcism, or adjuration of the spirit, was prescribed by Biblical texts, and the spiritual healing of Evens, carried out to a set ritual, brought about his relief and the restoration of normal family and communal functions. As has been noted a relapse occurred the following month, and a second exorcism performed, the results of which were suspected for some while after, as 'though he has ... been sorely assaulted, he has not been subdued but for a few minutes, on two or three occasions, when something has offended him, and he has yielded to *anger*.'[41]

Conclusion

This case, despite the lateness of its occurrence, highlights some of the ongoing problems of trying to understand witchcraft cases in the early modern period, such as the understanding of positions of the participants, their interactions with each other, and their contesting of meanings. Alternative accounts of the Evens affair could have greatly clarified a number of these points, for instance the sceptics reasoning of John Evens' action, in a way that the newspaper and private correspondence has done with the Lamb Inn affair and with the alleged possession of George Lukins. Contrary to other post-1736 cases of possession, Heaton's narrative sought to make no confessional capital out of the affair. Rather, Heaton saw the impact of his book as the refutation of contemporary scepticism and infidelity by proving, as he thought, the existence of spirits and the possibility that they might interfere in the natural order and subvert it. The case illustrates the changing response to traditional beliefs surrounding witchcraft and notions of possession during the early nineteenth century, following almost a century of legal disapproval surrounding the prosecution of witchcraft, Enlightenment scepticism, and changing attitudes within dissenting religions. Heaton's own leanings towards the supernatural may have engendered a certain sympathy with the Primitive Methodists, though Heaton remained a Wesleyan throughout his ministry. Certainly the fervour of the conversions engendered at revivals in his earlier years favours a more emotive and dramatic brand of evangelism.

The narrative portrays Heaton's earnest search for physical and psychological healing that he sought to bring to John Evens along the lines of Natural Philosophy, which he believed compatible with Christianity, and the conviction that he acted in the most selfless and honest way he could, according to his belief in 'Perfect Love,' Wesley's doctrine of a selfless, giving affection to all of humankind:

I thought it was more becoming a man and a christian, with sincerity, diligence, and patience, to investigate an intricate and momentous truth, and in the fear of God and love of man, to seek a distressed neighbour's relief, than to be discouraged from my duty by the frowns of the grave, the laughings of the thoughtless, or the reflections of the mistaken.[42]

Notes:

1. Keith Thomas, *Religion and the Decline of Magic* (London, 1971), 570 - 579.

2. Owen Davies, *Witchcraft, Magic and Culture 1736 – 1951* (Manchester, 1999), 18 – 27. Also Jonathan Barry, 'Public Infidelity and Private Belief?: The Discourse of Spirits in Enlightenment Bristol' in Owen Davies and Willem de Blécourt (eds.), *Beyond the Witch Trials: Witchcraft and Magic in Enlightenment Europe* (forthcoming 2004). My thanks to Jonathan Barry for providing me with a copy of the original manuscript version.

3. James Heaton, *The Extraordinary Affliction and Gracious Relief of a Little Boy* (Plymouth, 1822), 11. I am grateful to 'Mr. Lenkiewicz' - the late Robert Lenkiewicz, in whose library I first came across Heaton's narrative.

4. Mark 9: 17 - 26; Matthew 17: 14 - 21.

5. Heaton, *Extraordinary Affliction*, vi.

6. *The Imperial Magazine* 5 (March 1823), 270 - 272.

7. Biographical notes are taken from Heaton's Obituary, see *Wesleyan Methodist Magazine* 86 (1863), 479, 843.

8. James Heaton, *Memoir of Titus Close, Wesleyan-Methodist Minister* (London, 1836), 5.

9. C. W. Bracken, *A History of Plymouth & her Neighbours* (Plymouth, 1931), 182.

10. E. Welch, 'Dissenters' Meeting Houses in Plymouth to 1852' in *Report and Transactions of the Devonshire Association* 94 (1962), 582.

11. T. G. Hartley (ed.), *Hall's Circuits and Ministers* (London, n.d.), 327.

12. As the editor of early issues of the *Arminian Magazine*, Wesley included accounts of apparitions, witches, and magic as proofs of the supernatural. His *Journal* similarly records encounters with those who were believed to be afflicted by demons. See also James Sharpe, *Instruments of Darkness* (London, 1996), 253 - 255.

13. C. D. Field, 'The Mania of Methodism Reconsidered: Richard Polwhele's Polemic Against the Methodists, 1799 - 1836' in *Journal of the Royal Institution of Cornwall* 11: 4 (1997), 75.

14. Richard Lyne, *The Sinfulness and Idolatry of Charms, and of all Unbidden Christianlike Ways of Worshipping God* (Bodmin, 1817), 13, 33.

15. For an overview of the controversy see Owen Davies, 'Methodism, the Clergy, and the Popular Belief in Witchcraft and Magic' in *History* 82, No. 266 (1997), 252 - 265.

16. R. T. Davies, *Four Centuries of Witch Beliefs* (London, 1947), 190.

17. Henry Rack, 'Doctors, Demons and Early Methodist Healing' in W. J. Sheils (ed.), *The Church and Healing* (Oxford, 1982), 151.

18. Heaton, *Extraordinary Affliction*, 24, 25.

19. ibid, 21 - 23. No copies of the *Dock Telegraph* are extant from this period.

20. ibid, 63.

21. ibid, 30.

22. ibid, 30, 31.

23. ibid, 18.

24. *The Imperial Magazine* 5 (March 1823), 270 - 272.

25. For example, see Alexandra Walsham, *Providence in Early Modern England* (Oxford, 1999), 25-28.

26. Heaton, *Extraordinary Affliction*, 7.

27. ibid, 39.

28. ibid, 14.

29. ibid, 19.

30. ibid, 54.

31. ibid, 51.

32. ibid, 52.

33. Joseph Blagrave, *Blagrave's Astrological Practice of Physic* (London, 1671), 175.

34. Heaton, *Extraordinary Affliction*, 52.

35. ibid, 53.

36. James Sharpe, 'Disruption in the Well-Ordered Household : Age, Authority, and Possessed Young People' in P. Griffiths, A. Fox, and S. Hindle (eds.), *The Experience of Authority in Early Modern England* (Basingstoke, 1996), 196.

37. Heaton, *Extraordinary Affliction*, 30.

38. James Heaton, *Memoir of Titus Close, Wesleyan-Methodist Minister* (London, 1836), 8.

39. Heaton, *Extraordinary Affliction*, 85.

40. ibid, 61.

41. ibid, 96.

42. ibid, 63.

The Human Body in Southern Slavic Folk Sorcery

Andrija Filipovic and Anne M. Rader

In many charms, as in other rites, we often express a need to know with what part of the body one should commit a certain action: do we spit on the fourth finger of the left hand, do we touch something with a heel of the left foot, or cut hair from the back of the head? I have found within Slavonic sorcery that there is a principle of systematization that with its discrete rules does or doesn't allow communication of what we will. The instigation of will can be determined by a set of rules. These rules rise above one's will and function as rules of use, as rules of verbal language-of will.

In magical-religious texts, the body is not usually seen as a biological organization comprised of organs with specific functions, but above all it is seen as a spacious organized whole, with it's parts having a certain symbolic meaning. Thus, certain parts of the body become signs by which mythic contents are expressed.

The view we hold, based upon the above parameters allows a creation of analogies between the human body and other forms of the real world. This means that man, in his creation of the model of the world that surrounds him, puts forth his body as a measure of the universe. When bringing in the connection of the human body and universe, we create a base for the creation of cosmogonical myths, in which the body of the mythic hero, the First Human, gives birth to the universe. In the *Upanishads*, the cosmos is created from the parts of the body of Purusha: - from his *mouth* exited words; from his *eyes* came light, from light sun was made; from *ears*, the ability to hear, from this ability came the cardinal directions; from his *skin* grew hair, from *hair* plants were created; from *heart* came spirit, from spirit the *moon* was made; from the *navel* came apana, from apana – death; from his *phallus* flowed sperm, from sperm, was *water* created. In ancient India, they believed Purusha was a synonym for human.

Visantians interpreted the name of Adam as an abbreviation (ADAM), created of the Greek first letters in the words for East, West, North and South, concluding that man is a little universe (microcosm). In an apocryphal manuscript from Bosnia, "*Skazanije popa Ilije Ilica*", the creation of humankind is considered God's work; all was created of parts of the universe. God created *body* from earth, *eyes* of the sea, *blood* from dew, *mind* from clouds, *strength* from wind, *bones* of stone, *hair* of grass, *spirit* of the Holy Ghost.[1]

Formation of the symbolic picture of the human body is based on a series of binary oppositions, which are present in the texts of traditional culture as an operative aspect of mythic thinking, as I will explore in this article.

Naked – Clothed

Immediately after the birth of a baby, the child is considered to be on the border between culture and nature, and that is why it is not *dressed* but *swaddled*. The previously worn shirts of the mother or father are usually used for the first swaddling. This way, the marginal status of the child in the family is bridged. The swaddled child is not the same as the dressed, because the diaper wraps around the body, making it an undivided whole, and the cloth is sewn by the measure of the child's body. Until the baptism, the child is called *goljca, golco, kuslja* (meaning naked little thing), emphasizing his or her different status in his relationship to other people. Upon his/her baptism, the baby gets their name from their godfather and their shirt from their godmother, and with that, he or she is initiated from nature into culture.

One's name and clothes are seen as a measure of a human being and that is why they may be hidden when there is danger from malevolent spirits.

Because the opposite of the human world from the wild can be seen as an opposite between clothed and unclothed (naked) in terms of magical communication, where the direct contact of human with demonical beings is requested, man has to be unclothed when participating in magical rites. In Bulgarian history, men who "banished" the dragon from their village were naked. Also, among the Serbs, the blacksmith and his wife made tiny tools of iron, naked, at midnight, for magical protection.

Body-Soul

The idea that humans consist of *body* and *soul* is present in Slavic, as in many other

cultures across the world. After the death of the body, the soul leaves it and goes to the other world and the body decays. The relationship between the soul and body can be seen in dichotomies: inside/out, permanent/changeable, invisible/visible.

Among southern Slavic nations, the belief that the soul of some people can leave the body and return to it after some time is very widespread. According to this belief, such leave-taking can happen during the night at a specific hour. The people who have the power to do this usually have demonic characteristic, according to folklore, and they are the

enemies of humankind, called witches, or *mora*. But, they can also work for the benefit of the human race, such as the *Zdhuaci*, for example, who fight against the daemons of hail clouds. As a proof of the folk belief that some people with demonic characteristics can separate the body and soul, many people will testify to how they have seen how a witch can be stopped from *Macva*-separating her soul from her body. During the day, they say, if one suspects that a woman is a witch, a needle with a red string should be thrust in her shadow in the area of the head. If a woman is truly a witch, it is believed that she can't move from that place until sunset.[2]

There is a less-known traditional understanding of the soul leaving its body. In the Serbian-Bulgarian-Macedonian tradition of spellcrafting, a very archaic form of magical behavior has survived, in which the cunning man or women banishes a demonic force with her/his soul.³ This is done with a movement of the mouth-a yawn. That is why cunning-folk yawn during a healing ritual. If the cunning woman doesn't feel like yawning, she hasn't found any disease. In some charms involving children, a cunning man or woman may threaten demonic forces with the soul of a child's mother.

Everyday people cannot cast spells for themselves, only cunning folk can do it for them, often older women, among Serbs called *bajalice*, Croatians in Herzegovina - *mole* and *lice*, in *Kotari* in Dalmatia - *vidigoje*, in Macedonia - *basmarici, bajalici, bajaljki*, in Bulgaria - *bajacki, basmarki*, in Slovenia - *zagovarjalki*, Russia - *zagovoscici*, etc.⁴ Those who can do harm with spells are called in Serbia - *vracarice, vrazalice, cinjarice*, Monte Negro - *madjionice, carovnice*, Croatia - *coprnice*, Russia - *koldunje*.⁵ Knowledge of spellcrafting is transmitted only within the family, from elders to young, and according to this tradition, a young cunning woman begins working only after the old one stops. There are common ways of transmission of spellcrafting knowledge (in some cases *bajalice* transmit knowledge before puberty; in Bulgaria the old *bajalica* spits in the mouth of young one.) According to sayings of some cunning-folk, they have started to cast spells after the order of God's Mother, St. Petka, faeries, etc. which have come to them in dreams or during long illness and have discovered their ways of spellcraft. In some areas (eastern Serbia, *Banat*, western Herzegovina), a cunning woman, during a spell, falls into some kind of altered state of consciousness – a very sleepy trance-like state, losing consciousness. From this it is traditionally believed that, her soul, while in such state, is fighting with a demon of disease or visiting the faeries asking them for the return of health to the ill person. A Cunning woman has the obligation to keep a secret of spellcrafting and to always say any verbal part of spell correctly even if she sometimes does not understand it. Spell ("*basma*") is understood as an "instrument" of a special kind, which carries power since the Old Times and which assignment is to return balance. A

Cunning woman often does it in a symbolical way, creating some kind of parallel model, in which existing conditions, using specific magical procedures, translate into another - wanted state. According to assignation, spells can be sorted into spells for medical, economic and social life. As for the structure, spells can take the form of established phrases, prayers, beseeching or a developed, more complex, scheme.[6] For every occasion a unique spell exists but, in some cases, the text of one spell can be modified to suit a different need, with the cunning woman simply improvising. During spellcrafting, *bajalica* uses some tools, which have magical functions. They can be part of the non-verbal message of the spell - on one level, and on another – an illustration of cunning woman's intention (usually expressed in the form of a threat). The first group consists of: salt, eggs, flour, objects connected to fire, dead-man's things, parts of some animals and plants. The second group consists of: sharp tools (knife, axe, thorn, spindle), objects with strong smells (garlic, incense), cleaning tools (broom). Commonly, part of casting spells is the unusual behavior of participants. This behavior is, in some way, different than every-day, normal behavior. It is characterized by inverted behavior, such as silence, taking off clothes, spitting or swearing. Dragging some objects through a hollow tree, or their measuring has an important role in magical casting. Spells are cast in specific time and specific place, some cast during full, some during waxing moon. The day of the week is of some importance (very often spells are cast on Wednesday, Friday and Sunday); time of day (often some borderline time of day is chosen - morning just before sunrise, and night immediately after sunset, however some spells are cast in the middle of the night). Special marked places with some kind of ritual importance are often chosen for spell casting. Such places represent the boundary between common and alien space, starting from fireplace, doorstep, roof, fence, etc. Borderline places between land and water can be used as places for spellcrafting (wells, rivers, springs, watermill, bridge). "Unclean" places such are pig stys and graveyards are also used. Places with some kind of vertical line constantly present (chimney, standing stones, trees) are used for such activities too. In some instance Slavic ways of spellcrafting have been influenced by written magical literature (apocryphal prayers, curses, magical formulas). There are three lines of influence: Visantian (via Greek language), Roman-Germanic (via Latin and German) with only a little influence from Turkish, Arabian, Islamic sources.

The most archaic form of spell craft is present among Slavs in the Balkan-Carpathian area and in Northern Russia.

Horizontal Division of the Body

The body is divided into three parts horizontally: – head, chest and legs. There are many forms of magical healing which work using this system. In Macedonia, to heal irrational fear among children, a cunning woman places nine horseshoes near the head, chest and then knees. In *Levca* and *Temnic*, the cunning woman "replaces a cock for a man", for the magical healing of epilepsy. A midwife does this when the epileptic falls asleep. She will tear off the head of a young black cock that hasn't sung yet and bury the cock's head beneath the epileptic's head, while the body of the cock with the wings is buried beneath the epileptic's waist, and the cock's legs are buried beneath the epileptic's legs.[7]

Waist-Belt

The symbolic view of the human is usually based upon the clothed man. Clothing in traditional Slavic culture holds an importance for the *belt*, which separates the body into two parts: – the *upper* (clean) and *lower* (unclean) half. Because of this separation, the belt has a very important meaning; it becomes a medial element, which brings together two opposites. From this idea originates the very important role of the waist-belt in Slavic magic tradition. The cultural idea of girding one's waist has become a key element of cosmological Slavic myth, within which people believe that there is a world above us and underneath us. Those who live above us put the belt on just below their armpits, and those beneath us, put the belt around their thighs. But we, since we are in the middle world, gird our waists.[8]

Among simple folk in Russia in the 19th century, the belt was considered a sacred object because it was gifted upon baptism. It was considered rude if one prayed to God, ate and slept without the belt. In Herzegovina there still exists the custom of burying a child who has died with a belt around its waist. It is believed that if the child is buried without the belt, it couldn't have anything of its own in the other world.[9]

Because the belt is a boundary between two opposite principles, it has a very important role in magical practice. In eastern Serbia, if one wants to be protected from bullets, one must shoot down a piece of mistletoe from a tree and sew its twigs into one's belt.[10] In Bosnia, a child who cries a lot is thought to be cursed. The cursed child's waist is girded with a string woven with four colors – red, yellow, black and orange.[11] As a protection from night demons, known as *mora,* people put a belt over themselves during the night. When a *domacin*, who is a large property owner, suspects that there is *cuma* (an evil night spirit) in the village, he orders everyone to take off their belts, tie them together, and wrap them all around the houses. In Macedonia, for protection of the whole village, twin brothers till the ground around the village with a plough and twin oxen.

With the girdling of one's waist the opposition of up/down, clean/unclean, human/inhuman, is neutralized and thus, the possibility of conflict with malevolent spirits is neutralized too. For the same reason, Montenegros girdled their waists with a belt when they walked through the cemeteries and let it drag behind them.[12] People from Serbia, Bosnia and Macedonia think that if they approach a wolf, they should unbuckle their belt and they will surely save their lives. Other than the neutralization of the above said opposites, this custom makes the human himself a zoomorphic being, because the belt is used as a tail, and with it trailing behind, the difference between human and animal is negated.

The belt is also a horizontal axis and because of that it can take attributes from the female paradigm. The belt, together with a vertical axis; i.e. the height of a woman, creates a cross which point of intersection is the navel. Because of that, a belt is used in magical actions connected to giving birth.

Encircling a man, the belt is his measure too, and in archaic texts a man's measure can replace a real human. For example, if a man to whom Fates send illness cannot go to a doctor or nurse, he sends his belt.[13] In Kosovo, the rainbow is called "the belt" and it is thought that if one passes underneath it, s/he will change into the opposite sex: male will become female and vice versa.[14]

The Legs

The symbolic function of the legs is usually based on their connection to earth. A very important element is that they are seen as an ending of the body, since the head is the body's beginning. Because of that, a charm begins from the head, gradually banishing illness into the legs and from there – out of the body:

> "*Bezi urok iz glave na prsa,*
> "The curse runs from the head into the chest,
> *iz prsa na trbu,*
> from the chest into the belly,
> *iz trbua na bedra,*
> from the belly into the thighs,
> *iz bedra na tabane...*"
> from the thighs into the soles..."

There is a belief that above the head of a dying man, there is a guardian angel and below his feet, the devil, and each of them calls his soul.[16] The attack of malevolent beings usually begins from the legs. Here is a description of an attack of the night demon, *mora* from Herzegovina:

> "First, beginning from the toes on the left foot, a man feels some very heavy presence there: - something is pulling the toe and he feels it climbing on the leg; it feels like a huge stone falling on the leg. From the leg it goes into the stomach and, then, into the chest."[17]

Knees, heels, sock and shoes are also very important in magical actions. When people suspect that a strong wind is caused by the devil, they say: "Under the left knee!"[18] to banish the wind. In Bosnia, people believe that they can see witches if they, during the Easter dinner, spit the first bite of the dinner in the hand and look around. They believe that then they may see witches flying around glowing like sparks.[19] In Slavonia, some believe that if an old woman falls, it is because a male witch hit her in the knee.[20] There are many charms that use the touch of the heel for healing. The curses using the heel are usually used to cure diseases connected to the stomach. The most powerful heel is the one with which a cunning woman or man has killed a snake. The connection between shoes and the abundance of the earth can be seen in some Christmas customs – on Christmas Eve everyone take their shoes off before they go to bed so the crops grow evenly.[21] To protect oneself from spells, one should wear one red and one green sock.[22]

Vertical Division
Left and Right
Of all the opposites of the body, the most noticed one is the one concerning the left and the right side of the body. The right side is seen as a good, favorable, positive and as a male side; the left is marked as bad, unfavorable, negative, and a female side. Because of the communication with an unclean force, which goes with the same paradigm as the left side, spells are often cast with the left arm. "The left arm doesn't hold a cross", is a common expression in charms. For enhancing the powers, a cunning man would, when he sees the first snail in the spring, touch his head with the fourth finger on the left hand and say: "Whatever you are, go back!"

Front side – Back side of the Body
In spell crafting and divination, the front side of the body has these attributes – mine, human, and favorable, while the backside of the body is connected to the alien and inhuman.

For better communication with the spirit world, elements from the *backside of the body* are used: for an example, a sick man is wiped with the backside of his shirt. In love magic, cookies are made with water that has been trickled down one's spine and has been collected on one's bottom.[23] In the making of an amulet against ill luck, the hair from the backside of the head is used. The opposite front/back side of the body can be translated into the wider opposition of forward/backward (going backwards, spitting over the left shoulder while doing the spell).[24]

Center – Periphery of the Body
Hair and Nails

In folk magic, the nails and the hair are often used; sometimes hair from the beard and eyelashes too. All these elements can be sorted into peripheral opposition. The hair and the nails symbolize continuous birth and dying (expressed through constant growth and cutting) and through this, the symbol of perpetual change is expressed which is the goal of cunning-folk.

The hair is associated with the negative principle and the chthonic world. Because of that, there is a belief that one should not throw his hair into the water or else it will turn into snakes.[25] Among Serbs, after a death there is a custom that men must go without hats until the deceased is buried. After the burial ceremony they do not shave for 3 or 7 days.

The hair, like the nails, according to the *pars pro toto* principle, can be a substitute for humans. In a spell to cause a man's death, one has to take some of his hair, three nails from his toes and three from his fingers, a piece of his clothes and all is put into a rag doll made of the man's clothing and buried in the grave of an anonymous person.[26]

In charms, when an illness returns to a person, first, the cunning woman or man will hit him/her in the *nails*, then *joints*, *body* and *head* (*from the periphery toward the center*), and when the illness is banished from the person: - then it goes from *the brain into the bones*, from *the bones into the flesh*, from *the flesh into the skin*, from *the skin into the hair*, and from *the hair into the grass* (*from the center toward the periphery*).[27] Almost identical practices can be found among Germans: "A German adjuration addressed to a worm enjoins it to "go out" from the patient's marrow into his veins, then from his veins into his flesh, and so forth until is outside the body altogether."[28]

The picture of the world that surrounds humans is created by the same process of thoughts, which are also used for observance of one's own body and its situation in that same world. The key for understanding the world in mytho-poetic text is created on the perception of the human body and its status in the world space. The body becomes the heuristic model for the understanding of the cosmos.

The Voice
The Voice and the Light

The voice has had a very important role in the history of the Slavic culture. In cosmogonical myths, the voice is the beginning of the creation of the universe, because the light and the voice are opposites of the dark and silence. The first sign that a newborn baby has come into this world is its voice; and the first sound it hears is its voice. The voice separates it from the dark womb, but it leads it into the coldness of the world and risk. And later, as an adult, when this world threatens him or her in any period of his life, when it makes him or her incapable of dealing with hard situations, s/he raises their voice – in screams, cries, and pleadings. By spellcrafting; i.e. with the help of the words; that is the voice, the disturbance of the order in life, which is threatening to humans, is removed.

Among Slavs who live on the Balkans, the verbal part of the charm is called "*basma*". This word is of ancient Slavic origin and its root is *bha-*, which forms two major groups of words – one with the meaning "to speak", and the second "to light".[29] Independent of the hypothesis of semantic connections of these two verbs; in charms there are two opposite paradigms – the first are *the light and the speaking* (the sound) and the second is *the dark and the silence*. The first paradigm is attributed to humans and their social space, and the second – the wilderness and the chthonic world.[30]

In formulas for banishing unclean forces, the places to which those forces are sent are described as dark and where no voice can reach them (the voice of the rooster, the bell and the sound of an axe hitting the tree, most often).[31] During contact with such beings, accidental or otherwise, the person is obliged to be silent or else she can be severely hurt.

The spirit forces such as *ala*, werewolves, witches, and devils, are believed to endanger even the main sources of light – the Sun and the Moon. That is when there is an eclipse. People defend themselves during an eclipse with *shouting, ringing bells, hitting pots and other things*, or else complete darkness would reign.[32]

The Whispering and the Singing

Charms are often realized in vocal form, and, according to the rule, in a special vocal way. The most often way is whispering. Among Poles, the cunning woman lowers her head and very quietly whispers the charm. This way of spellcrafting was present even among ancient Assyrians and among other nations also; for example, the Hebrews. The whispering has a symbolic function. It can be seen as a spirit speaking i.e. the cunning woman is "an instrument", transmitter of an entity's language/speaking. In other words, she is "the gateway" through which, by speaking, a super-human force travels. It is enough for her to make contact with the power, which helps her, and to mark the cause of action. She describes the present situation, names the diseases, etc. in the charm. The helping power is often the Christian God, but among the Serbs the older system has survived and besides God, the helpers may be the Virgin Mary, and fairies who are like sisters to the cunning women.

There are other forms of spellcrafting also. In southern Serbia, some cunning-folk speak their charm in a monotone or even voice, which sounds more like singing than speaking. They fall into trance and, through the song, say the cure for the ill person. Some of them, after coming into the usual state of consciousness, cannot remember what they said while singing.[33] Some cunning-folk call for the help of their sister fairies, or even the soul of a drowned person.[34]

Here is an example of the concept of a charm having supernatural powers. This is the charm against the bite of poisonous snakes and it comes from Macedonia. As a charm, the song heard in a dream is used. Before spellcrafting, the person says: "My rooster lays the red eggs."[35] With this anti-behavior, the "upside down" model of the world is created, which should bring the neutralization of the human-snake's poison to a position of opposition, where the snake's poison is seen as an unclean spirit from the wild space.

Based upon the above listed examples, cunning-folks' singing and whispering can be connected because both transcend the simple, one-sided function of speaking as a social act, extending the possibility of communication with beings outside of the human world. The only difference is that one form "lowers below" the normal speaking (the whispering), and the second "rises above" it (the singing). Both forms demand a special emotional state (ecstasy or deep gravity. Among southern Slavs there are traces of the cunning-folk falling into trance similar to shamanistic journeying while whispering. In such forms of healing, *the voice* and *tears* have special symbolical meaning.

The Voice and the Soul

In a description of a charm against a curse, the cunning woman starts to yawn and tears start to drop from her eyes if she finds the disease she has been looking for. In Herzegovina, a cunning woman falls into a feverish state, sweats and bursts into tears. Sometimes even foam starts to fall from her mouth and cascades to the ground.[36] The usual rule is that the cunning woman speaks the charm with untied hair or, as among Vlahs in eastern Serbia, she is completely nude.[37] If this picture of a cunning woman is in contrast to the picture of some female mythological beings that cause diseases like the *forest* or *mountain mothers* and *babice*, one can see some striking similarities, also. These creatures are often depicted in the state of extreme rage and anger, with wide-open eyes and bared teeth. By sometimes bringing themselves into a special state of fury, cunning women take the "wild" upon themselves as the most convenient way to deal with the malevolent spirit force. In some charms, there are traces, which show that the cunning woman fights against the unclean force with her own *soul*, because of that, she constantly *yawns* and speaks the whole charm with the "whole voice", i.e. without a pause. Numerous examples show that *the voice* is seen as an outer manifestation of the spellcrafter's *soul*, which hunts down demons like a hunting dog.

The Voice and the Tears as the Axis Mundi

There are specific type of charms spread over the central Balkans among the Slavic population and partially among the Vlahs, which can be called "the story about suffering and healing of a man".[38] According to the contents, it can be divided into several groups.

The first group includes the charms against infected wounds, inflicted by sharp objects accidentally. These charms are present in eastern Serbia and western Bulgaria. They are formed by this model:

1. The person goes outdoors to collect herbs and hurts him/herself on some sharp object;
2. The wound gets infected and the person starts to cry because of the strong pain;
3. His/her voice goes high, up into the sky and the Virgin Mary hears it and asks about his/her trouble;
4. After the person repeats his/her story, the Virgin Mary soothes his/her pain and promises that a cunning man or woman will show up and ease the trouble.

The sharp objects are plants like *Dispacus silvester*, *Genistra germanica*, Hawthorn (*Crataegus sp.*). and things like the bone of the snake, the tooth of the wolf, the claw of an eagle, etc. These plants and parts of the animals have special magical function in other charms and magical rituals too.

The second group consists of charms, which differ from the first group by the cause of disease; in this group, the disease is caused by a malevolent spirit force on which a person stumbles upon in the field. Because of that, the circle of diseases is much bigger, and so is the action of the charms. Dangerous beings, which cause illness, are named thus: *ala, babice*, the three headed snake, and fairies. The sick man will also cry and his prayers are answered by his patron saint or even Christ.[39]

Except for the permanent structure, there is an archaic formula tied to the voice and the tears in these charms. The Virgin Mary or the saints help the suffering person only when she "screams up to the sky, and cries down to the earth". With this formula the symbolic union between the sky and the earth is created: - the endangered person builds up the cosmic axis, which means an expression of a need for correction of disturbed order. The creation of an axis means the bringing to life, the sacred time of the beginning, that is an archaic order in which everything has had its steady place and where no human being has been threatened by beings from an alien world. There is another level of symbolism here too: the axis is built up by real things, which are also the attributes of the Thunderer (the voice) and Mother Earth (the tears, moist). It is interesting that in some charms, the cosmic axis is symbolically created by the voice of a rooster and crying: "Roosters are crowing on the earth, while the crying goes high up to the sky".[40]

Magical Function of Genitals
The symbolic picture of the human in texts about folklore and ethnographic work is created on a binary principle. In the vertical perception; the strongest expressed opposition of the head/the legs, which is seen as binary opposition up/down, that is the beginning/the ending is translatable in the opposition clean/unclean. Because the final points on the human body are on the head and the legs, they become a person's "measure". Considering that it is believed that some people are capable to take away someone's "measure" with their evil eye; covering the head (with the hat or scarf) and wearing shoes (besides its pragmatic function), has the opposite symbolic effect - that of hiding "the measure" of the human body, as a way of protection against curses.

Under the much more severe rule of covering, which is very old and present in almost all nations worldwide, are the parts of the body from the navel or waist down including genitals and anus which must be covered at all times. These parts of the body have special status in the culture and except for the covering they are also forbidden to be spoken of in public. Some magical actions are, however, based on the intentional breaking of the rule of not showing and not naming the genitals.[41] The complete understanding of this phenomena would require an in depth discussion of marriage customs and beliefs connected to sex and birth giving but since that is not the topic, it will be only mentioned in passing here.

Mystery of Conception
As many researchers have noted, in some traditional cultures conception is a great secret. Among other "primitive" nations the connection between sex and conception is not understood, or conception is ascribed to unknown forces.[42]

In Serbian folk stories and poems there exists an international motif of "miracle conception", where the woman gets pregnant without sexual intercourse, usually when she tastes the powder of a dead man's skull.[43] Among Bulgarians the motif of becoming a hero from stone is widespread. The late V. Cajkanovic, an eminent Serbian folklorist, showed the unbreakable connection between marriage customs among Serbs and the cult of the ancestors.[44] He noticed that behind the diversity of marriage customs lies an inauguration of the bride into a new family unit, which consists of three parts: leaving the old family unit- coming into a new home- entering into a new family unit. The primary meaning of these rituals lies in getting consent from the ancestors, the protectors of home, and for the enlargement of family. The second part of marriage customs is the protection of the new couple from the forces of malevolent spirits. There's a connection between the ancestors and malevolent spirits. A couple can get in contact with them in spite of the boundary between the living and dead through the sexual act. With certainty one can say that contact is made during the first sexual intercourse. The defloration of the bride means opening the way into the world of the ancestors and direct contact with them because the female genitals are associated with a hole/abyss, and along with that, with the "gate" of the other world.

That is why, in a folk riddle, the bride is called *"pracijepaca"* and the groom is called *"pracijep"* (the one who's making cleft, who opens with a sharp and hard tool): "*Pracijepaca* and *pracijep*, between them a nice flower (couple and godfather)."[45]

The forcing of sex on a woman is called shattering.[46] Virginity is thus very important because the first sexual intercourse is seen as opening the way for the ancestors. Otherwise some other ancestors, who can be dangerous, may have already made contact and in such cases the bride is returned home with a broken ewer in her arms. This is a symbolic way to say that she isn't "whole". If the groom's family has decided to accept her, it is the family's duty to publicly announce, in a ritual way, that she isn't a virgin. These announcements are equal to those done when a child is born with a caul over its face. If the family does not ritually announce it, the child becomes a witch (as in demonic being, not a village cunning person).

So, the groom's first sexual intercourse with a bride means opening the gate of the chthonic world in a symbolic way. This is very risky for him, his family and community in general because some demonic dangerous force might come from that other world. This is why the bride is ushered into a groom's home accompanied with noise and uproar-to scare away any lurking daemonic forces.

In Bosnia, when people make noise around the bride and groom's room they are called wolves.[47] When we know that wolves are "keepers" of the boundary between wild and social space and that they are enemies of malevolent spirits, this magical action is then understandable.

The ancient symbolic view of a male's genitals as "penetrator" and the female's genitals as "abyss" shows that they are the only condition of conception which is seen as a gift of the chthonic world. At the same time, these body parts, symbolized, on a macro level, place the touch of this human world and the other world (shadow of ancestors) between clean and unclean and tabooed space-their showing and usage are controlled by community laws. Such a thought pattern dictates a fear of a possible irregular relationship between the living and dead, and an uncontrolled breakthrough of evil souls (unclean force) through the female abyss.

The Penis – The Devil – The Stone

For the reconstruction of the ancient beliefs about the genitals there is some importance of the paradigm of *the penis – the devil – the stone*, which can be noticed by comparing certain phraseological constructions in the Serbian language. There are some obscene expressions and vulgar names for the penis, with which the idea of "destruction" is expressed, similar to the expression "Go to hell".[48] A similar but emotionally stronger idea can be found in cursing followed by hitting a rock with another rock.[49] The wish for destruction of the cursed one is expressed as *capturing into the stone*.

It should be stressed that *the stone* has a very wide usage in the charms where it has the function of the mediator between the humans and an unclean force. Certain cultic *stones* in southern Serbia and Macedonia are famous because women who cannot have children will come to them and perform certain rituals such as crawling underneath. Symbolically, it could mean an "exchange" of the worlds – crawling underneath the stone a woman "travels" to the Otherworld and "dies" to return again to this world as a new woman capable of having children of her own. There is also another level of symbolism in this ritual. By crawling underneath the stone, a woman breaks into the chthonic space, imitating the entering of the penis into the vagina. Since the times of ancient Greeks and Romans, the usage of the hag stone in magic is widespread, and its chthonic characteristics are shown in those rituals where it is used.[50]

From medieval and later descriptions of "the meetings of the witches", very often obscene scenes are mentioned, with the devil presiding over them. Eroticism and temptation are the most important characteristics of this being. In one description, he is blamed for the spilling of semen during sleep: "He comes whenever, and the semen is spilled because of the dirty thoughts with which he fills the head of the one who dreams".[51] A euphemism for the witch is *the stone lady*.[52]

The motif that connects, at least on the first look, very different words/worlds, is the symbolic connection to the abyss and chthonic space.

The Genitals in the Model of Wonder

In the folk charms of the Slavs from the Balkans, from both Muslims and Orthodox Christians, there is a circle of certain charms which are created on the model of wonder; where actors have huge genitals and use them outside of the parameters of normal usage: - use them as a wand, as a dress, wearing them as bags over the shoulders. It is interesting that their real name is used despite the fact that it is very uncommon to use the real names of genitals in patriarchal society. This shows that these charms should be seen as a special form of magical speaking which is used only in special situations and only by the special person in question – the spellcrafter. The ones who usually have huge genitals in these charms are dogs, wolves, odd-looking and old men. All charms are against the evil eye. The model of wonder is created in them and this picture of wonder is produced to distract the attention of the one with the evil eye. Other than this, we can also speak about the older level of symbolism – the presence of an androgynous dog-like being who exists by itself and has no need to make contact with others. Thus the cursing (evil eye) is a form of taking someone's quality and with the breaking of the curse, it becomes formless.

Conclusion

Magic and religious notions of Slavonic custom show the human body as a spatially organized entity divided according to binary opposition. The body is divided into the upper (pure) half, which holds the head and chest, and the lower (impure) part, holding the rest of the body. The waist marks the boundary between the two parts, and thus has developed as a mediator, and has an important function in magic rituals. The body is also divided into the right (favorable) and left (unfavorable) side, the front ("one's own") and back ("another's"), the central (stable) and peripheral (changeable) part. The latter parts of the opposites (lower, left, back, peripheral) play a more important role in the performance of magic rituals, as they are associated with the space and spirits of the chthonic world. For this reason, specific parts of the human body are preferred above others in magic, such as the foot, left arm and leg, back of the head, back, heel, hair, nails, and body secretion.

The principle of symmetry is present in the perception of man – he is a single with pairs (eyes, ears, nostrils, arms, legs), as opposed to demons who are often represented as asymmetric. Man is comprised of body and soul, and differs from demons by his ability to speak, that is, his voice. In some incantations, voice and tears are elements that build the axis of the world (axis mundi) in a symbolic manner. Culture develops patterns that control contacts between the living and the dead. Since the dead affect fertility and fecundity, land and cattle, and the continuation of the family lineage, consummation of the marriage of the bride and groom is important, as a "clearing of the way" to the tree of the forefathers, thus the insistence on the virginity of the bride.

Notes-
Editor's note: where an English translation of a book or journal title is provided the authors have made this translation

1 Dusan Popovic, *Tragovi bogumilske jeresi u srpskom narodnom predanju (The Traces of Bogumil Heresy in Serbian Folk Tradition)* (Beograd: Karadzic IV, 1903), 178.

2 Sava Majstorovic, *Caranja u Macvi (Spells in Macva)* (Beograd: Raskovnik X, 1983), 19.

3 Vlastimir Stanimirovic, *Basme (Charms)* (Beograd: Arhiv SANU, 1993), 209.

4 The term 'cunning man or woman' is used after consulting Owen Davies, Cunning-Folk, Popular Magic in English History (London, Hambledon and London, 2003), see Ch.7 European Comparisons.

5 For comparison of cunning-folk names in different South Slavic nations see footnote number three in Joseph L. Conrad, *Bulgarian Magic Charms: Ritual, Form and Content* (Slavic and East European Journal, Vol. 31, No. 4, 1987), 559.

6 For systematic research of the structure of the charms see Joseph L. Conrad, *Magic Charms and Healing Rituals in Contemporary Yugoslavia* (Southeastern Europe, 10, No. 2, 1983), 99-120. and Joseph L. Conrad, *Bulgarian Magic Charms: Ritual, Form and Content* (Slavic and East European Journal, Vol. 31, No. 4, 1987), 548-562.

7 Stanoje M. Milatovic, *Narodna medicina Srba seljaka u Levcu i Temnicu (The Folk Medicine of Serbian Peasantry in Levca and Temnic)* (Beograd: SEZb, 1909), 364.

8 *Ibid.*, 450-451.

9 Nikola Begovic, *Zivot Srba granicara (The Life of Serbian Border-keepers)* (Beograd: Prosveta, 1986), 265.

10 Tihomir R. Djordjevic, *Zle oci u verovanju Juznih Slovena (The Evil-eye in the Beliefs of Southern Slavs)* (SEZb LIII, 1938), 203.

11 Stanko Sielski, *Hamajlija (The Amulet)* (Zagreb: Etnografska istrazivanja i gradja, 1941), 220.

12 V.M.G.Medakovic, *Zivot i obicaji Crnogoraca (The Life and Customs of Montenegroes)* (Novi Sad: JAZU, 1860), 180.

13 Milenko S. Filipovic, *Zivot i obicaji narodni u Visockoj nahiji (The Life and Folk Customs in Visocka nahija)* (Beograd: Prosveta, 1926), 188.

14 Tatomir Vukanovic, *Srbi na Kosovu II (Serbs on Kosovo)* (Vranje: Zbornik etnografskog muzeja, 1986), 457.

15 Josip Lovretic, *Otok (The Island)* (Zagreb: ZNZ, 1902), 153.

16 *Ibid.*, 199.

17 Aleksandar Petrovic, *Mora* (Beograd, GEM XI, 1936), 97.

18 Petar Z. Petrovic, *Zivot i obicaji narodni u Gruzi (Life and Folk Customs in Gruza)* (Beograd: SEZb LVIII, 1948), 334.

19 Tatomir Vukanovic, *Vjestice (Witches)* (Vranje, SEZb LXX, 1958), 956.

20 Josip Lovretic, *Otok (The Island)* (Zagreb: ZNZ, 1902), 143.

21 Petar Z. Petrovic, *Zivot i obicaji narodni u Gruzi (Life and Folk Customs in Gruza)* (Beograd: SEZb LVIII, 1948), 227-228.

22 Milorad Radunovic, *Ostala je rec (Only the Words Are Left)* (Beograd: SKZ, 1988), 324.

23 Radisav M. Djordjevic, *Da covek ide kao slep za zenom (A Man goes Blindly After a Woman)* (Nis: Kica III, 1907), 36.

24 Stanoje M. Milatovic, *Narodna medicina Srba seljaka u Levcu i Temnicu (The Folk Medicine of Serbian Peasantry in Levca and Temnic)* (Beograd: SEZb, 1909), 310.

25 Milorad Radunovic, *Ostala je rec (Only the Words Are Left)* (Beograd: SKZ, 1988), 330.

26 Stanoje M. Milatovic, *Narodna medicina Srba seljaka u Levcu i Temnicu (The Folk Medicine of Serbian Peasantry in Levca and Temnic)* (Beograd: SEZb, 1909), 292.

27 Vladimir Ardalic, *Basme iz Bukovice u Dalmaciiji (Charms from Bukovica in Dalmatia)* (Zagreb, ZNZ XVII, 1912), 359-360.

28 Richard Kieckhefer, *Magic in the Middle Ages* (Cambridge: Cambridge University press, 2000), 71.

29 See Joseph L. Conrad, *Magic Charms and Healing Rituals in Contemporary Yugoslavia* (Southeastern Europe, 10, No. 2, 1983), 101.

30 Ljubinko Radenkovic, *Simbolika sveta u narodnoj magiji Juznih Slovena (World Symbols in Southern Slavic Folk Sorcery)* (Nis: Prosveta, 1996), 27.

31 See Joseph L. Conrad, *Magic Charms and Healing Rituals in Contemporary Yugoslavia* (Southeastern Europe, 10, No. 2, 1983), 106, 111-112, 118; and Joseph L. Conrad, *Bulgarian Magic Charms: Ritual, Form and Content* (Slavic and East European Journal, Vol. 31, No. 4, 1987), 550, 554.

32 Nenad Dj. Jankovic, *Astronomija u predanjima, obicajima i umotvorinama Srba (Astronomy in the folk-stories, customs and sayings of Serbians)* (Beograd: SEZb LXIII, 1951), 111-112.

33 Dragutin M. Djordjevic, *Zivot i obicaji narodni u leskovackom kraju (Life and Folk Customs in the area of Leskovac)* (Leskovac: Prosveta, 1985), 146.

34 *Ibid.*, 147-149.

35 Stevan Simic, *Narodna medicina u Kratovu (Folk Medicine in Kratovo)* (Zagreb: ZNZ 42, 1964), 421.

36 Radmila Filipovic-Fabijanic, *Narodna medicina istocne Hercegovine (Folk Medicine of Eastern Herzegovina)* (Novi Sad: GZM, 1968), 47.

37 S.P.Gacovic, *O bajanju i vracanju Vlaha istocne Srbije (The Charms and Spells of the Vlahs of Eastern Serbia)* (Zajecar: Razvitak, 1986), 91.

38 See Joseph L. Conrad, *Magic Charms and Healing Rituals in Contemporary Yugoslavia* (Southeastern Europe, 10, No. 2, 1983), 115-116; and Joseph L. Conrad, *Bulgarian Magic Charms: Ritual, Form and Content* (Slavic and East European Journal, Vol. 31, No. 4, 1987), 557-558.

39 P.Sreckovic, *Zbornik popa Dragolja* (Beograd: SKA, 1890), 7.

40 Vlastimir Stanimirovic, *Basme (Charms)* (Beograd: Arhiv SANU, 1993), 292.

41 See Joseph L. Conrad, *Magic Charms and Healing Rituals in Contemporary Yugoslavia* (Southeastern Europe, 10, No. 2, 1983), 116-118; and Joseph L. Conrad, *Bulgarian Magic Charms: Ritual, Form and Content* (Slavic and East European Journal, Vol. 31, No. 4, 1987), 556-557.

42 E.Nojman, *Istinsko poreklo svesti (The True Origin of Consciousness)* (Beograd: Prosveta, 1994), 25.

43 Tihomir R. Djordjevic, *Deca u verovanjima i obicajima nasega naroda (The Children: Beliefs and Customs of our Nation)* (Nis: Prosveta, 1990), 23-29.

44 Veselin Cajkanovic, *Sabrana dela iz srpske religije i mitologije (Serbian Religion and Mythology: Collected Works)* (Beograd: SKZ, 1994), 133-135.

45 *Rjecnik hrvatskoga ili srpskoga jezika (Dictionary of the Croatian and Serbian Language)* (Zagreb: JAZU, 1980), 352.

46 *Ibid.,* 476.

47 Tihomir R. Djordjevic, *"Tovijine noci" u nasem narodu ("Tovija's Nights" in our Nation)* (Zagreb, ZNZ XXIX, 1933), 15.

48 *Recnik srpskohrvatksog knjizevnog i narodnog jezika (Dictionary of the Serbo-Croatian Literary and Folk Language)* (Beograd, SANU, 1992), 68.

49 *Rjecnik hrvatskoga ili srpskoga jezika (Dictionary of the Croatian and Serbian Language)* (Zagreb: JAZU, 1980), 857.

50 Ljubinko Radenkovic, *Narodna bajanja kod Junzih Slovena (Folk Charms among Southern Slavs)* (Beograd: Prosveta, 1995), 113-122.

51 *Rjecnik hrvatskoga ili srpskoga jezika (Dictionary of the Croatian and Serbian Language)* (Zagreb: JAZU, 1980), 82.

52 *Recnik srpskohrvatksog knjizevnog i narodnog jezika (Dictionary of the Serbo-Croatian Literary and Folk Language)* (Beograd, SANU, 1992), 157.

Four Glasses Of Water:

Magic considered as a 'culture' distinct from art, science or religion, and how this could help clarify discussion of the broad spectrum of magical, pagan, New Age and 'alternative' beliefs and practices

Lionel Snell

NB/ Lionel Snell is the everyday name of occult philosopher and author 'Ramsey Dukes'

This essay recognises an awareness among the media, academic, religious and scientific communities of an increasing public interest in 'alternative' beliefs and practices - ranging from alternative medicine, through New Age practices, astrology, Paganism, to formal ritual magic orders. It also notes that this phenomenon is usually dismissed as folly, sometimes seen as a threat, and sometimes both at once.

What is not seen is serious debate or public bridge-building between the two sides, as has been attempted, for example, in the 1990s dialogues between religion and science where a degree of mutual respect, if not full understanding, was often achieved [1].

What this essay proposes is that a recognition of magical thinking as a distinct 'culture' - in the popular sense in which art, science and religion are seen as distinct cultures - would help to clarify the nature of these alternative beliefs and provide a more fertile basis for understanding and dialogue between their practitioners and the rest of society.

The essay is based upon a public talk given by Ramsey Dukes at *Occulture* 2003 [2]. The talk was not addressing a specifically academic audience, and the resulting essay is not strictly academic in a number of respects.

Firstly it relies upon 'thought experiments' that ask 'what if?' rather than stating 'what actually' with full supporting references. Secondly it relies on a popular understanding of the terms art, religion and science without ever defining these terms. This is because it is argued that magical thinking does not rely on definitions that are closed in terms of sufficiency and necessity but rather on inductive classification that behaves more like a direction indicator. The main point being made is that categories can prove useful even when not strictly defined.

Although this puts a limit on the academic value of the essay, it does raise questions and suggest lines of enquiry that could prove very fruitful for the academic study of magic - hence its submission for this journal.

The Context

When The British Broadcasting Corporation screened *Magic - Art of Darkness* in April 2001 [3] - a programme on magic as practiced in modern Britain - the media response was mainly to show surprise at anyone taking the subject sufficiently seriously to merit a whole television programme (to appreciate the full scale of this insult, remember that the medium had already begun to devote many prime time hours to 'reality TV' programmes like *Big Brother*). This was reflected in the events and listings magazine *Time Out* headline 'Hocus Pocus - No Jocus' as well as the *Financial Times*' preview comment: 'You imagine that this will be the cue for a light-hearted look at the absurdities of suburban Aleister Crowleys, but this skilfully crafted documentary takes its subject rather seriously.'[4]

Rather than consider the possibility that the subject matter might deserve serious consideration, the only conclusion was that these apparently competent film makers must be cunningly presenting its subject seriously in order that we viewers could see for ourselves just how silly it really is. As the TV Listings magazine *Radio Times* put it 'a great film about not-so-great people, a clever sleight-of-hand that allows its subjects the freedom to expose their less salubrious side.' *The Times* reported[5]:

> The producer-director Paul Tikell disappeared completely, observing, recording, allowing the group to speak for themselves. He gave them all the rope they wanted and we watched them tie nooses with it. The more they tried to sound calm, serious, reasonable and in control, the more they sounded batty.

One wonders what such reviewers would think about a journal for the *academic* study of magic [6]!

The general tone of the reviews reflected an apparent assumption that the practice of magic is the extreme, and unpleasant, manifestation of an irrational tendency on the furthest fringes of society. This assumption does not square with the significant number of books on the subject to be found in most general bookshops throughout the UK. The *Radio Times* preview spoke of 'a sort of religion for those who don't have the discipline for real religions'. If discipline is the criterion, then they should consider the Golden Dawn curriculum, or some of Aleister Crowley's meditation exercises, and compare the standards demanded with the factual and spelling errors contained in, for example, the Times review.

It would have been good to hear rather more of the actual beliefs of the 'not-so-great people' featured in the programme, but this is not the way magic and the occult is handled by the media. It is usually the case that a 'serious' programme means one where scenes of magical ritual are layered between interviews with psychologists, historians, sociologists, theologians or clerics.[7] The emphasis is on a superficial display of what magicians *do*, contrasted with what experts *think*. We are given no insight into how magicians themselves think and the perceived role of magic in modern life.

Consider this description. 'I attended a ceremony of the death cult, in a temple surrounded by a field of buried corpses. The worshippers - apparently ordinary men and women from all walks of life, knelt before scenes of human torture and pretended to drink blood and devour human flesh while their children looked on in enforced silence.'

It is a faithful enough description of what happens every Sunday in my local church, and yet it conveys nothing of the significance of Christian communion and its place in village life. It does, however, mirror the way that the media continues to alienate the occult by focusing exclusively on what witches and magicians do without giving them a platform to explain why they do it and the extent to which their practices 'make sense'.

An Example From The Broader Context

Whereas magic itself is seen in these responses as something sinister and dangerous - albeit 'batty' - it is just the extreme end of a much wider 'irrational' tendency.

Here the media is less single-minded: on the one hand the 'serious' media will either pass over such subjects as astrology, feng-shui, crystals and alternative medicine or treat them with light-hearted detachment as fashionable crazes; while the popular media provide a wealth of material on these subjects, recognising them as every bit as real and relevant as the soap opera stories they also major on [8].

Here is an example of the light-hearted way one relatively serious journal addresses the subject of crystal healing in the Pagan community. It comes from the 'Feedback' column from *The New Scientist* [9] and begins:

> Crystal homeopathy combines the principles of homeopathic medicine with the healing power of crystals. That's the claim made by www.the-crystal-chamber.net... These crystals, while they were forming in caves over thousands of years, have picked up minute, homeopathic quantities of substances that will benefit you through their influence on your aura.
> Does this sound like complete garbage to you? A Feedback reader.... thought it did, so he posted a "provocative enquiry" at www.ukpagan.com, a site where believers in all things mystical gather to discuss matters of common interest....
> ...The response from ukpagan devotees was immediate and irate. Some were so rude the forum's moderators had to remove the posts. All insisted on the validity of their beliefs, some even referring to theoretical physics to support them. None questioned the claims of crystal homeopathy.

The person in question continued the on-line debate by quoting the actual wording of the website, taking its claims one by one and demolishing them as a cynical, scientifically unsound scam. But still he was opposed by ukpagan regulars. What was not announced until the end of the correspondence was the fact that the crystal homeopathy site was his own creation all along. 'Depressed by the abundance of absurd claims for quack alternative therapies, he had set up the site as a credulity experiment' according to the Feedback article [10].

The tone of the *New Scientist* piece is gleeful - a story that so neatly confirms the readers' prejudices does not merit closer analysis. Crystal healing is here assumed to be nonsense - rather than a dangerous challenge to the body of scientific truth - and here is a story that confirms the gullibility of its defenders. As nonsense it gets a light-hearted treatment and that is that.

The original perpetrator of the hoax, however, appeared to show much greater commitment to his cause. The website is good, an excellent piece of New Age promotion. Even though I myself had only come to the site after reading the *New Scientist* piece, I *wanted* a homeopathic crystal and almost felt healed by simply reading about the things! The creator of the site has since added an explanation of the hoax in which he claims that: 'It was all made up in a few hours'[11] and yet the original work of creating the site and following up the correspondence as he describes on the site reveals a significant investment in time and effort.

Could it be that the perpetrator was himself moved by something more than a light-hearted sense of fun? According to the *New Scientist* quote above, the purpose of the site was indeed to provide healing, but healing for his own depression occasioned by the 'abundance of absurd claims'. Putting myself in his place, it would be understandable that he might be seeking to reduce - rather than merely test - people's gullibility. Consider the effect that the bursting of the dotcom investment bubble has had on public opinion: commentators who were singing the praises of the 'new economy' a few years back now make a mockery of the phrase - so might not a public expose of the folly of crystal healing result in a similar awakening to reason?

Could it be that the motive behind this website was more than simple light-hearted fun, more even than self healing: was it also a desire to respond to something that was perceived as a threat to our rational culture? In his own words on the website he describes his contribution to ukpagan.com in these terms [12]:

> One time I even tried to assist people by telling them plain that it was nonsense. I adopted the username *disturber* — top scientist and arch-sceptic — and made a post to a suitable site, leading people to take a look at the stuff on offer. But the more *disturber* decried it, the less they wanted to know...

Let's see then how *disturber* addressed ukpagan. His opening posting was as follows [13]:

> Hi, just thought I'd disturb the comfy indolence of your minds with a provocative enquiry...
> With all your spells and deep insights into matters spiritual, and all your new age crystals and alternative therapies, can any of you people convince me that your semi-religious methods have ever had any effect whatsoever?
> Science can offer you the staggering magic of the computer screen that you are now looking at as testament to the validly of its method, but where are your proofs? Where are your triumphs? Where is the crystal that definitely healed a sickly person and didn't just provide vague emotional satisfaction?
> Take this clear nonsense that I recently found my sister (a ukpagan devotee) indulging in: www.the-crystal-chamber.net I mean, it is such transparent balderdash, yet she claims to feel its gentle healing powers, or something equally nebulous. Yet can she offer me any REAL proof of its effect? No, she can't... beyond its capacity to encourage wishful thinking, that is.

To what extent does this posting help set up a valid 'test for gullibility' as claimed, and to what extent does it actually amount to an opening salvo in a war of words? Phrases such as 'comfy indolence of your minds', 'all your spells and deep insights..' and 'vague emotional satisfaction' seem well formed to invoke the defensive emotional response that resulted.

If the purpose was simply to experiment, rather than to campaign, would an intelligent experimenter not have chosen a less inflammatory tone and simply ask: 'Is there anyone with experience on this forum who could help me decide if this crystal homeopathy website is bona fide or not?'?

Judged as a detached experiment to test human gullibility, the hoax has revealed little that is new - it has merely confirmed that if a minority group is addressed in a manner that reflects stereotypical attacks from the past, then you can expect a stereotypical reaction (as if, say, one were to conduct market research in a Jewish community while wearing a Nazi armband). But judged as an attack, it is much more successful. For the way the story is reported in New Scientist, and the way it would strike most casual readers, is that a clever hoax has made the ukpagan community look very silly indeed.

Changing the Context

I am suggesting that *disturber* and the commentator in *New Scientist* were responding to a perceived threat from a significantly large minority group that, as a healing technique, touches the fringes of science, has scientific pretensions and uses semi-scientific terminology and includes in its members those who could be accused of delivering 'bad science'. By setting up a hoax and challenging the group to defend it, the gullibility of that group has been demonstrated to the wider public.

Consider another significantly large minority group that also touches the fringes of science, has scientific pretensions and uses semi-scientific terminology and includes in its members those who could also be accused of delivering 'bad science' - namely science fiction fans.

What if *disturber*, instead of creating a very good New Age website, had written a very good science fiction novel that won an award as the best science fiction novel of the year. Then he announces that science fiction is 'bunk'; that his novel was deliberately based upon erroneous scientific models and unproven data and that no-one noticed or commented on this fact. What would the general public make of this 'test of gullibility'?

I propose that they would judge it as pretty silly. Rather than making the science fiction community look ridiculous, they would feel that the perpetrator had made a fool of himself and damaged his potentially lucrative career as a science fiction writer. The difference is that science fiction is not seen as a challenge to science, because it can be classified as 'literature'. Outside a small coterie of purists it would be felt that judging science fiction purely on the quality of its scientific validity is to miss the point.

Two Cultures

It has been suggested [14] that all that remains of CP Snow's legacy is two short phrases 'the corridors of power' and 'the two cultures' - the latter being the title of an article he wrote for *The New Statesman* in 1956, but it became better known in 1959 when he presented his Rede Lecture at Cambridge University 'The Two Cultures and the Scientific Revolution' [15] which was then published in *Encounter* magazine and became a major topic of intellectual debate in the English speaking world.

More significantly for the purposes of this article, it slipped into popular usage to describe the perceived gap between scientific and artistic understanding of our universe.

> The phrase has lived on as a vague popular shorthand for the rift - a matter of incomprehension tinged with hostility - that has grown up between scientists and literary intellectuals in the modern world. Lack of precision has been part of its appeal: to speak of "the two cultures" is to convey regret, censure, and - since one is bold enough to name and appreciate a presumably unfortunate circumstance - superiority all at once. [16]
> This rift was recognised in Richard Dawkins book *Unweaving the Rainbow* [17] - a title which traces the two cultures back to the previous century when the painter and critic Benjamin Haydon reported that Keats, at a dinner with Wordsworth toasted 'confusion to the memory of Newton, because he destroyed the poetry of the rainbow by reducing it to a prism'. In his book, Dawkins took up the debate from the scientific perspective and received very mixed reviews. According to Steven Rose in the

Guardian[18] 'it seems a bit churlish to continue to play the two cultures game in this embattled way.'

The last remark is significant, in that it illustrates the way that the term 'two cultures' has since helped to bridge the rift by giving it a label. Few scientists would feel a need to apologise nowadays for enjoying such irrational passions as football, opera, conceptual art or even religion. Rather than feeling a need to justify these in scientific terms, they simply recognise that, as humans, we have a need for a little of 'the other culture'. Scientists and public supporters of the rationalist cause only feel disturbed when there is evidence of a major public upsurge in more magical irrational pursuits at science's expense - as reflected in a *Financial Times* Halloween article by Richard Tomkins[19] which begins 'Oh well, I said to myself last Friday, bang goes the Enlightenment...' and later comments 'Where once science and reason seemed destined to prevail, we are experiencing an extraordinary upsurge in interest in spiritualism, mysticism, witchcraft, paganism, cults, sects and the paranormal.'

It is this useful bridge-building function that is most relevant to my thesis: by naming the demon of this abyss we gain control of it. What might have been felt as an uncomfortable dislocation between art and rationality in our lives can be and has been coped with (rather than dismissed) by labelling it as 'two cultures'.

By this means confrontation has been avoided, and art and science have been able to follow their separate paths in relative peace. A 1999 Channel 4 TV documentary *Two Cultures* returned to the debate with an updated perspective that reflects this evolution:

We may be grateful for the internet and mobile phones, but at the same time we are mightily more sceptical about science than in CP Snow's day. The Channel 4 film tries to span the two worlds by suggesting that there is really not much difference between art and science. Both explore the world around us, both try to find deep reasons and meanings art asks how and science why. If, 40 years ago, art was regarded as an irrelevant add-on, that's changed. Increasingly now ordinary people, not just elites, regard art as a central part of human life, the spiritual element that once was filled by religion.[20]

In this essay I will be challenging that last comment, which identifies the spiritual element with art, because I believe that the science/religion debates of the 90s have left us with an understanding of 3 cultures, even though they have not been encapsulated in so neat a phrase, and that the spiritual is still sought in forms other than artistic.

Four Glasses Of Water- A Thought Experiment
At this point in his talk, Ramsey Dukes took four identical tumblers and filled them all to the same level from a single jug of water. He then claimed that he would demonstrate his extraordinary magical powers by transforming them into four quite different and distinct objects before the very eyes of the audience. He then labelled the four objects now standing before him.

The first had been transformed into A GLASS OF WATER. The second into HOLY WATER. The third into HEALING WATER. The final glass had been transformed into AN OAK TREE.

At this point in the exposition it becomes necessary to invoke a demon. Now, this may not seem an appropriate introduction to an academic journal but the precedent has already been set by James Clark Maxwell (a fellow mathematician who didn't even claim to be a magician) in a thought experiment to challenge the second law of thermodynamics [21].

So picture this fiend - a sort of degenerate amalgam of *disturber*, Dawkins and numerous other arch-skeptics - that spends sleepless nights fuming about popular astrology, The X Files, Harry Potter and fantasy literature. It constantly petitions bookshops and the media to replace such rubbish with thoughtful scientific texts. At the first mention of homeopathy or crystal healing It rushes to pen vituperative letters about lack of scientific evidence, and at every Psychic Fair It is there heckling the speakers and handing out pamphlets decrying attempts to exploit human gullibility and ignorance.

So when Ramsey Dukes stands before this audience and claims that he has just manifested A GLASS OF WATER - the demon seizes the opportunity, and the glass, and takes the latter to a laboratory to conduct physical and chemical tests to disprove this magician's claim. Alas, poor demon, it turns out to be just a glass of water and so the score card reads 'Ramsey Dukes - 1 point; Demon - Nil'.

AN OAK TREE

So what about a more outrageous claim? That, with his fourth object, he has manifested AN OAK TREE? At this point he paused to read an extract from the Internet [22], as follows:

> In a room at Tate Modern there is a three-quarter full glass of water on a high shelf. It is a work by Michael Craig-Martin called An oak tree, 1973. Beside it there is the following text:
> Q. To begin with, could you describe this work?
> A. Yes, of course. What I've done is change a glass of water into a full-grown oak tree without altering the accidents of the glass of water.
> Q. The accidents?
> A. Yes. The colour, feel, weight, size ...
> Q. Do you mean that the glass of water is a symbol of an oak tree?
> A. No. It's not a symbol. I've changed the physical substance of the glass of water into that of an oak tree.
> Q. It looks like a glass of water.
> A. Of course it does. I didn't change its appearance. But it's not a glass of water, it's an oak tree.
> Q. Can you prove what you've claimed to have done?
> A. Well, yes and no. I claim to have maintained the physical form of the glass of water and, as you can see, I have. However, as one normally looks for evidence of physical change in terms of altered form, no such proof exists.
> Q. Haven't you simply called this glass of water an oak tree?
> A. Absolutely not. It is not a glass of water anymore. I have changed its actual substance. It would no longer be accurate to

call it a glass of water. One could call it anything one wished but that would not alter the fact that it is an oak tree.
Q. Isn't this just a case of the emperor's new clothes?
A. No. With the emperor's new clothes people claimed to see something that wasn't there because they felt they should. I would be very surprised if anyone told me they saw an oak tree.
Q. Was it difficult to effect the change?
A. No effort at all. But it took me years of work before I realised I could do it.
Q. When precisely did the glass of water become an oak tree?
A. When I put the water in the glass.
Q. Does this happen every time you fill a glass with water?
A. No, of course not. Only when I intend to change it into an oak tree.
Q. Then intention causes the change?
A. I would say it precipitates the change.
...and so on, ending with:
Q. How long will it continue to be an oak tree?
A. Until I change it.

To help the audience appreciate the nature of this miracle in the limited time available, he flashed before them a photocopy of a well-known Constable painting and asked them to say quickly what it was. Answer: 'The Hay Wain'.[23]

Then he pointed out that, according to the demon, they were wrong: all he had shown them was a cheap black and white image, whereas 'The Hay Wain' was a priceless oil painting now hanging in the National Gallery. And even that reality was no hay wain, in the sense that it is only a piece of canvas with paint on it. Had Turner named his painting 'Essex Pastorale' instead of 'The Hay Wain', then not only would the painting in the National Gallery be known as Essex Pastorale, but that photocopy too would be transformed into Essex Pastorale.

For we all know what we mean when we say that the piece of paper in his hand 'is The Hay Wain' - it is a meaningful statement despite the fact that a demon has rushed in to grab it and declare Dukes to be a fraud because it turns out to be just a piece of cheap paper with carbon marks upon it.

So too, he suggested, when he placed the label AN OAK TREE beside the fourth glass and the Demon rushed in to prove him a charlatan and that it was only a glass of water, then that demon had again missed the point. 'Ramsey Dukes - 2 points; Demon - Nil'.

Why? Because even the most rabid philistine who detests all conceptual art and everything it stands for, would still have a sense that it belongs in that despised 'Art' side of the cultural divide. So to attack it by doing scientific tests to prove my oak tree was only water is to make an even worse fool of oneself than 'the sucker who spends good money on this sort of nonsense'.

At this point, however, he drew attention to an interesting distinction. Having won their acceptance that the scrap of paper was, in a very real and useful sense, 'The Hay Wain', would they now allow him to sell it for the millions of pounds that the Hay Wain is worth? Of course not. But what if, instead of a poor photocopy, he got a superb craftsman to reproduce the original with such precision that not even the demon could distinguish it from the original - would they then buy it for millions?

The answer was again 'no'. Because as long as the original painting hangs in the gallery, anything else, however indistinguishable, from the original can be no more than a 'copy'.

This suggests that there is a sense in which in the 'art' culture it matters more what a work 'is' than what it 'does'; whereas in the science culture it matters more what it 'does' than what it 'is'.

To take the second instance: the fact that he might have filled the glass from a bottle clearly labelled 'water' (thereby illustrating that it really is water) is of less consequence to scientific investigation than the fact that the contents of the glass subsequently reacted in an appropriate way when tested physically and chemically. Whereas, in the case of the painting, it mattered less how accurately it responded to tests that proved it was identical to Constable's original, than the simple fact that it *was not* the original.

HOLY WATER

We now move to slightly trickier ground. He pointed to the glass labelled HOLY WATER and claimed that he had been in Rome yesterday, met the Pope and asked him to bless this water. It was, therefore, undeniably holy water.

He then invoked the image of the demon rushing to test the water and then grandly proclaiming that he was a fraud because the water in the glass proved to be no different chemically or physically from ordinary water. Was this a victory for the demon?

He suggested not, but added that it could well have been one hundred and fifty years earlier, around the time that Thomas H Huxley debated with Bishop Wilberforce at the 1860 meeting of The British Association for the Advancement of Science. In those days a claim that water blessed by the Pope could be shown to be in no way different from ordinary water might indeed have been seen as a defeat for religion. Even in the 1950s such a story might have created a stir, but surely only in the popular press. Because most thoughtful people were moving towards CP Snow's line of thinking: they would say that scientific tests on holy water have little to do with religion and the 'other culture'.

But nowadays, after all the 1990s debates about religion and science leading up to the millennium, he suggested that the demon's expose that my 'holy water' was no different from ordinary water would barely merit a mention even in a tabloid newspaper. For there is an increasing popular understanding that science and religion are quite different cultures - just as art and science are - and that such scientific attempts to 'disprove' religion in the old sense are simply missing the point.

So, once more, the score now reads: 'Ramsey Dukes, 3 points - Demon nil'.

But at this point the demon makes a discovery: Ramsey Dukes was not in Rome yesterday. It checked with the Vatican and confirmed that the Pope did not bless any water yesterday - so the story is a lie and he has at last been successfully exposed as a fraud. 'Ramsey Dukes 3 points - Demon 1 point'.

Because it seems that there is a sense in religion, as there was in his art example, in which it matters less what a thing *does* than what it *is*. The real test of holy water, like an original work of art, is not whether it responds differently to any physical or chemical tests. The test of holy water is whether it has actually been blessed by a priest. His water was not blessed by a priest, and so it was not holy water.

HEALING WATER

Now we enter the real battlefield. He pointed to the glass labelled HEALING WATER and explained that it was incredible healing water, taken from a secret sacred spring in the Celtic hills at a precise moment when a favourably aspected full moon is rising and according to an ancient ritual enacted by the celebrated magical genius Ramsey Dukes. 'Just feel that healing energy!'

Needless to say, the demon swoops in immediately to grab the water and return in triumph from its laboratory to announce that the healing water is in now way different from ordinary water. So, what's the score?

He felt pretty certain that the score now reads 'Ramsey Dukes 3 - Demon 2', because that scientific test is pretty damning for healing water. But he did have a reservation, because he suggested that it was only damning at a tabloid newspaper or popular TV documentary level. For a more educated public the demon's tests are not quite enough.

He proposed that, although there is broad denial of a thing called 'magic', there is a, so-far unacknowledged, beginning of an understanding of what it is about. More thoughtful critics have a hunch that magic is like science in the one sense that it matters more to magic what a thing *does* than what it *is*.

(Here I divert slightly to address a possible misunderstanding: 'but isn't holy water meant also to do something? namely to heal people?' My answer is that the healing power of holy water is a magical bonus rather than something innately religious. It would not serve as a test to prove the water was not holy water if it failed to heal, for the answer might be that 'it was not God's will to heal that person'. The real truth of holy water is whether it has been blessed by a priest, not whether it can heal, whereas 'healing water' that failed to heal in any sense would be condemned.)

So, damning though the demon's tests was, the real victory is only won when healing water is tested against ordinary water in a double blind test on a large number of sick people. And he predicted that the results will be little better than chance in favour of his water. The demon had its victory, because the healing water has now been shown not to have any significant healing effect.

Clearing the Battlefield of Its Dead

It is surely a dark day for magic when Ramsey Dukes admits that his amazing healing water probably doesn't heal? And yet this easy victory for the arch-skeptic demon presents problems analogous to those resulting from the recent triumph over the enemies of democracy in Iraq.

While I do recognise those who defend alternative healing practices by insisting that there is solid scientific evidence for their effectiveness, I am equally certain that the this body of evidence is not generally accepted by the scientific community. The impression there is more of a territorial war and, whenever science advances in full force upon any fringe group - whether astrology, homeopathy, popular psychology or whatever - there is either an outright defeat or else a capturing of the enemy forces. By that I mean that either the conclusion is 'no significant healing effect' or else, when some healing effect is noted, the healing principle is then isolated and taken into the scientific body of knowledge - as when a witch-doctor's herbal remedy is found to contain a previously unknown healing agent.

With reference to my earlier notion of 'bursting a bubble of irrationality', we might expect such a series of outright military victories to result in an erosion of magical beliefs and practices - a decline in public acceptance of astrology, homeopathy, alternative medicine and the 'all things mystical' referred to in the above *New Scientist* quotation. Instead we find that magical beliefs are holding their own and even gaining territory in the public imagination.

Could this reflect a profound ignorance about the nature of magical thinking, and a refusal to grant it recognition as a culture in its own right? That those waging this war are simply missing the point? Indeed, in the very process of denying such a culture, our society shows signs of recognising its key characteristics.

In the previous section I referred to the growing understanding among more thoughtful skeptics that it is not what healing water *is* that matters, so much as what it *does*. Once it was enough to point out that the process of manufacturing a homeopathic remedy could leave you with pure water and not one atom of the added principle, but now an intelligent critic knows that this is insufficient: the real test is whether the remedy heals or not. Another example: the magician likes to believe that the tarot pack represents a direct line of descent from the mystery wisdom of the ancient Egyptians, and it was once thought that all you had to do was reveal the historical truth that there is no such line of descent in order to debunk tarot divination. This does not work because, although the magician likes to believe the myth, the real value of tarot divination lies in the magician's perception of the uncanny way it can deliver images that match the magician's own subjective reading of events. In other words, the extent to which it works.

Consider the double-blind test itself. It involves a large number of people, some of whom receive the treatment and others who do not, but who receive some form of placebo replacement so that they do not themselves know if they are getting it or not. Where possible, it is also arranged that those administering the treatment do not know if they are giving the test subject or the placebo. From a scientific standpoint this is rock solid because:

1) Involving large numbers helps to dilute anomalies and deliver a statistically meaningful result.

2) The fact that the patients do not know whether they are getting the test treatment or not helps to eliminate subjective expectations from the healing process.

3) The fact that the experimenters themselves do not know who receives what until after the results are quantified, helps to eliminate the effect of 'desire for success' (either way) on the results.

From a magical point of view, however, the whole process can be seen as no more than a banishing ritual to exclude magic in order to prove that magic does not exist. In the very act of using it to disprove the existence of magic, the scientific community reveals a profound understanding of the greater power of magic; for the same double blind process is used to test scientific remedies too.

Thus, in the human activity of healing, science can be seen in two ways from two angles: on the one hand it has a mighty weapon against which magic is helpless; on the other hand science is a delicate thing that can only operate when magic is kept at bay. To return to the political analogy: for the Bush regime a multi-billion dollar programme of added security at airports across America is a victory *against* terrorism, but for many citizens who suffer the resulting inconvenience, it is a victory *for* terrorism and the terrorists gain greater influence as a consequence.

To understand how the double-blind test is an exorcism to drive out magic, consider how the healing water would be deployed in a magical culture. Dukes already told the audience about its magical provenance and the rituals used to reinforce its power. If one was motivated to use this water to heal an individual, one of the most powerful techniques would be to include that individual in the healing ritual so they were utterly involved and committed to the cure.

Does that mean the cure would not work at a distance? Of course not: if the patient could not be present then it is the strength of the magician's intent, the focus upon the recipient, that provides the magical link to support the healing.

Does that mean that one could not sell this remedy to persons unknown as a commercial product? Of course not: if that was the intention one would do what *disturber* did so well in his website, by providing labelling and packaging that told of the wonders of this water and how it had been produced by what a great magician, coupled with plentiful testimonials to its efficacy in support of the understanding that what matters in magic is what the remedy does more than what it is. In this way one would involve the buyers' commitment to the product, so that their belief in it provided the magical link for its effect.

Does that mean the remedy could not be used on an animal, or a skeptical patient who did not believe in it? Again, no problem as long as the person who administers the remedy has the belief and healing desire to effect the magical link between the patient and the creation of the remedy.

Some form of magical link is fundamental to the healing, and double blind process does all it can to eliminate all such links to produce a test that can be seen as a fair, objective trial, which eliminates spurious results due to extraneous factors. But the test can equally be seen as an ivory tower exercise that has no relevance to healing as practiced in real life. As irrelevant as a motor car test conducted with no petrol in the tank 'in order to eliminate extraneous factors'.

Subjectivity and Objectivity

I suggest that there is an even greater problem in this distinction between science and magic. Although both cultures share a common emphasis on effectiveness - what the remedy actually does - there is a divergence in the understanding of results.

Consider a magical group that performs a healing ritual for a beloved member of the group who has contracted a terminal illness. Next week the patient is visited by a member of the group who, in his heart of hearts does hope he will find the illness mysteriously eliminated to the bafflement of the medical profession. What often happens, however, is a more subjective healing of the situation. It could be that the patient still has only six months to live, as before, but that his whole life attitude has shifted. 'Doesn't it hurt anymore?'

asks the visitor. 'Yes, it hurts as much as ever' is the reply, 'but I realise now that I have been fighting this illness just as I have been fighting all my life. Suddenly it occurred to me that I have 6 months to live and so much I still want to enjoy. For the first time in my life I am absolutely sure of what I want...'

When something happens along similar lines, the tendency in magical and alternative healing circles is to feel that healing has indeed taken place, even if it was not what one might have hoped for at the start of the treatment. What's more, a healing experience of this nature often has a reciprocal effect, so that those involved in the healing process feel that they too have grown in understanding and humanity through witnessing the change in their friend. This subjective recognition of the result after the event goes against scientific principles of predictability and repeatability, and is likely to be dismissed as 'self delusion', 'fudging' or '*post hoc propter hoc* justification'.

A healing result along these lines is, presumably, the sort of thing that *disturber* refers to in his challenge when he asks 'Where is the crystal that definitely healed a sickly person and didn't just provide vague emotional satisfaction?' [24]

A *Wall Street Journal* opinion piece [25] called The Power of Modern Fads suggests that:

> In an age of instant communications, we become members of a huge worldwide tribe, in constant contact with the thoughts and emotions of our fellow members everywhere. This carries many blessings... But, like tribal societies throughout the ages, it's vulnerable to sudden surges of emotions, to shared if unexamined assumptions that harden into instant fads.
> And it concludes that:
> Fads, that is, have real consequences. And with tribal cohesion, it seems, there are not many to stand against them, least of all among guardians of the press. So serious people have to be careful to cling stubbornly to reality, to refuse to give the passing craze the benefit of suspension of belief.

Although the fads addressed in the article are more political than magical, the diagnosis and conclusion given would surely match the way a skeptic views popular acceptance of alternative healing. But the critical point is the meaning of the word 'reality' in the last sentence. Which is more 'real' to the family seeking healing: a carefully controlled scientific test in some distant laboratory situation, or a subjective transformation that completely alters the family's attitudes and life direction?

In the contest for the crown of 'reality' the former has the advantage of objectivity, but it is the latter that has the advantage of immediate relevance and visible effectiveness. Although both magic and science share the above described attachment to what things 'do' more than than what they 'are', this common function divides them more than it unites them (as in Oscar Wilde's oft-quoted observation that England and America are 'divided by a common language').

Indeed, I suggest that the greater value given to subjectivity is a common feature of art and magic, whereas the greater value of objectivity is common to religion and science. Although both science and magic agree that the real test of a procedure is whether it works, the conditions under which it is supposed to work, and the judgement of the results, diverge in the two cultures.

Although there is a sense (described above) in which art and religion agree in their emphasis on what a thing is being more important than what it does, there is also a parallel split along the subjective/objective fault-line. The holy water is holy because a priest blessed it - an objective fact. True, the Hay Wain is worth a fortune because it was painted by a great master, but here the divergence begins; because there is a much more subjective component in deciding who is a great master than there is in deciding who is a priest. And as you dig deeper into the art culture, rather than remaining on this commercial level, the more one is aware of the dominant emphasis on subjective judgement.

Compare also religion and magic: although there is some agreement in more liberal circles about the subjective nature of religious experience, there is far stronger support for the idea of God as an objective existing reality - even though the terms of reference are not those of the materialistic scientist. Religious people faced with the magician's subjective decision making - 'I'm working within the celtic pantheon at present' - find it quite disturbing ('a supermarket of beliefs') if not actually blasphemous.

These distinctions can be summarised in the following diagram, which matches the model suggested in *SSOTBME - an essay on magic* [26].

Understanding and Using this Model

I am proposing that this fourfold model can help to increase understanding between the cultures and reduce friction in the way that CP Snow's two culture model has already helped people cope with the gap between art and science. But first I must explain something about the model.

SSOTBME explored various differentiators between the cultures, one being [27] that art and magic relied more on 'right brain' activity while science in particular gave greater value to the 'left brain' as commonly understood. The relevance here is that the model is more typical of magical thinking in that it represents a spatial, fractal analysis rather than one based on four closed categories.

Magical categories tend to be fractal in the sense that each contains all the others - as in the fourfold division of the elements in which Fire can be subdivided into Earth of Fire, Water of Fire, Air of Fire, Fire of Fire and so on *ad lib*; or the I Ching in which a simple binary division into Yin or Yang becomes subdivided two more times to form trigrams and so on.

But scientific and academic thought prefers distinctions that are exclusive and well-defined. Thus I was approached after my talk with the question 'where does philosophy lie on your diagram?' - a question that comes naturally and yet it is the wrong question. Instead one should ask 'where does my diagram lie in philosophy?' - to which the answer would depend upon the standpoint.

THE FOUR CULTURES AS A COMPASS ROSE

The predominating qualities suggested here are those referred to in this essay plus others illustrated in *SSOTBME - an essay on magic*

Above the line
"It matters more what it is"
Judgement by intuition, or a sense of authority
Movement towards abstraction (spiritualisation)

Below the line
"It matters more what it does"
Judgement by observation
Movement from abstract towards manifestation

To the right of the line

Judgement by reason

Greater value of objective

Recognition of causes

Linear time

'Left brain' processing

Analysis into closed, discrete categories

Progress by denial

Questing

Honouring the repeatable

To the left of the line

Judgement by feeling

Greater value of subjective

Recognition of patterns

Cyclical time

'Right brain' processing

Analysis into interpenetrating fractal categories

Progress by affirmation

Cultivating

Honouring the exceptional

(Quadrants: religion, science, art, magic)

My answer, the one personal to my individual standpoint, would be that philosophy has its magical side (which I am practicing in this article) which is to seek solutions to life problems by exploring different ways to think about them, whereas a more scientific philosophy would insist on the quest towards ultimate truth, and a more religious philosophy would rather guide us towards the greatest good or the highest state for humankind, and a more artistic philosophy would be to celebrate pure philosophy for its own sake.

Thus the model should be seen not as a battle plan defining four distinct territories, but as a compass rose defining four directions. It can illuminate, but not answer, such questions as 'is psychotherapy science or magic?' because such placing of disciplines on the diagram depends upon one's standpoint - my school mathematics teacher who was a strict logician used to speak of the physics staff as 'the folklore department'!

This sort of thinking may not satisfy the need for clear boundaries and discrete categories, but it can help to bridge the gaps that such a need creates. I recall the pleasure that people got in the 1950s from debating 'whether the Modern Jazz Quartet was jazz or not', but I also recall some of the confusion and exclusion that resulted from such distinctions. I myself hugely enjoyed *disturber*'s campaign and the skill with which it was carried out (I salute good magic when I see it), but only regret when his prank is used by others as a weapon to bludgeon the faith out of someone who is beginning to enjoy crystal healing.

Instead, here is an example of how the model might help understanding. Let us imagine that a scientist has been struggling to solve a significant problem and senses that he is very close to the answer, but is suffering from late nights and exhaustion. He recognises this state - he has been in it before - where the answer is lurking just out of sight and he knows from experience that if he leaves the laboratory, has a good meal and a proper night's sleep, then he will almost certainly see the solution when he wakes up. The next morning he awakes in excitement, the answer is not only clear, it is beautifully simple and he spends the day tinkering with the theory and results to polish that beauty by balancing its parts and eliminating weak points. But when it comes down to writing up the work formally, all this detail will be omitted and the experiment described without any reference to feeling or will.

That sense of an answer lurking at the edge of vision - coupled with the experiential knowledge that it will be best grasped by ceasing to persist and getting a good night's sleep in expectation of discovery - is practical magic. To use more magical terminology: the truth is an errant spirit and it is more likely to be evoked if we cease to threaten it and adopt a more receptive state - and this is something the scientist has learned from experience by observing patterns of behaviour. Equally, his excitement and 'fudging' the results to bring out the beauty of his discovery is art. But when it comes to writing it up formally, he needs to be very careful to examine these origins and adjustments to his discovery by eliminating the elements of will, desire and other subjective factors. This is when the thinking process becomes truly scientific. And why does he work so hard? Maybe it is a sense of duty or monetary reward, but maybe also he believes that his work is important, that it helps humanity and the quest for truth - and this I would say is the religious aspect of his endeavour.

Analysing the operation in these terms offers two potential benefits. One is that it fosters understanding of the other cultures through discovering them within in one's own life - thus bridging the threatening abyss of otherness. Not that magic does not have its weird and whacky manifestations (indeed Ramsey Dukes is best known as a defender of the weirdest extremes of magical thinking), but that these can be recognised as just the further reaches of a territory that begins right here at home - and not intrinsically any more weird than the furthest extremes of art, science or religion.

The second benefit is that, while admitting these other cultures into the scientific process, they can be identified as such and dealt with appropriately. Admitting that 'the solution' might sometimes be better addressed as if it was a teasing, evasive spirit rather than an inert object waiting to be discovered, does not necessarily mean a slide into superstition. All it means is a different, practical approach towards handling one's own subjective states. Recognising this approach as 'magical', recognising the driving force for scientific endeavour as partly 'religious' and recognising the tidying and trimming process as partly 'artistic' - these three provide a pointer when it comes to eliminating extraneous factors in the final scientific presentation. This is surely better than attempting to deny that such factors as commercial funding, possible job losses or academic rivalry could possibly influence the results of scientific research?

The alternative - i.e. to continue to deny that there is a fourth, magical culture - means that we find ourselves forced to depend upon three new categories to paper over the gap. Namely: bad science, bad religion and bad art.

Bad science embraces not only the many magical disciplines seeking respectability in the name of science [28], but also the tendency to confuse statistical correlation with a proof of causality [29]. Bad religion covers all more magical faiths in today's 'supermarket of beliefs' that so worry traditional churchgoers. While bad art is a term that might be used not only for magical images which are built up by consciously incorporating symbols with a certain 'meaning', but also much commercial art. If a film or other work is constructed out of all the elements judged to invoke public adulation, then it should be recognised for what it really is: a magical talisman for invoking commercial success.

By all means let us subdivide science, religion and art (and magic too) along the good/bad axis if it helps our judgement, but let us first recognise what is *not* truly science, religion or art.

Conclusion

This *Journal for the Academic Study of Magic* is timely and significant in that it marks the beginning of a willingness to study magic without the twin seductions of passionate acceptance or equally passionate denial.

CP Snow's 'two cultures' helped us because the concept named a problem, thus helping both to identify it and also to lay it aside when necessary. A similar recognition of the factors that make religion and science essentially different has helped communication between the two - as when tests on the Turin Shroud are no longer seen simply as 'attacks' on the church but rather an act of co-operation over church history. In neither case has it been necessary to define the difference strictly in order to produce a useful result.

In this manner, a recognition of four cultures could help us to understand, assimilate (or lay aside) the whole spectrum of alternative beliefs and practices which are embraced by magical culture - rather than see them as a threatening tide poised to wash away all that Western Culture is believed to represent [30].

Notes

[1] I had in mind a number of now-forgotten radio and television documentaries on the subject. But see also the Science and Religion dialogues of The John Templeton Foundation (www.templeton.org) founded in 1987; or *Science and Theology* (SPCK/Fortress Press) and other works by John Polkinghorn, an Anglican priest and former Professor of Mathematical Physics at Cambridge University.

[2] Ramsey Dukes, *Four Glasses of Water - Post Secular Angst and the Denial of Magic*. Part of the Occulture festival, Saturday 19th July at the Sallis Benney Theatre, Brighton, Sussex, UK.

[3] *Magic - Art of Darkness*, BBC2, 9pm Thursday April 19th 2001

[4] Karl French, 'Television Preview' in *Financial Times,* Thursday April 19th 2001

[5] Paul Hoggart, 'Yesterdays Viewing' in *The Times,* Friday April 20th 2001

[6] Reference: the volume now in your hands.

[7] See *Beyond Entertainment? Research into the acceptability of alternative beliefs, psychic and occult phenomena on television* a report commissioned by the Independent Television Commission (ITC) in 2001. The ITC code does not permit portrayal of occult practices unless part of a 'legitimate investigation'. As the Astrological Association points out (www.astrologer.com/aanet/news/itc/itc_pr.htm) this means they can only be shown as being 'put on trial' - never to educate. According to the report's findings, the public has broadly positive perception of alternative healing and psychic subjects, but negative perception of 'the occult'. This is seen as reason to restrict coverage of the occult, rather than reason to educate with more positive understanding (as is sometimes attempted with other negative public perceptions of such subjects as immigration, homosexuality, addiction etc).

[8] See previous note for supposed public perception of occultism in relation to broader alternative ideas.

[9] Feedback, *The New Scientist*, March 1st 2003

[10] *ibid*

[11] See http://web.onetel.net.uk/~alwyne_k/chamber/#. This explanation has since been added to the original website www.the-crystal-chamber.net where it can be accessed under the title *HOAX DETAILS*.

[12] *ibid*

[13] See http://www.ukpagan.com/modules.php?op=modload&name=phpBB_14&file=index&action=viewtopic&topic=5492&152 for the full correspondence. Or else go to the end of the previous reference for a less tiresome link to the discussion.

[14] Roger Kimball, *"The two cultures" today*, The New Criterion, Vol 12, No 6, February 1994

[15] Reissued with additional material and introduction by Stefan Collini as *The Two Cultures* by Canto Books (Cambridge University Press) 1993.

[16] From Roger Kimball, *"The two cultures" today*, The New Criterion, Vol 12, No 6, February 1994.

[17] Richard Dawkins, *Unweaving the Rainbow, Science, Delusion and the Appetite for Wonder*, Penguin Books, 1999

[18] Stephen Rose, in a review of earlier edition of the above book in *The Guardian*, 17th October 1998.

[19] Richard Tomkins, 'Cold comfort from things that go bump in the night', *The Financial Times*, Friday October 31st, 2003.

[20] Polly Toynbee, from her column in *The Radio Times*, 8-14 May 1999.

[21] James Clark Maxwell, first Cavendish Professor of Physics, Cambridge University, 1871. For an account of 'Maxwell's Demon' see, for example, www.auburn.edu/~smith01/notes.maxdem.htm

[22] See http://www.cl.cam.ac.uk/users/ig206/oak_tree.html for the full text. I was told after the talk that the art work in question has since been relocated.

[23] John Constable, *The Hay Wain*, London, 1821. See http://www.nationalgallery.org.uk/cgi-bin/WebObjects.dll/CollectionPublisher.woa/wa/largeImage?workNumber=NG1207.

[24] See previous quotation reference note 10.

[25] Robert L Bartley, 'The Power of Modern Fads' in *The Wall Street Journal*, Monday, October 27, 2003.

[26] Ramsey Dukes, *SSOTBME Revised - an essay on magic*, The Mouse That Spins, London, 2002. In this book, and in the original talk, I suggested that the diagram illustrated another difference between magical and scientific thought, namely that magical thought relies more on pattern recognition than causality and so tends to see nested cycles where scientific thought sees linear developments. Thus a rationalist might recognise the place of magic in terms of an evolution of human thinking as: magic > art > religion > science (as I put it 'our primitive

ancestors did silly things (magic) for millennia, during which time they learnt to do silly things rather well (art). Then with increasing socialisation they learnt to do silly things with authority (religion), until finally they learnt to recognise the truth and now we have science.' But in my book I argue that the cycle continues and that magic is actually what follows after science.

[27] *ibid*, page 9.

[28] See Robert Todd Carroll, *Pseudoscience,* at http://www.skepdic.com/pseudosc.html. All the subjects dismissed in this website as 'pseudoscience' seem to me to be quite acceptable as magical theories or practices - including some such as Myers-Briggs Type Indicator whose practitioners might be horrified by my welcome into the magical quadrant!

[29] See *SSOTBME Revised* page 37, where this tendency was seen as a public reaction against the slow pace of scientific enquiry.

[30] As suggested in the *Financial Times* piece referred to in note 16.

The Land Near the Dark Cornish Sea:
The Development of Tintagel as a Celtic Pilgrimage Site

Amy Hale

'Celtic' spiritual tourism and pilgrimage has always been a feature of the Cornish tourist economy, but its relevance has increased in the past decade, especially as Cornwall has started to acknowledge its Celtic heritage and promote its Celtic cultural resources [1]. For some, Cornwall's Celticity is mainly a matter of Cornish ethnicity, but for others, primarily tourists, it has a spiritual, rather than ethnic implication. In 1993, John Lowerson described the quest for a metaphysical 'Celtic experience' that brings many people to Cornwall. Lowerson identifies Cornwall as a key site for spiritual Celtic tourism, along with places like Glastonbury, Lindisfarne, and Iona, all of which are also sites for more permanent communities which have settled in order to pursue spiritual interests [2]. Lowerson defines the New-Age tourists, as those who have a desire to escape from urbanity, are interested by pre-Christian Celtic religion, mythology, early Celtic Christianity, or the occult, and pursue those interests with a sort of 'neo-antiquarianism'[3]. This would certainly fit the profile of a spiritual visitor to Tintagel. Here, I will survey a number of historical threads of esoteric activity and influences that have converged to create an interrelated complex of pilgrimage sites in the North Cornwall area surrounding Tintagel. I will then examine the ways in which these seemingly disparate threads of magical activity become coherent, as the umbrella notion of 'Celtic' spirituality engulfs a variety of late twentieth century British esoteric trends.

North Cornwall and the area around Tintagel village in Cornwall is often said to have 'a mystical feel to it'. In fact, this 'mystical feel' is probably one of its major selling points as a tourist destination and in fact, any one of a hundred websites will refer to it. Within Cornwall, it is one of two geographical centers of spiritual tourism, pilgrimage and alternative religious activity, the other being West Cornwall where the highest concentration of megalithic monuments in the territory is located. Although Tintagel castle provides the focus of much of Tintagel's tourism, sites of mystical importance near the village of Tintagel are not confined to the medieval ruins of the fortress on a rocky headland. The neighboring villages of Boscastle, where the Museum of Witchcraft is located and Bossiney near St. Nectan's Kieve and the Rocky Valley mazes, also attract their share of visitors. In a sense, the three areas on the North Cornish coast create a geographical complex of sites that are functionally quite interrelated. That this group of sites is in Cornwall makes particular sense, given how that entire territory has been constructed by generations of holidaymakers as a sort of Celtic Otherworld; familiar yet exotic, and a place where you go for life changing transformation.[4]

In considering the reasons behind Tintagel's origins as a British mystical center in the twentieth century, the obvious first answer is the relationship between Tintagel and Arthurian legend, which parallels the reasons behind Glastonbury's emergence as a pilgrimage site. The implication of Arthur as a figure in nineteenth and twentieth century British esotericism is complex, multifaceted, and outside the scope of this article. Yet in many ways the early twentieth century mystical interpretations of Arthurian legend have now been submerged in the development of North Cornwall as a site of contemporary esoteric pilgrimage, which includes other phenomena and symbolism as well as Arthurian based mysticism. In some cases, the stories of the individuals and developments that laid the groundwork for activities in 'mystical Tintagel' have long since disappeared, leaving multiple layers of history and esoteric activity which are often not able to be unraveled by the visitor because they have not been included in histories or heritage interpretations of the village. Nevertheless, the variety of symbols represented in the North Cornwall area is not incongruent. We understand that Arthur, Goddess worship and the Museum of Witchcraft occupy the same semantic space, but why is not always immediately clear. Over the past eighty years, Tintagel has had the ability to stay relevant within the major trends and discourses of British esoterica, incorporating such themes as Goddess worship, ley lines, and Wicca. Tintagel, like Glastonbury, is a site that both encompasses and is emblematic of modern Celtic spirituality in Britain.

Tintagel and Arthur

Certainly it is Tintagel castle's longstanding association as the birthplace of King Arthur that inspired the development of the whole area as a tourist destination and a site of esoteric pilgrimage. Now, Tintagel, both the village and the castle itself, is a fascinating mix of symbols and images. The drama of the castle perched on the headland seems to contrast with the tourist kitsch that threatens to overwhelm the village. Those who are drawn to Tintagel for spiritual and aesthetic reflection are often frustrated with 'King Arthur's Car Park' and the proliferation of Arthur-based tourist shops, where one can purchase pewter Merlins, hastily glued to chunks of amethyst, as well as all manner of Celtic jewelry, scarves, wood carvings, and books. Some even take offense at King Arthur's Hall of Chivalry, which was originally built for the most noble of purposes, but unfortunately now has a rather undeserved reputation of being nothing but a tourist trap.

Tintagel's fame arguably began in 1136, with Geoffrey of Monmouth's medieval bestseller *The History of the Kings of Britain*, in which he identifies the place of Arthur's conception to the craggy promontory. *The History...* was one of the most influential and widely read works of the Middle Ages in Europe [5]. Geoffrey's translator, Lewis Thorpe states that 'the results of Geoffrey's *History* in 1136 were immediate and striking... it has had few, if any equals in the history of European literature' [6]. According to Geoffrey's account, King Uther Pendragon had fallen in love with Ygerna, wife of Gorlois, Duke of Cornwall. During a banquet at Pendragon's castle in London, Uther showered Ygerna with attention. This did not please Gorlois so he left Uther's gathering hastily, which so offended Uther that he vowed to ravage Gorlois' lands. Uther and his men went to Cornwall, and

Gorlois left Ygerna at his castle at Tintagel, while he hid at his fort Dimilioc, which lies about five and a half miles south-west of Tintagel. When Uther arrived he consulted Merlin about how to have his way with Ygerna. Merlin gave Uther a potion that would alter his appearance to that of Gorlois:

> They then set off for Tintagel and came to the Castle in the twilight. The moment the guard was told that his leader was approaching, he opened the gates and the men were let in. Who, indeed, could possibly have suspected anything, once it was thought that Gorlois had come? The King had spent that night with Ygerna and satisfied his desire by making love with her. . .That night she conceived Arthur, the most famous of men, who subsequently won great renown by his outstanding bravery.[7]

Although in Geoffrey's version Arthur was only conceived at Tintagel, most writers since have made Tintagel Arthur's birthplace, and even his residence.[8]

In truth, Geoffrey may have only been Tintagel's best-known publicist, for the site was most likely recognized as a center of some prominence far before that. The archaeological record of Tintagel indicates some sort of settlement on the headland from the fifth and sixth century A.D. Archaeologist Charles Thomas theorizes that the presence of pottery remains originating from the Mediterranean and North Africa indicates that Tintagel was the stronghold of the post-Roman kings of Dumnonia[9]. Thomas also argues that Tintagel's significance was retained in folk-memory which contributed to local legends placing Tintagel as the seat of Cornish kings[10]. The ruins of the fortress that are visible today originate from the first major medieval settlement on the site, which was begun c. 1230-40 A.D., by Richard, Earl of Cornwall, and reached the height of its prominence during the thirteenth century. Charles Thomas suggests that Richard chose the site perhaps because he wanted to capitalize on its legendary associations with Arthur.[11]

Although Tintagel has been connected with Arthurian legend since the twelfth century, the contemporary interest in its associations with Arthur begin in the Victorian era. In 1819 the distinguished English landscape painter Joseph Malord William Turner completed a romanticized sketch of the castle, capturing the image of a truly British vision of Arcadia. Parson Hawker of Morwenstow, famous for 'The Song of Western Men', better known as the Cornish anthem Trelawny, spent his honeymoon at Tintagel in 1823, which inspired the love of Arthurian legend which he was to share with Alfred Lord Tennyson later in his life. It also inspired the poem *The Quest of the Sangraal*, written forty years after his first visit and considered by Tennyson to be superior to his own 'Idylls of the King'.[12]

However, it was Tennyson's Arthurian works of the nineteenth century that ultimately had the most impact on Tintagel. In 1832 Tennyson published the earliest of his Arthurian poems, 'The Lady of Shallott', but he was already considering the idea of an epic Arthurian poem at this time.[13] In 1848 Tennyson visited the eccentric Hawker, and the two toured Tintagel. Ten years later, the first version of 'Idylls of the King' was published containing an account of Arthur's birth which Tennyson placed in Tintagel. Along with the reprinting of Malory's *Morte D'Arthur* in the early years of the nineteenth century, 'Idylls of the King' awoke the popular interest in Arthuriana in Britain during the second half of the nineteenth century, and which became a cultural preoccupation that has never really dissipated.

Until the 1880s, Tintagel was a sleepy remote village, known as Trevena—only the headland was called Tintagel. However, the influx of poets, painters, and writers forever changed the village. For centuries the economy of Trevena was based on agriculture and slate-quarrying, but in the 1880s boarding houses and hotels, such as King Arthur's Arms and the King Arthur Hotel, were built to serve the newly developing tourist trade.[14] In the 1920s and 30s Arthuriana was to take on a new profile in Cornwall with several distinct yet oddly interrelated events boosting Tintagel's profile, and laying the groundwork for the influx that was to later occur.

Although Tintagel has been an inspiration for artists and poets, which helped to boost the romantic appeal for tourists, Tintagel has also been serving British esotericists for almost as long. The development of Glastonbury and Tintagel as sites of spiritual pilgrimage is similar and linked. Tintagel is almost like Glastonbury's little sister. It is not nearly as commercial as Glastonbury in its trappings, yet it has its share of shops catering to spiritual tourists, dealing in esoteric books, candles, jewelry, tarot cards and incense, along with almost anything imaginable with Celtic designs on them. It is this story that is not always as accessible as that of the impact of Tennyson, but it may have actually had more impact on the village and its development.

Tintagel and the Archangel Michael
On 17 August, 1924 Tintagel was visited by philosopher Rudolph Steiner (1861-1925), whose theories about Tintagel's original function contributed to the area's mystique and reputation, although his theories are mainly lost on the public today. Steiner was a well-known Austrian occultist, mystic and philosopher who promoted a Western, Christ-based mysticism over that of Theosophy's Eastern based teachings. He was the founder of Anthroposophy, a spiritual system designed to elevate human consciousness to a more universal spirituality. Toward the end of his life, Steiner lectured in Torquay and London about the former role of Tintagel as a center of spiritual importance. Steiner believed that 'Arthur' was not a personal name but a priestly title, and that Tintagel was an ancient center of learning dedicated to studying planetary phenomena and communicating the knowledge of the cosmos gained by the megalithic monument builders.[15] Instead of merely being the birthplace of Arthur, Steiner viewed Tintagel as the home of Arthur and his twelve knights, each of whom represented a sign of the zodiac. The most important role of the ruling priests of Tintagel was to direct chosen souls to more fully experience the spiritual world. Steiner believed that the Arthurian priesthood was essentially a solar cult doing the work of the Archangel Michael, who, like Jesus and Merlin, was a solar entity administering the Cosmic Intelligence. He was a localized, Celtic articulation of a universal phenomenon.

That Steiner would link Arthur with a solar cult, essentially making him a British manifestation of a solar deity, would not have been unusual for the time. The Reverend Edward Davies in his 1809 *Mythology and Rites of the British Druids* argued that Arthur was a solar hero, and the idea received quite a bit of literary response throughout the nineteenth century. In the latter half of the nineteenth century the works of mythologist Max Müller were quite widely read and very popular with the European public. Müller's theory of solar mythology argued that because the movements of heavenly bodies must have been a main preoccupation with early societies that all mythological systems were invented to explain these phenomena. Thus, the symbolic origins of Arthur were interpreted as an aspect of a Celtic solar deity. It is quite likely that Steiner's views about Arthur's status were a continuation of popular mythological theory at the time.

Steiner argued that Tintagel, as a Michael site, would play a central role in regenerating the human spirit in the Michael Age. Inspired by Theosophical beliefs and the C.G. Harrison's 1896 collection of essays *The Transcendental Universe*, Steiner believed that in November of 1879 an event on the astral plane caused the Age of Gabriel to end, and the Age of Michael to begin.[16] This new Age of Michael would help foster the realization of God's vision and revitalize spirituality worldwide. Although this esoteric interpretation of Tintagel is not exactly apparent to visitors today, its status as a spiritual hotspot probably owes quite a bit to these initial theories, particularly with the reinterpretation and reinvigoration efforts of Wellesley Tudor Pole.

English esotericist Wellesley Tudor Pole is today probably most well known for his development of Glastonbury's Chalice Well Gardens in 1959. An advocate for Steiner's theories about the role of Michael in the spiritual life of Britain, Tudor Pole made the connection between Glastonbury and Tintagel as sites which had links with both Arthur and Michael. However, in the post WWII period, Tudor Pole wished to rejuvenate Britain's sacred sites by advocating a new era of pilgrimage, which he felt could help speed up earthly evolution, and help secure Britain's place as a spiritual world leader.[17] He called for an emphasis on sites that had been dedicated to St. Michael and suggested that pilgrims begin with St. Michael's Mount near Penzance, and then travel through Tintagel to Glastonbury Tor, also dedicated to St. Michael. Wellesley Tudor Pole's spiritual vision certainly had nativist overtones. In addition to his interest in Arthur and the Joseph of Aramathea legends about bringing the Holy Grail to Britain, he also considered St. George as a manifestation of the Archangel Michael, reinforcing England's position as a potential spiritual beacon which would help to rejuvenate a deflated and war-torn Europe.

Cornwall had a particular role in this transformation. Although today St. Piran is generally considered to be the patron saint of Cornwall, Piran is actually the patron saint of tinners (and drunkards). St. Michael is the patron saint of Cornwall, which puts Cornwall in the forefront of British spiritual development in the Michael Age.[18] That Tudor Pole would conflate Michael with the English icon St. George in Cornwall in 1951, the same year that the Cornish nationalist party *Mebyon Kernow* was founded, has a certain irony. Tudor Pole believed that St. Michael's Mount was a power nexus for all Michael power sites in Britain. What is interesting, is that Tudor Pole believed that Tintagel was a key stop for the Michael pilgrimage in Britain. Also ironic is the fact that although Steiner and Tudor Pole believed that Tintagel was the home of the preeminent Michael priesthood in Britain, there are no sites dedicated to Michael in Tintagel. Without doubt the Michael pilgrimage had taken hold by the late 1950s. Ithell Colquhoun writes of her own Michael pilgrimage in her 1957 mystical travelogue of Cornwall *The Living Stones*.[19] Her focus was only on the Michael sites in West Cornwall, but she does acknowledge the wider spread of sites dedicated to Michael sites throughout Cornwall. Although Colquhoun describes the sites well, she provides little in the way of mystical interpretation, nor does she indicate what rituals or meditations may have taken place along the way. In 1987 Cornwall County Council developed a St. Michael's Way pilgrimage route which is purported to be part of a pilgrimage route to Santiago de Compostela, but it only covers sites in West Cornwall.

It seems quite certain that Tintagel's association as a site for Arthur as British solar deity was well established in the British esoteric community by the late 1950s, and groups and individuals with occult leanings would probably visit the site with that understanding. However, the association with Michael now seems mostly lost, although the interest in Michael sites in Britain, Cornwall in particular, connected by the Michael ley line continues to develop. Alfred Watkins, who popularized the theory of ley lines in 1921, theorized that significant sites and monuments throughout Britain were connected in a travel network by a series of straight lines. They have since become a key feature of British New Age belief, which has adapted Watkins' theories to suggest that these sites are actually placed along some sort of magnetic or energy currents running underneath the earth's surface. The Michael ley line is believed by British earth mysteries enthusiasts to be an energy current which aligns a number of sites dedicated to St. Michael in a straight line from the east coast of England, through the South Western peninsula and Cornwall. Tintagel is not on the Michael ley line, but is still believed to be a 'power site'.[20]

King Arthur's Halls of Chivalry

There are other areas in Tintagel which have been the focus of esoteric activity. In 1928 custard magnate Frederick Glasscock, a Freemason, purchased what was then known as Trevena House and in 1929 began rebuilding the house into the King Arthur Halls of Chivalry. It was certainly a massive undertaking: the halls are substantial and fitted entirely with Cornish stone. It holds a very large carved granite throne for Arthur and two round tables, one entirely of granite, onto which are carved the shields of each of Arthur's twelve knights. In the front room of the Hall, several Pre-Raphaelite paintings by William Hatherell portraying scenes from Arthurian legend are displayed. The seventy-two intricate stained-glass windows in the Pre-Raphaelite style by Veronica Whall, (daughter of Christopher Whall, master of the Arts and Crafts movement) are incomparable. In addition to the stone work, the mural-sized paintings, and the stained glass, Glasscock also amassed an impressive collection of very rare manuscripts and literature dedicated to Arthurian legends and Welsh and Irish mythology, much of which is still on display in the hall, and is possibly one of the best private collections of its kind in Britain.

In 1932 the Halls were completed, and in 1933 the Hall was formally opened by the Bishop of Truro at a ceremony which over five hundred people attended. With the international publicity of the opening of the Halls coupled with the increase in Arthurian related tourism, it is no wonder that the *Western Morning News* reported local displeasure with the Cornish scholar Henry Jenner's attempts to discredit Tintagel by claiming that it could not possibly have been an Arthurian site.[21] The Halls were a significant manifestation of the Arthurmania that swept Britain in the late 1920s and really contains all of the visual hallmarks of that craze. It quickly became a significant attraction in Cornwall and must have influenced Cornish antiquarian Hambly Rowe's decision to hold the 1930 Arthurian Congress in Cornwall. As much as the Halls brought attention to Tintagel, they also had the effect of promoting other Arthurian sites in Cornwall, such as nearby Slaughter Bridge in Camelford where according to legend the final battle between Arthur and Mordred took place.

However, it was not Glasscock's intention to build a tourist trap. He loved Tintagel and was profoundly moved by its landscape, which inspired much more noble intentions. He intended to found a worldwide order along the lines of Freemasonry dedicated to reintroducing the ideals of chivalry to society. It is not clear whether or not his proposed society was in any way inspired by Steiner's influential lectures five years prior to the start of his project. If that was the case, there is little direct evidence of that now. Nevertheless, Glasscock had clearly designed a complex system of symbolism for the initiates of his society, The Fellowship of the Round Table, which is reflected in the stone shields and stained glass windows placed throughout the hall. Glasscock assigned each Knight of the Round Table a specific shield with a symbol on it and a set of attributes to which the initiate must aspire. These shields, with the attributes of each knight, are portrayed in stained glass panels lining the hallways of the large building. Unfortunately, the accompanying rituals and regalia are not available. According to the site's guidebook, Glasscock started the Fellowship in 1927 and had over 17,000 members worldwide[22]. Sadly, Glasscock died in 1934, a year after the Halls were completed, and the Fellowship ceased in 1936.

It is not well known whether or not the Halls were ever a focus for much esoteric activity. They have been held in private hands and not open to the public until the early 1990s. However, the Halls immense focus on Pre Raphaelite style art and themes is congruent with certain ways in which the spiritual aspects of Arthurian legend were visually represented in the 1920s and 1930s. The revival of interest in King Arthur during this period was associated with both British mysticism and the emerging Anglo Catholic movement, and the themes of Arthurian art conveyed both elements. Primarily this manifested in depictions of the Grail quest, but also in depictions of the divine feminine and in Grail angels, which responded to the growing popularity of Spiritualism throughout Britain, a movement characterized by communication with the dead through use of a medium.[23]

Although the Hall of Chivalry did not serve the society for which it was initially founded, it has served the Freemasons. Glasscock was a Freemason, and in 1952 the Freemasons took over the lodge, and continue to use it to this day. As the iconography of the Halls is overtly more quest oriented with its focus on chivalry and knights, it has an implicit, if not explicit, relevance to an initiatory order founded on the idea of revealing mysteries in the course of spiritual development. However, Tintagel is actually also home to a Co-Masonic lodge, as well, and one consisting only of women. According to documents in the archive of Ithell Colquhoun, the Lodge was called Lodge of the Holy Grail #5 and was certainly active by the early 1960s. It appears to have had a supplementary purpose related to Arthurian spiritual research in addition to traditional Masonic functioning. The bylaws of the Lodge state that the central purposes of the Lodge of the Holy Grail were:

1. To make research into the symbolism and legend of the Holy Grail and Arthurian Tradition.
2. To endeavour to attain to perfection in ritual.
3. To endeavour to apply in daily life the ideals set forth in the Quest of the Holy Grail.[24]

Residents of Tintagel say there is still what they refer to as an active 'women's lodge' which meets occasionally in a village hall, and not in the Halls of Chivalry where the men meet, although it is not known if they have retained their Arthurian researches. Today, the Halls are a popular tourist attraction, although they do not feature prominently as a site of particular spiritual focus. The connections between Glasscocks' Fellowship of the Round Table, and Freemasonry form a part of Tintagel's Arthur-focused esoteric history that still exists, yet is not overtly apparent today.

The Museum of Witchcraft

It is difficult to reconstruct the state of esoteric pilgrimage to the Tintagel area in the 1950s, but based on Ithell Colquhoun's 1957 description of a Tintagel pilgrimage and Wellesley Tudor Pole's work toward promoting

Tintagel as a spiritual center, we can guess that it certainly must have formed part of the tourist trade, even if a relatively small one. The Museum of Witchcraft was most likely initially established in Boscastle because of its proximity to Tintagel. Now the museum reinforces Tintagel's reputation as a mystical center. The Museum of Witchcraft has been in Boscastle since 1960, after having moved several times. Cecil Williamson, who established the museum in 1948, initially purchased the Museum's collection in the Isle of Man in the 1940s. He may have purchased some of the artifacts from Gerald Gardner, founder of modern Wicca, who was also living in the Isle of Man at the time. According to Williamson's accounts, he relocated the museum in Windsor in the early 1950s, and then claimed that representatives from the Royal family quietly paid for him to relocate somewhere far from Windsor Castle, although the current curator and owner of the Museum, Graham King admits that this cannot be verified.

It is not initially clear why Williamson chose Boscastle because there do not seem to be any particularly prominent legends associated with witches from Boscastle although there are certainly modern witches living there now. The answer may actually be quite mundane. Prior to that time, the attraction was one of several in Cornwall owned and operated by Williamson, including the Museum of Sorcery in Tintagel, which may have contained some of the collection now at Boscastle. Correspondence with Ithell Colquhoun from the late 1950s and early 1960s shows that Williamson was involved in a number of tourism enterprises, including the Museum of Smuggling, House of Cats, House of Shells, the Hangman's House and the Witches' House.[25] It may be that Boscastle's proximity to Tintagel made sense for the development of Williamson's most enduring attraction. It is clear from the signage made for the Museum of Sorcery that Williamson connected witchcraft with a legacy of Celtic magical practice in Tintagel, made famous by Merlin. The sign says 'Proof that Sorcerers are active today can be seen at The Museum of Sorcery'. Although the Museum of Sorcery in Tintagel was short lived, the Boscastle attraction has remained popular simultaneously establishing and reinforcing a legacy of witchcraft and sorcery in the North Cornwall area.

For people who believe that modern Witchcraft is a continuation of pre-Christian Celtic religion, the museum's existence in Boscastle is perfectly consistent with the esoteric interpretations of the Tintagel area that have emerged throughout this century. A 'witchy' theme now pervades the village. Paul Broadhurst's popular shops in Boscastle specializing in New Age books, incense, candles and Celtic art serve to draw together in one building the seemingly disparate yet connected threads of modern Witchcraft, Neo-Paganism, pre-Christian Celtic religion, and Arthurian legend.

Tintagel and Spiritual Tourism

Tintagel today is probably the first stop on the modern pilgrim's route in North Cornwall, followed by the Rocky Valley Mazes, St. Nectan's Kieve and the Museum of Witchcraft. A recent visitor's center is careful in its presentation of the history of the area and in integrating the Pagan viewpoint and relevance to the development of the village over the past century. This not only shows a great deal of tolerance and insight, it acknowledges the historic (and possibly also the economic) contributions of the wider esoteric community. There is certainly a good trade in Pagan and spiritual oriented merchandise, with a number of shops dealing specifically in books, accessories, and jewelry for the alternative spirituality market. The Pagan Federation regularly holds its Devon and Cornwall conference in the village or in neighboring Boscastle, and there are certainly hundreds of tours specializing in Sacred Sites, Paganism and New Age religions which feature the area as a focal point.

In the past decade, spiritual tourism in Cornwall has become more refined and more significant, despite the fact the tourism officials are rather reticent to capitalize on the market for esoteric tourism that exists. Although the comprehensive tourism strategy document written in 2001 specifically mentions the variety of Christian related tourism opportunities in Cornwall, esoteric or Pagan based tourism is completely absent from the document, despite the wide variety of independent tourism operators worldwide who offer esoteric based tourism experiences in Cornwall[26]. In fact, the Solar Eclipse of 1999 drew perhaps thousands to Cornwall for rituals and Pagan festivals, but very little of this was acknowledged in the press, and these events certainly were not promoted by the Cornish Tourist Board.

Interestingly, there was a set of esoteric, almost millennial beliefs linked with the Cornish eclipse worldwide that claimed that the time and place of this eclipse was so significant, that it would herald the second reign of King Arthur.[27] One might think that Tintagel would have been a center for eclipse activity, but it was not in the line of totality. Nevertheless, individual tour operators and tourism promoters are working to reach new niche markets, and pilgrimage and spiritual tourism is considered to be very desirable because it often attracts 'high spend' tourists.

So what do people hope to gain by coming to Tintagel today? In many ways Tintagel is a logical next stop from Glastonbury for the westward traveling pilgrim wanting to explore the mysteries of Britain. It is also a site for 'earth mysteries' enthusiasts such as Paul Broadhurst, Hamish Miller, and John Michell who claim that Tintagel is a power point situated on a ley line, which simplifies yet refines the theories of Steiner and Tudor Pole, and integrates the site into a more relevant and manageable British esoteric framework. Paul Broadhurst, who has probably written the most comprehensive work on the mystical associations of Tintagel, still argues in the same vein as Steiner that Arthur was the earthly embodiment of a Celtic solar deity, a hero priest king and the twelve segments of the Round Table represent the Zodiac demarcated onto sacred energy points in the landscape.[28] He maintains that pilgrims who visit the points can benefit from the energy there through celebrations at appropriate times of the year. At Tintagel those times would have been the summer and winter solstices, since Arthur is believed to have been a solar deity, and the solstices are the longest and shortest periods of sunlight during the year.[29] Again, this seems to be a refined and more contemporary interpretation of Tintagel's importance, one that will resonate with a variety of Pagan and earth-centered beliefs systems.

Now Tintagel castle itself seems mainly to be a place for reflection and meditation, less for ritual and offerings, which are more apparent at the neighboring sites of St. Nectan's Kieve and the Rocky Valley mazes. The primary site of ritual activity in Tintagel is probably Merlin's Cave beneath Tintagel castle. Merlin's Cave is actually a focal point for revelation and ritual, as it is supposed to be a womb like place to connect with essential feminine energies. Paul Broadhurst believes that Merlin's Cave near the castle ruins is a potent area for psychic experiences and visions. He reports having had one there himself.[30] This belief is echoed by a wide variety of tour groups that come to the area specifically to meditate and to experience inner revelation. Rituals done at Merlin's Cave often symbolically focus on the womb like aspect of the cave and often contain an element of 'rebirthing' where one emerges from a ritual or meditation as if born again.[31] Some 19th century texts place Merlin's Cave as the place where Arthur was washed up on the beach and found by Merlin, which supports more contemporary interpretations of the cave as a place of individual rebirth and transformation. This excerpt from a ritual travel diary compiled by Jim and Sherry Husfelt describes a visit to Merlin's Cave on August 10, 1999, the day before the solar eclipse in Cornwall. Here we can see the themes of the divine feminine, individual revelation and transformation :

> We were asked to enter his cave with respect. Following the footsteps of the Faery Queen, who was formerly guided by the purple serpent, we walked into the mother's womb. To my knowledge, none of us was blessed by any mythical guidance, but we each met with our own female within on a self-guided journey. The ocean and the cave worked in unison to remind us of the female power. Quietly merging with the stonewalls, the female aspect of our humanness presented herself. The flow of humans around us was like a river that pulsed to the depths of the cave, touching the rising tide and then surging back out again. As Pilgrims, we too surged out of the cave, but as we burst into the light of day, we gave birth to our female aspect. This sparkling new feeling glistened like the salt water meeting the sand, washing the tiny pebbles clean.[32]

Furthermore, tour groups which focus specifically on the Goddess or the divine feminine will often feature a visit to Merlin's Cave.[33]

Tintagel and Celtic Cornwall

One of the primary reasons that the above histories of esoteric Tintagel fit together is because they are implicitly, not explicitly, acceptable as 'Celtic' phenomena today. Despite what the academic criteria for 'authentic' cultural and historical Celticity may be[34], a wide range of phenomena embraced by esoteric practitioners worldwide are believed to be the survivals of an ancient Celtic spiritual inheritance. Although this has not always been explicit in the history of esoteric Tintagel, it is certainly the semantic thread that holds it together today. 'Celtic spirituality' is an umbrella phrase that can embrace a wide range of spiritual activity that practitioners associate with a real or imagined 'Celtic' past.[35] It can include such diverse groups as Neo-Druids, Wiccans, Celtic shamans, New Agers, New Age Travellers, Goddess worshippers, New Age Christians, and Pagan eco-warriors.

Although Arthur's Celtic credentials should be clear, some of the other constructions of Celtic Tintagel may not be as evident. A core belief of contemporary Celtic spirituality is the belief that the Celts were unusually close to the earth. This belief alone encompasses a variety of popular suppositions about pre Christian and early Celtic culture, including the belief that because the Celts were supposedly nature oriented that they were also a Goddess worshipping culture. Although Celtic cultures certainly did have Goddesses, they were not primarily Goddess-focused. Ironically, although Steiner originally touted Tintagel castle as the site of a solar God community, the same site today is most visited as a place where one can connect with divine feminine energies in Merlin's Cave. The Goddess associations of the Tintagel area are also supported by the nearby Rocky Valley mazes, which are believed to be survivals from a Goddess focused Celtic culture. Cheryl Straffon, a leading writer about sacred Goddess sites in Cornwall writes of them 'Mazes are a very potent example of a special spirit of place and they have traditionally been used as passageways into the meaning of the Goddess, leading the seeker deeper into the mysteries of the self.'[36]

Ley line and 'power site' theories are also important to practitioners of contemporary Celtic spirituality because they emphasize the perceived relationship between ancient people of Britain, particularly the Celts and the landscape of Britain, as well as the theory that Britain itself is actually alive and imbued with divine 'energy.' According to John Michell, who repopularized Watkins ley line theories in the 1960s with a New Age spin, the Druids worked a complex form of earth magic with this energy, which is most highly concentrated at sacred sites such as holy wells, and megalithic monuments. This is clearly consistent with the picture of Tintagel as an inherently holy place promoted by both Steiner and Tudor Pole. Michell claimed that Druids developed these magical techniques in systems involving tree and nature worship and divination.[37]

Likewise, modern witchcraft also fits neatly under the Celtic umbrella, as part of the religious narrative of Wicca is that it represents a number of religious survivals from pre-Christian Celtic religion.[38] As a result, although the Museum of Witchcraft may have been initially located in Boscastle out of convenience, today its proximity to Tintagel reinforces the area's overall association with an imagined Celtic religious inheritance. Again, Cornwall is an appropriate location for such an attraction. Not only is Cornwall a Celtic territory, within Britain it is considered to be a place that is slightly backward, unusually superstitious, and a place where there may still be people practicing the 'old ways'.[39] Indeed, folk collector Robert Hunt believed that superstition was a function of Cornwall's Celticity. That the Cornish were Celtic accounted for their 'backwardness' and superstitious nature, both of which made their folklore inherently more worthy of study:

> I have possessed the best possible opportunities for gathering up the folk-lore of a people, who, but a few generations since, had a language peculiarly their own,—a people who, like all the Celts, cling with sincere affection to the memories of the past, and who even now regard with jealously the introduction of any novelty and accept improvements slowly.[40]

Although the Museum itself does not have a variety of artifacts from actual Cornish folk practice, thematically it is suited to the ways in which Cornwall has been constructed as a Celtic territory.

Conclusion

Although the development of Tintagel as one of Britain's foremost sacred sites has rested on the sites' association with Arthurian legend, the way in which it functions for pilgrims, and the way in which that site's inherent sacredness has been interpreted has often been resultant on wider trends in

British esoteric thought. Currently its association as a site for Celtic spirituality allows for a variety of activity and belief, which is nevertheless perceived by visitors as coherent within a Celtic framework. As a result, Tintagel can stay relevant as a sacred site, even though the ghosts of former beliefs and theories are still present in the cultural landscape.

Notes

1 Cornwall County Council, *Cornwall Heritage and Culture Strategy* (Truro: Cornwall County Council, 2000).

2 John Lowerson, 'Celtic Tourism: Some Recent Magnets' in *Cornish Studies: Two* ed. by P. Payton (Exeter: University of Exeter Press, 1994), 131.

3 *Ibid.*

4 Amy Hale, 'Whose Celtic Cornwall: the ethnic Cornish vs. Celtic spirituality' in *Celtic Geographies,* ed. by Harvey, Jones, McEnroy, and Milligan (London: Routledge, 2002).

5 Geoffrey of Monmouth, *The History of the Kings of Britain,* trans. by Lewis Thorpe (London: Penguin Books, 1966) 207.

6 *Ibid,* 28

7 *Ibid,* 207

8 Charles Thomas, *Tintagel: Arthur and Archaeology* (London: B.T. Batsford Ltd 1993), 24.

9 *Ibid,* 87.

10 *Ibid.*

11 *Ibid.* 18

12 Piers Brendon, *Hawker of Morwenstow* (London: Anthony Mott, Ltd. 1975).

13 Paul Broadhurst. *Tintagel and the Arthurian Mythos* (Launceston, Cornwall: Pendragon Press, 1995) 31.

11 A.C. Canner, *The Parish of Tintagel: Some Historical Notes* (Middlesex: Friary Clark Ltd. 1982), 79.

15 Rudolph Steiner, *Karmic Relationships, Esoteric Studies Volume VIII* (London: Rudolph Steiner Press 1975, 1924), 31-45.

16 Rudolph Steiner, *Foundations of Esotericism* (London: Rudolph Steiner Press, 1983, 1905), 234-5.

17 Wellesley Tudor Pole, 'Preparing the way for the New Age' in ed. by anon. *Michael Prince of Heaven: Captain of the Angelic Hosts* (London: J.M. Watkins, 1951), 29.

18 Wellesley Tudor Pole, 'The Archangel Michael: leader of the angelic hosts of heaven' in ed. by anon. *Michael Prince of Heaven: Captain of the Angelic Hosts* (London: J.M. Watkins, 1951) 9-13.

19 Ithell Colquhoun, *The Living Stones* (London: Peter Owen Limited, 1957) 186-195.

20 Broadhurst, *Tintagel*, 157.

21 'Comment' *Western Morning News*, 10 June, 1933.

22 Don Hutchinson, *One Man's Dream: The Story of King Arthur's Great Halls* (Tintagel: Sword in the Stone Publishing, 1999).

23 Christine Poulson, *The Quest for the Grail: Arthurian Legend in British Art 1840-1920* (Manchester: Manchester University Press, 1999) 135.

24 Anon. 'By Laws of the Lodge of the Holy Grail #5' n.d.

25 Letter from Cecil Williamson to Ithell Colquhoun, 6 October, 1963.

26 The Objective One Partnership. *Objective One Tourism Proposal*, (Truro: Objective One Partnership 2001) 19.

27 Joseph E. Mason, 'Solar Eclipse 1999-Final Quest for the Holy Grail' <www.greatdreams.com/eclipse.htm> [accessed 15 October, 2003]

28 Broadhurst, *Tintagel*, 96

29 *Ibid*.

30 *Ibid*, 150

31 For examples see Ron Baker and Robert Baker ' Journey to Mystical England' <http://childrenoflight.com/england.htm.> [accessed 15 October, 2003] and SacredSites Tours <http://www.vibrational.com/sacredsites.htm> [accessed 15 October, 2003].

32 Jim Husfelt 'The Myth of the Sacred Millennial Journey of the Archangel Mikael (Michael), The Holy Grail and the Marriage of the Sun and Moon: the Total Solar Eclipse' (1999) <http://www.divinehumanity.com/media/The%20Myth%20of%20the%20Sacred%20Millennial%20Journey.htm > [accessed 1 December, 2003].

30 For examples of women centered and Goddess tourism at Merlin's Cave see The Spiritual Sanctuary website <http://www.spiritualsanctuary.com/england_pilgrimage.htm> [accessed 1 December, 2003], Soluna Tours <http://www.solunatours.com/wst-eng301.htm> [accessed 1 December, 2003], and Purple Mountain Tours <http://www.purplemountaintours.com/avalon.htm> [accessed 1 December 2003].

34 For a survey of these arguments see Amy Hale and Philip Payton 'Introduction' in *New Directions in Celtic Studies* ed. by Amy Hale and Philip Payton (Exeter: University of Exeter Press 2000) 1-14.

35 Marion Bowman, 'Celtic spirituality' in *New Directions in Celtic Studies* ed. by Amy Hale and Philip Payton (Exeter: University of Exeter Press 2000), 69-91.

36 Cheryl Straffon, *Pagan Cornwall: Land of the Goddess* (St. Just: Meyn Mamvro Publications, 1993) 44.

37 John Michell, *The New View Over Atlantis* (London: Thames and Hudson, 1995) 80.

38 For details on the role of the imagined Celtic past in Paganism and Wicca, see Hutton, Ronald. *Triumph of the Moon* (Oxford: Oxford University Press, 1999) also Bowman 'Celtic spirituality', 79.

39 The Cornwall Tourist Board website suggests that folk beliefs and practices in Cornwall not only still exist, but that some have been practiced continuously since the Bronze Age. For an example see <http://www.cornwalltouristboard.co.uk/heritage> [accessed 1 December, 2003].

40 Robert Hunt, *Popular Romances of the West of England: The Drolls, Traditions and Superstitions of Old Cornwall* (Lampeter, Wales: Llanerch Press, 1995, 1865), 23.

Trafficking with an 'onslaught of compulsive weirdness': [1]

Kenneth Grant and the Magickal revival
Dave Evans

The British occultist G. Kenneth Grant (1924-) has been variously applauded **"It's hard to name another single living individual who has done more to shape contemporary western thinking with regard to Magic"** [2] - and slated, with his sanity doubted: **"a schoolboy gone berserk on brimstone aftershave"** [3] - throughout his 50 year literary and magickal career. This article will briefly outline his early influences; literary output, examine some seeming factual and historical anomalies within his narrative and describe some of the broad influences that he has had on modern magic.

Grant had read very widely on occultism and Eastern philosophy by his early teens [4], and had been using his own personal magical symbol inspired by a powerful dream vision, since 1939 [5]. Since it was wartime, Grant volunteered for the army at 18, expecting to be **"sent to India where I had hopes of finding a guru"** [6]; which as Moore remarks, shows **"a grasp upon conventional worldly reality that was at best precarious"** [7]. However Grant developed an unspecified medical condition and was invalided out of the service aged 20.

Continuing his magical studies, Grant tried to meet the ageing magician Aleister Crowley by writing to Crowley's publishers, fruitlessly, as it turned out, as the address he took from the flyleaf of a book was a decade out of date. When Grant discovered London's *Atlantis Bookshop* he tried to gain an audience with Crowley through *Atlantis'* proprietor, Michael Houghton, who knew Crowley. Houghton refused to help (privately writing that Grant was **"mentally unstable"** [8]). Grant considered it to be because Houghton did not want to **"incur evil *karma*"** [9] from linking him to Crowley, but later modified this to a more pragmatic notion that **"Houghton had earmarked me for his own organization, *The Order of Hidden Masters*"** [10] and was thus trying to divert him from Crowley's influence, despite the apparent paradox of Houghton selling Grant numerous expensive Crowley books in the meantime.

Grant wrote instead to the publishers' addresses in these newer Crowley books and eventually his mail was forwarded. Grant and Crowley later met in the autumn of 1944, [11] and after several amicable meetings and a further exchange of letters Grant offered to work for Crowley as secretary-cum-personal assistant, in return for magickal instruction in *lieu* of pay. Crowley agreed, and in the early spring of 1945 Grant moved into in a lodge cottage in the grounds of *Netherwood*, the boarding house in Sussex where Crowley was then resident.

Crowley had an ambivalent relationship with Houghton and warned Grant (far too late, as it transpired) **"don't let *Atlantis* know you know me"** [12]. Grant busied himself working with and for Crowley for some months, dealing with Crowley's correspondence and daily needs, reading voraciously from Crowley's own library and magickal record, running errands to London, writing occult essays, performing rituals including ether-magnified magical path workings with Crowley [13] and becoming a high initiate of Crowley's magical order, the *Ordo Templi Orientis*, with Crowley writing in his diary: **"value of Grant. If I die or go to the USA, there must be a trained man to take care of the English OTO"** [14].

However Grant left *Netherwood* in June 1945 [15], after only a few months with Crowley, due to familial pressure to take on a 'proper' job [16]. In the face of this problem the financially bankrupt Crowley, by then reliant on supporters' donations to survive was unable to canvas sufficient funds to make Grant's position salaried. Crowley later wrote to Grant's father **"I am very sorry to part with Kenneth…I feel … that he is giving up his real future"** [17].

However the hard taskmaster Crowley had criticised Grant's secretarial failings regularly: **"it's all very unsatisfactory. You *must* put a sock in it if you still want to work with me for the Order"** [18]. Crowley also found Grant's verbosity and general flights of imagination **"a terrible defect in your outlook on life; you cannot be content with the simplicity of reality and fact; you have to go off into a pipe-dream"** [19]. However after Grant had left his employ, Crowley moderated this, in a letter to another OTO member, David Curwen: **"I feel that I may have treated him too severely"** [20].

Although Grant continued to correspond with, and support Crowley he never saw him again. Since much stock could be placed on Grant being a pupil of Crowley, it should be emphasised that their face-to-face association was not long, only a matter of months and thus although now regarded as an authority on Crowley he did not have a lengthy apprenticeship 'at the feet of the master', so to speak. Crowley died in 1947 and Grant attended his funeral.

In his *Ninth Arch*, published in 2003, Grant claims a biological relationship to Crowley: early in their relationship Aleister Crowley asked him **"it's a large clan, I know; but do you know Gregor Fergus Grant… my cousin?"** [21]. In Grant's book where this remark is published, from 1991, Grant does not footnote this with any commentary at all, let alone in the affirmative, which seems odd when 12 years later he claimed *distinct and long-term knowledge* of such a familial relationship. Gregor Grant is mentioned several times in various of Crowley's own volumes which were either jointly or solely posthumously re-edited for publication by Kenneth

Grant [22], but again no editor references are made there as to any familial link. It is indeed a large Clan: given the common nature of the surname Grant, any genealogical research to verify this claim would be pointless without considerable further information such as given names, birth dates and places.

This claimed link is through one Dr Phineas Marsh Black, a fictitious character in one of Grant's 'novels' (although confusingly the same novel is *dedicated to Phineas*) - both Grant's great-uncle [23] and a cousin of Gregor Grant, which would provide a very distanced familial, if not specifically *genetic*, link from Kenneth Grant to Crowley. Dr Black was allegedly a competitor with Crowley to find a particular ancient magic book, *The Grimoire of Clan Grant* [24], this being a record allegedly created over generations of the Grant Clan having magical traffic with otherworldly entities. Grant gives various details of Black in *Against the Light*, including a lifespan (1854-1957) and names one of Blacks' publications, as a medical doctor, which book has to date been untraceable [25]. This *Grimoire*, Phineas Marsh, Phineas Black or Phineas Marsh Black all fail to merit any mention in the index of Crowley's autobiography, *The Confessions* [26], which seems unusual given the 900-plus pages of very detailed autobiographical information given by Crowley therein, which covers often very brief and whimsical acquaintances and which would be expected to mention other prominent occultists with whom he ad any significant dealings, especially given Crowley's often vicious wit in criticising others in his field.

However a potential confounding factor might be that *this autobiography is a book edited by Kenneth Grant, and indexed by his wife Steffi Grant*, so there would have been ample opportunity to delete references to Black or the *Grimoire* if they wished to keep the matter secret for whatever purpose. However, neither does Phineas Marsh Black (or permutations thereof) nor the *Grant Grimoire* merit a mention in the indices of *seven major biographies of Crowley* [27] which predated publication of *The Ninth Arch*, and with which Kenneth Grant was *not* connected as editor. This would seem unusual if Phineas did indeed exist as an eminent occult researcher in contact with Crowley.

Perhaps more conclusively, none of the terms Phineas Black, Phineas Marsh Black or *The Grant Grimoire* appears in the index of <u>any</u> of Kenneth Grant's <u>own</u> books prior to 2003's *Ninth Arch,* which would seem unusual given the alleged vital importance of Phineas and the *Grimoire* throughout Grant's life.

Grant's life however did intersect with a very real and documented person after Crowley's death. There is not scope here to provide a full biographical background of Austin Osman Spare (1886-1956), instead the reader is directed to Grant's own masterwork *Zos Speaks* [28]. However, in brief, Spare was a much-feted artistic child prodigy, later a member of one of Crowley's magickal orders for a short time and the author of several books on art and magic, plus an arts magazine editor. Steffi Grant said she sought out Spare in 1949 and shortly afterwards introduced Kenneth to him [29]. By that time Spare was living a fairly Spartan existence in South London, having published no books for decades and living in virtual obscurity, eking out a living as a jobbing artist, sometime art tutor and quietly practicing and developing his method of visual, symbolic (sigilic) magic that was extremely innovative.

There are many problems with the easy academic or magical interpretation of Spare, in that he was, by today's standards, probably dyslexic [30] and **"Spare just invented, amalgamated or altered words to suit his meaning"** [31] : examples include **"there is a word precention meaning 'anticipated perception' or I've imagined it!"** [32], (he imagined it) and **"stectatorially"** [33].

To compound the problems of interpretation **"sometimes his spelling was very odd... Kenneth made a lot of tactful enquiries about the meaning"** [34] and he had **"cryptic handwriting"** [35]. Either or both of these factors make Grant's minute, lengthy and often cabbalistic interpretations of Spare's writings *potentially* fraught with error; such as investing them with arcane esoteric meanings that are perhaps simply not there. Elsewhere Grant's crucial misreading of a letter during his researches into Jack Parsons (an American occultist connected with Crowley) led to possibly similar problems [36]. Artist and Occultist Jan Fries believes that

"Spare's writings, and Grant's presentation of them, have been too cryptic for a mass audience. Numerous individuals and organisations have confused the basic simplicity of the method..." [37] and Matt Lee sees Spare's works as perhaps "artificially assimilated by Grant, to a particular, linear magical current, when they are more fluid than this should allow" [38]. Spare himself seems to have had some reservations about Grant's writings on occasion: "I think you are a trifle ambiguous for the ordinary reader" [39].

To further cloud the matter, Spare had recollections that "cannot be fully trusted...due to vagaries of memory" [40] for example his first book *Earth: Inferno* was privately printed as a run of 265 copies which took over a decade to find buyers for all copies, but he later recalled it as '500 that sold out immediately' [41] This seems to have been a lifelong problem: he failed his formal art examinations as a youth because "he could never remember technical terms for parts of the body" [42], and later in life he had problems reprising some of his unpublished textual works lost in the wartime bombing of his house, about which he lamented his "loss of memory (from the bombing injuries and general shock) and lousy normal memory" [43]. Even almost at the end of Spare's life, after 6 years of dealing with his handwritten papers intended for a book, Grant was still having troubles transcribing the words into typed text: "little of this last batch is intelligible to me" [44].

Even when Grant was confident that he did understand Spare, he was on occasion wrong: in early 1955, when he had been working with Spare's writing for five years, he wrote to Spare with horror at his discovery that he had made a continual transcription error, misreading "predicate" (a word Spare used a lot) for "predict", thus substantially changing meaning [45]. Spare's response that "I get mixed up with 'per' and 'pre'" [46] failed to make any sense of the matter, since *both* words begin with 'pre'.

Additionally, in many accounts of time spent with the Grants (and others) late in life there is a distinct feeling of Spare as an old man, almost exclusively inhabiting a bar-room environment, with the alcohol-based culture that implies ("a relentless round" of drinking as Steffi Grant recalled it [47], and this was despite the hedonistic Crowley's lifestyle warning to Kenneth about alcohol of a few years before **"Drink: at your age, the less the better"** [48]). Perhaps Spare was toying with young and possibly over-earnest acolytes, seeing how far his raconteur's act would go before any tall tales were 'found out'. As he said to his dear friend Frank Letchford, as a general philosophy: **"if you are going to tell a lie, tell a big one for it is more likely to be believed!"** [49] . There may not have been any particular malice implicit, it seemingly being done for his own plain amusement, perhaps to bring some interest to an immediately post-War austere lifestyle and/or simply providing entertainment which might justify the price of another drink. There was certainly stimulation to weave a good yarn: his narratives **"became more elaborate <u>with Kenneth's unfailing encouragement</u>… and the lateness of the hour, cosy pub, convivial company and the agreeable vapours of alcohol and tobacco"** [50] , with Letchford believing that Spare often told **"white lies…to boost a flagging ego"** [51] . So far as the shade of the lies is concerned, Spare variously had told Letchford that during World War One he had once been stuck in a pile of corpses in 'no man's land' between the opposing armies' trenches, had contracted malaria in West Africa, and was aboard a troopship that was torpedoed. Much later Letchford checked Spare's war record and found all of these tales to be complete falsehoods [52] .

Yet despite all the public bar verbosity, Spare said he found **"pleasure in destroying words… reducing a concept to its most simple verbal form"** [53] . Grant, by comparison, does the opposite in his general writing, making almost an art-form of complexity and learned ideas, an example being **"This symbolism, although apparently complex, is simple, as may be seen by equating it with the well-known Buddhist formula: First there IS (i.e. *Malkuth*)- Form (i.e. presence of Object). Then there is NOT (i.e. *Kether*) – Void (i.e. presence of Subject). Then there IS (i.e. *Ain*)- Neither Form nor Void, but absence of the presence of both Object and Subject (i.e. the Absolute Absence, or Void)."** [54] Crowley had also apparently earlier twice rebuked him for verbosity and other related faults in his use of language: **"I wanted an** answer, not a sermon!"** [55], and **"you must learn to be systematic & accurate and unambiguous"** [56].

Perhaps this is learned behaviour: Grant's mentor Crowley was not shy of codifying and making matters obscure: **"The verses of... several... of the Holy Books of Thelema are numbered from nought (the** *ain* [57] or zero) **instead of from one"** [58] so that a verse numbered four is *sometimes but not always* actually the fifth; for example. Then later, when Aleister Crowley might refer back, perhaps to 'the fourth verse' of that piece of writing, one is often not sure which verse he means.

As well as being a very creative performer with his anecdotes, the financially-straitened Spare was **"streetwise"** with his money, with an eye for a bargain and likely sources of income well before he met Grant [59], and he was not averse to subtly pitting Grant against other potential buyers in order to manifest quicker sales of his artworks [60]. He also became aware that very cheap bric-a-brac items (such as pseudo-ethnic carvings) that he purchased from flea markets as content or background for the scenes of his pictures then became very saleable in themselves once the picture was completed, for being 'one of his models'. Although dyslexics sometimes also have genuine cognitive problems with numbering, Spare also *deliberately* and fraudulently mis-dated some artworks for sale; two contemporary and just-completed sketches were signed and dated many years apart to suit the intended buyer who was keen to acquire 'Spare originals from different artistic periods' in one fell swoop and at a seemingly favourable price [61].

There is also plausible speculation that Spare's 'Zen-like' detachment from material life in middle-age, so lauded by some of his *post-mortem* admirers as a sign of his holiness and magickal commitment to a higher plane, may have instead been a necessary and expedient withdrawal from artistic society and the up-market art publication scene. This is believed by Naylor to be due to rumours of extensive plagiarism and fraud (which appear now to be accurate), which may have prevented many other artists and editors from ever risking their reputations by working with him again on any publication projects. Naylor believes that this also casts doubt on the veracity of Spare's claimed 'psychic automatic' drawings, and mentions that some of his illustrations as an official war artist (during and just after World War One) were banned since some scenes he depicted were either highly inaccurate or completely fake [62]. In any case, Spare's subsequent choice of home, in poverty-stricken South London was from **"force of circumstances, lack of cash"** and a wish not to be disturbed [63] rather than any 'class-conscious' act or spiritual retreat from Bohemian 'arty' London.

One particular aspect of 'Spare's world according to Grant' is found severely lacking under scrutiny; Spare's relationship with a 'Mrs Patterson', who supposedly taught him a hereditary form of witchcraft, but about whom no independent information can be found. In 1975 Grant wrote that Spare **"was extremely reticent about Mrs. Paterson. All that I was able to elicit from him during the eight years of friendship was that she was very old when he met her and that she claimed descent from a line of Salem (New England) witches that Cotton Mather had failed to eradicate"** [64]. Despite this apparent dearth of information, in subsequent books Grant has written a considerable amount about Mrs Patterson, investing her with particular magical abilities and heritage in great detail, which in light of his comment does not seem to have come from Spare (and Patterson was an old woman in Spare's early life, so would have been long dead by the time Grant first met Spare). In addition, the veracity of those tried at Salem in the 17th Century being any kind of 'witches' - in the modern understanding of the word as someone with 'real magical powers'- has been largely discredited.

In a challenging article, Cantu demonstrates how this initially scant information on Patterson has been drip-fed over several decades by Grant, often when convenient to him, as confirmatory 'evidence' of his own published magickal theories, and that very little independent information about Patterson survives [65]. Often when writers quote Spare **"by his own account…(of) Mrs Patterson"** [66] they are actually reliant on the accuracy and honesty of Grant's account of something Spare may or may not have said, either in exactly the words given, *or at all*. Equally, much of the seemingly Grant-corroborative information from Spare's old friend and financier Frank Letchford is corroborative simply because it derives from Grant's accounts, rather than being a confirmatory remark heard direct from Spare [67], since

Letchford wrote only that **"Austin mentioned the woman in vague terms to myself"** [68]. Letchford was an avid reader and was certainly aware of Grant's later writings about Spare in general [69]. It seems unusual that Mrs. Patterson, who was *supposedly, according to Grant,* so very influential in Spare's life would not have been a major topic of conversation between Spare and such a dear friend as Letchford, given the latter's interest in spiritual matters.

Grant has said that Spare said very little about Patterson, however there is a lot of ill-provenanced detail about her in Grant's books. If Grant's remark is *not* true then there is an alternative possibility, that Spare was spinning a special yarn to Grant that was particularly tailored to Grant's occult interests. This is not without precedent. To others **"Austin liked to believe (without much foundation) that he was descended from an illegitimate son born to Lord Nelson and Lady Hamilton… objects belonging to the Admiral were sold by Spare when he was in financial stress (a fairly frequent state)"** [70]. This seems to be both a flight of fancy and a useful way to earn money from the credulous by profitably recycling various 'naval' artifacts that Spare probably picked up cheaply from London bric-a-brac shops. Given Grant's overwhelming occult fascination, what better way to keep him interested than to claim to have had a powerful witch-figure as a childhood mentor, a character perhaps nominally based on a local fortune-teller recalled from Spare's youth, but whose magical attributes and abilities were considerably 'beefed-up' in the repetitive re-telling?

Perhaps equally surprising, given that they were two such close and contemporary associates of Spare, Grant and Frank Letchford first met at a hospital; only shortly before the seriously ill and by then mostly unconscious Spare died in 1956, so there was never scope for a 3-way confirmatory conversation about Patterson, magic or anything else [71]. Whatever the source, this gradual accretion of 'facts' onto the name of Mrs. Patterson reached such a point that Grant's emerging and expanding mythos of 'Patterson the great witch' was taken up by others who created a probably spurious link between her to an extant coven of modern witches, and this 'news' was breathlessly ushered back into Grant's writings as independent supporting evidence of his own beliefs about Patterson the Witch [72], when it may instead merely be an evolving and distorted 'Chinese Whisper' that had finally returned to its progenitor, or at least, publisher. Since Grant and Letchford, two of Spare's closest confidantes, have both written on occasion that Spare didn't speak much about Mrs. Patterson, then if these comments are both true the main source of 'information' about her seems to be Grant himself, who never met her. An alternative is that Grant was prey to Spare's possibly bar-room fuelled elaborate recreation of Patterson and that much of his subsequent mythologising of her, by repeating some tall stories of Spare's, and incorporating these into his own system has distorted his own magical writings considerably.

In any case some kind of recognisable witchcraft element to Spare's work may be totally spurious: **"since the publication ...of** *Zos Speaks!* **the fallacy of subsuming Spare the magician within some 'tradition' becomes clear; look at the texts - where is the witchcraft, exactly? Even the text of** (Spare's book) *'Witches' Sabbath'* **refers explicitly to** *'Ehr'* **...** *Lao Tzu,* **the Taoist sage"** [73].

Letchford, a mystically-interested writer, bibliophile and appreciator of art rather than outright practicing occultist, gave a different, somewhat more rounded view of Spare than others, being **"especially keen to communicate his** (Spare's) **humanism, often lost on somberly-garbed seekers after sigillic mysteries"** [74], similarly Semple's book *Zos Kia* attempted to **"reconcile the rather austere yet joyful... mystical philosophy we find in** *The Book of Pleasure* **with the image of the skulduggerous sorcerer which emerges in the works of Kenneth Grant."** [75]. This view has considerable plausibility, since Spare did not know what the *Qliphoth* was in 1955 [76], this being a technical Cabbalistic term, and one <u>absolutely central</u> to the dark magickal work that Grant was engaged in with his *Typhonian OTO* in the same year and onwards to the present. Such a knowledge gap for a member of Grant's Order would perhaps be of the same magnitude to a practicing Christian not knowing anything about Judas.

An additional temporal problem with Grant's adoption of Spare as another magickal mentor is his claim to have co-founded the magickal group the

Zos Kia Cultus with Spare, based on Spare's methods, in 1948 [77], when Grant's own published correspondence indicates he did not actually meet Spare until 1949 [78].

The final thing to remember about Grant's work with Spare is that it was *never finished*, Spare had been variably in poor health for some years, but was taken very suddenly seriously ill and died in a very short space of time, so his remaining notes were only partial at the time of his death [79], and Grant has had the metaphorical task of reconstructing a jigsaw without benefit of a full picture as a guideline. This might explain why he took nearly 20 years to produce his first major book about Spare and over 40 years to produce the second.

All of these factors imply that the enigmatic Spare was cryptically hard to understand, often a sharp businessman under the guise of a mystic (and probably *vice-versa*) and suffered several problems with his memory. He was shrewd to the point of creating some very tall tales, often within an alcohol-fuelled culture, and Grant's work with him was unfinished, yet considerably 'varnished' (and perhaps manipulated to fit a *Typhonian* Magickal schema which might have been inappropriate) so far as accuracy, selectivity and honesty of reporting when it was published. Thus without denying their magical veracity, any all-encompassing view of both Grant's and Spare's works must include these considerations as a major *caveat*.

Perhaps oddly, despite Grant's major role and truly Herculean effort in preserving and then promoting Austin Spare materials and methods; and the efficacy with which he regards them in his own practice, his magickal order the *Typhonian OTO* do not currently formally incorporate any Austin Spare techniques into their teachings or ritual work [80].

Publications "these aren't just books about Magick; these books are Magick" [81]

After Crowley and then Spare had died, Grant began in earnest on his major writing work. He had exclusive access to Spare's unpublished written works, having been bequeathed them in Spare's will, and his remit to use Crowley's unpublished and published archive was all but unchecked since

Grant worked directly with Crowley's literary executors on editing and reproducing several of the Beast's major books. He also wrote his own pieces for publication, and apart from miscellaneous articles and essays this currently extends to over a dozen, usually hefty books. Bogdan sees him as **"perhaps (the) most original and prolific English author of the post-modern occultist genre"** [82].

Grant's occult publications are as follows: *The Carfax Monographs*, a limited print run of only sets of 100 illustrated articles published in a series of ten installments between 1959 and 1963. These were reprinted in one slim volume as *Hidden Lore* in 1989.

The Magical Revival (1972, reprinted 1991) was Grant's first mainstream occult book to be published in an appreciable number of copies, and was the first volume of the nine *Typhonian Trilogies*. As well as the historical slant to the title and content, *Magical Revival* can also be seen as a manifesto for the future of magick, encouraging interested parties to become involved.

Aleister Crowley and the Hidden God followed in 1973 (reprinted 1992), being volume 2 of the *Typhonian Trilogies*. It deals with the sex-magickal system of Crowley (much of it previously unpublished), Tantra and some of the methods within the *Typhonian* OTO.

Images and Oracles of Austin Osman Spare (1975) was a groundbreaking collection of the art and writings of Spare, the result of almost 20 years' work by Grant. It was not a rapid or high selling title initially, being remaindered [83] before becoming a very sought-after volume, with scarce copies later consistently selling on the second-hand market for very many times the original cover price. A long-awaited 2003 reprint of the work seemed destined for the same *kudos* only weeks after publication.

Cults of the Shadow (1975, reprinted 1994), was *Typhonian Trilogies* volume 3. The First trilogy ended with Grant providing details of, and his theories of the linkages between Left-Hand path magical cults (both those currently in existence, and historical) and his own practices. These included Crowley and Spare's work, Voodoo cults and Eastern Tantric groups.

Nightside of Eden (1977, reprinted 1994) was *Typhonian Trilogies* volume 4: Part One of the book discusses various dense magickal formulae in Grant's (by now usual) complex and gnomic manner, including detailed cabbalistic exegesis. Part Two details the numerous branches of *The Tunnels Of Set*, a dark and dangerous magickal realm explored by Grant using the formulae examined in Part One. Reaction was mixed, and polarized; readers either hated it, Suster deriding him as **"ignorant... perverted ... *Tunnels of Set* ? Sewers of shit... those who accept Grant's statements ... are eating his used lavatory paper"** [84], or loved him: believing that in general Grant in the 1970s was **"practically alone in offering new contributions to the literature of magick"** [85].

Outside the Circles of Time (1980) was *Typhonian Trilogies* volume 5; covering similar materials as before, with the addition of a discussion of 'Ufology' with relation to occultism, some autobiographical information, and a great deal about insectoid symbolism, which prompted one critic to highlight a plausible belief held in some quarters that as well as him being actually insane, there are errors of fact: Grant **"went totally loopy... it's biologically incorrect some of the things he says about honey bees"** [86]. The same critic who lauded him for his huge contribution during the 1970s wrote **"while he gets high marks for originality, his manner of exegesis is difficult for the beginner, and his later books are progressively bizarre"** [87]. Another, anonymous, reviewer remarks, **"while parts are inaccurate in the strict historical sense, it remains a valuable source"** [88].

Grant then either lost or had completed his publication contract with Muller and no new material by him appeared in book form for eleven years, until 1991's *Remembering Aleister Crowley*, a thin and rather expensive volume of diary entries, correspondence, photographs and general memoirs of Grant's short time with Crowley. His new publisher, *Skoob*, reissued several of his previous volumes in the early 1990s, and *The Trilogies* resumed with *Hecate's Fountain* in 1992 (*Typhonian Trilogies* volume 6). In this book Grant gives many anecdotes of the workings of the New Isis Lodge, with the preliminary comment that: **"It would seem that almost all successful magick manifests as a ricochet, a sidekick to group ceremonies...**

or to isolated magickal workings. I call this peculiarity a *tangential tantrum*" [89]. He then devotes much of the book to the various magickal accidents, including insanity and many deaths, believed to be directly as a consequence of ritual work, that his group encountered. On occasion these deaths were due to seemingly very bizarre circumstances, with evoked alien entities being culpable. Quite how these deaths, illnesses and injuries can be viewed as successes is debatable. Before an extremely hostile review of the book draws to a close, Suster castigated the body count and injury list as being the results of **"crass magical incompetence"**, for which he says Grant seems almost proud [90].

Outer Gateways (1994) continued the *Typhonian Trilogies*, being volume 7. Part One of the book covers Grant's theories regarding the older prehistory of *Typhonian* traditions from around the world, with relation to Crowley, Spare and the works of HP Lovecraft and the book concludes with the entire text of, and a lengthy analysis of a clairvoyantly-received text, *The Wisdom of S'lba*.

Against the Light: A Nightside Narrative (1997) is a novel, involving one 'Kenneth Grant' as a character. There is a major emergent academic problem that is highlighted at this point in reading any of Grant's *supposedly* fictional work as pure fiction, since elsewhere he makes comments about this book being both **"quasi-autobiographical"** [91] and a **"magical biography"** [92]. This implies strongly that many of the events in the 'novel' actually happened, although Grant does not specify which events come under this heading. With this book Grant changed publishers again to *Starfire*, the *Typhonian OTO's* own imprint, where he remains, apart from the following for *Fulgur* Ltd, a specialist publisher on Austin Spare matters.

Zos Speaks! Encounters with Austin Osman Spare (co-authored with Steffi Grant, 1998), was a weighty and presumably comprehensive collection of 7 years' worth of chronological diary entries and correspondence (from 1949 to Spare's death in 1956), photographs, illustrations and Grant's reconstruction of Spare's magical techniques and philosophical aphorisms.

Beyond the Mauve Zone (1999) was *Typhonian Trilogies* volume 8. The Mauve Zone is a magickal realm which Grant claims to have explored, and believes to be a place accessed by all manner of mystics, mages and artists over the ages; many of which he discusses in detail. He does this by now familiar blend of cabbalistic permutations and with repetitive reference to 'the usual suspects', Spare, Lovecraft and Crowley; plus some contemporary occultists from around the world who had contacted him in previous years to compare notes.

Snakewand and the Darker Strain (2000) was two stories in one volume, describing African sorceries, voodoo and the like. It is not clear whether any elements of these stories are partly autobiographical.

The Ninth Arch (2003) was *Typhonian Trilogies* volume 9, and final volume in the three trilogies. It comprises more of Grant's continued convoluted cabbalistic interpretations and musings on Crowley, Spare, Lovecraft *et al* and then a lengthy verse-by-verse analysis of some more material, called the *Book of the Spider*, received by mediumistic methods from the era of the New Isis magickal group; similar to the format of *The Wisdom of S'lba* in *Outer Gateways* (above).

Gamaliel and Dance, Doll, Dance! (2003) was his most recent product, and another example of Grant's 'fiction', being two supposedly fictional stories in one volume, one tale of a vampire and one about a Tantric sexual group. Again, it is not clear whether any elements of these stories are partly autobiographical.

Despite this wealth of titles, and his editorial work on Crowley re-issues, publishing life has not been all plain sailing for Grant, however. After often slow sales in the earlier years and some temporary remaindering of titles in bookshops Grant's works are now all much sought-after and of considerable resale/collector value, and one of his staunchest critics concedes that all of Grant's books are **"graced by artwork of the utmost distinction"** [93] and beautifully presented, a lesson learned probably from Crowley's consummately high publication standards [94]. The mere thought of a *paperback* mass-market standard Kenneth Grant volume would be anathema.

Despite the several lengthy gaps between books (and in some cases between publishers) this amounts to a considerable and detailed *corpus*. Some of these gaps are perhaps explained by major preparatory work before the publication dates of his edited editions of works by Aleister Crowley, and Grant's own *Zos Speaks* was the result of four decades' work. Bogdan believes that **"the works of Kenneth Grant… can be seen as a modern '*lesemysterium*' - a mystery one experiences while reading the books"** [95] which provides a **"consciousness-jerking shift",** according to Phil Hine [96]. Grant himself simply summarised his books as primarily to **"prepare people for encounters with unfamiliar states of consciousness… extra-, sub-, and ultra-terrestrial encounters"** [97], (whatever those distinctions actually *mean*) although one critic sees those states of consciousness induced as being more mundane, and painful: **"one might suspect that he is employed by the makers of headache relieving medications"** [98].

The Magical System: "Mercury rules the sphere of mental magick; his image is the dog and the ape, both notorious masturbators" [99]

Although Grant states explicitly that his magick is a system of ceremonial and ritual magick that primarily relates to psychosexual mysteries [100], for the most part little specific unequivocal detail is given, and certainly no actual full instructions of how to perform these rituals. Although in some instances it may be impossible to describe, **"because the formula may not be communicated in dualistic language, but only in the depths of the dream itself"** [101], primarily his books are at most only partially, and often obliquely descriptive of the work done, rather than a set of prescriptive instructions, with the main focus of his description being on the underlying theory and experienced effects.

Fact versus fiction: "knowledge that appears to have been channeled rather than researched" [102]

Grant has written a considerable quantity, and in a seemingly impressive and learned fashion, but there has been doubt cast on the verifiable content: **"Grant...has a knack for creating glamours, weaving mystique for specific ends."** [103] Colin Wilson was captivated, but read Grant's books **"without believing more than one word in ten"** [104].

Grant is also an avid proponent of referring to documents that the reader simply cannot access themselves, such as 'secret grimoires' (usually un-named) or restricted papers that are only circulated within the exclusive membership of small magickal groups, themselves often un-named [105]. While on first appearance this may be seen as helpful in offering the reader a small taste of literature inside a magickal order, it raises the doubt as to whether this is just not some kind of magical one-upmanship, and relies totally on trust in the reader as to whether such documents, and groups, really exist.

Given Grant's track record for veracity, this stance is perhaps asking too much of the reader's credulity: he has been criticised, mildly, for being not strictly accurate historically in one book. (*Outside the Circles of Time*, see above). This sentiment may be hardened, and extended to his entire output, as simple errors of fact are common, for example Grant, writing of Aleister Crowley and Victor Neuberg's dark magickal adventures in 1909 with Enochian entities, describes these as being the same magical arenas **"partially explored two centuries earlier by Dee and Kelley"** [106]. This places Dee's life dates to the 1700s, which is wrong by approximately one hundred years (John Dee, 1527- 1609 [107]). This seems a slipshod factual mistake for Grant to have made, especially in the light of Grant's seemingly expert knowledge of *Necronomical* matters and him presumably knowing something about Dee, the latter's *Liber Loagaeth* [108] being a real historical book, to which the *Necronomicon*, if it existed at all, may have had similar content.

Grant's use of references to support his ideas is also not a strictly academic exercise, since he gives equal weight to a mix of citations from learned history, anthropology and physical science disciplines, quotes from fictional authors such as Sax Rohmer (1893-1959) [109] and HP Lovecraft, ancient historical manuscripts from the British Museum [110], The actor Bela Lugosi

(1882-1956)[111], the occult symbolism which he sees within Salvador Dali's [112] (1904-1989) artwork, the supposed magickal voodoo rhythms within the music of Count Basie (1904-1984)[113], a considerable number of linguistic puns and wordplay[114], the early vampire film *Nosferatu*[115], and perhaps most bizarrely a cat called Tibbles[116], from whose name he makes some important cabbalistic links to HP Lovecraft, Crowley and Madame Blavatsky.

Suster sees it as laughable that Grant **"casually assumes… as facts… (that) Atlantis and Lemuria existed"**[117], when in the continued absence of credible archaeological records they are still regarded as mythology in most academic quarters. Grant also regularly uses the works of the 'Reverend' Montague Summers (1880-1948) as an authoritative source, however Summers is now largely seen as someone who fairly indiscriminately collected and published (with a missionary slant) a great deal of 'information' about the Satanic evil which he believed to be manifest in largely folkloric sources. It also appears that he was not a 'real' Priest in any conventional terms and so despite giving a public face of being a devout devil- and witch-hunting clergyman, who would have been more at home in the 16th than the 20th Century, it appears that Summers' works are at best to be treated with caution[118]. Just as Grant seems almost fixated on seeing significant cabbalistic links in every cat and every piece of horror fiction, Summers was just as insistent that malefic witches lurked behind every hedgerow and Satan crouched in every shadow.

Those above are areas in which Grant *may* perhaps have been aware of his historical errors, or the reliance on (academically) dubious source materials, however in a tale of a magical ritual in 1949, (first published in 1977) Grant makes a huge and knowing factual error in detailing the fates of various of those who took part. This was apparently an aborted group ritual which 'short-circuited', resulting in unfortunate consequences to the participants, including some mysterious deaths almost immediately afterwards and **"Gardner was himself not long in following suit"**[119]. Gerald Gardner died in 1964, and Grant must certainly be aware that he lived for at least five more years after the ritual in 1949, since the two men were in contact by letter at various points after the ritual and it was in 1954 that Grant claims to have personally introduced Gardner to Austin Spare [120]. This would appear to be a knowing distortion of facts, with possibly the only matter in question being whether either of five or fifteen years later after 1949 constitutes 'not long' when writing in terms of a human lifespan.

I was able to proffer this question (among several others regarding his work) to Mr Grant by letter in 2002. Having outlined the problem with the physical death date I made the suggestion that his talk of Gardner's death 'soon afterwards' was a symbolic comment, in that this was around the date when Gardner withdrew from the OTO arena and took on his role within the revival or recreation of the modern witchcraft movement, which could be seen as a 'death' so far as OTO-style magick was concerned. Mr Grant replied, citing the complexity of my questions as a whole (some of which were, I believed, simple yes-no matters) needing **"a book, no less, to meaningfully explicate the queries"** and invoked his understandable unwillingness to breach confidence to provide me with excerpts from **"confidential correspondence over the years, some of which would still leave questions incompletely explained"** [121]. From this I concluded that Mr Grant did not mean a simple, physical death being involved, and the question was one or both of too difficult, or inappropriate, for me to examine further as I may be unequipped to recognise, let alone *understand* any answer that I might uncover. Perhaps the Gardner tale and other apparent bendings of historical data is an example of Starr's view that Grant **"recycles ideas and refits them to his real science of the universe, which is unconstrained by the limits of academic knowledge"** [122].

While Grant makes errors that can be highlighted with reference to history, his many other magical theories described in his books are supported by the results of ritual and trance experiment and detailed cabbalistic exegesis. Neither of these, although common and valid occult techniques, would be considered as valid *academic* methods of research, although accepting as historical fact that the practitioners *believed* in both the veracity of techniques and the results would be a valid approach.

Aside from Cabbalistic workings, Grant's more general tales of magical life are often rather lurid, seemingly without complete justification, and imply a tendency to exaggerate and-or make wild claims, aside from the 'many deaths after ritual' element discussed above. The artist and occultist Ithell Colquhoun said that Kenneth Grant **"makes the** (Magical Order of the) **Inner Light set-up sound more exciting that any impression of it which I received,"** [123] and Suster said, in general that **"it is difficult to take Mr. Grant's claims seriously"** [124]. Grant himself tries to give some degree of clarification about the reality of his writings: **"by fantasy is here meant the fantastic or 'impossible'"** [125], and, in more detail: **"terms such as vampirism, cannibalism, death, sleep etc., connote operations applicable not to terrestrial levels, but to alien dimensions ... confusion arises principally from an interpretation in mundane terms of concepts not relating to mundane dimensions. This leads certainly to ludicrous and sometimes dangerous results"** [126], the former implies that much of it is outside the realm of earthly verification, and the latter point being that the effects of supposed fictionality in magic can be totally real to those who believe in it, and subsequent practical magical mistakes made can thus be dangerous, leading to one becoming a casualty, as Moore has so elegantly and beautifully named, in *Wizard of Oz*-esque terminology **"Yellow Brick Roadkill"** [127]. Moore continues to provide useful analysis of Grant, seeing all of his books as being **"an apparent deliberate blurring of the line between describing Separate Reality and writing Magic Fiction, if there ever really was a line to blur"** [128].

Bertiaux, one of Grant's magickal collaborators adds a further useful remark: **"there is the cosmic world of the imagination, and that is what we are talking about when we discuss our magical creations and discoveries... there is the world of archetypal images... which is 'between' the world of sense-perception and the world of the abstract essences of ideas in the mind of God"** [129], so in other words, very little of this material may happen 'really, on earth, as written', even if it is presented as such.

Regardless of the earthly reality aspect, it appears that among practitioners both the risks and rewards of such a magical approach are regarded as commensurately greater than other, 'safer' occult practices: Grant's books **"despite, or possibly because of their forays into dementia, have** more genuine occult power than works produced by <u>more conventionally coherent authors</u>"[130]. Although controversial in many ways within occultism, perhaps Grant's most frowned-upon quality is his insistence on citing HP Lovecraft and other authors, these being nominally fictional writers, as presenting highly relevant occult 'facts', and his then performing rituals to contact Lovecraftian entities.

Grant's accounts of various rituals are in many respects reminiscent of the unearthly referents sometimes described in early-modern accounts of the alleged Witches' Sabbat. An important difference here is not one of content, but of context. Unlike many historical witch-trial transcripts, which were very often written by hostile, clerically-biased scribes, during (or closely following) intimidation or torture of the accused; and adhering to an ecclesiastical agenda of seeing the Devil ever-present in the world, Grant's accounts are his own, freely written, albeit perhaps some time after the event in some cases, and *electively published* in a country where his activities are not outside the law.

To an extent, modern academics looking into occultism, when examining such claims are in a similar interpretative position to the early-modern judiciary: Ginzburg discusses the legal problems inherent with trying witches who claimed to have been to the witches Sabbat (especially when they make a seemingly impossible, or magical claim, such as having *flown* there, for example) and perhaps consorted with the Devil. A major consideration in Law at the time being whether this act had been physical, or imaginal, but Ginzburg concludes, **"even if the sabbat <u>had</u> been a purely mental phenomenon (and this cannot be proved) its importance for the historian would not be diminished"**[131]. In the same way, Grant's accounts of ritual are important, whether they 'really' happened 'on earth' or as now seems more likely, on some 'astral plane' since the imagery has since been written, printed and circulated, thus entering the consciousness of a great many occultists, who will themselves have developed their own ideas as to what plane of existence such events occurred on. Gaskill remarks on the academic problems inherent in exploring **"alternative and contrasting definitions of what too often we confidently call 'the truth'"**[132] and the manner in which cultural boundaries and memes often determine truth, at least as much as perception and historical record within that cultural group is concerned. Grant himself remarked, **"I am very exact in matters of occultism and would not make any statement I could not substantiate either historically <u>or magically</u>"** [133], which appears to give equal weight to *either* discipline, and thus either view of what is 'real', and implies that the two disciplines are not mutually conducive.

In any case, such magical writing satisfies needs that are **"are not necessarily the same to ... believers and to observers (particularly historians)"** [134]. Whether it 'happened' or not in the materialist, earthly, historically-supportable sense becomes almost immaterial to the effects on the readers, and in any case, as Heelas points out, **"the academic study of religion *must* remain *neutral* in regard to ultimate truth"** [135] such as this.

Conclusions: "no-one could doubt that Kenneth Grant is one hell of a meanass occultist" [136]

Despite a tendency to write profusely while revealing little of his actual methods, Grant has consistently excited considerable interest among occult writers and practitioners, however two Crowley biographers (Colin Wilson and Roger Hutchinson [137]) inexcusably fail to mention Grant *at all*. However Wilson has subsequently written, briefly, about Grant and says that he was aware of him 20 years before the Crowley biography was published [138], while other Crowley biographers (Booth for example [139]) only mention him in passing, as a *post mortem* editor of Crowley's works. Perhaps surprisingly, there has as yet been no published biography (or autobiography) of Grant. This may relate to him being apparently **"obsessively secretive about his personal life, refusing to release biographical details ... (he) prefers to live the life of a scholar and recluse"** [140]. A rare published interview provides a rather stilted glance at the man, being it was conducted by an anonymous interviewer, for a magazine friendly to Grant (being run by his publisher at the time) and only gives what appears to be a truncated discussion [141].

Grant's output, while not monstrous in terms of sheer page count accrued over more than 50 years, seems to be scattered widely- books, monographs, translations of his work into several languages, art exhibition catalogues, some very sale-enhancing 'guest introductions' to the books of lesser-known writers, encyclopaedia entries and journal articles; many of which are no longer obtainable, such as a series of pieces on Eastern thought in journals published in India in the early 1950s [142]. In the late 1960s he wrote some populist magazine articles including calls for magickal discipline and will in the use of drugs, not as hippy 'kicks' [143] and promoted the magical use of Tantric sex [144]. As with many magicians, his work has inspired a distinctly novel Tarot Deck [145].

Grant has an advantage over many writers on occultism in that as well as being a pupil of Crowley and Spare he has continued access to a great deal of unpublished materials from those prominent occultists, being literary executor of the latter and closely involved with the executors of the former.[146]

Gerald Suster summarises Grant's writing as, **"mystified, one tries to read ... concluding that if he wishes to conceal, he should keep silent; and if he wishes to reveal, he should learn how to write"** [147], however Starr exhorts hard work from the reader as a prerequisite: **"if we don't apply ourselves to understand his work, we have only ourselves to blame if we cannot perceive his vision"** [148], which again implies a Darwinian approach to the readership. Understanding Grant *is* far from simple, however it appears that the necessary work to comprehend is worthwhile for occultists: **"Grant's images impart a wisdom or an experience not found in more easily accessible models"** [149], and his writings are of **"inestimable value"** and **"transaeonic"** [150], the latter comment meaning that they are of use and appeal to a wide range of occultists who might otherwise have major 'doctrinal differences' in their reading matter. A convenient, if crude, metaphor might be that 'if Crowley was a Pope, then Grant was his Cardinal, and yet Grant's published works have been appreciated by Protestants, Mormons, Muslims and Jews'.

Grant's apparent command of a broad range of magickal methods and fine use of language seems to goad his critics to either attempt to emulate his wordiness, or failing that to descend to base crudities; for example his later books are seen by Moore as **"an information soup, an overwhelming** and hallucinatory bouillon of arcane fact, mystic speculation and apparent outright fantasy"[151], while the late Gerald Suster simply called some of it 'shit', as mentioned above. Dave Lee perhaps provides a middle view: **"Grant explores the refuse left behind by the Great Man of solar religion. Whilst such a pastime is not to every magician's taste, the importance of this work is that it adds to our conception of totality"** [152]. Another reasoned view comes from Sennitt, who attacks some criticism of Grant which is **"misplaced; he has been accused of everything from over-glamourising the occult to being anti-evolutionary"** [153].

Grant is **"as fascinating and ultimately mystifying as a giant squid in a cocktail dress"** [154], a troubling enigma, the last surviving writer and practitioner to have known and worked with Britain's 20th Century's 'great triumvirate' of influential occultists: Aleister Crowley, Austin Spare and Gerald Gardner (and being the secretary and/or archivist of the former two). His place in occult history would be assured, simply for that, regardless of the *caveats* discussed above such as the numerous potential and actual problems inherent in Grant's interpretation of the works of the enigmatic, dyslexic, slippery, multi-faceted and absent-minded Austin Spare, his seeming leading role in the creation or transmission of an expanding fable around 'Mrs. Patterson the great witch mother', and his cryptic comments on the often equally unfathomable Aleister Crowley. To this should also be added the interpretation problems added by Grant's own idiosyncrasies of cabbalistic method, his historical re-interpretation and the worrying (to the academic) width of what he considers to be valid source materials and the withholding of a great deal of detail about his actual methods. However, quite how Grant will be eventually assessed is a moot point; anywhere between Magus and maniac, depending upon each viewers' perspective, and the clarifying or revelatory effect of any texts which might emerge after his death. To a large extent, the question of sanity or sanctity is not an area that can be approached academically- as Heelas remarks, **"if people say they are Enlightened… the academic simply does not have the tools to assess the claim"** [155]. Regardless of what Grant may or may not be, his influence has been immense, and his magickal systems are in use across a broad range of occult disciplines.

Despite heated discussion and divided opinions about his veracity and methods, Grant continues to consistently provide highly stimulating, contentious and unusual fare for magickians to both read and work with. His *corpus* remains a convoluted and multidisciplinary challenge to academics, covering as it does, Cabbala, Hebrew, Sanskrit, history, magick, voodoo, mediumship, astronomy, astrology, Tantra, Eastern and Western philosophies, literature (including what was once published as 'pulp fiction'), linguistics, etymology, Egyptology, folklore, zoology, 'Ufology', alchemy, religious studies and conspiracy theory. To further add to the task of interpretation, much of this is provided in a far from straightforward, and often seemingly counterfactual manner, with tidbits of information about various events being spread often across several books; requiring painstaking reconstruction to gain a clear(er) picture.

In summary, regardless of any occasionally dubious factually-supportable 'truth' in his works, Grant might be seen to be providing a vital service. In a world where comparative 'truths' compete with eachother and there is perhaps no absolute truth, there is a social situation where people *need* magic- just as some need to believe in a God, or conversely that there is no God, or that friendly aliens orbit the planet in spaceships, *that 'fictional' characters are somehow ' real'*, or a thousand other viewpoints. As Gaskill points out: **"it will never be proven that God and the Devil are scholastic fictions... sheer *desire* to imagine an enchanted universe would inevitably be indulged in, and the idea would catch on"** [156]. Grant, in writing about magic with such aplomb, *provides* magic in huge doses for those who wish to believe, and gives any number of detailed jumping-off points for those occultists with the will to experiment, and the historian of modern occultism simply cannot ignore Mr Grant's work.

Notes

1 Alan Moore, Beyond our Ken (a review of Kenneth Grant, Against the Light), in *Kaos*, 14, London, Kaos-Babalon Press, 2002, p 155- 162, p 156

2 *Ibid,* p 162

3 *Ibid,* p 156

4 John Symonds, *The King of the Shadow Realm. Aleister Crowley, his life and magic*, London, Duckworth, 1989, p 570-572

5 Richard Kaczynski, *Perdurabo: the life of Aleister Crowley*, Tempe, Arizona, New Falcon, 2002, p 440

6 Kenneth Grant, *Remembering Aleister Crowley*, London, Skoob, 1991, p v

7 Moore, *Kaos*, 14, p 156

8 Kaczynski, *Perdurabo*, p 440

9 Kenneth Grant, *Outside the Circles of Time*, London, Muller, 1980, p 87.

10 Grant, *Remembering*, p 1

11 *Ibid*, p 6

12 *Ibid*, Aleister Crowley to Kenneth Grant, Letter of 22-2-1945

13 Lawrence Sutin, *Do What Thou Wilt: A life of Aleister Crowley*, New York, St Martins, 200, p 406

14 Symonds, *King of the Shadow Realm*, p 572

15 *Ibid*, p 570-572

16 Sutin, *Do What Thou Wilt*, p 406

17 Grant, *Remembering*, Letter from Aleister Crowley to Kenneth Grant's father 14-5-1945

18 *Ibid*, p 40, Letter from Aleister Crowley to Kenneth Grant, 21-06-45, emphasis original

19 *Ibid*, Letter from Aleister Crowley to Kenneth Grant, 15-2-1945

20 *Ibid*, Letter from Aleister Crowley to David Curwen, 22-1-46

21 *Ibid*, p 3, Letter from Aleister Crowley to Kenneth Grant, 27-11-1944

22 For example Aleister Crowley, *Magick without tears*, Scottsdale, Arizona, New Falcon, 1991, p 357. This volume originally appeared as 'Aleister Explains Everything' in 1954

23 Kenneth Grant, *The Ninth Arch*, London, Starfire, 2002, p 498

24 *Ibid*, p 411-412

25 Kenneth Grant, *Against the Light: a Nightside narrative*, London, Starfire, 1997, p ix, the questionable book being Phineas March Black, *Clinical Studies in Senescence and Diseases of Memory*, Edinburgh, 1886 via an un-named publisher.

26 Aleister Crowley (John Symonds and Kenneth Grant, Eds.), *The Confessions of Aleister Crowley*, London, Routledge, 1979

27 These being John Symonds. *The Great Beast*, St Albans, Mayflower, 1973; John Symonds, *The King of the Shadow Realm. Aleister Crowley, his life and magic*, London, Duckworth, 1989; Richard Kaczynski, *Perdurabo: the life of Aleister Crowley*, Tempe, Arizona, New Falcon, 2002; Martin Booth, *A Magick Life*, London, Hodder & Stoughton, 2000; Colin Wilson *Aleister Crowley: the nature of the Beast*, Wellingborough, Aquarian, 1987; Roger Hutchinson, *Aleister*

Crowley: the Beast demystified, Edinburgh, Mainstream, 1999, and Susan Roberts, *The Magicians of the Golden Dawn*, Chicago, Contemporary Books, 1978.

28 Kenneth & Steffi Grant, *Zos Speaks! Encounters with Austin Osman Spare*, London, Fulgur, 1998.

29 *Ibid*, p 30

30 Kenneth Grant, *Beyond the Mauve Zone*, London, Starfire, 1999, p 33

31 Grant, *Zos Speaks!*, p 20

32 *Ibid*, p 129, p 284 fn 119

33 *Ibid*, p 123

34 *Ibid*, p 20

35 Gavin Semple, *Study for a portrait of Frank Letchford*, London, Fulgur, 2002, p 18

36 Kenneth Grant, Hecate's Fountain, Skoob, London, 1992, p 25, citing Correspondence between Jack Parsons and his 'elemental' Marjorie Cameron, letter of 27-1-1950. The letters were handwritten originally, and Grant does not mention that 'backside' may actually read **"blackside"** (www.babalon.net). This is presumably because 'backside' fits better into Grant's magical worldview of the 'other', or 'back' side of the cabalistic Tree of Life being so important to his system.

37 Jan Fries, *Visual Magick*, Oxford, Mandrake, 1992, p 42. In this instance Fries is talking about sigilisation techniques.

38 Matt Lee, 'Memories of a sorcerer': notes on Gilles Deleuze, Felix Guattari, Austin Osman Spare and anomalous sorceries, *Journal for the Academic Study of Magic*, 1, 2003, p 102-130, p 124, Emphasis added

39 Grant, *Zos Speaks!*, p 68

40 Keith Richmond, Discord in the garden of Janus: Aleister Crowley and Austin Osman Spare, in *Austin Osman Spare: Artist, Occultist, Sensualist*, Bury St Edmunds, Beskin, 1999, no page numbering

41 Sunny Shah, *An Edwardian Blake: an introduction to the Life and Works of Austin Osman Spare*, Thame, Oxon, Mandrake Press, 1996, p 20

42 Frank Letchford, *Austin Osman Spare, From the Inferno to Zos*, Volume 3, Thame, Oxon, First Impressions, 1995, p 44

43 Grant, *Zos Speaks!*, p 93, Emphasis added

44 *Ibid*, p 128

45 *Ibid*, p 129

46 *Ibid*,

47 *Ibid*, p 13

48 Grant, *Remembering*, p 15

49 Letchford, *From the Inferno to Zos*, Volume 3, p 69

50 Grant, *Zos Speaks!* p 15, Emphasis added

51 Letchford, *From the Inferno to Zos*, Volume 3, p 87

52 *Ibid*, p 103

53 Grant, *Zos Speaks!*, p 20

54 Kenneth Grant, *Nightside of Eden*, Skoob, London, 1994, p 40. Malkuth, Kether etc need to be defined somewhere. The capitalisation used may also hide a code, in the same way that Crowley used to, in the sentence above Grant may be alluding to the magical order the AA, *Argentum Astrum*, by his use of capitals.

55 Grant, *Remembering*, p 58

56 *Ibid*, p 38.

57 Cabbalistic term, meaning **"neither Form nor Void, but absence of the presence of both Object and Subject (i.e. the Absolute Absence, or Void."** Kenneth Grant, *Nightside of Eden*, Skoob, London, 1994, p 40

58 Grant, *Nightside*, p 36, fn 7

59 Frank Letchford, The search for a Guru, *Skoob Occult Review*, 3, 1990, p 30-36, p 31

60 Gavin Semple, *Study for a portrait of Frank Letchford*, London, Fulgur, 2002, p 21

61 Richmond, Discord in the garden of Janus, in *Austin Osman Spare: artist, Occultist, Sensualist*, Bury St Edmunds, Beskin, 1999, no page numbering, *fn* 58

62 For an extensive discussion of Spare's alleged plagiarism see A.R.Naylor, *Stealing the Fire from Heaven*, Thame, Oxon, IHO, 2002, especially pages p 9-22

63 Grant, *Zos Speaks!* p 16-17

64 Kenneth Grant, Introduction to Austin Osman Spare, *The Book of Pleasure*, 1975. (Online) Fulgur website http://www.fulgur.org/articles/grant1975.html

65 David Cantu, A brief evolution of "Mrs Patterson", witch mentor to Austin Osman Spare, in Joel Biroco (Ed.), *Kaos 14*, London, Kaos-Babalon Press, 2002, p 38-41, p 38.

There is a lead that I am pursuing from a possible Patterson descendant -with a likely Mrs. Patterson being described as having a large occult library, including a rare 14th Century alchemical treatise which sold for a very large sum of money after her death, and it seems her family was associated with Watkins Occult bookshop in London very early in the 20th Century. However further information, including a hoped-for birth certificate from which to make further enquiries, is likely to be slow in emerging due to internal divisions and communication breaks within that family. It is only after such information should become available that the depth of any link with Austin Spare will become researchable.

66 Richmond, Discord in the garden of Janus, in *Austin Osman Spare: Artist, Occultist, Sensualist*, Bury St Edmunds, Beskin, 1999, no page numbering

67 Correspondence between David Cantu and Joel Biroco, in *Kaos 14*, London, Kaos-Babalon Press, 2002, p 42-44

68 Letchford, *From the Inferno to Zos*, Volume 3, p 147, Emphasis added

69 My own copy of Grant's *Aleister Crowley and the Hidden God* came from a sale of the library of Mr. Letchford after his death. It has been well-thumbed **by somebody**, and he had taken the trouble to cover it in a second dust jacket to preserve it.

70 Letchford, *From the Inferno to Zos*, Volume 3, 1995, p 35

71 Semple, *Study for a portrait of Frank Letchford*, p 21

72 Ronald Hutton, *Triumph of the Moon*, Oxford, Oxford University Press, 1999, p 303 and Kenneth Grant, *Outer Gateways*, London, Skoob, 1994, p 17-31

73 Hermetic Com website, An Interview with Gavin Semple, February 2001 http://www.hermetic.com/spare/semple-interview.html

74 Semple, *Study for a portrait of Frank Letchford*, p 29

75 Hermetic Com, Interview with Gavin Semple,

76 Grant, *Zos Speaks!* p 135.

77 Kenneth Grant, *Outside the Circles of Time*, London, Muller, 1980, p 140 *fn* 10

78 Grant, *Zos Speaks!*, p 29

79 *Ibid*, p 150

80 Michael Staley, personal communication, October 2001. Mr. Staley is a senior official in the Typhonian OTO of Kenneth Grant, and runs their publication arm, Starfire.

81 Nema (Margaret Ingalls), *Maat Magick: a guide to self-initiation*, York Beach, Weiser, 1995, p 218

82 Henrik Bogdan, *Kenneth Grant A bibliography- from 1948*, Academia Esoterica Press, Gothenburg, 2003, p viii

83 Sunny Shah, *An Edwardian Blake: an introduction to the Life and Works of Austin Osman Spare*, Thame, Oxon, Mandrake Press, 1996, p 12

84 Gerald Suster, Letters, *Nox*, 5, 1987, p 7-8

85 Kaczynski, *Perdurabo*, p 461

86 Uncarved website: Current 93: Interview with David Tibet, June 1989 http://www.uncarved.demon.co.uk/music/OOOc93.html

87 Kaczynski, *Perdurabo*, p 461, Emphasis added

88 Anon, Review of Kenneth Grant, Outside the Circles of Time, *Cincinnati Journal of Ceremonial Magick*, 1, 5, 1983, p 76, Emphasis added

89 Kenneth Grant, *Hecate's Fountain*, Skoob, London, 1992, p i, italics authors own.

90 Gerald Suster, Barking up the wrong tree: Review of Kenneth Grant, Hecate's Fountain, *Skoob Esoterica Anthology*, 1, London, Skoob, 1995, p 187-190, p 190

91 Grant, *Ninth Arch*, p 85

92 *Ibid*, p 260

93 Suster, Barking up the wrong tree, *Skoob Esoterica Anthology*, 1, p 187

94 For an superb examination of the ritualisation and elaborate quality of the publication process by Crowley, see Timothy d'arch Smith, *Books of the Beast*, Oxford, Mandrake, 1991, chapter 1

95 Bogdan, *Kenneth Grant*, p viii

96 Phil Hine, Review of Kenneth Grant, Hecate's Fountain, *The Occult Observer*, 2, 3, Winter 1992, p 56-7

97 Anon, Interview with Kenneth Grant, *Skoob Occult Review*, 3, 1990, p 5-7, p 5

98 Frater M.E.D, Review of Hecate's Fountain, Online http://www.geocities.com/Athens/Parthenon/7069/grant6.html

99 Grant, *Nightside*, p 150.

100 *Ibid*, introduction, p xi

101 *Ibid*, p 181, footnote 16

102 Moore, Beyond our Ken, *Kaos* 14, p 155- 162, p 155

103 Hermetic Com website, An Interview with Gavin Semple, February 2001 http://www.hermetic.com/spare/semple-interview.html

104 Colin Wilson, Tentacles across time, *Skoob Esoterica Anthology*, 1, London, Skoob, 1995, p 13- 15, p 13

105 Grant, *Nightside*, p 90 *fin* 37

106 Kenneth Grant, *Hecate's Fountain*, Skoob, London, 1992, p 5

107 Benjamin Woolley, *The Queen's conjuror: the science and Magic of Dr Dee*, London, HarperCollins, 2001, p 3, p 322. The exact birth and death dates are open to debate, as discussed by Woolley, but are not so wrong as to make Grant's comment remotely accurate.

108 John Dee, *Liber Loagaeth, or Liber Mystorium, Sextus et Sanctus*, Approximately 1583, British Library Sloane Ms A3189. Online at www.esotericarchives.com/dee/sl3189.htm

109 Sax Rohmer: pen name of Arthur Henry Sarsfield Ward, a **"prolific mystery writer best known for the master criminal Fu Manchu"** among his characters,

with his first successful novel being published in 1913 and his numerous works including some occult fiction remaining best-sellers into the 1950s. Kirijasto Website. www.kirijasto.sci.fi/rohmer.htm Ward was a member of the Hermetic Order of the Golden Dawn

110 For example Grant, *Ninth Arch*, p 512

111 Most famous for his horror film roles such as Dracula, the Hungarian Bela Lugosi (Bela Ferenc Dezso Blasko) was at the height of his fame in the 1920s and 1930s. EOFFTV.com website. www.eofftv.com/names/l/lugosi_bela_main.htm

112 Salvador Dali, Famous Spanish Cubist and Futurist artist. Grant makes *seventeen* references to Dali in one book alone (Grant, *Outside the Circles of Time*, London, Muller, 1980)

113 For example Grant, *Nightside*, p 148. William "Count" Basie: an extremely popular 20th Century Black American Jazz and Swing Pianist and Band Leader who reached the height of his fame on either side of World War II. Harlem Org Website, www.harlem.org/people/basie.html

114 For example Grant, *Ninth Arch*, p 337, where Grant equates a Chinese character called Li Sing with one of his mediums, Margaret Leesing

115 Grant, *Ninth Arch*, p 509

116 *Ibid*, p 490. This may seem particularly strange to include as a source, but at least Grant does not go so far as to write *an entire occult book* about mystical cats, as was done by Mama San Ra-Ab Rampa in *Pussywillow*, London, Corgi, 1965. Mrs Rampa was the wife of T Lobsang Rampa, the probably fraudulent 'Tibetan Lama' who published numerous spurious occult titles in the 1960s

117 Suster, Barking up the wrong tree, *Skoob Esoterica Anthology*, 1, p 188

118 d'arch Smith, *Books of the Beast*, p 37-46

119 Grant, *Nightside*, p 124 (Skoob 1994 edition, original 1977)

120 Grant, *Zos Speaks!*, numerous mentions in correspondence, p 86-97

121 Kenneth Grant, personal communication, 17-7-2002

122 Martin Starr, Foreword to Henrik Bogdan, *Kenneth Grant A bibliography-from 1948*, Academia Esoterica Press, Gothenburg, 2003, p vi, Emphasis added.

123 Ithell Colquhoun, *Sword of Wisdom: MacGregor Mathers and the Golden Dawn*, London, Spearman, 1975, p 189

124 Gerald Suster, *The Legacy of the Beast: the life, work and influence of Aleister Crowley*, London, WH Allen, 1988, p 216

125 Kenneth Grant, *Hecate's Fountain*, Skoob, London, 1992, p 221

126 *Ibid*, p 197

127 Moore, Beyond our Ken, in *Kaos* 14, p 155-162, p 161

128 *Ibid*, p 156

129 Michael Bertiaux, La Couleuvre Noire Course, Section GG, Part 2, paper 2. In Kenneth Grant, *Hecate's Fountain*, Skoob, London, 1992, p 197

130 Moore, Beyond our Ken, in *Kaos* 14, p 161, Emphasis added

131 Carlo Ginzburg (John & Anne Tedeschi, Trans.) *The Night Battles, Witchcraft and Agrarian cults in the Sixteenth and Seventeenth Centuries*, Baltimore, Johns Hopkins University Press , p *xiv* Emphasis added

132 Malcolm Gaskill, *Hellish Nell; last of Britain's Witches*, London, Fourth Estate, 2001, p 2

133 . Letter from Kenneth Grant to Cecil Williamson, 25-6-1951, Museum of Witchcraft Archive. Emphasis added.

134 Bengt Ankarloo & Stuart Clark, Introduction to *The Athlone History of Witchcraft and Magic in Europe, Volume 6: The Twentieth Century*, London, Athlone, 1999, p vii

135 Paul Heelas, *The New Age movement*, Oxford, Blackwell, 1996, p 6, Emphasis original

136 Herman Skelder, "Laughing stock" danger of worshipping strange entities, in *Kaos 14*, p 35-37, p 36

137 Colin Wilson *Aleister Crowley: the nature of the Beast*, Wellingborough, Aquarian, 1987; Roger Hutchinson, *Aleister Crowley: the Beast demystified*, Edinburgh, Mainstream, 1999

138 Colin Wilson, Tentacles across time, *Skoob Esoterica Anthology*, 1, London, Skoob, 1995, p 13- 15, p 13

139 Martin Booth, *A Magick Life*, London, Hodder & Stoughton, 2000

140 Wilson, Tentacles across time, *Skoob Esoterica Anthology*, 1, p 14

141 Anon, Interview with Kenneth Grant, *Skoob Occult Review*, 3, 1990, p 5-7

142 Bogdan, *Kenneth Grant A bibliography*, p 11

143 Kenneth Grant, The Golden Dawn, *International Times*, 33, June 14-27 1968, no page numbering

144 Kenneth Grant, Love Under Will, *International Times*, 49, January 31-February 13, 1969, p 18

145 Linda Falorio & Fred Fowler, Shadow Tarot, *Cincinnati Journal of Magick*, 7, 1989, p 48-9

146 Kenneth Grant, *The Magical Revival*, London, Frederick Muller, 1972, p 1-2

147 Suster, *Legacy of the Beast*, p 215

148 Martin Starr, Foreword to: Henrik Bogdan, *Kenneth Grant A bibliography-from 1948*, Academia Esoterica Press, Gothenburg, 2003, p vii

149 Stephen Sennitt, Editorial, *Nox*, 2, 1986, p 3

150 Anon, Foreword to Cincinnati Journal of Ceremonial Magick, 1, 5, 1983, p 6

151 Moore, Beyond our Ken, *Kaos* 14, p 155

152 Dave Lee, What is magick for? *Nox*, 5 p 11-16, p 13, the 'Great Man' presumably being Crowley

153 Stephen Sennitt, Editorial, *Nox*, 2, 1986, p 3

154 Moore, Beyond our Ken, *Kaos* 14, p 155

155 Paul Heelas, *The New Age movement*, Oxford, Blackwell, 1996, p 6

156 Gaskill, *Hellish Nell*, p 364

Magic through the Linguistic Lenses of Greek *mágos*, Indo-European **mag(h)-*, Sanskrit *māyā* and Pharaonic Egyptian *Ḥeka*.

Aaron Cheak

> You look up when you desire to be exalted. And I look down, because I am exalted.
>
> - Nietzsche.[1]

Magic, like religion, is notoriously difficult to define. No scholarly consensus can be said to exist, a fact compounded by the increasing tendency in recent studies to deconstruct the very category of magic rather than provide a constructive or at least heuristic definition of it. What is presented here is a return to a philological basis of description, but one which attempts to extend the linguistic analysis beyond the confines of a single language/culture. We will therefore approach magic by considering some of its semantic and etymological aspects, with specific attention to i) Persian *magu-* and Greek *mágos* in Hellenistic antiquity, ii) the proposed Indo-European root of *magu-* and its cognates, iii) the root and cognates of Sanskrit *mā* as basis of the concept of *māyā*, and iv) the Egyptian concept of *heka* and its signification in Egyptian cosmogony and theology. Finally, we will conclude by identifying a number of motifs which are felt to adumbrate a broader definition of magic, yet which nevertheless remain consistent with the examples discussed. Before we turn to this, however, some discussion of the nature of scholarship on magic needs to be ventured.

Magic and Religion : To Separate or not to Separate?

Einar Thomassen has remarked that, as far as the history of religions is concerned, magic is the black sheep in the discipline's family of theoretical concepts.[2] This, it is suggested, explains why one of the first scholarly tasks was the conceptual separation of magic from religion, followed by the reduction of it to a social reality.[3] While scholars are increasingly realising the arbitrary nature of the magic-religion dichotomy, it appears that there is ultimately no consensus as to whether religion and magic are conceptually identical or separate. Yet evidence from the ancient world alone compounds the ambiguity.

Scholars have become increasingly aware of the dual tendency to compare magic, unfavourably, not only to religion, but also to science.[4] Magic, it seems, has suffered at the hands of polemicists since as far back as Plato, the term being denigrated in order to exalt either logocentric paradigms on one hand (philosophy, science), or communally sanctioned 'irrationalities' on the other (religion).[5] In the words of Johnathan Z. Smith, magic has become 'doubly dichotomized.'[6] The positivist-evolutionist tendency to plot magic, religion and science (in that order) upon an ascending hierarchy (proceeding from the irrational to the rational) further enables magic to be chronologically subsumed by either of its opposites.[7] Hence, magic is either erroneous religion subsumed by righteous religion (as per Gnosticism and Christianity), or pseudo-science subsumed by true science (as per alchemy and chemistry). Further permutations are also possible. Magic has been understood in terms of specific lacks or excesses that have been overcome by suitably evolved forms of religion and science,[8] or conversely in terms of a *devolution* from such evolved forms of religion or science (i.e., when the chronological record did not support an evolutionist view). Either way, we are confronted with an understanding of magic which proceeds from an arbitrarily constructed vantage. While some evidence supports the perspective gained from such a vantage, other evidence does not, and it is hence toward a more relativistic paradigm that post-existentialist scholars have turned when confronted with the ultimate elusiveness or contingency of any 'solid' authority. Indeed, there is a tendency to abandon any claim to the validity of categories beyond the narrow limits of their demonstrable socio-cultural construction, and a climate of over-specialisation has ensued to compensate for previous over-generalisation.

Coequal with this dual dichotomization is the so-called 'grand dichotomy' that has informed Modernist scholarship (most notably in the legacy of Tylor and Frazer).[9] In other words, a gulf is seen to divide 'us' from 'them,' separating the rationalist West from that which is Other.[10] Under the aegis of Post-Modernism in general, and social anthropology in particular,[11] the projection of such Modernist religious categories is widely (and rhetorically) disparaged. Hence a seemingly reactive oscillation toward the opposite pole has developed, an orientation which prefers to see all grand or universal understandings of reality as utterly contingent social-constructs. Extreme ethnocentricism is accordingly replaced with extreme cultural relativism. Yet it would seem that the tendency to deconstruct the category of magic, while it usefully exposes the prejudices of those who use the term in an etic sense, does little to clarify what it may have meant to those who used it in an emic sense.[12] Indeed, in spite of the increasing popularity of the 'social-construction-of-religious-categories' approach,[13] other scholars have spoken for the validity and usefulness of the more traditional taxonomy. So while recognition of the arbitrary nature of this dichotomy is apparent, so too is the recognition of this dichotomy as an emic distinction in some of the studied cultures. With this comes the necessity to distinguish between the dichotomies created in the process of scholarship (i.e. etic distinctions) and those evident within the material studied (i.e. emic distinctions).[14] Ultimately however, a lack of consensus prevails about the so-called demise of the grand dichotomy, for some maintain that our religious categories may nevertheless provide useful heuristic tools. That is to say, our dichotomous categories, instead of being simply abandoned or rejected as products of a

Western ethnocentric bias, may be more usefully refined and contextualised, rather than unthinkingly universalised.[15]

The refinement rather than deconstruction of our religious categories is somewhat justified in so far as ancient cultures exhibit emic examples of equivalent distinctions. That the conceptual separation of magic and religion antedates Early Modern theology[16] is suggested most notably by recent studies of magic in Antiquity. Here the two-fold polemic which pits both religion and science against magic is viewed not merely as a retroactive projection of Modern prejudices but, as H. S. Versnal and Fritz Graf have shown, is in fact evident in the Classical world.[17] That Greek philosophers and doctors began to distinguish themselves over and against magicians as early as the fifth century B.C.E. effectively displaces the Protestant and positivist-evolutionist models that are generally viewed as the prototypes for this dichotomising. Moreover, it argues for an understanding of these categories as far more deeply entrenched in Western culture than previously appreciated.

If the presence of our categories in fifth century B.C.E. Greece effectively deposes the social anthropologist myth that projected religious categories are a Modern (if not Modernist) construct. Jens Braavig's identification of the magic-religion dichotomy in Hindu and Buddhist sources effectively demonstrates the existence of non-Western examples.[18] Hence, the recognition that the magic-religion dichotomy is present in both pre-Reformation and non-Western contexts may be seen as reasonable justification for the use of the categories as a general heuristic tool, but only in so far as care is taken to contextualise the categories rather than to universalise them.

Yet we will do well to remember that while such a theoretical distinction between religion and magic constitutes the Western (i.e. Greco-Roman, Judaeo-Christian) bias, this distinction, even in light of the supporting non-Western examples supplied by Braarvig, cannot be extended to *all* non-Western cultures.[19] Hence, following from the views that i) an 'unconscious clinging' to our received categories is counterproductive, and ii) deconstruction of these categories tends to preclude any meaningful understanding of our subject, a more (self-)conscious use of definitions or categories is posited in order to actually facilitate an understanding of magic in any positive or meaningful manner.[20]

Realizing that magic can neither be conclusively separated or identified with religion in a universal sense, other scholars have looked toward more fluid models of the relationship magic-religion. In accordance with a generally neglected aspect of Mauss' theory,[21] Goode,[22] has usefully suggested that a continuum rather than a chasm exists between the polarised opposites of magic and religion.[23] The dichotomy still exists, but it is mediated. The notion thus arises that any given magical or religious phenomenon may be plotted somewhere along the continuum, usually closer to one pole than the other, but only rarely at either extreme. Such a view allows religion and magic to blend and overlap. While this model is valuable, Thomassen's suggestion that an essential *intertextuality* characterizes the magic-religion relationship is perhaps a more nuanced restatement of the position.[24] Even when an emic distinction is seen to exist between magic and religion, magic is still informed by the religious and vice versa. Indeed, so much of the difficulty in distinguishing magic and religion is due to the fact that often both are deeply informed by each other's conventions. At the very least, recognition of the fundamental intertextuality of the magic-religion relationship seems enough to avoid many of the pitfalls typically engendered when attempting to account for their conceptual separateness or unity.

A Question of Semantics
Persian *magu-*; Greek *mágos*

The origins of the Western concept of magic lie in Greek antiquity. The native term for magician in archaic Greece was *góēs*, 'sorcerer,' which referred to a socially marginal figure connected with the passage of the dead between worlds and to indigenous purificatory practises of a probable shamanic nature.[25] In such a context we find healing in Homeric Greece inextricably bound to magic, the term *phármakon*, 'medicine, poison' being ascribed by Homer to medico-magical practises.[26] This evidence suggests that a blurring of spiritual and physical technologies is evident in the archaic period,[27] seemingly evincing a fundamental conflation of the dualities that would later be recapitulated in the symbolism of alchemy (e.g. medicine-poison, healing-death etc.).

By the fifth century B.C.E., a foreign loanword came to predominate in Greek descriptions of magic. Derived from the Iranian (Old Persian *maguš*, Avestan *moγu*, Elamite *ma-ku-iš*),[28] and apparently signifying a 'member of the tribe,'[29] the term *mágos* is a designation specifically understood by the Greeks as well as by scholars as referring to a member of the learned Median priest-class of Archaemenid Persia.[30] More generally, the West-Iranian Magi typically had the reputation in classical antiquity of being wise men heir to ancient wisdom.[31] Though the Persian priest, on closer scrutiny, seems to have been a ritual specialist rather than a 'magician,' their practises were nevertheless seen as foreign and alien to the civic religion known to the Greeks.[32] Over time the exotic and barbarous dimension of the Greek perception became emphasised over the ethnographic realities,[33] a change which accounts for the subsequent employment of magic (Greek *mageía*) to characterise religious practises or ideologies deemed aberrant, fraudulent or Other. Terms such as *mágos* and *mageía* thus came to possess a dual meaning, referring on one hand to Persian priests (regarded with some prestige), and on the other to religious practices diverging from civic religiosity (regarded as errant).[34] This latter sense of magician came to refer particularly to itinerant ritual specialists who offered religious services for a fee.[35] The general notion of the Magus however, came to be regarded with simultaneous opprobrium and respect.

A century after Herodotus, a dual polemic arises against magic, indicating a shift in awareness whereby philosophy and medicine begin to be distinguished from the domain of magic. These tendencies are respectively exemplified in the writings of Plato and the Hippocratics; in both cases the methods of magic, which bordered on the domains of both the numinous and the medical, became displaced as the disciplines of theological philosophy and medicine were rationalised.[36] By late antiquity, magic had become well established as a term of disparagement.[37] Competing religious factions contemporaneous with nascent Christianity bear witness to a particularly intense need for polemical denigration of religious alternatives. Amidst such a climate, the term *mágos* became a polemical term *par excellence*. As Segal has shown, the would-be prophet had great need to simultaneously i) prove his numinous authority and ii) distinguish himself from the stigma of magic.[38] Thus a strong sense of ambivalence came to characterise the charismatic philosopher and divine-man (e.g. Jesus, Apollonius etc.), who could become a sage, sorcerer or charlatan depending on one's perspective (or bias).[39] Indeed, a very fine and, it would seem, arbitrary line separates the exercise of spiritual power from the practise of magic, to the point where the magic-religion distinction in late antiquity was based increasingly upon a politico-religious expediency oriented towards monopolisation of the *numen*.

INDO-EUROPEAN *mag(h)-

Despite the vicissitudes of the word *mágos* in the Graeco-Roman world, the question remains: what was its original significance? The Old Persian term is of uncertain etymology.[40] The most probable Indo-European root of 'magic' is *mag(h)-*,[41] which refers primarily to the ideas of ability and power. This is certainly the semantic field attested in Pokorny's *Indogermanisches etymologisches Wörterbuch*, which glosses Indo-European *magh-* as '*können*' (can/could, to be able), '*vermögen*,' (to do, to be able/capable), '*helfen*' (to help, assist), and Indo-European *magh-ti-* as '*Macht*' (power, might).[42] Mann's *An Indo-European Comparative Dictionary* lists two senses of *mag(h)-*, the first of which refers to 'charm, delight,' and the second to 'contrivance, invention.'[43]

Cognates of *mag(h)-* permit a more nuanced view. Among the Indo-Iranian languages, we find Indic *maghá-*, 'power, strength/force, wealth, gift,'[44] *maghávan-, maghávat-*, 'strong, powerful';[45] Iranian *magu-*, Old Persian *maguš*, 'magician.'[46] The Thraco-Phrygian languages, preserved only in Armenian, give us *marthankh*, 'aid, means of help.'[47] The Greek lexicon furnishes *mêkhos*, (Doric *mâkhos*, poetic *mēkhar*), 'aid,'[48] as well as *mēkhanḗ*, (Doric *mâkhaná*), 'device, art,'[49] whence Latin *machina*, 'machine, mechanism, aid, tool' (figuratively: 'cunning trick or ruse').[50] The Germanic languages provide two of the senses attributable to the Indo-European root *mag(h)-*. The first, glossed generally with the modern German cognate, '*mögen*' (to want to, like to), is attested in Gothic *magan*, Old Icelandic *mega, muga*, Old Frisian *muga*, Middle Low German *mögen*, and Old High German *magan, mugan*. The second appears to be derived from Proto-Germanic *mag- (to be able, to have power), which in Germanic forms *mah-tiz and *mag-ena.[51] Examples, which include Gothic *mag, mahts*, Old Icelandic *magn, megin*, Anglo-Saxon *mæg*, Old Saxon *megin*, Old High German *magan* and Old Frisian *mei*, are glossed variously as 'power, most important thing,'[52] or 'strength.'[53] Among the Baltic languages we find Lithuanian *māgulas*, 'numerous, many,'[54] Latvian m āžs, 'fantasy,'[55] Old Church Slavonic *mogo, mošti*, 'can, to be able; to do,'[56] and *moštъ* (Russian *močъ*), 'power, strength.'[57]

What this string of 'barbarous' words suggests is that magic may primarily find its etymological basis in concepts of power, ability and facility. Magic might best be conceived as stemming from a semantic field which suggests i) empowerment, ii) effectiveness, and iii) that which speeds, aids or quickens power, ability and effectiveness. From the foregoing we may therefore surmise, with Jean Gebser, that:

> There is a word group correlating among others the words 'make,' 'mechanism,' 'machine,' and 'might,' which all share a common Indo-European root *mag(h)-*. It is our conjecture that the word 'magic,' a Greek borrowing of Persian origin, belongs to the same field and thus shares the common root.[58]

That said, it is necessary to reiterate that the presumed connection of the name Magi with the reconstructed Indo-European root *mag(h)-* is by no means certain. Due to the tentativeness of the premise, it seems prudent to temporarily undervalue its place in our discussion pending supporting evidence. Therefore, to supplement our understanding of magic, and to provide independent descriptive vantages, we will turn to two examples which are linguistically unrelated to the Persian-Greek loanword and its proposed cognates.

SANSKRIT *māyā*

Little evidence appears forthcoming to suggest that the Sanskrit term for magic, *māyā*, is connected to the Indo-European root discussed above.[59] The agreed etymology of *māyā* derives it from the Sanskrit root *mā*, the primary meaning of which is 'to measure, mete out, mark off.' Further permutations give i) to measure across/traverse; ii) to measure by any standard, to compare; iii) to correspond in measure; iv) to measure out, apportion, grant; v) to help anyone, anything; vi) to prepare, arrange, fashion, form, build, make; vii) to show display, exhibit; and viii) to be measured, to cause to be measured or built, measure, build, erect.[60] The Sanskrit root is expandable to the broader Indo-European root, *med-, which describes the concept of measure in the context of ancient Indo-European notions of law. According to Emile Benveniste, the Indo-European root *med- forms the basis of the Greek concepts 'to take care of' (*medomai*) and 'meditate, reflect, invent' (*mēdomai*); the Latinised Oscan concept of 'magistrate' (*med-dix*); the Latin concepts of 'heal' (*medeor, medeo*),[61] and 'measure, moderation' (*modus, modestus*); and lastly two Germanic concepts: 'to measure' (Gothic *mitan*, Old High German *mezzan*, German *messen*) and 'to reflect, make plans' (Gothic *miton*, Old High German *mezzon*, German *ermessen*). As has been indicated, the notion which is posited to unify these diverse lexemes is that of *measure*. However, this is not a measure of material dimension, but an ethical measure which is imposed *on* things. As Benveniste points out, it is:

> ... a measure of which one is master and which implies reflexion and choice, and also presupposes a decision. In short, it is not something to do with measurement but with moderation, that is to say a measure applied to something to which measure is unknown, a measure of limitation and constraint [...] which is applied to a disorderly situation.[62]

Hence, *med-* suggests a 'tried and tested measure which brings order into a confused situation.' This is apparently the root meaning of the derived verbs signifying 'to heal,' which stem less from the notion of 'giving health,' and more from the concept of 'submitting a disturbed organism to given rules,' or 'bringing order into a state of confusion.'[63] The measure of *māyā* then, is presumably to be understood in the sense of 'taking measures,' and may be conceived as a process which rectifies and orders according to the dictates or juridical customs of sovereign power. As scholars such as Georges Dumézil have argued,[64] divine sovereignty is dually composed in Indo-

European ideology, consisting of a spiritual authority on one hand (the so-called magico-religious function), and a temporal power on the other (the regal-juridical function).⁶⁵ In the former case, sovereign control is executed via magic, in the latter via law and war.

All this is to suggest that the root *mā* is semantically centred in controlling measures exercised by sovereign divinity. We may justifiably expand this conception to include the very process that *establishes* the order which divine sovereignty seeks to maintain. Thus, beyond the senses denoting rectification and 'healing' exist those designating creation: 'fashion, form, make, build.' Furthermore, permutations such as 'show, display, exhibit' (Monier-Williams) and 'measure of limitation' (Benveniste) suggest the cosmogonic process of differentiation. That is to say, 'show, display and exhibit' refer to appearance, and hence manifestation; 'measure of limitation' to the process of demarcation or delineation. These terms therefore indicate the process whereby the invisible is made visible, the unmanifest manifest, the unlimited limited, and so on.⁶⁶ Let us refine our position by turning to the mythic and philosophical expressions of *māyā*.

Jan Gonda observes that a central meaning may be discerned amidst the polyvalent uses and shades of meaning which adhere to *māyā*.⁶⁷ While it is a fact that, in Sanskrit literature, one is able to distinguish between a pre-Vedic *māyā* (which is more 'mythic,' as exemplified in the magical exploits of Rudra and Indra) and a Vedāntic *māyā* (which is more 'philosophical,' notable chiefly in early Upanishadic thought), care must be taken to avoid emphasising one to the exclusion of the other.⁶⁸ Thus, both the subjugating power of Indra's magical net, and the Brahminic doctrine of phenomenal reality as an illusory veil obscuring absolute reality, must equally inform our understanding of *māyā*. Indeed, it is possible to define *māyā*, after Jan Gonda, in a way that accounts for both change *and* continuity. *Māyā* may thus be discerned as an 'incomprehensible wisdom and power enabling its possessor, or being able itself, to create, devise, contrive, effect, or do something.'⁶⁹ It does not always refer to illusions or false-reality, nor does it *necessarily* deal with the issue of phenomenal versus absolute reality (i.e. *māyā* vs. *brahman*).⁷⁰ Instead, the mythic dimension of *māyā* seems to converge upon the exercise of miraculous power which results in the creation of concrete form.⁷¹ Accordingly, *māyā* encompasses power, process and tangible result. That is to say, it is usefully understood in terms of i) the *power* which engenders an appearance, ii) the performative *act* of engendering an appearance, and iii) the resultant *appearance* itself.⁷² Not insignificantly, these three aspects of *māyā* can be usefully compared to the notions of *śakti* ('power'),⁷³ *karman* ('to act, do') and *prakṛti* ('material form').⁷⁴

It is necessary to emphasise that such a power is in essence amoral. That is to say, *māyā* acquires moral duality only insofar as 'good' or 'evil' agents employ it (e.g. *devas*, 'gods,' or *asuras*, 'anti-gods').⁷⁵ This instrumentality of *māyā* finds its most immediate expression in the form of Indra's net (*indrajālam*). Like Varuṇa's noose (to which it is often assimilated), it exists primarily as a symbol of divine superiority, and hence sovereignty.⁷⁶ Its overmastering power is well represented in *Atharvaveda* 8.8.5-8:

> The Atmosphere was the net ; the great quarters [were] the net-stakes ; therewith encircling [them], the mighty one (çakrá) scattered away the army of the barbarians (dáśu). [...]
> Since great [is] the net of the great mighty one, the vigorous (vāgnínīvant) – therewith do thou crowd (ubj) down upon all [our] foes, that no one soever of them may be released. [...]
> Great, O Indra, hero (çū́ra), is the net of thee that art great, that art worth a thousand, that hast hundred-fold heroism ; therewith encircling the army of the barbarians, the mighty one slew a hundred, a thousand, ten thousand, a hundred million. [...]
> This great world was the net of the great mighty one ; by that net of Indra do I encircle all yon men with darkness.⁷⁷

Elsewhere, Indra's net is synonymous with *māyā*, conveying concepts such as 'magic,' 'spectacular feat,' or 'creation of phantasms.'⁷⁸ Whether employed by gods or anti-gods, *māyā* is used to engender bewildering form (appearance, manifestation), or to modify, disguise or otherwise alter the appearance of a given form.⁷⁹ This is most explicit in the divine ability to shape-shift: 'By his uncanny powers (*māyā*) does Indra/ Rove around in many a form.'⁸⁰

Ultimately, it is not a difficult transition from *māyā* as 'outward appearance' to *māyā* as 'phenomenal reality,' and in this way the mythological *māyā* finds continuation in a manner which is applicable to the cosmos as a whole.[81] The philosophical dimension of *māyā* may thus be seen to converge upon the Upanishadic doctrine of the emanation of the phenomenal world by *brahman*. If anything, the shift reveals the pronounced metaphysical orientation which the Upanishads brought to Indian thought. Thus, in conceiving reality on an increasingly cosmological scale, the meaning of *māyā* is not so much transformed, but widened to signify the entire matrix of phenomenal appearance. This much is present in the passage from the *Atharvaveda* cited above ('This great world was the net of the great mighty one'). However, in the Upanishads, this phenomenal matrix is distinguished sharply from the absolute (i.e. the godhead), from which it is typically seen as either a derived form, or as an illusory veil.[82] This power is well characterised as 'hiding reality and projecting a pseudo-reality.'[83] Yet *māyā* retains its sense of bewildering appearance, paired with a subjugating valence; in its wider application, it bequeaths to the phenomenal world the same qualities of bewilderment and confusion as are engendered by the *māyā*-wielding gods of the *Ṛg Veda* upon their spectators.

PHARAONIC EGYPTIAN *ḥeka*

Egyptologists are fortunate that the traditional Pharaonic Egyptian term for magic, *ḥk3* (*ḥeka*), via its Coptic descendent (*ḥik*), came to be identified by the Egyptians with the Greek notion of magic (Greek *mageía*, Coptic *magia*),[84] thereby eliminating the problems usually besetting the use of Western categories in the study of other cultures. That being said, the Egyptian concept of magic is very different from that typically adhering to the received Western understanding (which as we have seen is largely a product of Graeco-Roman and Judaic-Christian perspectives).[85]

According to H. te Velde, *ḥeka*, stemming from the verb *hwi-k3* initially concerned the one who 'strikes' (*hwi*, 'to strike') the doubles or vital essences (*k3w*, '*kas*') of the creator god. That is to say, the one who consecrates, dedicates, or initiates the *kas* to life on earth.[86] Following from this, Robert Ritner suggests that the original significance of *ḥeka* is thus the 'consecration of images.'[87] In the context of Egyptian ceremonial, this takes on particular significance, for not only is the root meaning of *ntr* (the Egyptian term for god) also 'image,' but the Pharaoh, the priest, and the objects employed by them in ritual are so many embodiments of divine realities. Comments Ritner:

> The 'imagistic' process is shown repeatedly on Egyptian temple reliefs in which the king's ritual presentation of food, diadems and prisoners is a *reflection* of the god's granting of life, prosperity, and victory, each object being a tangible image of its abstract counterpart. The essential unity of the divine and royal actor is concretely embodied in the person of the Pharaoh, who is at once god and living image, expressed theologically in such names as [...] 'The living image of Amon/Re.' Obviously Pharaoh cannot perform every rite in all temples, and thus these were performed by *his* image, the priest. It is the priesthood which composed, collected and performed rites and spells for both public and private ceremonies, not merely imitating gods, but becoming them. By an intricate series of consciously elaborated imagery, humans may exploit the powers of the primordial gods.[88]

That royal and priestly action is homologous with divine action therefore suggests a functional identity by which humans can be magically assimilated to gods. The divine power to act at a distance is perhaps reflected in the word translated as 'spells' (*3ḥw*, or *akhu*), which is traceable to a verbal root signifying both 'to be effective,' and 'to shine.'[89] Accordingly, spells have the literal nuance of 'effective things,' and, concomitant with this, they may also denote an *emanation*. The latter notion seems to be justified insofar as it is consistent with the role of magic in Egyptian cosmogony and theogony.

Ḥeka, in addition to being a concept, is also personified as a god, and throughout Egyptian texts, no real distinction seems to be made between the concept of 'magic' (*ḥeka*), the title 'magician' (*ḥeka*) and the god 'Magic' (Ḥeka).[90] The divine personification is portrayed in Spell 261 of the *Coffin Texts* as the son of the Creator, as well as the causal, animating force of the gods:

> I am he whom the Unique Lord made before two things
> ('duality') had yet come into being in this land by sending forth his
> unique eye when he was alone, by the going forth from his mouth
> ... when he put Hu ('Logos') upon his mouth.
> I am indeed the son of Him who gave birth to the universe ('the
> All'), who was born before his mother yet existed. I am the
> protection of that which the Unique Lord has ordained. I am he
> who caused the Ennead to live ... I have seated myself, O bulls of
> heaven, in this my great dignity as Lord of *kas*, heir of Re-Atum.[91]

In the cosmogonic and theogonic process (which is cyclic, recurring with each dawn), Ḥeka as the first-born son of Re-Atum, is in actuality 'the hypostasis of the creator's own power which begets the natural order,' and as such may be seen to reside within the creative word itself (i.e. 'logos,' personified as Hu).[92] Ḥeka is therefore coeval or consubstantial with his father, and while Ḥeka manifests as the son of Atum-Re, he does not do so as a newly created god, but as the expression (cf. *b3* or *ba*) of the vital essence or power (*ka*) of the creator himself.[93] The epithets of Ḥeka, such as 'First-born son (of the creator-god)' and 'Eldest Magician,' are therefore explicable by virtue of his provenance as the primordial power which initiates, permeates, animates and ultimately actualises existence.[94] Just as the creator must precede the theogony, so too must his creative force, personified as Ḥeka, necessarily antedate the divine forces that it brings into being (to include 'rival' first-born deities such as Shu).[95]

Of course, Ḥeka's primacy as a personification of divine creative power does not preclude other roles. This is most notable in the chthonic journey of the solar bark, where Ḥeka protects the sun-god against nocturnal dangers, the most formidable of which is the eternally regenerating serpent of chaos and non-existence, Apophis.[96] In the tenth hour of the Book of Gates, for instance, we find the god Ḥeka wielding nets to constrain and control Apophis, thereby effecting the dominance of divine order over primeval chaos through magical binding.[97] Thus, the power which establishes the ordered universe at daybreak, inherent both to the generation and animation of existence, is wielded by night to defend the created order and destroy its enemies.

It is thus apparent that the force embodied as Ḥeka, like the net wielded by Indra, is an ultimately bivalent force. This follows from its instrumentality, and as such it may be understood as an essentially unadulterated power. Indeed, lexical evidence tells us that as early as the twentieth dynasty, the phonetic rendering of the god's name was often replaced with the emblem of the lion's hind-quarters (*pḥty*), to which is ascribed the meaning of 'strength/power.'[98]

Thus, the concept of *ḥeka* is primarily understandable as a bivalent force inherent in the *ka* or vital essence, and able to be emanated to effect creative/apotropaic and destructive influence. Like *mag(h)*- and *māyā*, it is deeply bound with notions of power, effectiveness and the ability to *do*. Therefore, evidence philologically unrelated to Indo-European *mag(h)*- serves to consolidate, via cultural if not linguistic parallel, the tentative identification of Persian *magu*- with the semantic field of strength and ability. Moreover, the instrumentality of magic, expressed in both the *Atharvaeda* and the *Book of Gates* as a binding net, seems to correlate well enough with the notion of 'mechanism' or 'tool' attributable to *mag(h)*-. Additionally, while *māyā* and *ḥeka* are without doubt forces of domineering subjugation, their destructive valence is compensated by their connection to the sovereign creative force that underpins the phenomenal cosmos. Overall, we can begin to see a basic facility between the numinous and the concrete.

Between Essence and Manifestation

By way of conclusion, we will draw attention to a few motifs which may reveal additional meaning. It should be noted that such can only be preliminary to a more encompassing theory of magic, and should not be mistaken for a comprehensive nor universal definition. At most, I seek to articulate some of the common underpinnings discernable in the material presented above. Where appropriate, I will cross-reference material outside the bounds of the present discussion in order to further consolidate the significance of the motifs identified.

As we have seen, the semantic complex of power-ability-effectiveness is evident beyond the proposed cognates of *mágos*. Magic, as apprehended through the linguistic lenses of **mag(h)-*, *māyā* and *ḥeka*, all converge on the power to *do*.[99] In the latter two examples, this is closely connected with the power of affecting and effecting *appearance* (e.g. phenomenal reality, living image). This sense is not explicit in the Indo-European derivatives of **mag(h)-*; only the Latvian cognate *māžs*, 'phantasy,' gives us a comparable sense. Yet, in the predominantly Greek-influenced magical tradition of Western Europe (of which the Florentine Neoplatonists are representative), it is precisely the notion of *phantasía*, 'imagination' that is discernable as a fundamental magical concept.[100] Here it is worth noting that the Greek term *phantasía* (derived from the verb *phaínō*, 'to appear, to be apparent, to come to light') is bound to the notion of that which is *phenomenal* (*phainómenon*). Derived from the same verb is *phantázō*, 'to take a definite appearance, to take shape – as of a spectre, or to give oneself an appearance, to exalt oneself.'[101] All this pertains quite transparently to phenomenology. Of this, we may extrapolate two orders: A first, which simply signifies manifestation, and a second, which seems to recall the Vedic understanding of *māyā* as an ability or power to affect an appearance in the phenomenal world. One pertains to the manifest world itself (i.e. the world of phenomena), and the other to something *beyond* the world of appearances which is able to reveal itself in phenomenal form (e.g. as in a theophany).

The primacy of *power* in our discussion of magic has some further implications that require explication. The deep and fundamental connection of magic to power provides the basis upon which we may understand much of its attendant symbology. This is most notably structured in terms of a divine-human continuum. The scale of being from human to god is functionally equivalent to a scale of power. Relative positions on this scale are sufficient to account for the duality of god and human, immortal and mortal, subjugator and subjugated, master and slave, and so on. Moreover, it also provides the basis of initiation, which is not only founded upon ontological transition, but accounts for the strong presence of *liminality* in the mechanics and symbology of magic.[102] Thus, to acquire magical power is equivalent to making the transitions which result in self-deification, as was explicitly the case in Egypt where identification with the deity was fundamental to the mechanics of magic.[103] More power meant more ability, more effectiveness, and was analogous to more ontological freedom in the cosmos. Conversely, less power meant less ability, effectiveness and freedom in the cosmos. Almost unanimously, this conception of reality is overwhelmingly cast in the symbolism of binding; fettering and unfettering thus become the currency of subjugation and liberation upon the scale of being. Magically, this finds diverse expression: Indra's net, the bound prisoner motif in Egyptian ritual, the Greek *katádesmos* and Roman *defixio*, Giordano Bruno's *vinculum*, to name but a few.[104] Moreover, it is here where we can most clearly see the boundaries between religion and magic dissolve, as is suggested, for instance, in the root meanings of *religō* ('tie up, fasten') or *yoga* ('to yoke').[105] Even in philosophy, the will to power has been expressed (by Nietzsche) as *Selbstüberwindung*, literally 'self over-winding.'[106]

Finally, that the magician could effect a resonance or identification of human and god on the scale of being suggests, as it were, some *bond* between these dimensions of existence. This is implicit in so far as the divine power of magic actually gives rise to the manifest or phenomenal world, whether emanated as cosmogony or projected as a bewildering veil. Thus the impetus toward divine power, like Gnosis, may be conceived as a return to an original or primordial condition;[107] it is tantamount to a reversal of the cosmogony, a withdrawal of projected delusions. Indo-European traditions are less anticosmic; rather than a 'fall' from spirit to matter to be rectified by salvific ascent, the transition is viewed as an eternally recurring shift between microcosmic and macrocosmic orders of manifestation (the basic substance of each condition being identical, merely constituted differently at different moments in the cosmic cycle).[108] Grounds exist to suggest that the theogony sung by the Persian Magi during ritual sacrifice[109] bespoke the creative phase of precisely this cosmogony.[110] Egyptian processes of eternally-regenerating creation are not entirely dissimilar. All this is to suggest that the bond between essence and manifestation is cyclic, as reflected in the phases of interiorisation and objectification, union and separation, 'love and strife.'[111] Esotericism and exotericism, magic and religion, may well be seen as complimentary, any distinction between them being one of relative orientation.

Be that as it may, it is enough to establish that the path to attaining divine power is centripetal, while the path of *exercising* divine power is centrifugal. Our etymologies affirm that magic is most closely related to the latter phase. What is fundamental to magic is sufficient *mastery* over the process, which brings us back to the concepts of power, ability, and effectiveness (**mag(h)-*). Whether magic is the vital power consubstantial with divinity and responsible for the generation and animation of the phenomenal world (*ḥeka*), or the bewildering power of appearances which conceals and reveals absolute reality (*māyā*), mastery over this power enables both the trans-empirical manipulation of phenomenal reality (hence magic as commonly understood), and the 'shifting of the veil' to reveal absolute reality (hence self-deifying Gnosis).

Notes

[1] Friedrich Wilhelm Nietzsche, *Werke : Kritische Gesamtausgabe*, ed. Giorgio Colli and Mazzino Montinari (Berlin: De Gruyter, 1967-8), VI.I, 45: 'Ihr seht nach Oben, wenn ihr nach Erhebung verlangt. Und ich sehe hinab, weil ich erhoben bin.' Translation, R.J. Hollingdale.

[2] Einar Thomassen, 'Is Magic a Subclass of Ritual?' in *The World of Ancient Magic : Papers from the First International Samson Eitrem Seminar at the Norwegian Institute at Athens, 4-8 May 1997*, ed. Hugo Montgomery, Einar Thomassen, and David R. Jordan, *Papers from the Norwegian Institute at Athens ; 4* (Bergen: The Norwegian Institute at Athens, 1999), 55-6.

[3] Cf. Emile Durkheim, *The Elementary Forms of the Religious Life*, trans. Joseph Ward Swain (London: Allen and Unwin, 1915), 44 ff; James George Frazer, *The Golden Bough : A Study in Magic and Religion*, 3rd ed., vol. 1, The Magic Art and the Evolution of Kings (London: Macmillan, 1911; reprint, 1963), 234 ff; Marcel Mauss, *A General Theory of Magic*, trans. Robert Brain (London: Routledge and Kegan Paul, 1972), 24.

[4] Cf. the articles collected in Jacob Neusner, Ernest S. Frerichs, and Paul Virgil McCracken Flesher, eds., *Religion, Science, and Magic : In Concert and in Conflict* (New York: Oxford University Press, 1989).

[5] For discussion of issues surrounding rationality, see Stanley Jeyaraja Tambiah, *Magic, Science, Religion, and the Scope of Rationality, Lewis Henry Morgan Lectures ; 1981.* (Cambridge, U.K.: Cambridge University Press, 1990).

[6] Jonathan Z. Smith, 'Trading Places,' in *Ancient Magic and Ritual Power*, ed. Marvin W. Meyer and Paul Allan Mirecki, *Religions in the Greco-Roman World ; 129* (Leiden: E.J. Brill, 1995), 13-14.

[7] Frazer conjectures that magic is the earliest and most primitive form of human thought: 'just as on the material side of human culture there has everywhere been

an Age of Stone, so on the intellectual side there has everywhere been an Age of Magic.' See Frazer, *The Golden Bough*, 232-40. For discussion, see Smith, 'Trading Places,' 13-15.

⁸ Smith, 'Trading Places,' 14-15.

⁹ For Tylor, see Edward Burnett Tylor, *Primitive Culture : Researches into the Development of Mythology, Philosophy, Religion, Language, Art and Custom*, 2 vols. (London: Murray, 1871), I, 116.

¹⁰ See Jens Braarvig, 'Magic : Reconsidering the Grand Dichotomy,' in *The World of Ancient Magic: Papers from the First International Samson Eitrem Seminar at the Norwegian Institute at Athens, 4-8 May 1997*, ed. Hugo Montgomery, Einar Thomassen, and David R. Jordan (1999), 21 n.1.

¹¹ See E. E. Evans-Pritchard's 'The Morphology and Function of Magic : A Comparative Study of Trobriand and Zande Ritual and Spells,' *American Anthropologist* 31 (1929): 619-41; 'Witchcraft (Mangu) among the A-Zande,' *Sudan Notes and Records* 12 (1929): 163-249; and *Witchcraft, Oracles and Magic among the Azande* (Oxford: Clarendon Press, 1937), passim.

¹² On the original formulation of the terms 'emic' and 'etic' (derived from 'phonemic' and 'phonetic'), see Kenneth L. Pike, *Language in Relation to a Unified Theory of the Structure of Human Behavior*, Preliminary ed. (Glendale, Ill.: Summer Institute of Linguistics, 1954). It should be noted that in the kind of linguistic analysis that we will be advancing, such distinctions can become lost to the extent that lexical items are removed from their original contexts.

¹³ Cf. discussion in David Frankfurter, 'The Dynamics of Ritual Expertise in Antiquity and Beyond : Towards a New Taxonomy of Magicians,' in *Magic and Ritual in the Ancient World*, ed. Paul Allan Mirecki and Marvin W. Meyer, *Religions in the Graeco-Roman World ; 141* (Leiden: E.J. Brill, 2002), 159.

¹⁴ Braarvig, 'Magic : Reconsidering the Grand Dichotomy,' 27-8. Recent years have seen the scholar and practitioner of magic coincide in the same individual, as is the case, for instance for Susan Greenwood, on which see her *Magic, Witchcraft and the Otherworld : An Anthropology* (Oxford ; New York: Berg, 2000), 11-19. This is not an exclusively modern phenomenon, however; Apuleius also blurs the boundary with the dual perspectives displayed in his *Apologia* and *Metamorphoses*.

¹⁵ Braarvig, 'Magic : Reconsidering the Grand Dichotomy,' 22-3.

¹⁶ Cf. Keith Vivian Thomas, *Religion and the Decline of Magic : Studies in Popular Beliefs in Sixteenth and Seventeenth Century England* (London: Weidenfeld & Nicolson, 1971), 641 ff.

¹⁷ Fritz Graf, 'Excluding the Charming: The Development of the Greek Concept of Magic,' in *Ancient Magic and Ritual Power*, ed. Marvin W. Meyer and Paul Allan Mirecki, *Religions in the Greco-Roman World ; 129* (Leiden: E.J. Brill, 1995), 30-35; H. S. Versnel, 'Some Reflections on the Relationship Magic-Religion,' *Numen* 38 (1991): 188-92.

¹⁸ Braarvig, 'Magic : Reconsidering the Grand Dichotomy,' 44-5. Braavig discusses

Bhavya as an apologist for the religious rather than magical use of mantras in mahāyāna Buddhism.

[19] Hence the approach of Robert Ritner, who, with no pretence of universality, responds by explicitly adopting a working definition advanced from a self-acknowledged Modern Western perspective, a definition which is proclaimed as serviceable only for examining cultures purely from our own cultural vantage. See Robert Kriech Ritner, 'The Religious, Social and Legal Parameters of Traditional Egyptian Magic,' in *Ancient Magic and Ritual Power*, ed. Marvin W. Meyer and Paul Allan Mirecki, *Religions in the Greco-Roman World ; 129* (Leiden: E.J. Brill, 1995), 44-5. Here Ritner defines magic as: 'any activity which seeks to obtain its goal by methods outside the simple laws of cause and effect.' Moreover, Ritner's study of ancient Egyptian magic shows, contrary to evidence for the separation of magic and religion, that magic (or *ḥeka*), was actually *central* to Egyptian religion, thereby providing a finite historical counter-example to the validity of Western categories. See Ritner, *The Mechanics of Ancient Egyptian Magical Practice, Studies in Ancient Oriental Civilization ; No. 54* (Chicago, Ill.: Oriental Institute of University of Chicago, 1993), 4-28, 192-249.

[20] Braarvig, 'Magic : Reconsidering the Grand Dichotomy,' 21 ff.

[21] In Mauss's words, we have: 'two extremes which form the differing poles of magic religion: the pole of sacrifice and the pole of evil spells.' Commenting further, he adds that: 'A continuity thus exists between magic and religion. Yet despite this interrelationship, an awareness of their differences is also present, which thereby influences how they are practised.' Consequently, Mauss reasons that these consciously expressed differences enable some kind of classification to be made.

[22] William J. Goode, 'Magic and Religion : A Continuum,' *Ethnos* 14, no. 2-4 (1949): 176 ff.

[23] Cf. discussion in Versnel, 'Magic-Religion,' 181, 87.

[24] Thomassen, 'Is Magic a Subclass of Ritual?'

[25] Cf. Ritner's conclusion (in accordance with van Gennep) that for ancient Egyptian temple practice, 'magic' in fact comprised the *techniques* of 'religion' (i.e. official cult), from which it was inseparable. Ritner, *Mechanics*, 247.

[26] For the shamanic nature of the archaic Greek magician (*góēs*), see Walter Burkert, "ΓΟΗΣ : Zum griechischen 'Schamanismus'," *Rheinisches Museum* 105 (1962): 36-55. For Greek shamanism in general, see E. R. Dodds, *The Greeks and the Irrational, Sather Classical Lectures, v. 25* (Berkeley: University of California Press, 1951), 135-78.

[27] Graf, "Excluding the Charming," 36-7. According to Graf, the Homeric *phármakon* was a drug possessing supernatural effect, and employed toward both criminal and medical ends (e.g. poisoning and healing). This existed alongside the *epoidē* or 'incantation,' a verbal utterance with supernatural effect (mostly positive/medical).

[28] *Ibid.*, 36-40.

[29] See Hjalmar Frisk, *Griechisches etymologisches Wörterbuch, Indogermanische*

Bibliothek. 2. Reihe, Wörterbücher. (Heidelberg: C. Winter, 1960), II, 156; Albert de Jong, *Traditions of the Magi : Zoroastrianism in Greek and Latin Literature, Religions in the Graeco-Roman World v. 133*. (Leiden: E.J. Brill, 1997), 394-5. The Iranian loanword reached Greece in the sixth century B.C.E., on which see Burkert, „ΓΟΗΣ," 38.

[30] Jong, *Traditions of the Magi*, 387.

[31] The chief classical account of the Magi is Herodotus' *Histories*, where the Magi (Greek *Mágoi*) are mentioned as one among several Medean tribes (1.101). Others include the Busae, the Paretaceni, the Struchates, the Arizanti, and the Budii. For text and translation, see Herodotus, *Herodotus*, trans. A. D. Godley, *Loeb Classical Library*. (London: Heinemann, 1920). For secondary accounts of the Magi, see Elias J. Bickerman and H. Tadmor, "Darius I, Pseudo-Smerdis and the Magi," *Athenaeum* 59 (1978): 239-61; Gherardo Gnoli, "Magi," in *The Encyclopedia of Religion*, ed. Mircea Eliade (New York: Macmillan, 1993), IX, 79-81; Jong, *Traditions of the Magi*, 387-413. For the development of the meaning of *mágos* in the classical world see Arthur Darby Nock, "Paul and the Magus," in *Arthur Darby Nock : Essays on Religion and the Ancient World* (Oxford: Clarendon Press, 1972), I, 308-330. See also Graf, "Excluding the Charming," 30-33; Graf, *Magic in the Ancient World*, 26 ff; Peter Kingsley, "Meetings with Magi : Iranian Themes among the Greeks, from Xanthus of Lydia to Plato's Academy," *Journal of the Royal Asiatic Society* 5 (1995): 173-209.

[32] This was certainly the case for Plato (*First Alcibiades*, 122 E f, 123 A) as it was for Apuleius (*Apology*, 25.10).

[33] Various attributes and practices of the Magi are recorded in Herodotus, to include royal dream interpretation, rites of exposure, killing of noxious creatures, offering of libations, sacrifice, and sorcery. See Herodotus' *Histories*, 1.107, 1.120, 1.128, 7.19, 7.37 (dream interpretation), 1.140 (rites of exposure, killing of noxious animals), 7.43 (offering of libations), 7.113 (sacrifice), and 7.191 (sacrifice, sorcery).

[34] Graf, *Magic in the Ancient World*, 29.

[35] The Magus was also conceived as a charlatan, fraud or quack. See Nock, "Paul and the Magus," 301 ff, 23-4.

[36] Walter Burkert, "Itinerant Diviners and Magicians : A Neglected Element in Cultural Contacts," in *The Greek Renaissance of the Eighth Century B.C. : Tradition and Innovation : Proceedings of the Second International Symposium at the Swedish Institute in Athens, 1-5 June, 1981*, ed. Robin Hägg (Stockholm: Svenska institutet i Athen, 1983), 116, 18.

[37] For Plato, see in particular *Laws*, 10.909 B. For the Hippocratics, see Hippocrates and Heraclitus, *Hippocrates : With an English Translation by W.H.S. Jones and E.T. Withington, Loeb Classical Library*. (London: Heinemann, 1923), II, 140-1. See discussion in Graf, *Magic in the Ancient World*, 20-7; Graf, "Theories of Magic in Antiquity," in *Magic and Ritual in the Ancient World*, ed. Paul Allan Mirecki and Marvin W. Meyer, *Religions in the Graeco-Roman World ; 141* (Leiden: E.J. Brill,

2002), 97-9.

[38] For discussion of the understanding of magic contemporaneous with Jesus, see Morton Smith, *Jesus the Magician*, 1st ed. (San Francisco: Harper & Row, 1978), 68-91.

[39] Segal, "Hellenistic Magic : Some Questions of Definition," 355 ff.

[40] Graf, *Magic in the Ancient World*, 232-3.

[41] Gnoli, "Magi," 79.

[42] In historical linguistics, an asterix before a lexeme denotes a word that has been reconstructed by scholars; while unattested, it is proposed as a root of attested forms.

[43] Julius Pokorny, *Indogermanisches etymologisches Wörterbuch* (Bern: Francke, 1951), II, 695.

[44] Stuart Edward Mann, *An Indo-European Comparative Dictionary* (Hamburg: H. Buske, 1984), 726.

[45] Pokorny, *IeW*, II, 695: 'Macht, Kraft, Reichtum, Gabe.'

[46] *Ibid*: 'kräftig.'

[47] *Ibid*: 'Magier, Zauberer.'

[48] *Ibid*: 'Hilfsmittel.'

[49] *Ibid*: 'Hilfsmittel.'

[50] Mann, *ICD*, 726. Cf. *magh-* as 'contrivance, invention.'

[51] Pokorny, *IeW*, II, 695: 'Hilfsmittel, Werkzeug, List.'

[52] Stephen E. Flowers, *Runes and Magic : Magical Formulaic Elements in the Older Runic Tradition* (New York: P. Lang, 1986), 127; Friedrich Kluge and Elmar Seebold, *Etymologisches Wörterbuch der deutschen Sprache*, 22. Aufl. / ed. (Berlin: Walter de Gruyter, 1989), 453; Jan de Vries, *Altgermanische Religionsgeschichte*, Grundriss der germanischen Philologie. (Berlin: Walter de Gruyter, 1956), I, 275 ff.

[53] Pokorny, *IeW*, II, 695: 'Macht, Hauptsache.'

[54] *Ibid*: 'Kraft.'

[55] *Ibid*: 'zahlreich, viel.'

[56] Mann, *ICD*, 726. Usually attested in the plural: *mā• i*, 'fantasies.'

[57] Pokorny, *IeW*, II, 695: 'können, vermögen.'

[58] *Ibid*: 'Macht, Stärke.'

[59] Gebser, *The Ever-Present Origin*, 46.

[60] While *māyā* has in the past been connected to I-E **mag(h)-*, more recent scholarly consensus deems this unlikely. However, due to the nature of the evidence, the position cannot be wholly excluded, if only for the reasons that a) where the Indo-European root and the Sanskrit term differ phonetically (a voiced palatal stop versus a palatal semivowel), they nevertheless share the same *place* of articulation (i.e. the palate), and b) *māyā* came to possess the dual meaning of 'magic' and 'illusion' as did *mágos* in the Graeco-Roman world. Be that as it may, the cognates or *māyā* are with Zend Avestan *mā*; Greek *metron*, *metreo*, *medomai*;

Latin *mētior, mensus, mensura, medeo/r*; Slavic *mera*; and Lithuanian *merà*. Cf. Emile Benveniste and Jean Lallot, *Indo-European Language and Society, Studies in General Linguistics*. (London: Faber, 1973), 400; Monier Monier-Williams, Ernst Leumann, and Carl Cappeller, *A Sanskrit-English Dictionary : Etymologically and Philologically Arranged with Special Reference to Cognate Indo-European Languages*, New ed. (Oxford: Clarendon Press, 1976), 804.

[61] Monier-Williams, Leumann, and Cappeller, *Sanskrit-English Dictionary*, 804.

[62] Some derived forms: *medicare, medicatio, medicina, medicamentum, remedium*.

[63] Benveniste and Lallot, *Indo-European Language and Society*, 403.

[64] *Ibid.*, 405.

[65] See in particular Georges Dumézil, *Mitra-Varuna : An Essay on Two Indo-European Representations of Sovereignty*, 2nd ed. (New York: Zone Books, 1988), passim. For general discussion of Dumézil's theories, see C. Scott Littleton, *The New Comparative Mythology : An Anthropological Assessment of the Theories of Georges Dumézil*, Rev. ed. (Berkeley: University of California Press, 1973), passim.

[66] Cf. the excellent exegesis on this motif by Ananda K. Coomaraswamy, *Spiritual Authority and Temporal Power in the Indian Theory of Government, American Oriental Series ; v. 22*. (New Haven, Conn.: American Oriental Society, 1942), passim.

[67] In this light, the Greek and Germanic cognates which give us 'reflect, invent, make plans' seem to indicate a microcosmic reflection of a homologous macrocosmic process. That is to say, from an inner or unmanifest activity (*med*itation, *men*-tation) is derived an outer or manifest expression (taking measures).

[68] J. Gonda, *Change and Continuity in Indian Religion* (The Hague: Mouton, 1965), 192-3: 'It cannot however be said that the idea itself has in the course of the last twenty-three hundred centuries or so been essentially modified. What was at first intuitively understood and imperfectly formulated, elucidated by popular similes, or intimated by means of mythological imagery, underwent, in later times, a process of intellectualization, of deepening and broadening; the very core of the concept, however, remained unaffected.'

[69] *Ibid.*, 164-5.

[70] *Ibid.*, 166. In this connection, it is well to note that Indra, whom we see to figure prominently the mythic expression of *māyā*, is in Dumézil's schema the second-function god, i.e. the king-warrior who is characterised by activity (*rājas*), that is, one who enacts or *does*.

[71] *Ibid*.

[72] Teun Goudriaan, *Māyā Divine and Human : A Study of Magic and Its Religious Foundations in Sanskrit Texts, with Particular Attention to a Fragment on Vishnu's Māyā Preserved in Bali*, 1st ed. (Delhi: Motilal Banarsidass, 1978), 2. Creation of concrete form may take human or non-human forms.

[73] On *māyā* as outward appearance, cf. Ṛg Veda 6.58.1: *víśvā hí māyā́ ávasi svadhāvo bhadrā́ te pūshann ihá rātír astu*. For edition, see Theodor Aufrecht, ed.,

Die Hymnen des Rigveda, 4. Aufl. / ed., 2 vols. (Wiesbaden: Harrassowitz, 1968), I, 448.

[74] Cf. the tantric Śakti as personification as the Lord's creative power.

[75] Goudriaan, *Māyā*, 3-4.

[76] Cf. *su-māyā-*, 'good *māyā*,' and *durmāyu-*, 'bad *māyā*,' as discussed in Gonda, *Change and Continuity*, 167.

[77] Goudriaan, *Māyā*, 215. The motif of *māyā* as a magic net (*māyājāla*) is traceable to the *Atharvaveda*.

[78] Translation, William Dwight Whitney, *Atharva-Veda-Samhita*, 2nd Indian reprint ed., 2 vols., *Harvard Oriental Series ; V.7 ; V.8.* (Delhi: Motilal Banarsidass, 1971), II, 504, parenthesis and square brackets Whitney, square brackets marking ellipses, mine (here I have only removed editorial commentary between the translated passages).

[79] Goudriaan, *Māyā*, 214.

[80] *Ibid.*, 2-3.

[81] *Ṛg Veda* 6.47.18: '*rūpáṃ-rūpam prátirūpo babhūva tád asya rūpám praticákshaṇāya / índro māyā́bhiḥ pururū́pa īyate yuktā́ hy asyā́ hárayaḥ śatā́ dáśa*' For edition, see Aufrecht, ed., *Rigveda*, I, 437. See also *Bṛhadāraṇyka Upaniṣad* 2.5.19. Text and translation in *Brhadaranyaka Upanisad : Containing the Original Text with Word-by-Word Meanings, Translation, Notes and Introduction*, 2nd ed., Upanisad Series. (Mylapore: Sri Ramakrishna Math, 1951), 177-8.

[82] Gonda, *Change and Continuity*, 171.

[83] Teun Goudriaan, " Māyā," in *The Encyclopedia of Religion*, ed. Mircea Eliade (New York: Macmillan, 1993), IX, 297.

[84] Gonda, *Change and Continuity*, 184-5.

[85] This occurred in Coptic Christian times. A passage from the 'Martyrdom of Saint George' is cited by Ritner as representative of the identification, also attested in the Coptic translation of *Acts* 8: 9 to describe the 'magic' of Simon Magus (*rhik* 'to do *hik*' = Greek *mageúon*). See Ritner, *Mechanics*, 14-15; Ritner, "Traditional Egyptian Magic," 48. On the derivation of Coptic *hik* see Jaroslav Černy, *Coptic Etymological Dictionary* (Cambridge, U.K.: Cambridge University Press, 1976), 276. For Coptic usage and Greek parallels, see Walter Ewing Crum, *A Coptic Dictionary : Compiled with the Help of Many Scholars* (Oxford: The Clarendon Press, 1939), 661.

[86] The inadequacy of Western theories of magic in relation to ḥeka is discussed in W. Gutekunst, "Zauber(er) (-Mittel, -Praktiken, -Spruch)," in *Lexikon der Ägyptologie*, ed. Wolfgang Helck, Eberhard Otto, and Wolfhart Westendorf (Wiesbaden: O. Harrassowitz, 1972), VI, cols. 1321-6; Ritner, *Mechanics*, 4-28, 192-249.

[87] Herman te Velde, "The God Heka in Egyptian Theology," *Jaarbericht ex Oriente Lux* 21 (1970): 179-80. The sense of 'initiation' (i.e. a beginning) may well be

reflected in the native or 'folk' etymology from Esna, which derives ḥk3 from ḥ(3.t)-k3(.t), 'first work'. Cf. Ritner, *Mechanics*, 25.

[88] Ritner, "Traditional Egyptian Magic," 49.

[89] *Ibid.*, 50-1, italics Ritner

[90] Cf. Fifth hour, fifth scene in *The Book of the Amduat*: 'may your ... magic shine.' For text and (German) translation, see Erik Hornung, *Das Amduat : Die Schrift des verborgenen Raumes*, 3 vols. (Wiesbaden: Harrassowitz, 1963), I, 180, II, 98: ‚Mögen eure Worte entstehen und mögen eure Zauber leuchten (*sšp*).' On the relationship of ḥk3 to 3ḥw, and the sense 'effective; bright,' see Ritner, *Mechanics*, 30, 34; te Velde, "Heka," 176-7.

[91] Ritner, *Mechanics*, 16; te Velde, "Heka," 177.

[92] Translation: Ritner, *Mechanics*, 17. See also Raymond Oliver Faulkner, ed., *The Ancient Egyptian Coffin Texts* (Warminster, U.K.: Aris & Phillips, 1973), I, 199-201; te Velde, „Heka," 180. Ritner and te Velde appear to lend the most precise renditions of the passage under consideration.

[93] Ritner, *Mechanics*, 17. On Ḥeka as preceding creation, see discussion in Erik Hornung, *Conceptions of God in Ancient Egypt : The One and the Many* (Ithaca: Cornell University Press, 1982), 208-9; Ritner, *Mechanics*, 17; te Velde, "Heka," 176.

[94] On Ḥeka as a hypostasis or personification of the creator's power, see Hans Bonnet, *Reallexikon der ägyptischen Religionsgeschichte* (Berlin: De Gruyter, 1952), 301; Ritner, *Mechanics*, 17; te Velde, "Heka," 180-1. The connection of *ḥeka* with the vital essence (*ka*) is variously attested. At the birth of the Pharaoh, the child and his *ka* are brought to the god Ḥeka, who brings them to Ennead of gods. H?eka probably bestows magical protection via consecrating or initiating vital potential. Elsewhere, Ḥeka is one of the fourteen *kas* of the Pharaoh, and one of the 14 *kas* and 7 *bas* of Re. See te Velde, "Heka," 178-82.

[95] Ritner, *Mechanics*, 25. It is worth noting that the native etymology ('first work') appears to be consistent with these epithets. On the generative power of Ḥeka in the cosmogony, see *Coffin Texts* spell 648: 'It was Heka ... who created the mountains and knit the firmament together.' Translation: Faulkner, *Coffin Texts*, 223-4.

[96] te Velde, "Heka," 180-3. It has been rightly recognised that the fundamental consubstantiality of magical power underpins the significance of the creator's bodily fluids (notably saliva), a motif which informs practices down to the *Greek Magical Papyri*. See Ritner, *Mechanics*, 74 ff.

[97] Ritner, *Mechanics*, 18-20.

[98] Hornung, *Conceptions of God*, 208.

[99] Ritner, *Mechanics*, 25-6; te Velde, "Heka," 184-5. Te Velde glosses *pḥty* as 'physical strength, sexual power, creative power.'

[100] This much was clear to Mauss (based on somewhat different evidence). Marcel Mauss's theory of magic first appeared in French as early as 1904, later to be published in his *Sociologie et Anthropologie* in 1950, and translated into English

in 1972. For editions, see Henri Hubert and Marcel Mauss, "Esquisse d'une théorie générale de la magie," *Année sociologique* 7 (1904); Mauss, *A General Theory of Magic*. Here magic and technology are seen as different kinds of ability, magic being etymologically connected with the semantic notion of 'to do,' as attested in the examples of Sanskrit *karman, kṛtya*, Latin *factum* and German *Zauber*. This sense of effectiveness attributed to the magical rite was seen as indistinguishable from the *effectiveness* of techniques commonly found in arts, crafts etc. While the arts and crafts themselves are 'universally distinguished' from magic, Mauss suggests that rites might be distinguished as *'traditional actions whose effectiveness is sui generis'* (Mauss, *A General Theory of Magic*, 19-20, emphasis Mauss). Magic then, while essentially the art of doing things, is more specifically the art of 'pure production *ex nihilo*.' A magician is able to achieve with word and gesture what technique achieves with labour: 'A magician does nothing, or almost nothing, but makes everyone believe that he is doing everything' (*A General Theory of Magic*, 141-2).

[101] The Renaissance Neoplatonists from Ficino to Bruno are particularly representative. For a magisterial treatment of magic and phantasmology in Renaissance thought, see Ioan P. Culianu, *Eros and Magin in the Renaissance*, trans. Margaret Cook (Chicago: Chicago University Press, 1987), passim. See also the chapters on the *vis imaginativa* in Antoine Faivre, *Theosophy, Imagination, Tradition : Studies in Western Esotericism*, SUNY Series in Western Esoteric Traditions (Albany, NY: State University of New York Press, 2000), 99-167. For the theoretical exposition of the imaginal as a mediating reality with its own ontological verity, see Henry Corbin, *Mundus Imaginalis: Or, the Imaginary and the Imaginal* (Ipswich: Golgonooza Press, 1976), passim.

[102] Murray Wright Bundy, *The Theory of Imagination in Classical and Mediaeval Thought* (Norwood, Pa.: Norwood Editions, 1977), 12.

[103] For the general theory of liminality and initiation, see Arnold van Gennep, *The Rites of Passage* (London: Routledge & Kegan Paul, 1960); Victor Turner, *The Ritual Process : Structure and Anti-Structure, Lewis Henry Morgan Lectures ; 1966.* (London: Routledge & Kegan Paul, 1969). For discussion of liminality in the mechanics and symbology of magic, see Graf, *Magic in the Ancient World*, 106 ff; Sarah Iles Johnston, "Crossroads," *Zeitschrift für Papyrologie und Epigraphik* 88 (1991): 217-24; H. S. Versnel, "The Poetics of the Magical Charm : An Essay on the Power of Words," in *Magic and Ritual in the Ancient World*, ed. Paul Allan Mirecki and Marvin W. Meyer, *Religions in the Graeco-Roman World ; 141* (Leiden: E. J. Brill, 2002), 145-51.

[104] Derived practices continue down through to the Theurgy of the *Chaldaean Oracles*, the *Mithras Liturgy* and the *Greek Magical Papyri* in general.

[105] For the bound-prisoner motif and the function of binding in Egyptian magic, see Ritner, *Mechanics*, 113-44. For binding in Graeco-Roman execration texts, see John G. Gager, ed., *Curse Tablets and Binding Spells from the Ancient World* (New York:

Oxford University Press, 1992); see also the discussion in Graf, *Magic in the Ancient World*, 118-26. For Bruno, see "On Magic" and "A General Account of Bonding" in Giordano Bruno, *Cause, Principle, and Unity*, trans. Robert de Lucca and Richard J. Blackwell, *Cambridge Texts in the History of Philosophy* (Cambridge, U.K.: Cambridge University Press, 1998), 105-42, 45-76; For discussion see Culianu, *Eros and Magic*, 95-9. In Hebrew, magic and binding cohere in the terms *hōbēr, habārīm*, on which see Peter Schäfer, "Magic and Religion in Ancient Judaism," in *Envisioning Magic : A Princeton Seminar and Symposium*, ed. Peter Schäfer and Hans G. Kippenberg, *Studies in the History of Religions, 75* (Leiden: E.J. Brill, 1997), 27; However, cf. comments in W. Robertson Smith, "On the Forms of Divination and Magic Enumerated in Deut. XVIII. 10, 11 (Part II)," *The Journal of Philology* 14 (1885): 123. In Nordic myth, fetters of war and sorcery are described in *Hávamál* 148-9, *Gróagaldr* 10, and chapter 7 of *Heimskringla*; among the epithets of Óðin are Haptaguð (fetter-god) and Haptsoenir (fetter-loosner). For further examples and discussion, see Mircea Eliade, 'The "God Who Binds" and the Symbolism of Knots,' in *Images and Symbols : Studies in Religious Symbolism* (Princeton, N.J.: Princeton University Press, 1991), 92-124.

[106] Eliade, 'The "God Who Binds",' 115.

[107] Nietzsche, *Werke : Kritische Gesamtausgabe*, 6.1: 8: „Der Mensch ist Etwas, das Überwunden werden soll. Was habt ihr gethan, ihn zu überwinden?'

[108] On this theme, see Hans Jonas, "Myth and Mysticism : A Study of Objectification and Interiorization in Religious Thought," *Journal of Religion* 49, no. 4 (1969): 315-29.

[109] Bruce Lincoln, *Myth, Cosmos, and Society : Indo-European Themes of Creation and Destruction* (Cambridge, Mass.: Harvard University Press, 1986), 5.

[110] Herodotus, *Herodotus*, 1.131-2.

[111] Lincoln, *Myth, Cosmos, Society*, 53-6.

[112] On love and strife, cf. Empedocles:

> There is a double birth of what is mortal, and a double passing away; for the uniting of all things brings one generation into being and destroys it, and the other is reared and scattered as they are again being divided. And these things never cease their continual exchange of position, at one time all coming together into one through love, at another again being borne away from each other by strife's repulsion.

Text and translation, M. R. Wright, ed., *Empedocles, the Extant Fragments* (New Haven: Yale University Press, 1981), 96-7, 166.

Research Notes

Although the JSM encourages longer articles, the following is an example of the type of succinct, thought-provoking and detailed shorter piece that we would be delighted to see in our new 'Research Notes' category: The symbolism of the pierced heart
Joyce Froome

The beginning of the 20th Century was the golden age of the greetings postcard, a time when this interesting popular art form reached extraordinary heights of tasteful sentimentality. A typical Valentine's Day card of the period shows a charming, realistically childlike Cupid, with golden wings, seated on a wall. Attached to the wall is a target, with a heart as a bull's-eye, with a golden arrow sticking out of it.[1]

This is the image of the pierced heart at its most innocent. Indeed, a great deal of artistic skill has gone into creating that impression of innocence. It is all the more startling, therefore, to discover that at around the same time Margaret Murray (no less) was collecting a very different, and literally blood-soaked, example of heart symbolism:

> "When you greatly wish to summon a person you must cut out a heart of red flannel, and thoroughly soak it with your blood. Stick a needle through it. At the stroke of midnight you must throw it into the fire saying:
> 'It is not this heart I wish to burn
> But the heart of (-) I wish to turn.

> May he (she) neither eat nor drink nor sleep
> Until with me he/she come to speak.'"[2]

Two different uses of the symbolism of the pierced heart, with clearly a huge gulf between them. How can the same basic image take such divergent forms?

In Classical times it was never specified that Cupid shot his victims through the heart. Indeed, the Greek and Roman cultures did not attach any particular importance to the heart as an organ. By the time of Chaucer, however, the heart was clearly associated with love. *Troilus and Criseyde* contains lines referring to Troilus being shot by Cupid –

> "At which the God of Love gan loken rowe
> At which the God of Love began to consider angrily
> Right for despit, and shop for to ben wroken.
> Full of scorn, and plotted revenge.
> He kidde anon his bowe nas naught broken;
> He soon showed that his bow was not broken;
> For sodeynly he hitte hym atte fulle" –
> For suddenly he struck him squarely.
> and just twenty lines later describes Troilus's heart as being on fire with love –
> "Yet with a look his herte wex a-fere,
> Yet with a look his heart was on fire,
> That he that now was moost in pride above,
> So he that just now was most in pride above,
> Wax sodeynly moost subgit unto love."[3]
> Was suddenly most subject unto love.

Interestingly, though, the two concepts are not directly connected – Cupid is not described as shooting Troilus through the heart.

However, there has been some speculation that the stylised heart-shape of European art may in fact have derived from the shape of flint arrowheads. These were believed, possibly from as early as Roman times, to be elf arrows. Being shot by an elf was, together with witchcraft, a common explanation for any mysterious illness, and wearing a flint arrowhead was thought to offer magical protection.[4] It is a curious thought that the very shape of the heart symbol may derive from the arrow that pierces it. But it is also worth noting the yoni-like quality of the shape, which, with the phallic quality of the arrow, suggests a degree of sexual symbolism.

In the 16th century, St Teresa of Avila described a mystical experience during which an angel fired a flaming arrow into her heart. This undoubtedly helped to fix the image of the pierced heart in the popular imagination. In 1612, the ballad *King Cophetua and the Beggar Maid*, published in Richard Johnson's *Crown Garland of Goulden Roses*, includes the lines:

> "The blinded boy, that shootes so trim,
> From heaven downe did hie;
> He drew a dart and shot at him,
> In place where he did lye:
> Which soone did pierse him to the quicke.
> And when he felt the arrow pricke,
> Which in his tender heart did sticke,
> He looketh as he would dye."[5]

Michael Maier's alchemical work *Tripus Aureus*, published in 1618, contains a picture of Cupid firing an arrow at a heart held by Venus.[6] Also, by this period, interesting variations on the basic symbolism were already appearing. Daniel Cramer's Rosicrucian book *Societas Iesu et Rosae Crucis Vera*, published in 1617, contains pictures of a heart with a sword cutting into it, a heart nailed to a cross, and a heart resting on a bed of thorns.[7] In the second half of the 17th century, Ste Marguerite Marie Alacoque introduced the idea of the Sacred Heart of Jesus. A picture drawn by the saint in 1685, now in the Monastery of the Visitation at Turin, shows the Heart surrounded by the Crown of Thorns, with the Cross emerging from the top of it, and pierced by the three nails of the Crucifixion.[8]

And the symbolism was also already being used for darker and less mystical purposes. An early account of English witchcraft, *The Examination of John Walsh*, from 1566, describes the making of clay images:

"They use to take the earth of a new made grave, the ryb bone of a man or woman burned to ashes… and a blacke Spider, with an inner pith of an elder, tempered all in water, in which water the sayd Todes must fyrst be washed. And after al ceremonies ended, they put a pricke, that is a pyn or a thorne in any member wher they wold have the party greved. And if the sayde prycke be put to the hart, the party dieth within nine daies."[9]

The pamphlet *The Most Cruell and Bloody Murther committed by an Inkeepers Wife, called Annis Dell…With the severall Witchcrafts, and most damnable practises of one Johane Harrison and her Daughter*, dating from 1606, describes (with rather odd punctuation) how Johane Harrison had some kind of anatomical drawing, which she pricked with a needle to injure her victims, "and those whome she intended to kill had the same in effect. If she gave a pricke in the middle of ye parchment, where she had placed the heart."[10] Thomas Middleton's play *The Witch* also contains a memorable reference to a disembodied wax heart:

"Is the hart of wax
Stuck full of magique needles?"[11]

The 17th century also saw the development of a form of counter-magic for use against witches – the witch bottle. These were usually stoneware bottles, known as bellarmines, with a face on the side. This face was intended by the manufacturers to be purely decorative, but it seems to have inspired the use of the bottles for magical purposes. According to a number of 17th century accounts, if someone was believed to have been cursed by a witch, one of these bottles would be filled with the victim's urine, together with iron nails or pins, various other ingredients such as hair and nail parings, and often, although not always, a cloth heart pierced with pins. The bottle would then be buried or heated, turning the witch's magic back on herself (or himself) and tormenting her with urinary problems.[12] In fact, so many of these bottles have been found, it seems likely that they may often have been

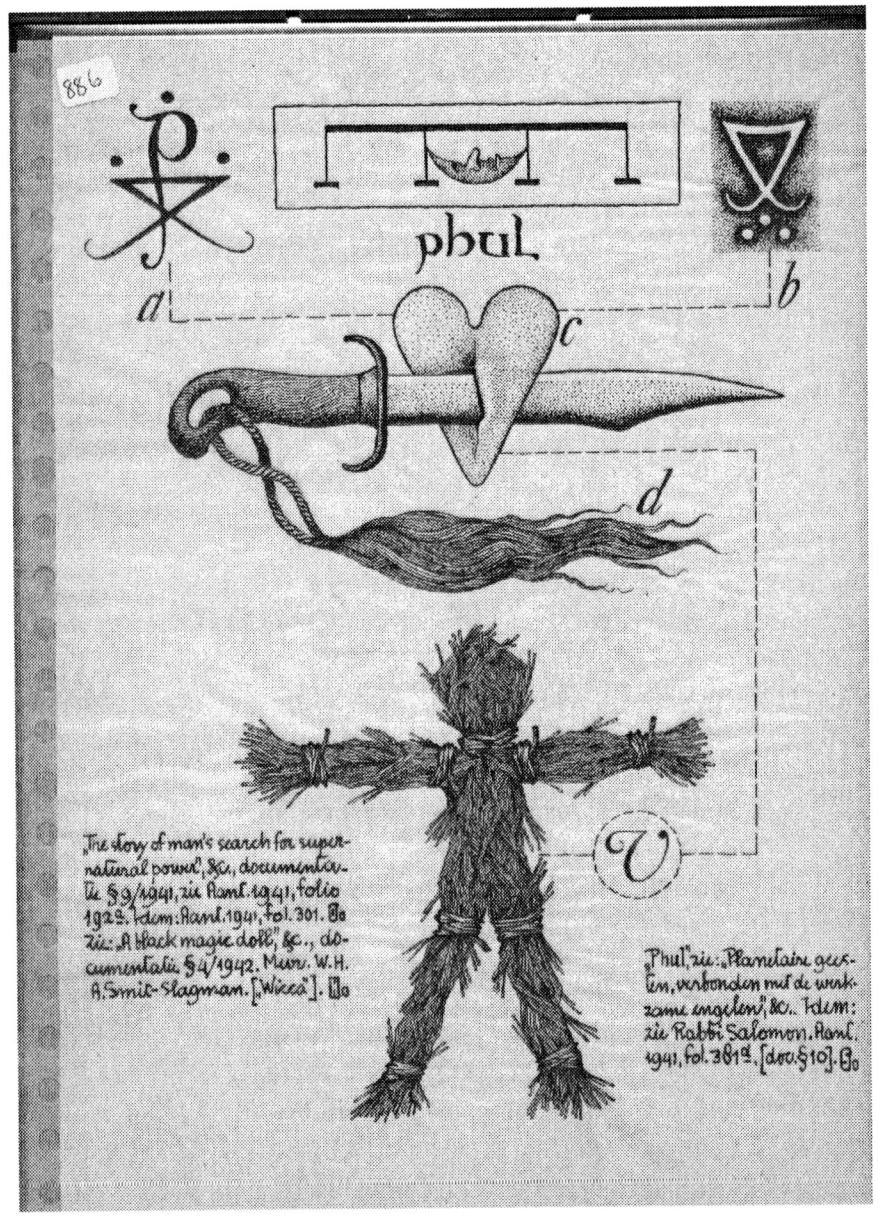

used as a general protection against witchcraft, rather than against specific cases of bewitchment.[13]

Thus the 17th century seems to have witnessed an explosion of symbolism elaborating on the basic image of the pierced heart. And interestingly, when we next have a similar wealth of evidence, in the late 19th/early 20th centuries, we see a similar bewildering variety. And in spite of the intervention of the Age of Reason and the Industrial Revolution, there are many striking resemblances.

In the 19th century The Sacred Heart of Jesus was firmly established as a symbol invoked for its miraculous powers, particularly of healing.[14] In the early 20th century, the Rosicrucian symbolism was taken up in the Rider Waite Tarot, with the three of swords showing the swords piercing a heart – a bold, stark image rather uncharacteristic of the pack as a whole. A.E. Waite, of course, was a member of the Rosicrucian-influenced Golden Dawn, and wrote a book on Rosicrucianism that mentions Daniel Cramer's work.[15] A similar image appears in one of the pictures in the Richel Collection at the Museum of Witchcraft in Boscastle, Cornwall. This is a collection of artefacts and documents originally amassed by a Dutch occultist during the first half of the 20th century, and mainly linked to ritual magic. The picture shows a cutlass or large dagger driven through a heart shape that appears to have been cut out of metal. A dotted line connects it to a straw poppet labelled 'a black magic doll'. Does this make the pierced heart a curse in this case? At any rate, an image with Rosicrucian echoes is linked physically in this document to an image associated with witchcraft and folk magic.

The Museum of Witchcraft also has a felt heart pierced with pins, and with nail clippings attached, very similar to the cloth hearts found in witch bottles, although here it is undoubtedly a curse rather than counter-magic. Interestingly, though witch bottles were still in use in this period, they were now usually ordinary glass bottles, and those that have survived seem not to have contained cloth hearts.[16] This may be an example of magical symbolism actually becoming simplified – since the main ingredient of a witch bottle was urine, and the aim was to cause urinary problems, the use of a cloth heart may have died out because it complicated the symbolism unnecessarily.

In fact another kind of heart symbolism had now gained popularity as a form of protection magic – the use of an animal heart pierced with pins or thorns. This development is probably a case of heart symbolism being imposed on the very ancient magical practice of animal sacrifice. *The Evil Eye*, by Frederick Thomas Elworthy, first published in 1895 – a very informative book about folk traditions of the period – gives a number of examples:[17]

"Some of the old people declared it to have been a custom when a pig died from the 'overlooking' of a witch to have its heart stuck full of pins and white thorns, and to put it up the chimney, in the belief that as the heart dried and withered so would that of the malignant person who had 'ill wisht' the pig. As long as that lasted no witch could have power over the pigs belonging to that house."

"The other day I was at the Court House, East Quantoxhead, and was shown in the chimney of a now disused kitchen – suspended – a sheep's heart stuck full of pins. I think Captain L – told me that this was done by persons who thought themselves 'overlooked' or 'ill-wished'; also to prevent the descent of witches down the chimney."

"A sheep's heart was stuck full of pins and roasted before the fire. While this was being done, the assembled people chanted the following incantation:-

'It is not this heart I wish to burn,
But the person's heart I wish to turn,
Wishing them neither rest nor peace
Till they are dead and gone.'

….After this had gone on far into the night, the inevitable 'black cat' jumped out from somewhere, and was pronounced to be the fiend which had been exorcised."

This last example is particularly interesting because of its resemblance to the summoning spell mentioned at the start of this article.

Another invaluable book of the time, *Pins and Pincushions* by E.D. Longman and S. Loch (published in 1911), also mentions another form of heart protection magic – the custom of keeping heart-shaped pincushions in kitchens to ward off ill fortune, and of giving sailors a heart-shaped pincushion to protect them on their voyages. The authors relate both these customs to the belief that the heart offered protection against storms.[18] (Could this – like the apparent link between the heart shape and flint arrowheads – be connected to the significance attached to flint artefacts? Stone axes were believed to be thunderbolts and to protect against lightning.)[19] On the other hand, a witch described in *The Evil Eye* carried a heart-shaped pad into which she would stick a pin to curse anyone who offended her.[20]

Onions were sometimes substituted for hearts. Elworthy mentions "an onion… found hidden in a chimney, with a paper stuck round it by numberless pins; on this was written the name of a well-known and highly-respected gentleman."[21] Curiously, when it came to love magic, the use of onions, rather than hearts, seems to have been the norm. *Pins and Pincushions* cites two examples:[22]

"If a lover did not visit his sweetheart as often as she wished, she roasted an onion stuck full of an ounce of pins. The pins must have never been through paper, and were supposed to prick his wandering heart and bring him to his lady's feet."

"On St Thomas' Eve in Derbyshire girls used to procure a large red onion, into which, after it was peeled, they stuck nine pins, and said:-

> 'Good St Thomas, do me right,
> Send me my true love this night,
> In his clothes and his array
> Which he weareth every day.'

One pin was placed in the centre, and the other eight stuck round it. The centre one was given the name of the 'true love'. The onion thus prepared was placed under the pillow on going to bed, and the girl dreamt of the right person."

In case any reader should think that a young lady might be too squeamish to use an animal heart in love magic, *Household Tales with Other Traditional Remains*, by Sydney Oldall Addy (1895), relates the grim story of a girl who stuck pins in a live frog, kept him in a box for a week (by which time he was dead), then kept the remains until only bones were left, and took out a small key-shaped bone:

"[she] got into the company of the young man she wanted, fastened the bone to his coat, and said:

> 'I do not want to hurt this frog
> But my true lover's heart to turn
> Wishing that he no rest may find
> Till he come to me and speak his mind.'
> After this he had a week's torture, as the frog had" [before agreeing to marry her].[23]

Although obviously there may have been many examples of love magic using animal hearts or cloth hearts that went unrecorded, or that I just haven't discovered, it seems strange that these examples *avoid* using any heart symbolism more explicit than an onion – even though in the case of the spell using the unfortunate frog the wording of the charm is so similar to other forms of pierced heart magic we have encountered.

But is the symbolism of Cupid's arrow piercing a heart, as appears on Valentine's Day cards, simply an evocative classical reference, or does it have a magical element? The Museum of Witchcraft has three interesting and relevant charms in the Richel Collection.

Two consist of oyster shells painted with two hearts joined by an arrow, together with other symbols derived from astrology and ritual magic. The obvious interpretation of these charms is that they are a form of love magic. However, a description of one of the charms, in the notebooks that came to the Museum with them, refers to its power to protect against lightning. This of course echoes the use of heart-shaped pincushions described in *Pins and Pincushions*. Also, the letters AGLA, which are inscribed on it, are a word of power derived from ritual magic but also often used in folk magic as a protection charm.[24] But why the use of two hearts joined together, not to mention the oyster shell, if there isn't an element of love magic involved? The third charm is a kind of triangular box, painted with a single heart transfixed by an arrow, with the initials J and F, Hebrew letters, and, again, the letters AGLA. The box contains pubic hair, making it clearly an example of love magic. In this case the letters AGLA may simply be empowering the charm, but this does clearly demonstrate the (often confusing) complexity of magical symbolism, particularly in areas where elements of ritual magic and folk magic are combined.

Of course, as well as Valentine's Day cards, the arrow and heart was a popular subject for tattoos (which themselves involve piercing with a needle, and have connotations of initiation). The arrow and heart was definitely regarded as an essentially sentimental image even at the height of its romantic use, and there was humour to be had from the contrast between its sentimentality and the toughness implied by having a tattoo. A good example can be found in John Masefield's 1927 children's book *The Midnight Folk*:

"If this should come after my death into the hands of the police, let them know that Twiney Pricker was from the northern parts, a sailmaker by profession and speaks in the northern way, lobster-eyed and blue of both eyes, wears his beard in the Newgate fringe fashion, has two teeth missing from the upper jaw on left side, being hit with a pot in a dispute about the victuals. He has also a lady's heart transfixed with arrow on chest in gunpowder, also the fat ox of Bedford on his right arm."[25]

An interesting detail in this description is that the tattoo is described as a *lady's* heart. It might be supposed that if a man has a heart transfixed with an arrow tattooed on his chest (or, for that matter, sends a lady a card featuring a heart transfixed with an arrow), he is making a statement that *his* heart has been pierced by love for *her*. If, however, the heart is *her* heart, things look a little different. Is he in fact practising love magic, and trying to gain power over her?

Ultimately the pierced heart is a very dramatic power symbol. Think of the apparently invincible and immortal vampire, destroyed by a stake through the heart – an idea popularised, of course, in Bram Stoker's *Dracula* in 1897. The concept of power links all the many variations of the symbol. And while we appear to be dealing with two different kinds of power – divine power, in the more mythological and mystical aspects of the symbol, and the more dubious type of magical power in the spells and charms – is that really the case? In *Between the Living and the Dead*, Eva Pocs convincingly argues that magical beliefs are inextricably linked to beliefs about the Otherworld.[26] The ordinary person's pragmatic use of magic to obtain practical results ultimately derives from beliefs about the spiritual realm.

Magic covers a sweeping range of practices and purposes, from Granny Boswell, in a moment of political irritability, making a Tory activist's car break down,[27] to the *Sworn Book* of Honorius promising a vision of God.[28] The study of magical symbolism asks us to confront the challenge this presents. In myth, and even in modern fantasy fiction such as *The Lord of the Rings* and *Harry Potter*, magic is something done by beings who are themselves at least semi-supernatural. But in history, the most ordinary people have believed that there were ways for them to access that power.

In the symbolism of the pierced heart, it may be an arrow fired by an angel that is doing the piercing, or a simple pin; and the heart may be the heart of Christ or the heart of a sheep. Are we in the realm of the spiritual or the psychological? Or should we, perhaps, reassess our ideas about the boundary between them?[29]

Notes

1 Pamela E. Apkarian-Russell, *Postmarked Yesteryear: art of the holiday postcard* (Portland, Oregon: Collectors Press, Inc., 2001), 51

2 Caroline Oates and Juliette Wood, *A Coven of Scholars: Margaret Murray and her Working Methods* (London: FLS Books, 1998), 57

3 F.N. Robinson (Ed.), *The Works of Geoffrey Chaucer* (London: Oxford University Press, 1957), 391-392

4 Keriann Godwin, Museum of Witchcraft, Cornwall, personal communication. Audrey L. Meaney, *Anglo-Saxon Amulets and Curing Stones* (Oxford: BAR British Series 96, 1981), 98,120; quoting W.W. Skeat, *Snake-stones and Stone Thunderbolts as Subjects for Systematic Investigation*, (Folklore XXIII, 1912) 64. Ralph Merrifield, *The Archaeology of Ritual and Magic* (London: B.T. Batsford Ltd., 1987), 16

5 Beverley Nichols, *A Book of Old Ballads* (London: Hutchinson & Co (Publishers) Ltd, 1934), 74

6 Stanislas Klossowski de Rola, *The Golden Game: Alchemical Engravings of the Seventeenth Century* (London: Thames and Hudson, 1988), 121 (Ill. No. 99)

7 Adam McLean (Ed.), *The Rosicrucian Emblems of Daniel Cramer* (Edinburgh: Magnum Opus Hermetic Source Works, 1980), 27,29,39

8 Emile Grillot de Givry, *Illustrated Anthology of Sorcery, Magic and Alchemy* (New York: Mallard Press, 1991, 1929), 217

9 Marion Gibson, *Early Modern Witches: Witchcraft Cases in Contemporary Writing* (London: Routledge, 2000), 31

10 Gibson, *Early Modern Witches*, 153

11 Thomas Middleton, *The Witch* (ed. Elizabeth Schafer) (London: A. & C. Black, 1994)

12 Merrifield, *Archaeology*, 163-175

13 Graham King, Curator, Museum of Witchcraft, personal communication.

14 Ken Arnold, Martha Baldwin and John Mack, *Abracadabra – The Magic of Medicine. An exhibition at the Wellcome Institute for the History of Medicine* (London: The Wellcome Trust, 1996), 18, 19, 28

15 McLean, *Rosicrucian Emblems*, 1

16 Merrifield, *Archaeology*, 163-175

17 Frederick Thomas Elworthy, *The Evil Eye* (London: John Murray, 1895), 53, 55, 56

18 E.D. Longman and S. Loch, *Pins and Pincushions* (London: Longmans, Green & Co., 1911) 183-5, and Plate XXXIX 1 & 2

19 Merrifield, *Archaeology*, 9-14

20 Elworthy, *Evil Eye*, 54

21 Elworthy, *Evil Eye*, 54-5

22 Longman and Loch, *Pins*, 40-41, 46-47

23 Jacqueline Simpson & Steve Roud, *A Dictionary of English Folklore* (Oxford: Oxford University Press, 2000), 218

24 Merrifield, *Archaeology*, 162

25 John Masefield, *The Midnight Folk* (London: William Heinemann Ltd, 1927), 94

26 Eva Pocs, *Between the Living and the Dead: Seers and Witches in the Early Modern Age* (Budapest: Central European University Press, 1999)

27 Kelvin I. Jones, *An Joan the Crone. The History and Craft of the Cornish Witch* (Penzance: Oakmagic Publications, 1999), 41-42

28 Robert Mathiesen, 'A Thirteenth-Century Ritual to Attain the Beatific Vision from the Sworn Book of Honorius of Thebes', in *Conjuring Spirits – Texts and Traditions of Medieval Ritual Magic*, ed. by Claire Fanger (Stroud, Gloucestershire: Sutton Publishing, 1998), 143-162

29 This research would not have been possible without access to the Museum of Witchcraft and its extensive library. My thanks to Graham King, the curator, and all the museum team, for their invaluable assistance, ideas and suggestions.

Shamanic Motifs in Fin-de-Siècle Russian Art: The Case of Nicholas Roerich

John McCannon

We shall endure only if we create a new antiquity for ourselves.

— Hugo von Hofmannsthal

In a 1915 canvas entitled *The Commands of Heaven*, nine fur-clad shamans come face-to-face with the elemental forces that surge through their prehistoric world. Standing in a forlorn, rocky landscape of dull reds and browns, the elders reach up to the sky, their arms outstretched. The air billows with clouds, which seem alive with a dynamic, knowing presence. Whether the shamans are attempting to control or propitiate the wild, natural forces around them is not at first glance apparent.

The artist who painted *The Commands of Heaven*, Nicholas Roerich, was one of *fin-de-siècle* Russia's foremost painters: a member of the renowned World of Art Society and a stage designer for Diaghilev's Ballets Russes. He was also a skilled amateur archaeologist of some note; a prominent explorer of Tibet, Central Asia, and the Himalayas; two times a nominee for the Nobel Peace Prize; and, most germane to the purposes of this essay, one of the many turn-of-the-century intellectuals in Russia who developed a strong attraction to occult mysticism.[1] Indeed, even in a climate where interest in esoteric and alternative forms of spirituality was common, Roerich stood out for the intensity and literalism of his beliefs. With his wife Helena, Roerich went on to found an occult discipline of his own, the Theosophically-derived Agni Yoga, which still flourishes worldwide, especially in Russia, India, and, to a degree, the United States.

Integral to Roerich's artistic vision, his archaeological theories, and his spiritual beliefs was a fascination with shamans and shamanic practices. It should be noted at the outset that, like most of his peers (and like many "new age" enthusiasts today), Roerich tended to be somewhat inexact in his definition of "shamanism." Likewise, he subscribed to a universalizing conception of shamanism based on the assumption that shamanic traditions worldwide follow a single, even generic, set of practices and principles. Such a conception is largely at variance with most present-day anthropological and religious-studies scholarship, which argues that shamanic rituals and cosmologies vary significantly from culture to culture, even closely-related or neighboring ones.[2] To be fair to Roerich, much of the scholarship of his own day was more tolerant, even welcoming, of the sort of broad definitions and generalizations he favored. Moreover, as a painter, Roerich felt perfectly justified in taking a certain degree of artistic and philosophical license with ethnographic reality.

Whatever the case, between his graduation from the Imperial Academy of Arts in 1897 and his emigration from Russia in 1917-1918, Roerich painted literally dozens of scenes related to shamanism, and his famous designs for Igor Stravinsky's *The Rite of Spring*, the libretto of which Roerich co-wrote, are imbued with shamanic motifs. Roerich's many essays, poems, and short stories from these years reflect the same interest—often providing an interpretive key to his paintings and designs.

Roerich's interest in shamans and shamanism stemmed from several sources. To begin with, attraction to shamanism was very much in vogue among Roerich's fellow artists, whether for aesthetic, academic, or spiritual reasons. Secondly, Roerich's own understanding of shamanism changed over time, shifting from a culturally particular focus on the ancient Slavs to a more generalized perspective that took in all of Eurasia. This paralleled his evolving archaeological, philosophical, and spiritual conviction that the world's major faiths, religions, and traditions all reflected a single, universal truth that had united the peoples of Europe and Asia at the dawn of time. To understand shamanism, Roerich believed, was a step toward understanding this deeper, primal truth. Finally, devoting artistic attention to shamanism, whether in Slavic, Siberian, or universalized form, allowed Roerich the opportunity to reinforce one of his central philosophical messages: the idealization of the Stone Age as an era of spiritual purity, harmonious communalism, and balance between humanity and the natural environment. This essay will address each of these issues in turn.

Fashionable Shamanism in **Fin-de-Siècle** *Russia*

In recent years, sharper scholarly focus has been fixed on what one historian calls "fashionable occultism" in *fin-de-siècle* Russia.[3] As in the wider Western world during the late nineteenth and early twentieth centuries, occult practices and alternative forms of spirituality pervaded Russian life, whether at the highest levels of the Imperial court or among the bohemians and intellectuals who comprised Russia's artistic elite. Indeed, one could argue that it was in Russia that turn-of-the-century occultism reached its most fevered and most apocalyptic pitch. Theologian Georges Florovsky remembered of his homeland during these years that:

> Once more dreams floated, and the soul, captivated by them, worshipped unknown gods. It was a time of searching and temptations. Paths strangely crossed and diverged, contradictions reigned, while the anxiety of the conscience intensified.[4]

No observer of the Russian scene at this time, scholarly or otherwise, fails to make note of the occult's cultural and intellectual prominence.

Multitudinous forms of occultism—Spiritualism, Theosophy, Anthroposophy, astrology, Swedenborgianism, fortune-telling, and more—were everywhere to be seen in Russia during the late 1800s and early 1900s. If one includes mystical and non-doctrinal interpretations of Judeo-Christian belief, the sway of alternative faiths over the Russian mind during the *fin de siècle* was all the stronger. Between 1881 and 1918, more than thirty journals and periodicals dedicated to occultist themes and topics were published in Russia, despite the opposition of the Orthodox Church and many government officials.[5] By 1913, more than thirty-five officially registered groups, clubs, and societies had formed for the purpose of studying and/or practicing occultism.[6] Such a number comes nowhere near to accounting for the many small, informal circles that convened privately or secretly. The legalization of political parties and civic groups and the lifting of censorship, both of which followed the 1905 Revolution, had the effect of bringing Russian occultism even more into the open. In this climate of what one historian refers to as a sense of "frenzied eschatological doom," the fascination that Russia's Silver-Age artists and thinkers felt for the occult neared the point of obsession.[7] Astutely, the leading authority on the Russian Theosophical movement states that attempting to understand early twentieth-century Russian culture without taking the prevalence of the occult into consideration "is comparable to trying to understand medieval art while ignorant of Christianity."[8]

One aspect of this "fashionable occultism" was what one might call a "fashionable shamanism." A number of Russian artists and thinkers were drawn to shamanism, viewing it variously as an academic subject, an artistic inspiration, a means of understanding one's own cultural roots, and a model of spiritual practice to emulate. This tendency—to turn away from what many considered to be a soulless, materialistic age of industry, mechanization, and cold rationality to ancient forms of paganism (not necessarily in their authentic form, but as they were popularly understood) for artistic, even spiritual, insight—was by no means peculiar to Russian intellectuals. The Celtic Revival's appropriation of druidic images and motifs is but one of many examples of this phenomenon, as is Wagner's operatic retelling of Germanic myth.

In keeping with this trend, the Russian poet Ivan Konevskoi drew upon the *Kalevala*, the Finnish national epic, and a romanticized understanding of Finno-Ugric shamanism in composing his own verses of 1904 and 1905.[9] Attempts to express "transrationality" (*zaum*) in verse inspired Futurist Velimir Khlebnikov to study the linguistic structure of Siberian shamans' ritual utterances.[10] The young Kandinsky spent a number of months conducting archaeological and ethnographic research into the shamanic practices of the Zyrian (Komi) people, non-Slavic inhabitants of Russia's northwest Arctic coast.[11] Much like their European counterparts, many Russian Symbolists—Andrei Bely, Alexander Blok, Vyacheslav Ivanov, Dmitrii Merezhkovsky, Zinaida Gippius, and Maximilian Voloshin, among others—flushed with exhilaration from their encounter with the works of Nietzsche and Wagner, and in full revolt against their own era of Darwinian science and Apollonian refinement, dedicated themselves to the task of recapturing what they believed to be the pure, magical, Dionysian spirituality of bygone ages.[12] What historian of religions Mircea Eliade would later characterize famously (and, as far as most present-day scholars are concerned, misleadingly) as the "ritual ecstasy" of the Siberian shaman was readily interpreted by Russian artists as fundamentally Dionysian.[13]

Other factors helped give rise to "fashionable shamanism" in Silver-Age Russia. Several avant-garde painters appropriated the art and artifacts of the ancient peoples (both Slavic and non-Slavic) of the Eurasian landmass in much the same way that Western artists like Gauguin and Picasso so famously appropriated "primitive" modes of representation from Oceania and Africa: not just for its primeval vitality, but also for the way it fused that vitality, whether beautiful or stark, with a non-representational manner of presentation.[14] Russia's Neo-Primitivists, for instance, led by Natalia Goncharova and Mikhail Larionov, paid great attention to old forms of Russian and indigenous art, including icons and woodcuts, but pre-Christian and ancient works as well. Pavel Kuznetsov's attempt to emulate the "native" style of painting in his scenes of Central Asia further illustrates this general trend.

Scholarly and popular interest also converged where shamanism was concerned. From the middle of the nineteenth century onward, a host of archaeologists, explorers, and ethnographers—among them Grigorii Potanin, Nikolai Korkunov, archaeologists A. A. Spitsyn and M. I. Rostovtsev, and the famed explorer Nikolai Przhevalskii—greatly expanded the academic understanding and public awareness of Russia's prehistoric past. They also did the same with respect to the Russian Empire's eastern frontiers, awakening a widespread fascination with the myriad of non-Russian peoples who lived under, or were in the process of being brought under, Russian rule. The exotic appeal of Mongolia, Central Asia, the approaches to India and China, and the parts of Siberia that joined Russia to those regions stimulated within the Russian mindset a variant of the "orientalist" tendency that featured so prominently in Western culture overall.[15] Among the many forms this Russian orientalism took was an interest in the bewildering mix of faiths, folklores, and ritual practices found in the broad swath of Eurasia that encompasses Siberia, Central Asia, Mongolia, and the Himalayas. Of these, shamanism was among the most compelling to Russian scholars and armchair travelers alike.

Increased attraction to Asiatic religions also bolstered popular interest in shamanism. Even today, it is no simple matter for scholars to unravel the tangled interrelationships between Hinduism, Islam, the various forms of Buddhism, and even Christianity (especially the Nestorian variant) on one hand, and indigenous religious practices throughout Asia.[16] For turn-of-the-century intellectuals and artists not armed with twenty-first-century anthropological knowledge or methodology—and more concerned in many cases with exotic flavor and aesthetic appeal than with ethnographic precision—it was easy to homogenize Eastern faiths, by ignoring or failing to see important differences in detail. Among the "fashionable" set (as distinct from the more disciplined and academically scrupulous orientalists working in Russia), to be interested in one Asiatic religion often meant to be indiscriminately interested in others. In any event, such interest grew rapidly in Russia during the late 1800s and early 1900s. Hindu classics such as the *Bhagavad-Gita*, the *Ramayana*, and the *Upanishads* were translated into Russian. Mahayana ("Great Vehicle") and Vajyarana ("Thunderbolt Path") forms of Buddhism gained a higher profile among the Russian elite during the *fin de siècle*. The Buryat lama and herbalist Pyotr Badmaev became a major figure at the Romanov court, creating a fashion for Tibetan medicine in St. Petersburg. Likewise, the lama Agvan Dorjiev stirred up interest in Buddhism among the members of Russian high society; he also served secretly as a diplomatic liaison between Nicholas II and the 13th Dalai Lama (and possibly as an intelligence operative). Between 1909 and 1915, Dorjiev supported and advised the construction of a Buddhist temple in Petersburg (a project with which Roerich was involved). Because Russian enthusiasts, much like their Western counterparts, perceived Buddhist worship among Tibetans, Mongolians, Buryats, Kalmyks, and related groups to be syncretically linked with indigenous religious practices throughout Central Asia and the Himalayas, the activities of figures such as Dorjiev and Badmaev had the indirect effect of calling more attention to shamanism.[17]

More broadly, the Asiatic face of Siberian shamanism entranced members of those cultural movements whose artistic agendas included an emphasis on the Russian Empire's multi-ethnic heritage. Most notable here are the Scythian and Eurasianist movements. Although neither of these became formal associations until World War I, Scythian and Eurasianist *impulses* had made themselves felt since the late 1800s. As its name suggests, the Eurasianist movement viewed Russia not as a European civilization, but one whose roots were dug in deeply throughout the vast Eurasian landmass. Scythianism, a prominent variety of Russian orientalism, took its name from Indo-Iranic warrior nomads who, from 700 to 200 BC, inhabited a vast territory ranging from Central Asia to the Black Sea. Many turn-of-the-century artists and intellectuals in Russia, wishing to highlight their country's differences from Europe, claimed the Scythians as ancestors of sorts. Archaeological and ethnographic analysis from the 1930s onward suggests that, while the Scyths formed part of a Greco-Iranic cultural substratum that influenced the Slavs centuries later, only in the most indirect (or metaphoric) sense can they be considered the Russians' forebears.[18] During the *fin de siècle*, however, evidence on this question was not so clear-cut, and many believed at the time that the Scyths were literal ancestors of the Russians. Either way, the Scyths served metaphorically to allow Russians to identify themselves with a barbaric, passionate intensity that set them apart from their supposedly more refined European cousins. Those whose work displayed a Scythian sensibility included poets and writers like Blok, Bely, Alexei Remizov, Valerii Briusov, Sergei Gorodetskii, and Jurgis Baltrushaitis, as well as composers Sergei Prokofiev, Vladimir Senilov, and Igor Stravinsky. Even Rimsky-Korsakov, with his orientalist fantasies, had something of a Scythian outlook. Both the Scythians and Eurasianists focused a great deal of their intellectual and artistic attention on Siberia and Central Asia, and were as a matter of course interested in those regions' shamanic traditions.

Shamanism and Roerich's Vision of History

Throughout his career, Roerich was considered to be one of Russia's most adept painterly interpreters of ancient history and prehistory. He was also respected for his expertise as an archaeologist, folklorist, and ethnographer.[19] How to conceive of the distant past, and how to draw lessons from it for the present and future, were central questions in Roerich's art and philosophy. His understanding of shamanism was conditioned by his understanding of these larger questions.

As early as his student years at the Imperial Academy of Arts, Roerich strove to uncover what he considered to be the Asiatic roots of Russian culture. A key influence here was the critic and scholar Vladimir Stasov, best known for championing composers such as Mussorgsky and Rimsky-Korsakov, as well as the painters of the so-called "Wanderers" movement. In the field of literature, Stasov advanced a famous theory about the development of medieval Russia's epic poetry (*byliny*). The *byliny*, he argued, strongly resembled the great sagas of Persia and India, especially the *Shahnameh* and the *Mahabharata*, in their structure and morphology. Likewise, Stasov argued that old Russia's decorative arts had a distinctly Eastern cast to them.[20] Whatever the truth of Stasov's theories, they were highly regarded in their time, and Roerich, who came to know Stasov personally, subscribed to them wholeheartedly. Deeply embedded in Roerich's developing views of history and archaeology, then, was a preoccupation with the question of linguistic, religious, and cultural diffusion throughout Eurasia.

For similar reasons, Roerich became interested in the "North," as a transnational cultural space including Slavic Russia, Norse Scandinavia, and the Baltic and Finno-Ugric portions of northeastern Europe. Roerich's conception of the distant past took in the prevailing scholarly view that Indo-Iranic languages, folkways, art, and religious practices had spread westward from South and Central Asia, eventually reaching the Mediterranean and all of Europe. In addition, non-Indo-European cultures, among them various Turkic and Mongol peoples, had played an important role in this process. As time passed, Roerich came to believe that the Siberian-Central Asian-Mongolian wilderness was the possible origin of human culture.[21]

On one level, Roerich's theories squared perfectly well with respectable anthropological and ethnographic scholarship—certainly the scholarship of his own time and, to a point, that of today. Linguistic, archaeological, and ethnographic research had shown beyond doubt that the mountains and steppes of Central Asia, southern Siberia, and Mongolia were the original homelands of ethnicities whose migratory spread throughout Eurasia had covered an enormous territorial expanse. Furthermore, as a host of explorers and scholars, including Sir Aurel Stein and Sven Hedin, were busy proving, these lands had acted for centuries as a vast cauldron of cultural interchange, brimming over with the ferment of mutual religious, linguistic, artistic, and folkloric influence. Even Roerich's speculations about the origins of humankind were not outside the academic mainstream of the day. Some of the great paleontologists of the early twentieth century, Roy Chapman Andrews and Pierre Teilhard de Chardin, were open to the possibility, based on the fossil record, that Central Asia or Mongolia had been the birthplace of the human species itself.

Over time, however, Roerich's thinking about the past became more poetic and, ultimately, more fanciful. Roerich had always believed that the best scholarship was that informed by what he felt to be the deeper insight of the artist—a view he expressed as early as 1898, in the article "Art and Archaeology," in the journal *Art and Artistic Industry*.[22] But it was his increasingly pronounced occult inclination that brought about the real change in his views. By no later than 1905, Roerich and his wife were engrossed with Hinduism, Buddhism, and Theosophy, and their dedication to mysticism steadily deepened as the years went by.

Consequently, Roerich's artistic handling of ancient history took on a new form. As a student and journeyman artist, Roerich had gained his renown as a scrupulously accurate painter of Slavic and northern primevalism. His graduation piece, *The Messenger* (1897), along with *Idols* (1901), *Visitors from Overseas* (1901-1902), *Slavs on the Dnieper* (1905), and many others, were considered brilliant evocations of a long-dead era, when the Slavs migrated into the Russian-Ukrainian heartland and intermingled with the Viking, or Varangian, traders who blazed a southward path to Byzantium through the Slavic lands. Gradually, however, Roerich would dispense with his Slavic particularism and move on to a more Eurasian, pan-cultural universalism. This by no means meant that he lost his interest in Russia. What he did was to fit Russia into the larger vision of history outlined above. When he painted Russia after 1905, it was generally with the intention of examining the ways that old Russia had interacted with other cultures. For example, his set and costume designs for the 1909 production of Borodin's opera *Prince Igor*, which depicts the twelfth-century clash between the Russians and the Polovtsy, their nomadic foes from the Asiatic steppe, juxtaposed east and west in vivid fashion. On several occasions, Roerich provided sets and costumes for various productions of Rimsky-Korsakov's *The Snow Maiden*. Although *The Snow Maiden* is quintessentially a product of Russian folklore, Roerich took the opportunity to advance his (and Stasov's) thesis about the Asiatic roots of Russian culture by presenting the shepherd boy Lel—whom Roerich considered to be an avatar of the Hindu demigod Krishna—in Asiatic form.

Roerich's artistic rendering of shamans and shamanistic practice underwent a similar evolution. His earlier scenes of pagan ritual are distinctly Slavic in appearance. All of the accoutrements highlighted in his several versions of *Idols*, for instance—with their carved and brightly painted wooden totems, clustered in a sacred circle, surrounded by fenceposts hung with horses' skulls—are consistent with the religious objects depicted in his many paintings of Stone-Age Slavic settlements. *Gathering of the Elders* (1898), which shows convocation of ancient Russian wise men and healers, would not be out of place in the pages of an ethnography textbook.

Over time, however, influenced largely by the ecumenical teachings of Vivekananda and Ramakrishna, Roerich became convinced that all religions and faiths were reflections of a single higher truth. He became further convinced that ancient peoples throughout Eurasia had perceived that higher truth more clearly than their descendants did, and far more clearly than twentieth-century humankind could. Famous essays such as "Joy in Art" (1908-1909), which Roerich published in the famed "thick" journal *Herald of Europe* (*Vestnik Evropy*), praised the virtues of life during the Neolithic Era—and spoke of all Neolithic cultures sharing similar religious beliefs and artistic tastes.[23] Here, Roerich's historical and archaeological theories, his artistic convictions, and his spiritual beliefs converged. As a symbolic representation of an ancient faith that transcended boundaries and linked Russia with a broader Eurasian tradition, shamanism was ideal. The fact that Roerich was convinced of shamanism's validity as a pathway toward enlightenment and its actual efficacy as a magical force made it all the more appealing to him.

Roerich's new approach was in evidence no later than 1905. Three canvases that, at first glance, might appear to be straightforward historical works in fact reveal Roerich's budding conviction that there was true wisdom to be found in the pagan practices of the Stone-Age north. All three depict the mysteries of shamanic ritual. In *Sorcerers*, figures clad in wolfskins gather around a circle of magic stones. *The Conjuration by Water* shows a man standing alone on a rocky shore, thick furs protecting him from the winter chill. His arms raised, he calls to the river flowing by, and the waters rise up as if in reply. In *Fiery Spell*, the shadow of a spell-caster looms large against the wall of a cave as he himself kneels before a sacred fire and gestures to it. Many more such scenes, culminating in Roerich's designs for *The Rite of Spring*, would follow over time.

Noteworthy was the fact that Roerich's wise men, elders, and shamans were taking on a form that was less recognizably Russian or Slavic and more indeterminate. One way that Roerich made his shamanic figures more universal was to make them appear more generally northern. This was the case not only with the canvases discussed in the previous paragraph, but also *By the Sacred Stone Sits an Unknown Elder* (1910), in which an old hermit meditates in front of a forest hut, and *The Sorceress* (1916), which depicts a crone, bent with age and leaning on a cane, gathering herbs in the woods. Judging from the colors and patterns of her dress, the sorceress could be Slavic, but she could also be Finnish, Baltic, Lappish, or Scandinavian. The same ambiguity features in many of the depictions of shamanism Roerich turned out during World War I.

In 1907, with *Earthly Spell*, Roerich experimented with a look that was even more hyperborean. In this grey, green, and blue nighttime scene, Roerich depicts three fur-clad figures, walking along what appears to be the crest of the earth. The crescent moon rides high in the chilly northern sky. Strewn about the ground are stones covered with mysterious signs, including a thick circular band containing three orbs (a symbol to which Roerich later attached great meaning). The men are shamans engaged in some kind of ritual; reindeer antlers protrude from the headdress worn by the figure in the middle. What remains indeterminate is the shamans' cultural identity. They are clearly from Siberia or the high north. Are they Inuit or Yakut? Tungus (Evenki) or Chukchi? Some other ethnicity altogether? No answer is provided, but their faces are distinctly Asiatic, a further indication of Roerich's pan-cultural inclinations.

Roerich includes Asia in other paintings that touch on shamanic subject matter, even if the Asiatic touch is not immediately apparent. Beginning in 1911, as Roerich worked concurrently on his sets and designs for *The Rite of Spring*—which, ostensibly Russian in character, was, at least to Roerich, a project that spoke to a more universal spirituality—he painted a series of scenes in which a piper in Slavic folk costume charms bears with the beauty of his music. The first of these paintings is entitled *Human Forefathers*, a reference to the Slavic pagan belief that humankind descended from bears.[24] *Our Ancestors* (1919) deals with the same motif, albeit in a color scheme, brown and orange, different from the pastel greens, blues, and purples he used in 1911. While, on the face of it, this might seem to be a purely Russian handling of pagan belief, the strong equation that Roerich made between Lel, the archetypal musician-lover-charmer from Russian folklore, with Krishna adds an Asiatic flavor to these scenes. Indeed, *The Magic of Beasts*, a variant of *Human Forefathers* painted in 1943, shows the piper with facial features that are unmistakably Asian.

Another cultural hybrid, joining northern with Asiatic, is *The Snake Charmer*, painted sometime during the 1910s. Here, a fur-clad shaman, standing on the rocky shore of a northern sea, makes use of a magic stick to mesmerize a large serpent. While the visual and geographic references are to Siberia or the Arctic, the symbolic reference is most definitely meant to be wider, triggering associations with India and Asia more generally. Roerich's 1916 canvas, *St. Pantaleimon*, can be decoded similarly. Pantaleimon is famed in the Orthodox canon as a great healer, and Roerich depicts him as a kindly old man gathering herbs. The cultural context is Greco-Slavic, and the physical landscape in which Pantaleimon appears is an idyllic northern glade. However, the less obvious subtext is Himalayan: Roerich felt a lifelong fascination for the practice of Tibetan medicine—reinforced by the fame of Dr. Badmaev in St. Petersburg during the twilight years of the Romanov dynasty—and he included the motif of the virtuous, magic-working herbalist in literally dozens of his paintings. In effect, Pantaleimon is a shaman, a figure of deeper antiquity, wilder magic, and broader Eurasian provenance, cloaked in the trappings of a Christian saint.

East meets north, Eurasian cultures stem from one and the same source, and Russia mediates between them all. Roerich considered this to be historical fact, artistic truth, and spiritual verity. Roerich found many ways to express this conviction in his art and writings. The figure of the shaman, however, who he felt was present in the religious and cultural history of all Eurasian peoples—and hence a common factor linking all of them—proved a particularly useful means for doing so.

Shamanism, Stone-Age Culture, and Archaic Communalism
In his landmark history of turn-of-the-century Vienna, Carl E. Schorske notes that, in the face of what seemed to many to be the atomizing, dehumanizing forces of the modern era, a common response was to look backward and dream of the past, as a time when communities were more

tightly-knit and human interactions were more meaningful. In particular, Schorske traces the impulses that led to the creation of three very different political movements—Georg Schönerer's Pan-Germanism, Karl Lueger's Christian Socialism, and Theodor Herzl's Zionism—back to this common longing.[25] The same dreams are readily discernable in the work of innumerable authors, artists, and intellectuals from the late 1800s and the 1900s: Wagner, John Ruskin, William Morris, the Pre-Raphaelites, D. H. Lawrence, and a host of others besides.

The Russians, particularly Symbolists and the retrospective dreamers of the World of Art movement, were no exception. Evocation of the distant past—be it the ancient Mediterranean, as in Léon Bakst's designs for the Ballets Russes, the scenes from Cimmerian antiquity that graced the work of Konstantin Bogaevsky, or the medievalist, fairy-tale fantasies of Ivan Bilibin, to cite only a few examples—was not simply a matter of creating picturesque atmosphere. Often, it served to express a very specific yearning: the desire to live in an imagined past, free from the perceived threats and concerns of the twentieth century's encroaching menace.

Most definitely, Roerich's artistic treatment of the past had much to do with his revulsion at what he considered the baser characteristics of the age he lived in: soulless materialism, shallow vulgarity, and an inability to comprehend, much less create, true beauty. As a young man, Roerich had eagerly devoured the writings of John Ruskin, and under the patronage of Princess Maria Tenisheva, he had become even more deeply committed to the Arts-and-Crafts ideals of William Morris, especially the Ruskin-Morris tendency to identify more with the past than the present. Roerich was, for a time, a dedicated medievalist, and even later, he never lost his liking for medieval art.

Over time, however, his first love became the Stone Age, which he idealized in many ways and on several levels. His handling of the shamanic theme, of course, touched on all of these. Aesthetically, Roerich transposed his admiration of medieval art and architecture to the Neolithic era, arguing enthusiastically and vociferously that the art and artifacts, and even the folk practices and rituals, of the Stone Age had a beauty and sophistication to them that had gone unappreciated and misunderstood for too long.[26] Roerich's historical and archaeological thinking about the Stone Age also led him to idealize the era. Pioneering thinkers in the fields of anthropology and sociology, including Lucien Lévy-Bruhl, Edward E. Evans-Pritchard, Emile Durkheim, Sir James Frazer, and Claude Lévi-Strauss had, in various ways, postulated that Neolithic people, secure in their innate sensitivity to what was sacred and what was not—and joined together securely by the ties of kinship and community—were the most contented humans ever to live.[27] Such ideas have since been called into question by more recent research and changing views. As the prominent British archaeologist Alisdair Whittle has forcefully stated, it is erroneous in the extreme to "envisage the Neolithic as some far-off Arcadia."[28] However, in Roerich's own time, and for a long while, the notions that primeval humanity understood even the most mundane elements of earthly existence in spiritual terms, and that the bonds of community among ancient peoples were tighter than during later stages of social development, were fundamental and enduring tenets of anthropological scholarship.

A sizable cohort of Russian artists and thinkers, especially those Symbolists interested in recapturing the Dionysian spirit of the ancient past, subscribed to this sort of thinking. The poet Vyacheslav Ivanov wrote of emulating the people of antiquity, who lived in a time when, in his words, "Every form of life was sacred and there was no action that would not be linked with the worship of divine power....Like a gigantic shadow, the deity was inseparable from man. Truly, everything was 'full of gods'."[29] Roerich believed this on several levels. On a strictly academic basis, he would have agreed fully with the assessment of Mircea Eliade that, "Ultimately, for the man of archaic society, the very fact of living in the world has a religious value."[30] Aesthetically, of course, it was entirely possible to appreciate abstractly this belief in the world as a divine space—without necessarily sharing it—and admire that belief for making the lives of primitive peoples spiritually and socially meaningful.

Ultimately, though, as he grew more attracted to the occult, Roerich came to believe not just that ancient peoples *thought themselves* to be living in a world where the sacred and the spiritual were regularly made manifest. He came to believe that they *actually did* live in such a world. In other words, the men and women of the Stone Age had been blessed with genuine insight, a fully awakened consciousness, that twentieth-century humanity, to its misfortune, had lost. In Roerich's eyes, shamanism would come to seem truly magical, not merely symbolically so.

To one degree or another, this emerging viewpoint underpins every painting or stage design in which Roerich deals with shamanism, magic, or spell-casting. It also had much to do with the key shift that Roerich made during the 1900s and early 1910s from an artistic outlook grounded in geographic and historical specificity—namely, Slavic primevalism and northern prehistory—to one oriented more toward metaphoric generality and the quest to uncover in his painting a metaphysical otherworld of truth and beauty. Roerich now began to conceive of the Stone Age as a time when a single, universal proto-culture, nothing less than an *ur*-culture for all of humanity, or at least all of Eurasia, spanned the globe. What was more, the people of this culture lived in an ideally communal fashion: they existed in harmony with their natural environment, they were attuned to the forces of spiritual purity that surrounded them, and they interacted with each other in fruitful cooperation.

To pinpoint precisely when Roerich moved from, first, the depiction of primitivism as a historical phenomenon to, second, a metaphorical appreciation of the primitive worldview, then, finally, to a literal belief in that worldview is difficult, if not impossible. Judging from his paintings, his essays, and his early poetry, it seems that faithfulness to history, at least as he perceived it, was Roerich's main motivation until around 1905. Over the next few years, his geographic interests widened, and his aesthetic identification with the Stone Age deepened. By 1909-1910, certainly not much later, Roerich's occult identification with the ancient past—more universally and pantheistically conceived—seems to have become paramount. This last development therefore coincides with the years Roerich spent working with Igor Stravinsky on the libretto, sets, and costumes for *The Rite of Spring*, which is better understood as an attempt, at least on Roerich's part, to reproduce the rituals and customs of not just a *Slavic* primevalism, but a more widely *Eurasian* primevalism.

Whatever the case, what kind of world do Roerich's shamans live in, and what is the shaman's purpose in that world, whether that world was cloaked in geographic symbolism that was Slavic, Asian, northern, or universal? Physically, the Stone-Age realms that that Roerich's shamans inhabit are typically wild, and more than occasionally bleak. The elder world, Roerich tells us, is fraught with peril and charged with elemental forces beyond human understanding. One of Roerich's most famous paintings on this theme, *Heavenly Battle* (2 versions, 1909 and 1912), overwhelms the onlooker, who, facing the picture, stands directly in the path of a gathering tempest. Massive banks of clouds, tinged with gold, violet, and blue-green, billow and roil above low-lying, verdant hills and the shore of a lake. One can imagine a titanic struggle about to take place. Huddled in the lower right-hand corner are the wooden huts and outbuildings of a small village. The scene is at once beautiful and unsettling. The presence of humankind, embodied in the tiny cluster of frail dwellings, seems dwarfed, even menaced, by the elemental might of nature—not only by the coming storm, but by the vast emptiness of the surrounding hills.

And yet this is a world and an era that Roerich prefers to his own. However dangerous the Stone Age might have been, it was, Roerich believed, more spiritually untainted than the corrupted and morally impoverished modern age. One might have to struggle to survive, but life in the distant past was, to Roerich, nonetheless preferable to the deadening and decadent existence that people led in the twentieth century. Two things above all made this rigorous, robust life superior in Roerich's view to modern existence: communal solidarity, which provided social cohesiveness, and the spiritual leadership of the shaman.

Regarding the question of communalism, Roerich's most eloquent written statement on the topic—and a useful key to many of his paintings from this period—is his essay "Joy in Art" (1908-1909).[31] A long, many-faceted piece, "Joy in Art" says much about many things, among them, Russia's place in the broader context of Eurasian cultural development. As he progresses, Roerich goes back further and further in time, excavating in prose the artistic legacy of every historical period, until he comes at last to the Stone Age. "The dark depths of the Bronze and Brass ages defy our understanding," he maintains, but the Stone Age is a time of "clear truth."[32] "Stone-age man gave birth to the beginning of all brilliant cultures," Roerich insists, "only he was able to do this." "Joy in Art" climaxes in a rhapsodic description, in effect a word-painting, of a holiday scene in a Stone-Age settlement:

> Let us turn one last time to the expansive quality of life in the age of stone.
> A lake. At the mouth of a river stands a row of houses. Does not the refinement of their decoration remind you of the houses of Japan, of India? The dwellings, flints, furs, the wicker fences, the urns, a dark body are all bathed in a beautiful iridescence. Roofs with high chimneys are covered with yellowing reeds, hides, and furs, thatched with some kind of marvelous wattleing. The tops have been secured with patterned plates cut from wood.
> Trophies of the best hunts have been hung from the edges of the roofs. A white skull wards off the evil eye.
> The walls of the houses are ornamented in yellow, red, white, and black tones. There are hearths within and without. Above the hearths, pottery, gorgeously patterned pottery, brown and grey-black. On the shore there are dugouts and nets. The nets are

> woven long and fine. Hides are drying on the kilns: bear, wolf, lynx, fox, beaver, sable, ermine…
>
> It is a holiday. Let it be the one when the victory of the springtime sun was celebrated. When the people went out into the woods, to spend long periods of time admiring the trees. When, out of the first grasses, they made fragrant wreaths and adorned themselves with them. When they played upon horns and pipes [dudki] of bone and wood. In the crowd, clothing, furs, and floral garlands intermingle. Beautifully decorated footwear, made of reeds and hides, shuffle side by side. In the circle dance [khorovod], amber pendants, braid, stone beads, and white talismans made of animals' teeth flash.
>
> The people rejoiced. Among them art was born. They were near to us. They almost certainly sang. And their songs were heard beyond the lake and on all of the islands. And enormous fires flickered in yellow patches. Near the fires, the dark crowd moved. The waters, turbulent by day, have calmed and become lilac-blue. And amid the nocturnal rejoicing, the silhouettes of dugouts swiftly glide on the lake.[33]

Roerich goes on to assure us that, "Of the Stone Age we will someday know more. We will better understand and more justly assess this era. And the Stone Age, better understood, will tell us much."[34]

A handful of critics understood right away the more universalist, more metaphysical direction Roerich was beginning to take in his paintings representing prehistory. Writing for *The Golden Fleece* (*Zolotoe runo*), Alexander Rostislavov remarked that Roerich, for the moment Russia's most "individualistic" painter, was turning out work that was not only more "fantastical," but more deeply situated in the past: "Miraculously, he perceives and understands the beauty of bygone eras… he comprehends the remote culture that is so puzzling to the rest of us."[35] Similarly, the antiquarian Nikolai Wrangel would praise Roerich's unique insight into the long-buried past: "From a high peak, Roerich, with his keen eye, gazes upon a faraway truth. The grey mists that conceal the mysteries of bygone centuries are no obstacle to his understanding."³⁶ One commentator in particular, Sergei Makovsky, perceived what kind of social structure Roerich was trying to portray in his primevalist scenes. Makovsky wrote for *The Golden Fleece*, and later served as editor-in-chief of *Apollo* (*Apollon*); he was also well-acquainted with Roerich personally.

Writing in 1907 about Roerich's recent paintings of past eras, Makovsky proposed that, although Roerich had been categorized as a painter of historical Russia, he was in the process of becoming something more.³⁷ Makovsky observed that human figures in many of Roerich's canvases—when they appeared at all—were blending more and more into the natural world surrounding them. As this happened, the facial features of the men and women Roerich painted were becoming less distinct: either depersonalized or barely visible. Roerich's humans had no personal identity; instead, they coexisted in a primitive oneness. To Makovsky, this facelessness, this lack of individuality, was intentional: it was Roerich's way of placing humankind in balance with nature and with itself. As Makovsky described Roerich's characters, "They are without names. And they do not think, they do not feel on their own… they live with a collective mind and a collective feeling, together with the trees, the stones, and the creatures of antiquity." Makovsky then turned to the question of exactly when and where these scenes existed: "Who is he, this 'faceless one'? What epoch is reflected in his blind soul?" Conventional wisdom would have it that Roerich was painting Kievan Rus, or old Muscovy, or appanage (*udel'naia*) Russia. But Makovsky replied:

> If you like. But that is not important, although it is customary to consider Roerich a 'national painter.' It is not important, because for him the national-historical theme is only decoration. Roerich's 'man' is not a Russian, or a Slav, or a Varangian. He is Ancient Man, the primeval barbarian of the earth.

Makovsky's insight was to understand how Roerich was beginning to incorporate the theme of communalism in his themes of the past. Like Makovsky, the Symbolist poet Maximilian Voloshin, made note of the increasingly universalist nature of Roerich's depiction of the past. He also drew attention to the more prominent role that magic and ritual seemed to be playing in Roerich's painting. When the inaugural number of the journal *Apollo* appeared in October 1909, Voloshin contributed an essay entitled "Archaism and Russian Painting."[38] Here, the poet profiled three artists—Roerich, Léon Bakst, and Konstantin Bogaevsky—whose work drew them back to the far reaches of antiquity. Voloshin's appreciation of all three painters had much to do with his typically Symbolist view of ancient cultures as lost worlds best examined through the prism of dreams and poetic mysticism than scientific empiricism. Thematically, he linked his three subjects by opening with a quotation from the Jewish *Kabbala*: "Stone becomes vegetable. Vegetable becomes beast. Beast becomes man. Man becomes demon. And the demon becomes a god."[39] All three artists have a place in this progression. Bakst represents the human element, Bogaevsky the vegetative. Delving back to the very origins of humankind, Roerich worked in stone.

Like Makovsky, Voloshin called attention to the facelessness of the human figures in Roerich's northern and archaic scenes. To Voloshin, this was an indication of the communal oneness that Makovsky had noted. In addition, this quality went hand in glove with the ambitious, even cosmic, chronological scale on which Roerich practiced his art. While Bakst's ancient tableaux recalled the Greco-Mediterranean empires of Troy and Knossos, and Bogaevsky's works put the viewer in mind of Cimmerian and Scythian southlands, Roerich's subject was a far older and more severe landscape, "in which time is measured out by geological epochs."[40] It was a rocky world of flints and fossils, "only just emerging from the dead layers of seemingly eternal glaciers."[41] "This is a land that still preserves its primordial essence," Voloshin asserts.[42] The inhabitants, like the landscape, appear to be part of the stone itself. They also are just beginning to stir to life. Having penetrated the hidden secrets of humanity's earliest days, Roerich deserves to be considered "the mightiest...and boldest" of artists.[43] If Voloshin understood how humankind fit into Roerich's Stone Age, he, even more so than Makovsky, understood Roerich's attempts to infuse his portraits of the era with a magical quality. In a manner typical of the Russian Symbolists—many of whose perceptions of antiquity were poetic, even

Atlantis- or Stonehenge-besotted in the most fanciful ways, rather than academically exact—Voloshin notes that Roerich's archaic landscapes remind him of the standing stones, mengirs, dolmens, and temples of the earth's eldest cultures, among them the Celts, the Mayans, and the Egyptians.[44] Voloshin's reference to the *Kabbala*, of course, places Roerich, as the artist of stone, at the base of his cosmological scheme.

How did shamanism fit into Roerich's conception of Stone-Age communalism? In Roerich's eyes, it was the leadership of the shaman that enabled humankind to survive—and, beyond that, to attain spiritual maturity—in what he saw as the harsh conditions of the Stone Age. One of the functions of shamanic practice, in Roerich's view of things, was to preserve what he imagined had been the precarious balance between humanity and the vast, untamed environment in which it existed. The ritual power of shamanic magic relieves the starkness of the archaic landscape in which Roerich's subjects dwell. Another of the shaman's purposes was to weld the community into a more unified whole. Finally, shamans and shamanism helped to raise the level of the community's spiritual awareness, putting humankind in closer touch with the magical, elemental energies that modern humanity could no longer feel or detect.

All these functions were reflected in many of Roerich's paintings, stage designs, essays, and poems from 1905 through World War I and the Russian revolutions of 1917. Early examples include the spells and incantations Roerich depicts in the abovementioned *Sorcerers*, *Fiery Spell*, and *The Conjuration by Water*, all of which date from 1905. The subtext of Roerich's designs for *The Rite of Spring*—independent of anything that Stravinsky or Vaclav Nijinsky, Roerich's collaborators, might have wished to communicate by means of music or choreography—was to demonstrate not just the savage, ecstatic beauty of ancient Slavic ritual, but the power of shamanic magic to foster communal solidarity and, furthermore, to allow mankind to reach an accord with the overwhelming forces of nature.

During World War I, Roerich turned increasingly to the subject of incantation and spell-casting. In *The Command*, from 1915, a lone, fur-clad wizard extends his hands over a river rushing past him, binding the waters to his will by the power of his magic. *The Commands of Heaven* (1915) and *The Sorceress* (1916), each introduced at earlier points in this paper, fall into this category as well. Another cluster of paintings demonstrates the heightened sensitivity to spiritual truth that Roerich believed ancient humankind to possess. For example, in *The Omen* (1915), a man on a hilltop gazes at the sky, reading portents in the shapes of the clouds passing overhead. In similar works, ancient peoples show themselves able to decipher hidden messages all around them—concealed not just in the form of clouds in the sky, but also rocks and boulders in the shape of human faces (as in *The Holy Island*, from 1917), rune-like fissures and cracks in mountainsides and geological formations, and constellations in the heavens (as in 1912's *Starry Runes*). All are tangible symbols of spiritual truths that Roerich believed were obvious to the inhabitants of Stone Age Eurasia: a time and place where the "sacred signs"[45] (to which Roerich dedicated so much of his poetry before and during World War I) could be read by all.

In all of these instances, whether in his writing or in his painting, Roerich communicated his conviction that the ancients had indeed lived surrounded by supernatural forces, hidden spirits, and pagan gods. At first he believed this in an artistic and metaphoric sense. Then, as time passed, he became convinced, quite literally, that the ancients had perceived correctly—that they did not merely *believe* that they existed in a god-filled world, but that they *did* exist in such a world. Exactly when Roerich crossed this line is unclear. But it is indisputable that, in either case, the shamanic motif was central to the way Roerich expressed his thoughts on this matter.

From Communalism to Hierarchy: An Epilogue

How long-lasting was Roerich's commitment to the communalist principle he professed in his paintings and writings? If anything, that commitment deepened in the long run. From December 1916, when he left St. Petersburg, to January 1918, when the new Soviet Union closed its borders to the west, Roerich and his family lived in a state of self-imposed semi-exile. Weary of wartime misery, fearful of political developments at home, and plagued by an inflammation of the lungs, Roerich moved away from the capital to the lakes and woods of Karelia, on the frontier between Russia and Finland. There, he painted a series of northern landscapes, pored over Hindu and Buddhist texts, as well as the poetry of Rabindranath Tagore, and dreamed of India.

In addition, the political turmoil that his country underwent in 1917—its plummeting military fortunes, the fall of the tsarist regime in the spring, and the Bolshevik takeover in the autumn—focused Roerich's mind more intently on the question of social organization. By now, the ideas that he had expressed—and continued to express—in those paintings dealing with the shamanic theme were stated even more explicitly and more forcefully.

Roerich's feelings are most apparent in his essays "Unity" (*Edinstvo*) and "Soul-Creation" (*Dukhotvorchestvo*), both from late 1917, as well as a series of heavy-hearted, soul-searching letters he exchanged with friends and colleagues, including fellow World of Art painter Alexandre Benois, the historian and collector A. P. Ivanov, and the playwright Leonid Andreyev.[46] As the Bolsheviks came to power in Russia and the prospects of civil war loomed, Roerich attributed much of his society's problems to atomization. Paradoxically, he wrote, the more men and women congregated into mobs and crowds, the more disaggregated each individual became. To a certain degree anticipating Ortega y Gasset's famous critique of twentieth-century mass society, Roerich insisted that the modern mob was "mindless" and "animalistic." While one might join the crowd out of fear or for one's own short-term, base advantage, all one gained was the illusion of collectivity, and all one accomplished was to isolate oneself further. The so-called "communism" offered by Lenin and the Bolsheviks was nothing more than dictatorship in disguise.

The antidote, Roerich argued, was exactly the type of *authentic* collectivity that he had been painting and writing about for years. The only hope Russia had for the future was to look backwards to antiquity. The *true* communalism that humankind had enjoyed during the Stone Age, together with a reverent appreciation of the healing power of art and culture, would be the salvation of Russia in this debased, degraded age of war, mass hysteria, and political demagoguery.

As a result, Roerich spent the next few years as a supporter of the White campaign against the fledgling Soviet government. (Later, by the mid-to-late 1920s, Roerich's attitude toward the USSR became more ambiguous, involving at the least a resigned belief that it was Russia's destiny to endure the stresses and strains of Soviet rule and perhaps, for a time, a hope that Soviet communism could somehow be reconciled philosophically and in practice with a more modern conception of Buddhism). As Roerich and his wife Helena formalized the tenets of their own occultist discipline, Agni Yoga, one of the principles they embedded most firmly within that discipline was that of hierarchy. Indeed, one of the tomes that make up the thirteen-volume "Agni Yoga" collection is entitled exactly that: *Hierarchy*.

A charge that is frequently levelled against modern occultists is that they all too readily incline toward hierarchalism. Writing of W. B. Yeats and the occult vision the poet outlines in his mystical screed, *A Vision*, no less a figure than George Orwell complained that "the very concept of occultism carries with it the idea that knowledge must be a secret thing, limited to a small circle of initiates." Therefore, Orwell continues, "hatred of democracy and a tendency to believe in crystal-gazing...go together."[47] As much as the Russian philosopher Nikolai Berdiaev empathized with the urge to embrace the primitivist "cosmism" that Roerich embraced, he argued that this urge must be resisted. Cosmism and occultism might provide the comforting *illusion* of joy, ecstasy, and communion with mystery, but they destroy human individuality: in Berdiaev's words, they "lead to the dissolution of human personality."[48] "Cosmism," Berdiaev insists, "has in fact a reactionary character, above all a spiritually reactionary character. It exalts the idea of organism and the organic."[49]

Whether Roerich was among the "primitivists" and "cosmists" that Berdiaev had specifically in mind when he wrote these words is impossible to tell. There is no doubt, though, that Berdiaev was referring in general to the cultural substream in Silver-Age Russia to which Roerich belonged. And because, in the end, Roerich took his "cosmism" to much greater extremes than any of his compeers, Berdiaev's words, in a sense, apply better to him than to anyone else Berdiaev might have been thinking of. It would be unfair to go so far as to say of Roerich, as Orwell does of Yeats, that "his tendency is Fascist...he is a great hater of democracy"(indeed, it is hardly fair even to say it of Yeats).[50] It is true, however, that, as time went on, Roerich saw himself more and more as the spiritual leader of a community— a small one, to be sure, but one that would hopefully grow—to which he imparted wisdom and insight, by means of his art and his teachings. Such wisdom and insight would shield his followers from the spiritual dangers and pitfalls of modern existence and prepare them for the cosmic changes he believed were soon to come. In this fashion, Roerich was no longer simply making use of the shamanic motif in his art. He had refashioned himself into a latter-day shaman, and he continued to portray himself as such to the end of his days.

Original Painting Details:
The Commands of Heaven (1915). Tempera on board, 29.5 x 38.5 inches. State Russian Museum, St. Petersburg.

"The Great Sacrifice," entr'acte curtain for The Rite of Spring (1910-1913). Tempera on canvas, 29 x 32 inches. Bolling Collection, Miami, Florida.
Heavenly Battle (1909 and 1912). Tempera on board, 26 x 37.5 inches. State Russian Museum, St. Petersburg.

Notes:
1 Despite Roerich's importance, no full-length academic study of his life exists in English. The best approximation is Jacqueline Decter, *Messenger of Beauty: The Life and Visionary Art of Nicholas Roerich* (Rochester, Vt.: Park Street Press, 1997), a beautifully illustrated but thinly and inadequately researched album of Roerich's paintings. Studies that deal with various aspects of Roerich's life and art include Robert C. Williams, *Russian Art and American Money* (Cambridge: Harvard University Press, 1980); Charles J. Errico and J. Samuel Walker, "The New Deal and the Guru," *American Heritage* 40, no. 2 (March 1989): 92-99; Robert A. Rupen, "Mongolia, Tibet, and Buddhism, or, A Tale of Two Roerichs," *Canada-Mongolia Review* 5, no. 1 (April 1979): 1-36; Karl E. Meyer and Shareen Blair Brysac, *Tournament of Shadows: The Great Game and the Race for Empire in Central Asia* (Washington, D.C.: Counterpoint, 1999); Millicent Hodson, "Nijinsky's Choreographic Method: Visual Sources from Roerich for *Le Sacre du Printemps*," *Dance Research Journal* 18, no. 2 (Winter 1986-1987): 7-15; Kenneth Archer, "The Theatrical Designs of Nicholas Roerich: Problems of Identification" (M.A. thesis, University of Antioch, 1985); and idem, *Nicholas Roerich: East and West* (Bournemouth: Parkstone, 1999). Roerich is routinely mentioned—albeit often in passing—in English- and Russian-language works on art and theater history, especially in conjunction with his role in designing the sets and costumes for the famous premiere of Stravinsky's *The Rite of Spring*. Russian biographies, which tend to be weak in their treatment of Roerich's occult interests (as well as the controversies those interests stirred up in the United States and during his Asian travels), include L. V. Korotkina, *Rerikh* (St. Petersburg: Khudozhnik Rossii, 1996); P. F. Belikov and V. P. Kniazeva, *N. K. Rerikh* (Samara: Agni, 1996); and E. I. Poliakova, *Nikolai Rerikh* (Moscow: Iskusstvo, 1985). Roerich's own voluminous writings are available in Russian in a variety of editions, the most recent being published by the International Center of the Roerichs (MTsR) in Moscow. Specialized studies touching on various themes of Roerich's art have been appearing with steadily increasing frequency in Russia over the last decade. Among the best is E. P. Iakovleva, *Teatral'no-dekoratsionnoe iskusstvo N. K. Rerikha* (Samara: Agni, 1996).

2 Exactly what constitutes "shamanism" remains a point of contention among scholars, not to mention authors writing for popular audiences (whether or not the popular audience in question consists of "new age" adherents). The term "shaman" is thought to be Siberian, specifically Tungus, in origin, although some argue that the word comes from Pali or Chinese [Ronald Hutton, *Shamans: Siberian Spirituality and the Western Imagination* (London: Hambledon and London, 2001), 113-15]. When Westerners first encountered the word in the late seventeenth century, they began to use it as an umbrella term to describe any ritual specialist in Siberia who entered a trance-like or ecstatic state for the purpose of transacting with spirits. Despite the fact that Siberian tribes themselves used a variety of terms to describe such ritual specialists, scholars and lay people alike continued to use the term "shaman" as a catch-all descriptor for them. Likewise, although the ritual practices and religious worldviews of Siberian ethnic groups varied considerably, they came more and more to be lumped under the single category of "shamanism." The scholarship of the very early 1900s, with which Roerich would have been familiar, would have supported such a universalizing view.

The universalist view of shamanism became even more prominent later in the century (ironically, just as most anthropological and ethnographic scholarship was beginning to emphasize specificity and difference). Both popular and scholarly perceptions of shamanism have been indelibly stamped by the imprint of historian of religions Mircea Eliade, whose *Shamanism* (Princeton: Princeton University Press, 1974) remains one of the most widely-read books on the subject. Despite his undisputed erudition, however, Eliade, for a variety of personal and political reasons, put forward a view of shamanism that further universalized the shaman by defining him or her as any practitioner of what Eliade referred to as "ritual ecstasy." Eliade went on to propose that most, if not all, "primitive" societies incorporate some form of "shamanism" into their religious life. The tremendous influence that Eliade's ideas have enjoyed both in and out of academe has led to even broader theorization and speculation—some of it rigorous, some of it fanciful in the extreme—about the global universality of "shamanism" (the blockbuster success of Carlos Castaneda's highly controversial, but best-selling, "Don Juan" books is but one illustration of how far this reasoning has been taken).

This essay adheres to a more particularist view of shamanism and, consequently, considers the universalist perception of shamanism—and certainly Roerich's perception of it—to be flawed. It needs to be noted, however, that however skewed Roerich's views of shamanism may seem by today's scholarly standards, they were well within the scholarly mainstream of his own day, and they are not dissimilar to the Eliade metanarrative—which, despite its faults, has enjoyed and continues to enjoy wide acceptance.

On shamanism in general, see Hutton, *Shamanism*, 60-61, 113-27, which provides a useful critique of the universalist view, as well as Gloria Flaherty, *Shamanism and the Eighteenth Century* (Princeton: Princeton University Press, 1992); Uno Homberg-Harva, *Finno-Ugric Mythology and Siberian Mythology* (Boston: Archaeological Institute of America, 1927); A. F. Anisimov, *Kosmologicheskie predstavleniia narodov Severa* (Moscow: Nauka, 1959); L. P. Potapov, *Etnicheskii sostav i proiskhozhdenie Altaitsev* (Leningrad: Nauka, 1969); Marjorie Mandelstam Balzer, ed., *Shamanic Worlds: Rituals and Lore of Siberia and Central Asia* (Armonk, N.Y.: M. E. Sharpe, 1996); Robert J. Harvey, *Shamans/Neo-Shamans: Ecstasy, Alternative Archaeologies and Contemporary Pagans* (London: Routledge, 2003); G. Harvey, *Shamanism* (London: Routledge, 2003); Alice Beck Kehoe, *Shamans and Religion: An Anthropological Exploration in Critical Thinking* (Prospect Heights, Ill.: Waveland, 2000); D. C. Noel, *The Soul of Shamanism: Western Fantasies, Imaginal Realities* (New York: Continuum, 1997); Clark Chilson and Peter Knecht, eds., *Shamans in Asia* (London: Routledge, 2003); Caroline Humphrey and U. Onon, *Shamans and Elders: Experience, Knowledge, and Power among the Daur Mongols* (Oxford: Clarendon, 1996); and J.-P. Roux, *La Religion des Turcs et des Mongols* (Paris: Payot, 1984).

3 See, for example, W. Bruce Lincoln, *Between Heaven and Hell* (New York: Viking, 1998), 273-87; Maria Carlson, *"No Religion Higher Than Truth": A History of the Theosophical Movement in Russia, 1875-1922* (Princeton: Princeton University Press, 1993); idem, "Fashionable Occultism: The World of Russian Composer Aleksandr Scriabin," *Journal of the International Institute* 7, no. 3 (Summer 2001); Bernice Glatzer Rosenthal, ed., *The Occult in Russian and Soviet Culture* (Ithaca: Cornell University Press, 1997); James Webb, *The Occult Underground* (La Salle, Ill.: Open Court, 1974), 154-174; Peter Washington, *Madame Blavatsky's Baboon: A History of the Mystics, Mediums, and Misfits Who Brought Spiritualism to America* (New York: Schoken, 1995), 163-169; Robert C. Williams, *Artists in Revolution: Portraits of the Russian Avant-Garde, 1905-1925* (Bloomington: Indiana University Press, 1977), 101-127; and Orlando Figes, *A People's Tragedy: A History of the Russian Revolution* (New York: Viking, 1996), 208-209.

4 Georges Florovsky, *Ways of Russian Theology* (Vadiz, 1989), II:233-34.

5 Carlson, *"No Religion Higher Than Truth"*, 3-8.

6 *Ibid.*

7 The quotation comes from Washington, *Madame Blavatsky's Baboon*, 160. Readers unfamiliar with the history of the arts in Russia should note that the label "Silver Age" is commonly applied to the period lasting approximately from 1880 to 1920. The reference is in contrast to the so-called "Golden Age" of Russian arts and letters, which is considered to have begun with Pushkin's rise and concluded with Dostoevsky's death and the end of Tolstoy's most productive years as a

writer. Both labels are, of course, inexact and subjective, but they have sufficient currency to serve as a convenient shorthand. "Silver Age" is therefore used in this essay as a culturally-specific substitute for "turn-of-the-century" and *"fin-de-siècle."*

8 Maria Carlson, "Fashionable Occultism," 1-2.

9 Joan Delaney Grossman, "The Transformation Myth in Russian Modernism," in Peter I. Barta, ed., *Metamorphosis in Russian Modernism* (New York: Central European University Press, 2000), 41-60.

10 Bernice Glatzer Rosenthal, *New Myth, New World: From Nietzsche to Stalinism* (University Park: Pennsylvania State University Press, 2002), 106.

11 Peg Weiss, *Kandinsky and Old Russia* (New Haven: Yale University Press, 1995). In "Shamanic Elements in Some Early Eighteenth-Century Russian Woodcuts," *Slavic Review* 52, no. 4 (Winter 1993): 725-745, Dianne E. Farrell traces even more deeply the interaction between Finno-Ugric shamanism and Russian culture.

12 Rosenthal, *New Myth, New World*, 1-60; Rosamund Bartlett, *Wagner and Russia* (Cambridge: Cambridge University Press, 1995).

13 See endnote 2 for discussion of Eliade's interpretation of shamanism. It should go without saying that the Russian Symbolists' conception of shamanism as "Dionysian" was mythopoetic rather than scholarly.

14 On the wider point of Western artists' appropriation, even cultural colonization, of "primitive" art, see Roger Benjamin, "Matisse in Morocco: A Colonizing Aesthetic?" *Art in America* 78 (November 1990): 157-64, 211-13; Stephen F. Eisenman, *Gauguin's Skirt* (London: Thames and Hudson, 1997); Charles Harrison, et al., *Primitivism, Cubism, Abstraction: The Early Twentieth Century* (New Haven: Yale University Press, 1994); Patricia Leighten, "The White Peril and l'art negre: Picasso, Primitivism and Anti-Colonialism," *Art Bulletin* 72, no. 4 (December 1990); Jill Lloyd, *German Expressionism: Primitivism and Modernity* (New Haven: Yale University Press, 1991); and Marianna Torgovnick, *Gone Primitive: Savage Intellects, Modern Lives* (Chicago: University of Chicago Press, 1990).

15 On the application of Edward Said's famous "orientalism" thesis [*Orientalism* (New York: Vintage, 1979)] to the study of Russian imperialism, see Daniel Brower and Edward J. Lazzerini, eds., *Russia's Orient: Imperial Borderlands and Peoples, 1700-1917* (Bloomington: Indiana University Press, 1997).

16 For a useful survey of this problem, begin with Hutton, *Shamans*, 19-22, 62-63, 113-20, 129, 138.

17 See Carlson, *"No Religion Higher Than Truth"*, 296-305.

18 For an introduction to Scythian and Eurasianist trends in Russian culture, see W. Bruce Lincoln *Between Heaven and Hell* (New York: Viking, 1998); James H.

Billington, *The Icon and the Axe* (New York: Vintage, 1970); and Orlando Figes, *Natasha's Dance* (London: Allan Lane, 2002). Historian George Vernadsky, art historian N. P. Kondakov, and poet Nikolai Gumilev were among the major exponents of the Eurasian thesis. Gumilev's son Lev, a prominent historian, has written a massive and popular body of work outlining Eurasianist theories of history (contemporary editions are now being issued with Roerich's paintings as illustrations). See George Vernadsky, *Ancient Russia* (New Haven: Yale University Press, 1943); M. T. Rostovtzeff, *Iranians and Greeks in South Russia* (New York: Russell, 1963) [orig. 1918]; A. L. Mongait, *Archaeology in the USSR* (Harmondsworth: Penguin, 1961), 130-32, 153-63; Lev N. Gumilev, *Drevniaia Rus' i velikaia step'* (Moscow: ACT, 2001); and S. G. Kliashtornyi and T. I. Sultanov, *Gosudarstva i narody evraiziiskikh stepei: Drevnost' i srednevekov'e* (St. Petersburg: Institute of Oriental Studies, 2000).

19 Roerich was inducted into the Russian Archaeological Society and gave lectures at the Imperial Archaeological Institute. He regularly worked at excavations in the Novgorod, Pskov, Iaroslavl', Tver', and Vologda regions. For samples of Roerich's archaeological writings, see "Na kurgane," *Sobranie sochinenii* (Moscow: Sytin, 1914), 1-26; "The Closed Eye," *Fiery Stronghold* (Boston: Stratford, 1933), 56-63; and "Iskusstvo i arkheologiia," *Iskusstvo i khudozhestvennaia promyshlennost'* 3 (December 1898): 185-94, and 4-5 (January-February 1899): 251-66.

20 V. V. Stasov, "Proiskhozhdenie russkikh bylin," *Vestnik Evropy* (1868). On Stasov's books *Russian Folk Ornament* (1872) and *Slavic and Oriental Ornament* (1884-1887), see Alison Hilton, *Russian Folk Art* (Bloomington: Indiana University Press, 1995), 223, 320n24.

21 For more on Roerich's thinking on this topic, see John McCannon, "In Search of Primeval Russia: Stylistic Evolution in the Landscapes of Nicholas Roerich," *Ecumene* 7, no. 3 (July 2000): 271-97; and idem, "By the Shores of White Waters: The Altai and Its Place in the Spiritual Geopolitics of Nicholas Roerich," *Sibirica: Journal of Siberian Studies* 2, no. 2 (October 2002): 167-90.

22 Roerich, "Iskusstvo i arkheologiia," op. cit.

23 Roerich, "Radost' iskusstvu," *Vestnik Evropy* 2 (April 1909): 508-33. Reprinted in Roerich, *Sobranie sochinenii*, 116-53; and idem, *Adamant* (New York: Corona Mundi, 1922), 108-39.

24 N. S. Shaparova, *Kratkaia entsiklopediia slavianskoi mifologii* (Moscow: Astrel', 2001), 353-55; E. F. Konev, *Slavianskaia mifologiia* (Minsk: Kharvest, 2003), 73-75; Jack V. Haney, *An Introduction to the Russian Folktale* (Armonk, N.Y.: M. E. Sharpe, 1999), 65-71, 89-90.

25 Carl E. Schorske, *Fin-de-Siècle Vienna: Politics and Culture* (New York: Knopf, 1980), 167.

26 Among other works, see Roerich, "Radost' iskusstvu," op. cit.; idem, "Iskusstvo i arkheologiia," op. cit., idem, "K prirode," *Sobranie sochinenii*, 80-90; idem, "Obedneli my," *Sobranie sochinenii*, 103-15; idem, "Zakliatoe zver'e," *Niva* 18 (1909): 311.

27 See, for example, Emile Durkheim, *The Elementary Forms of the Religious Life* (New York: Free Press, 1965); Edward E. Evans-Pritchard, *Theories of Primitive Religion* (Oxford: Clarendon, 1966); James Frazer, *The New Golden Bough*, ed. Theodor H. Gaster (New York: Mentor, 1964); Claude Lévi-Strauss, *The Savage Mind* (Chicago: University of Chicago Press, 1966); Lucien Lévy-Bruhl, *Primitive Mentality* (New York: Macmillan, 1923); Octavio Paz, *The Labyrinth of Solitude* (New York: Grove, 1986), 226. In *Europe in the Neolithic: The Creation of New Worlds* (Cambridge: Cambridge University Press, 1996), Alisdair Whittle complains that, until comparatively recently, the scholarly orthodoxy regarding everyday life in the Stone Age had it that "from spirits, ancestors and other beings came a sense of the sacred, and this, rather than anything secular, guided people's values and ideals....The values and ideals of cooperation, sharing, solidarity, mutuality, honour and esteem were central to the way of life" [355]. It is this orthodoxy that Whittle and most contemporary archaeologists have worked to dispel.

28 Whittle, *Europe in the Neolithic*, 7. On how the older, romanticized view of Stone-Age life has largely, if not altogether, dropped out of the scholarship, also see, among other sources, Whittle, *Problems in Neolithic Archaeology* (Cambridge: Cambridge University Press, 1988), 164-84; D. Bruce Dickson, *The Dawn of Belief: Religion in the Upper Paleolithic of Southwestern Europe* (Tuscon: University of Arizona Press, 1990), 1-27, 123-96; Paul M. Dolukhanov, *Ecology and Economy in Neolithic Eastern Europe* (New York: St. Martin's Press, 1978); Barry Cunliffe, ed., *The Oxford Illustrated History of Prehistoric Europe* (Oxford: Oxford University Press, 2001); Kristian Kristiansen, *Europe Before Prehistory* (Cambridge: Cambridge University Press, 1998); and Clive Gamble, *The Palaeolithic Societies of Europe* (Cambridge: Cambridge University Press, 1999).

29 V. Ivanov, "Religiia Dionisia: ee proiskhozhdenie i vliianiia," *Voprosy zhizni* (June 1905): 190.

30 Mircea Eliade, *Occultism, Witchcraft, and Cultural Fashions* (Chicago: University of Chicago Press, 1976), 21.

31 Roerich, "Radost' iskusstvu," *Vestnik Evropy* 2 (April 1909): 508-33. Also in *Sobranie sochinenii*, 116-53; and *Adamant* (New York: Corona Mundi, 1924), 108-24, 125-39.

32 Roerich, "Joy in Art," *Adamant*, 123.

33 Roerich, "Radost' iskusstvu," *Sobranie sochinenii*, 150-51.

34 *Ibid.*, 152.

35 Aleksandr Rostislavov, "Individualizm Rerikha," *Zolotoe runo* 4 (1907): 8-10.

36 N. N. Vrangel', "Otblesk bylogo," *Russkii bibliofil* 5 (1916): 5-10.

37 S. K. Makovskii, "N. Rerikh," *Zolotoe runo* 4 (1907): 3-7.

38 Maksimilian Voloshin, "Arkhaizm i russkoi zhivopisi: Rerikh, Bogaevskii i Bakst," *Apollon* 1 (October 1909): 43-53.

39 *Ibid.*, 43.

40 *Ibid.*, 50.

41 *Ibid.*

42 *Ibid.*

43 *Ibid.*, 53.

44 Here, of course, Voloshin writes as a poet and an art critic, not as an archaeologist. However, at the time, even the academic understanding of prehistoric megaliths and megalithic cultures—or at least much of that understanding—was confused and speculative, informed by dubious anthropological and linguistic conclusions, as well as wild guesses based on surface similarities and slight likenesses. Indeed, even today, scholarly work on the subject, not to mention popular writing, is not always immune to this sort of vaporous theorizing. For a sense of how writing on megalithic artifacts has evolved over time, start with Jean McMann's chapter, "Antiquarians, Archaeologists, and Astro-Mystics," in *Riddles of the Stone Age* (London: Thames and Hudson, 1980), 138-45; and continue with Whittle, *Problems in Neolithic Archaeology*, 164-84; and Mark Patton, *Statements in Stone: Monuments and Society in Neolithic Brittany* (London: Routledge, 1993), 1-17.

45 See "Zakliatiia," *Sobranie sochinenii*, 321-23. These verses comprise the first three parts of what eventually became the poetic cycle *Flowers of Morya* [*Tsvety Morii*] (Berlin: Slovo, 1921).

46 Roerich, *Listy dnevnika (1942-1947)* (Moscow: MTsR, 1995), 599-600; idem, *Puti blagosloveniia* (Riga, 1924), 228; E. G. Soini, "Perepiska N. K. Rerikha s sovremennikami," *Sever* 4 (1981): 109-10.

47 George Orwell, "W. B. Yeats," *The Penguin Essays of George Orwell* (London: Penguin, 1994), 236-37.

48 Nikolai Berdiaev, *Slavery and Freedom* (New York: Charles Scribner's Sons, 1944), 34-35.

49 *Ibid.*, 101.

50 Orwell, *op. cit.*

Feature Book Review Section: Shamanism

In this and subsequent issues of the JSM we intend to pick a subject and review some of the significant recent titles in that area. This issue concentrates on contemporary approaches to Shamanism:

Nine Worlds of Seid-Magic: Ecstasy and Neo-Shamanism in North European Paganism, by Jenny Blain, Routledge, 2002, ISBN 0415256518 £15.99 208 pages

Work on North European Paganism has been somewhat lacking in quantity (though not quality) in recent years, and Jenny Blain's *Nine Worlds of Seid-Magic* is thus a timely publication. It is also a valuable one. What Blain presents us with is an insider ethnography which if perhaps a little dry at times, is intelligent, sensitive and lucid. On a theoretical level moreover, *Nine Worlds* constitutes a significant contribution to our field of study in that Seid magic is placed by Blain within the longstanding anthropological literature on shamanism. Thus through *Nine Worlds*, Seid magic (and perhaps magic more generally) is brought firmly into the realms of the academically respectable while our understanding of it is significantly furthered through a specific focus on its shamanistic nature. I must also say how rewarding it is to read the work of a scholar of magic who is prepared to engage with postmodernism; Blain's study is informed by some of the most up-to-date social and cultural theory and yet the work does not degenerate into either the self-refutation or the excessive agnosticism that have given the more postmodern social science a bad name.

Doubtless the author will be criticised for her taxonomy, both explicit and implicit. In Blain's portrayal of it, Seid magic is sharply separated from the wider Hermetic tradition in which all contemporary western magic is carried out; it is also rather sharply separated from neo-shamanism generally, and neo-paganism generally; and finally, it is rather sharply separated from alternative spirituality generally. Moreover, those of a more positivist cast of mind may be inclined to attack this study for deploying too loose a definition of its theoretical cornerstone, shamanism. However, anyone who has ever thought or written about any aspect of contemporary magic will have struggled with matters of definition and taxonomy, and criticism on such grounds is perhaps inevitable for us all. It would be a shame if such relatively minor problems were to detract from a long overdue book-length anthropological study of North European Paganism, produced by an insightful individual who is better placed than many to represent contemporary Seid magic.

William Redwood

Robert J. Wallis, *Shamans / Neo-Shamans: Ecstasy, alternative archaeologies and contemporary Pagans.* **London, Routledge. 306 pages, ISBN 0415302021. £19.99 / $29.95 softback. £60.00 / $95.00 hardback.**

As an exposition and appraisal of European and North American neo-Shamanisms, and of anthropological and archaeological perspectives on their construction and practice, Wallis' book does a wonderful job of systematically reviewing the complexity of issues and interests surrounding the topic.

But in accommodating the plurality of viewpoints surrounding neo-Shamanisms, Wallis sometimes leaves himself little space for manoeuvre in delineating possible solutions to the problems discussed. This is also evident in the introductory chapter, where Wallis introduces queer theory as a possible framework within which to recast contemporary (and often dismissive) scholarly debates surrounding the 'authenticity' of neo-Shamanisms. While an interesting and potentially illuminating approach, the usefulness of this theoretical trope is never really developed elsewhere in the volume, and the significance of queer theory is only again reappraised in the concluding chapter. In a similar vein, the book attempts to institute a self-reflexive and experiential study of the subject; and while Wallis makes clear his own position - as a neo-Shamanic practitioner - within the field of study, the manner in which the author's own presence is located within the ethnographic landscape he seeks to elucidate is not always made obvious or explicit. In this respect, the book forms more of a prolegomenon to what Wallis otherwise claims is an 'autoarchaeological' approach to neo-Shamanisms.

Following the introduction, Wallis offers an overview of Eliade, Castaneda and Michael Harner as key sources having shaped Euro-American neo-Shamanisms. This forms a springboard from which to appraise neo-Shamanisms in chapter two, subsequently developed and contextualised through 'ethnographic fragments' of contemporary Druid and Heathen Shamanisms in chapter three. Rounding off the first part of the book, chapter four includes an assessment of historical and archaeological sources informing neo-Shamanistic practice and belief. There, Wallis highlights the failure within academic discourse to take heed of neo-Shamanisms beyond labelling them as neo-colonial and/or part of the 'New Age' fringe. Whilst Wallis is cognisant and critical of the cultural appropriation and historical revisionism that is certainly evident in certain sectors of Western neo-Shamanisms, he makes a strong counter-argument, highlighting the need to reconsider 'appropriationist' analyses on a number of counts: that in terms of cosmological outlook and praxis, 'modern' Western Shamanisms are not always unrelated to the 'traditional' or 'indigenous' Shamanisms from which they draw inspiration; and that this is not necessarily a case of unreflective recreation or appropriation on the part of practitioners - some of who, Wallis demonstrates, are acutely aware of and responsive to the problems entailed by their interpretations of the past and of other cultures.

Marking a shift in focus, but one which continues to iterate issues surrounding the problematised 'authenticity' of neo-Shamanisms, chapters five, six and seven introduce the prickly and contested areas of access to 'sacred sites', the reburial of ancestral remains, and the encounter between neo-

Shamanisms and contemporary (non-Western) indigenous groups. Here, the reflexivity attributed to (some) neo-Shamans is, however, often denied to those within the academic community in their dealings with practitioners. That many academics and site managers are unsympathetic to the claims of neo-shamans is no doubt the case (and Wallis does offer plentiful evidence to suggest that this is so), and given one of the central aims of the book - the call for a more 'engaged' study of neo-Shamanisms - this is understandable.

This (valid) critique of current scholarly accounts of neo-Shamanisms seems, however, problematic in one particular: the book tends to reproduce a view that, in this reviewer's mind, continues to dog analytical accounts of Western magic and paganism (particularly those produced by openly pagan academics): namely the manner in which the "West" is depicted as a monolithic epistemological and philosophical entity, in relation to which 'alternative spiritualities' emerge as sites of resistance; even if academic studies are more often than not informed by methodological agnosticism, Wallis' claim that the philosophical orientation of the West is largely informed by atheism seems to be too much of an overgeneralisation. Magical or (for wont of a better word) "non-rational" beliefs have informed and continue to inform Western cultural formations - and in all fairness this is something which Wallis acknowledges *vis a vis* neo-Shamanisms. But in highlighting the (sometimes) anti-hegemonic qualities of neo-Shamanisms, the problem remains of representing these 'alternative spiritualities' as marginalised, unusual or exotic, and distinct from some imagined "mainstream" - something which Wallis is clearly keen to avoid. It is around these areas that a more substantive discussion of the relevance of queer theory would, perhaps, have been appropriate. On the other side of the coin, that indigenous Shamanic sources (from which neo-Shamanisms are partially constructed) may be enmeshed in equally asymmetrical and hegemonic sets of power relations is not really addressed. However, Wallis' astute insights concerning academic accounts of the encounter between neo-Shamanisms and contemporary non-Western Shamanisms - accounts which hold the negative transformation of the latter in favour of the former as the invariable outcome of such encounters - makes for thought-provoking reading, and calls into question long-held essentialist concepts of culture.

The above criticisms are not, however, meant to eclipse what otherwise amounts to an excellent and rigorously researched piece - particularly impressive is Wallis' extensive bibliography, which should prove invaluable to students of neo-Shamanisms. The book certainly represents a significant contribution to (and recasting of) current debates informing both the study and practice of neo-Shamanisms, and one which does seek to critically incorporate the depth and complexity of the phenomenon. Despite some of the aforementioned (and rather minor) reservations, this reviewer for one has no compunction in heartily applauding Wallis' call for a closer, dialogic engagement between practitioners and scholars of neo-Shamanisms.

Justin Woodman

Shamans – Siberian Spirituality and the Western Imagination, Ronald Hutton Hambledon and London, 2002, ISBN: 1 85285 324 7 £ 16.95

"Shamans" is that precious gem, a specialist text with wide appeal, even to readers whose knowledge of Siberia stops at the 1908 Tunguska meteorite (the Tungusic family of languages is mentioned often). Shamans were practitioners of healing and divination (clairvoyance) in the Siberian world, a windswept Garden of Eden where primal human dramas have been played out since the dawn of time.

The traditions of a reticent oral culture are fragile stuff in the hands of Western researchers—especially those who try to foist a linear framework on customs they dimly understand. Bringing their own agendas to the table, these scholars draw expansive conclusions from narrow data sets. Hutton corrects this tendency to generalize – his entire book, as he says, tends against a definitive resolution of certain issues.

He ensures this by asking questions to which the only fit answer is "perhaps," "sometimes," or "it depends". Did the Shamans use props, costumes? Did public performance hold the key to their work? Did they eat hallucinogens (mushrooms?). Was shamanism male-dominated (not always!)? Hereditary or trained? With the pleasing chink of ice cubes tumbling into a highball glass, Hutton assembles his arguments point-by-point, pole-vaulting across endless thickets of definition, ambiguity, and downright mendacity in the source materials at his disposal.

Spiritual *journeys* form a recurrent theme of this book. Whether working with spirit-helpers, or by shape-shifting and taking animal form, the shamans—after achieving the requisite trance state—would venture into the spirit world to coax back the wandering souls of sick fellow villagers. If their village itself was at war with rival tribes, these expeditions into the unknown healed the torn fabric of the community, or readied a counterstrike against the enemy. Day-trips into the ether also served an advisory function, as the shamans could then assess livestock headcounts, identify the closest waterholes, et cetera.

According to certain legends, practitioners of shamanism achieved full spiritual status only after undergoing destruction followed by resurrection. Sound familiar? The shamans' voyages into the hierarchically structured spirit world distantly but instantly reminded this reviewer of Dante's journey in the *Divine Comedy*. For centuries, sentimental Westerners have enjoyed drawing analogies between Siberian spirituality and their own mythologies. To give one example, some magicians on the frosty steppes used strings and cords to mark out pathways on the ground to help wandering spirits return home. The theory went that spirits travel along accustomed routes, set in straight lines across the physical landscape. Forteans and folklorists in the U.K. have pondered whether these guide-ropes correspond to "ley lines" in the Western tradition.

These comparisons break down on closer inspection. The oracles of Ancient Greece gave advice too, and they exhibited supernatural behaviour in a trance state… but that doesn't make shamans Delphic oracles. As Hutton cautions, idle analogies between superficially similar phenomena in far-flung countries are great fun but a slim basis for scholarship. Many authors have gotten into deep, hot water by speculating on whether and how shamanistic practices spread around the globe, or if they developed independently. In any subject—particularly in a borderland topic such as this—these conjectures must be performed with care and scrupulous respect for the evidence.

Hutton, so careful to avoid the traps that ensnare others, generally sidesteps the issue of whether the shamans did real magic; although it is clear that many of these people attempted superhuman feats of the coal-walking variety (sticking hot knives into their skin). And "Siberian Spirituality" reminds us of certain truths we in the West minimize or ignore – such as the power of rhythm and percussion to shake the atmosphere in a room and galvanize the audience's attention.

Ancient accounts—so often presumed to be automatically misleading—are helpful here in pinpointing the earliest appearance of Siberian shamans and their performances. Note that the initial reaction of foreign chroniclers has been to stress the strangeness of these local customs, rather than to draw non-existent comparisons with life back home. Sentimental 20th century researchers have poked and prodded these native peoples with their stethoscopes and may—who knows?—have contaminated their subjects in the process. To the extent they exist today at all, shamans and their accessories are reduced to kitsch, dishonourably reminiscent of Native American smoke signals and feathered headdresses.

Complicating the researcher's task is the absence of any feedback loop to act as a reality check—for shamans have tended to be shy with strangers, for good reason. The 20th century saw the rise of Soviet communism, which fancied itself the protector of aboriginal peoples but actually wrought its own brand of havoc, stamping out local customs and peoples with a passion. For suspicious minds in Moscow, the odysseys of Siberian shamans must have a sent a message – not of liberation exactly, but certainly of constraints overcome, bonds cast aside, and independence from the Politburo rulebook. As Hutton says: "If the stories are to be believed, Evenk shamans joined the wealthier clansmen in opposing Soviet propaganda, and encouraging their people to avoid the new hospitals, burn schools and slaughter collectivised reindeer herds."

Lethal consequences ensued for anyone or anything remotely viewed as a threat to Moscow's authority. The starvation of the Ukrainian peasantry was scandalously effective but left barely a footprint on Soviet records. The Communist authorities were a bit more frank about their plans for the Siberian Shamans, and this candour spilled over into the visual arts.

"In the Museum of the History of Religion and Atheism at Leningrad there hung during the 1980s a classic Soviet Realist painting entitled 'The Triumph of Enlightenment over Superstition' (…) It portrayed an Evenk shaman, caught in the act of performing an act of magical healing for a patient lying on a bed in a native hut, cowering defeated before a Russian flying doctor. The latter has just burst through the door and is standing, medical bag in hand, young, square-shouldered, clean-cut and firm-jawed, and dominating the scene with his physical as well as his professional presence."

In the field of academia, the writing was also on the wall. One scholar argued that the shamans must be exterminated, *but that records must be taken first.* The typical Soviet scholar's mix of excellent formal skills combined with vicious ideological blinkers led to especially unhappy results where Siberian shamans were concerned. Which is not to say that USSR scholarship is useless, merely that it must be handled with care.

While the Soviet boot left its heel-marks in Siberian faces, there are forces more powerful than Communist oppression. Shamanism may rise again some day. It came before us, and may outlast us. There is much that we now know – but much we still don't understand.

Neil L. Inglis

Margaret Stutley, *Shamanism: An Introduction.* **London: Routledge 2003. 134 pages. ISBN 0-415-27318-8 paperback. £7.99 / $14.95**

and

Jan Fries, *Helrunar: A Manual of Rune Magick* Oxford: Mandrake of Oxford (1993, revised and reissued 2002). 448 pages. ISBN 1869928-199 paperback Over 130 black and white line illustrations by the author £14.99 / $25

'Shamans' in Siberia were first encountered by explorers in the sixteenth century and their reports over the next three hundred year or so consistently represent shamans in a variety of derogatory terms, from Petrovich's (2001 [1672]) charge that the shaman is 'a villain of a magician who calls demons' and Gmelin's (2001 [1751]) judgment that 'shamans deserve perpetual labour for their hocus-pocus', to the notion that 'shamans are impostors who claim they consult with the devil–and who are sometimes close to the mark' (Diderot et al. 2001 [1765]). Siberian shamans endured centuries of persecution, first under the Tsars and then communism; those that survived kept their practices hidden or attempted to keep at bay the spirits which plagued them to take up the shaman's vocation.

Attitudes to shamans have changed, in the West at least, since the first half of the twentieth century when anthropological reports presented shamans in a more sensitive light and when, from the psychedelic 1960s onwards, various 'classic' texts made shamanic worlds appealing to popular culture. In particular, the publication in English of Mircea Eliade's *Shamanism: Archaic Techniques of Ecstasy* (1989[1964]) put shamans – as an '-ism' – on the global map in the history of religions, as, allegedly, the oldest, simplest, most primitive and widespread of all religions. At this time also, Carlos Castaneda (e.g. 1968) began producing what has become a very long list of volumes chronicling his relationship with a Mexican 'shaman', *Don Juan*; with detailed explanations of entheogen use, these books were suitably attractive to a generation seeking alternative spiritualities and/or the next 'trip'. Sometime later, Michael Harner's *The Way of the Shaman* (1990[1980]) took the ultimate step in not only making the exotic worlds of shamans accessible, but also offering shamanic techniques Westerners could try for themselves. Over some 350 years, Western perceptions of shamans have transformed from 'conjurers of devils' and 'tricksters', even mentally ill and socially aberrant, to shamans as inherently 'spiritual', in harmony with nature, and exemplary of the exotic Other.

In recent years, studies on shamans have problematised and theorised how shamans are understood ethnographically, and hence produced groundbreaking interpretative insights, such as Taussig's (1987) Marxist approach and the provision of historical contexts (e.g. papers in Thomas and Humphrey 1994), in addition to specific ethnographies (e.g. Atkinson 1989; Humphrey 1996) and the contributions of archaeologists (e.g. papers in Price 2001a) and studies on rock art (e.g Dowson 1999). Unfortunately, one of the most recent volumes on shamanisms, Margaret Stutley's *Shamanism: An Introduction*, does not stand out as one of these ground-breaking studies; it does succeed in reproducing a number of negative stereotypes and exemplifies how not to introduce shamanisms.

It is now widely agreed that 'shamanism' is a constructed term, which has been used by scholars from a variety of disciplines to examine various specific 'religious' and/or 'healing' social practices in a variety of indigenous communities. This does not mean, however, that anthropologists have 'invented' shamans and that therefore shamans do not exist. The term 'shaman' derives from the Tungus speaking communities of Siberia; the key to understanding shamans and to applying the term 'shamanism' effectively (and sensitively), in Siberia and beyond, lies in its diversity. Even among the Tungus speakers, people we might label shamans may be termed very differently in each community, with very different social standing, functions and practices.

Taking such variety into account, it is difficult to 'define' what a shaman is, or to pin shamans down to a list of features which can be ticked-off. The situation is further compounded when the term shaman is taken outside Siberia and applied for comparative purposes to other indigenous peoples, from Australia and South America, to Palaeolithic and Viking age western Europe – indeed shamans have been identified on every continent and in almost any culture from prehistory to the present. This tells us something significant about ourselves as much as it informs us about shamans: Westerners have found shamans fascinating, fantastic, odd and Other since first contact, and, with the Modernist ethic in hand, have determined to 'find' shamans everywhere – the search for similarities is a task in generalising and as such it is a misconceived, modernist endeavour. This need not mean 'shamanism' can not be a useful term; it need not mean there are not shamans outside Siberia. It does mean we have to approach both the term 'shaman', and shamans themselves, carefully, sensitively, and with critical reflexivity.

Stutley's approach, overall, neglects this post-modern shift in anthropological thought, with its emphasis on diversity, nuance and difference, and instead reifies the Modernist principle of identifying similarities across space and time. This is research in the vein of Eliade whose pioneering work has been invaluable, but is now much outdated. Stutely's introduction is short (at 134 pages) but conciseness need not be at the expense of accuracy of representation. Identifying similarities tells us nothing about shamans in their specific community contexts or about the complexity of engagements between shamans and their communities. This book does not succeed in introducing shamanisms adequately to a general audience – an uncompromising review which requires evidence.

The title of the volume, 'Shamanism', is agreeable, though I would prefer to see a pluralisation in acknowledgement that shamanisms are not singular and 'all the same'; the problematising and theorising of the term can be done after this, perhaps in the first pages of the book – though it is not. The sub-title, 'An Introduction', is also suitable: there are numerous books on shamans which purport to provide an introduction but are exclusively by Western (neo-Shamanic) practitioners whose perspectives are valid but often biased away from specific shamanic traditions towards general, pragmatic matters of practice and technique. An introduction to shamanisms by an academic is welcomed (though Harvey's 2003 reader has already established itself as a modern classic). Stutley may be 'a leading scholar of world religions and folk tradition' with expertise in Hinduism and Biblical theology, but the substance of this book indicates she is by no means a leading scholar on shamanisms.

The introduction, in theorising shamanisms' diversity a little, is the (marginally) best chapter in the book. Stutley suggests '[s]hamansim should not be thought of as a single centrally organized religion, as there are many variations' (p2). Yet the definition of 'shamanism' immediately following this comment makes no reference to social context, so removing community specificity and replacing diversity of approach with a generalising, misleading metanarrative. We are then informed, quite correctly, that '[t]he name "shamanism" was invented by Europeans, so giving the impression that there was only one fixed belief system' (p3), again drawing attention to the way in which shamanisms are not singular and entirely similar cross-culturally. Yet, apparently, 'recent research indicates that shamanism represents the earliest religious experiences of mankind and therefore is important for the understanding of all human culture' (p4). Stutley contradicts herself and misunderstands 'recent research'. Recent research suggests, for example, that certain altered conscious states are neurologically-derived and may therefore be consistent cross-culturally as the somatic origin of certain religious experiences since at least the emergence of modern humans. This might signal altered consciousness, but not 'shamanism', as the 'earliest religious experiences of mankind (sic.)' with implications for examining certain, though not all, 'human culture'; although a majority of human cultures institutionalise altered consciousness in various socially sanctioned ways, not all of them are shamanic. Again, Stutley disregards the diversity of shamanisms, not to mention human cultures more generally, in favour of a metanarrative which locates 'shamanism' as the single primordial, primitive religion and ancestor to all religions. Rather than informing us about shamans past and present, this approach epitomises the positioning of shamanism as 'one of the phenomena against which modern western civilization has defined itself' (Hutton 2001:viii).

Given these recent theoretical, methodological and interpretative developments, it seems incumbent on any new volume on shamanisms, particularly a volume which introduces the topic, to appraise and dispel rather than reify the many stereotypes there are of shamans. Against this end, Stutley appears to follow Ioan Lewis' by (correctly in my view) including possession states as part of the shaman's repertoire in some examples; but this material is presented in a way which gives no background to the debates, an understanding of which is essential to appreciating similarities and (most importantly) differences between shamanic, mediumistic and possession states, and those shamans who move fluidly between them. Stutley is careless, also, in making general statements without providing specific examples, and where actual cases are cited these are listed one after the other, check-list style, imposing yet greater homogeneity on diverse practices. As a result, the entire volume reads like a list of notes, a poorly researched and unfinished manuscript.

To support this claim, I could, for example, discuss in some depth Stutley's discussion of 'Transvestism' and 'Androgynous male and female shamans' which, rather than deconstructing Eurocentric, binary notions of sex which conflate sex and gender, actually reinforces these categories and so neglects and homogenises issues of gender diversity and nuance in shamanic communities with multiple gendered 'changing ones' (for a scholarly approach, see e.g. Roscoe 1998). In a similar vein, I might address the concept of 'an archaic Mother-cult' (p66), involving 'maternal cosmogonic cults whose formation apparently can be traced back to the period in which the view of Earth as a supernatural female took shape' (p62), which is, by all scholarly accounts, seriously outdated (e.g. Meskell 1995). I could also comment on the lack of discussion of neo-Shamans – Modern Westerners engaging with indigenous and prehistoric shamanisms for personal and community empowerment (e.g. Wallis 2003): taking the readership for the volume into account, which includes, according to the rear cover, 'Mind/Body/Spirit', making no discussion of neo-Shamans is surprisingly short-sighted. Restricted to a short book review, however, I offer instead two examples where Stutley's volume interfaces with my own specialist areas: shamanisms and rock art, and shamanistic aspects of Northern religions.

Shamanisms and Rock Art:

'Shamanism' is, Stutley contends, important for understanding the 'symbolism of the ancient rock paintings of Eurasia…Mircea Eliade and some other writers see an early form of shamanism in the Lascaux cave paintings, especially in the depiction of a bird, a tutelary spirit, perched on a pole… The figures depict ancestors, spirits, heroes, shamans and animals (p4). This Lascaux shaft-scene is one 'which Horst Kirchmer (sic.) suggests represents a shamanic trance, but not all scholars agree with this interpretation' (99). Stutley is, according to her note 11, here citing Eliade (1989[1964]: 481), who in turn has cited Kirchner's 1952 article (*Anthropos* XLVII:244-86). I would deem such second-hand referencing as poor practice among undergraduates, let alone among 'leading scholars'; but also, in confining her research in this instance to Eliade whose work is itself outmoded, Stutley is consequently unfamiliar with current developments in rock art research which has not only proposed sophisticated methodologies for approaching altered consciousness in prehistory (e.g. Lewis-Williams & Dowson 1988) but also debated vociferously the use of the term 'shaman' in such contexts (for a review see Wallis 2002), with the result that the shamanistic approach now stands as one of the most rigorous in interpretative archaeology. Unfortunately, for readers new to shamanisms and rock art, Stutley's slight volume is based on debates of five decades ago.

Furthermore, with such comments as 'The human horned figures on Finnish and Siberian rock paintings probably depict people shamanizing' (p109) alongside those cited above, readers might assume all Eurasian (and potentially worldwide) rock art is shamanistic, which is simply not the case – yet another stereotype of shamanisms is, then, reproduced and reinforced. Worse still, on a more general note, Stutley typecasts (a singular) prehistory as an era in which 'a mystical solidarity exists between human beings and animals' (p18). While early Native Americans arguably contributed to the extinction of various megafauna and the last tree on Easter Island was cut down by the indigenous population, Stutley reifies the stereotype that shamans are the primitive care-takers of the Earth, environmentally friendly and 'green', neglecting the complex relations indigenous communities (past and present) have with what Westerners term 'nature'.

Shamanisms and Northern Religion:

Stutley makes reference to 'shamanism' in Northern religion, specifically among the Norse, twice. First, in chapter 2, with regard to the god Odin whose knowledge of runes, self-sacrifice and 'poetic art and magic', as well as the berserker and Wolf-head warriors dedicated to him, may relate to shamanic trances (p35-36). In the second instance, the phenomenon of Odin's warriors wearing wolf-skins and thereby transforming into 'werewolves' is repeated in chapter 9 (p112). In both instances, the sole supporting reference (chapter 2 notes 12, 13, and chapter 9 note 3) is Rudolf Simek's (1993) *Dictionary of Northern Mythology*. This work is arguably a classic, but as a Professor of German, not all of Simek's sources and interpretations, particularly from archaeology and especially regarding 'shamanism', are reliable or current. Stutley is treading on thin ice by using only a dictionary in place of primary sources: I reiterate again that an accessible introduction to shamanisms should be no less scholarly than a small print-run of an ethnographic volume on a specific shamanic tradition; indeed, extra care and attention is required in an introductory volume precisely because so many stereotypes exist about shamans. In restricting her research to Simek (she might at least have commented on Eliade's discussion of 'shamanism' among German tribes and then not have neglected to mention comparable issues and debates for the 'Celts'), Stutley overlooks a significant amount of recent literature which has problematised and theorised the notion of shamanisms and altered consciousness in the Viking and preceding eras in northwest Europe (e.g. especially Price 2001b). Indeed, the most detailed account of shamanic-like activity is that of *seidr* in the saga of Erik the Red, and despite recent discussions (e.g. the principally Blain 2002), we hear nothing of this or the neo-Shamanic reconstruction of seidr.

The rear cover blurb states that shamanism is 'one of the world's most ancient, notorious and frequently misrepresented spiritual traditions', but rather than offer corrections to this imbalance, *Shamanism: An Introduction* can only be recommended as an introduction to how shamanisms should not be introduced and to what shamanisms are not. Three volumes published over the last three years are prominent in providing with far greater critical analysis, what Stutley's volume lacks. For a detailed and respected academic introduction to the topic, I recommend Graham Harvey's (2003) *Shamanism: A Reader* as a matter of course, which contains pertinent readings from all over the world and has wide chronological scope – and achieves this without compromising diversity and difference. For Siberia especially, see Ronald Hutton's excellent *Shamans: Siberian Spirituality and the Western Imagination* (2001, reviewed elsewhere in JSM 2), a truly engaging and lively read and imparting necessary material on this 'locus classicus' for the first time in English. Also on Siberia, but spreading its net further still, the papers in Jeremy Narby and Francis Huxley's (2001) *Shamans Through Time* are also essential reading, again providing access to some obscure but relevant records, though the presentation is not as nuanced as that of Harvey or Hutton, particularly with regard to the definition/constitution of 'shamanism'. For neo-Shamans, on the other hand – perhaps the greatest consumers of books on shamans over academics – these volumes offer limited information on how to practice shamanism: attending to this much neglected issue which has a number of significant implications for academics, I return to the theme of Germanic shamanisms with Jan Fries's book *Helrunar: A Manual of Rune Magick*.

In the year 98CE, the Roman Senator P. Cornelius Tacitus wrote an ethnographic treatise in which he describes divination in the lands of *Germania*:

> They retain the highest opinion for omens and the casting of lots. Their method of casting lots is always identical: they cut off a branch of a nut-bearing tree and cut it into strips, which they inscribe with various marks and cast entirely at random onto a white cloth...[The] priest...gazing heavenwards, picks up three strips one at a time and interprets their meaning from the inscribed signs (Germania 10, translated by Mattingly 1948).

The 'marks' and 'signs' Tacitus describes may be runes (e.g. Elliott 1989 [1959]), but not all scholars are convinced (e.g. Page 1995). They might agree that the runes were more than simply an alphabet or script and that archaeological and historical contexts indicate at least a magical significance (e.g. Pollington 1995). Among contemporary Heathens, neo-Shamans and other Pagans, however, Tacitus' evocative description is a source par excellence for the use of 'runes' as an ancient oracular device, and these modern practitioners use the runes as magical tools for divination and self-empowerment in their daily lives (e.g. Gundarsson 1990; Pennick 1992, 1999; Aswynn 1994). Etymologically the old English *rūn* means 'mystery, secrecy, hidden knowledge', and clearly, approaching the use and meaning of the runes in antiquity is, for all contemporary interpreters, ever enigmatic and mysterious. To make matters worse, these interpreters must inevitably grapple with the troubling recent historic background: well known symbols appropriated by the SS, for instance, include the two Sowilo (SS) runes which comprised its insignia. The search for Anglo-Saxon and Germanic paganism has been rife with prejudice, nationalism and romantic assumptions, sometimes with dubious references to so-called 'Indo-European' origins. Academics tend now to avoid these issues in favour of perceived empirical approaches, but meanwhile neo-Nazi groups re-appropriate such symbols and some contemporary Heathens themselves have become embroiled in 'blood-and-soil' issues. So it is refreshing to read Jan Fries' work, *Helrunar*, which stands alone, in a different league from books before it, and attitudes towards, the runes.

The first thing to strike me when I picked up the 1993 edition of this book soon after its publication was Fries' energetic and economic style. On the one hand, he encourages beginners to experiment: 'Now I hope that you are eager to try this out here and now. Of course I cannot tell you exactly what and how you should do it, as you are a person with unique talents and hangups. I don't know which symbols get you going...You will have to experiment to find out' (p299). And on the other, he swiftly dismisses some established protocols among occult practitioners. Discussing preparations for ritual, for example, Fries argues: 'Esoteric literature abounds with complicated rules as to what invocation to use, what garments to wear, where and when to work the divination and so on. As very few of these rules make any sense save in giving beginners a complicated ritual to believe in, I will not bother to burden you with them. (A shrug, a smile - do what you wilt!)' (p243). Later, we are told: 'Now we come to the real goodies...the time honoured method of astral projection. Start with an open mind. Maybe you have read about astral projection before. Most of what you have read will certainly be dubious rubbish describing in fine esoteric prose things that the authors have no direct experience of. If you expect astral projection to be like that, based only on gossip and hearsay, you may be in for some disappointments (p294). Essentially, Fries advocates a 'freestyle' approach to runes – if it is functional and hands-on, and if it works for you, do it.

In this vein, Fries refuses to be bogged down by the blood-and-soil issues which inevitably emerge in discussions of runes, but does not shy away from them – he explicitly distances contemporary Heathenry from the

National Socialist politics of the past, simply dismisses blood-and-soil issues as unfortunate nonsense, and draws attention to similarities between the runes and other visual culture over thousands of years from all over Western Europe in order to remove national(ist) boundaries and make the runes accessible. Fries also rebuffs issues of authenticity and validity by acknowledging that his volume is based more on inspiration and personal insight than scholarly thought; he thus succeeds in providing 'a manual of rune magick' for the contemporary practitioner which engages with the past to inspire practices for the present: 'It is not our job to resurrect some "genuine old tradition". There are witches and pagans who search for this fantastic entity, thinking that the old way may offer a safety that they cannot find in modern times. I do not believe that any such tradition exists, nor do I think that it is needed...We have to find new solutions that suit the new aeon' (p98). *Helrunar* ('one who "runes" or makes rune magick') follows his previous book *Visual Magick: A Manual of Freestyle Shamanism* (1992) which also has a lively, engaging style. Freestyle shamanism, applied to runecraft is, for Fries, the use of altered consciousness and the personal insight derived therefrom, combined with a shamanic reading of the Norse myths, particularly the exploits of the god Odin who, Fries and others agree, received the runes in a painful initiatory and otherworldly vision. Into this, Fries weaves a significant element of Thelemic Magick – hence he employs Crowley's orthography 'magick' and definition of magick as the science and art of causing change to occur in conformity with Will. Fries is deeply influenced by Austin Osman Spare also, as evident in his spectacular artwork which profusely illustrates the book and is itself in no small part trance-derived.

For the contemporary practitioner, all of this makes for an eclectic synthesis of ancient lore and Modern magick which is equally plain-speaking and captivating, and, thanks to various allusions to eroticism and the 'dark side' of runic practices, rather exciting: 'Most civilized people feel a deep horror at the idea of excitement and wild vibration welling up from the hips and thighs, even leading to all-body spasms; and the notion of releasing control to some savage spirit seems downright indecent. Spirits, after all, have their own codes of proper behaviour' (p273). Fries' Runecraft is in many ways

Pagan – actively celebrating nature, life and somatic pleasures – with numerous references to sex magick techniques, ecstatic trances and practicing out of doors: 'To learn about runes one should not only practice at home but go and dare the wilderness..."Giving oneself" (gebo) means to open up to new experience. To walk in the woods, by day and by night, and in all kinds of weather. To feel the passage of the seasons. To be cold, to get wet with rain or snow, to lose one's way, to stumble around in the dark, to rest in the sun, to flow with the fog and to dance with the wind...Nature religion is sterile without nature experience (p140-141). But there are other, more eclectic influences: in 'runic yoga', for example, body postures which allude to rune-shapes can be assumed to invoke runic 'energies'. These postures are derived from such Germanic material culture as inscriptions on the Golden Gallehús Horns from South Jutland, and the interpretations of these postures are of course informed also by Hindu yoga – with an earthier, less transcendental, Northern European edge. Rune 'sounds', the intoning of each rune name (in Old English, Icelandic, etc), and associated sounds, may be combined with the postures, and both postures and sounds are used to induce altered consciousness and other self-empowering states. Clearly, this approach takes the runes into a realm well beyond that of academic discourse, and perhaps far beyond their original uses in antiquity.

For the academic examining contemporary Heathen and/or wider Pagan uses of runes and magic/k, Fries' volume, in its 'freestyle' approach, is markedly different – positively so – from the staid and perhaps more conservative (though equally as valid) approaches taken by other practitioner writers on runes (e.g. Thorsson 1984; Linsell 1992), though its approach is by no means as systematic. But for the academic studying runes and their meaning in the past, Fries' book, which itself offers perspectives on the past (as well as suggesting interpretations of the past for the present), will no doubt appear too eclectic, 'alternative' and poorly referenced. For instance, Fries happily conflates a variety of time periods and cultures, which is disconcerting from an archaeological point of view. He suggests that we might view rune-like images 'as root symbols of humanity; signs that express certain basic structures of consciousness and experience, which have been discovered and applied during all periods of human development' (p25). For Fries, these proto-runes may have emerged in Palaeolithic cave art some 10-20,000 years or more before the archaeologically-known Germanic rune scripts. Without theoretical and methodological rigour, such generalizing is speculation presented-as-fact. In a similar way, the diverse Germanic peoples themselves, from Icelanders and Anglo-Saxons to Goths, along with Celts, Etruscans and others, are homogenised as essentially the same. Such deconstruction of ethnic boundaries for the purposes of overall consistency and accessibility is common in books on runes and the pagan religions of northwest Europe generally (e.g. Bates 1996), but it is difficult for academic specialists to contend with such avoidance of cultural specificity, diversity and difference.

There are a number of other statements-presented-as-fact which will unsettle archaeologists, such as 'the standing stone or menhir symbolizes the phallus of the sky god, while the dolmen, or barrow grave, symbolizes the sacred womb of the earth mother' (p79) – there is no evidence to suggest this is the case: the dichotomous, binary male-female definition of gender is a Modern Western construct rather than cross-cultural consistency, and the 'goddess' interpretation (as advocated by academics e.g. Crawford 1957; Gimbutas 1974) is one which scholars have problematised over some years for being similarly universalising and which homogenises artifacts, periods, places and peoples without foundation (e.g. Meskell 1995). It might be argued that popular authors of so-called 'fringe theories' tend to stand by their interpretations, as facts, over the years, in the face of widespread criticism – but not Fries. The 2002 edition of *Helrunar* is a revised and expanded version of the 1993 book (still, unfortunately, not without numerous typographical errors). In the new material, Fries confesses his errors with regard to timescales, the conflation of cultures, 'great goddess' speculations, and so on. Regarding the 'horned god', for example, he reflects: 'That there are lots of different horned deities in Europe is a fact that is not generally found in books on wicca...This may not fit wiccan dogma, but it should fit the minds of all free-thinking pagans who care to discover how many different religious possibilities were explored in ancient Europe...More than ever the modern pagan ought to be aware that the old religions of ancient Europe were not a single system but a flourishing variety of local customs and beliefs which changed repeatedly in the passage of the centuries' (p421-427). This marks a heartening break from other practitioner literature on runes which reproduces the same stereotypes over and over again. I have one critical point though: the further reading in this section is surprisingly slight and, in an English language edition, restricted primarily to German texts when significant moves forward have been made for understanding religion(s) in a variety of prehistoric periods across Europe – with implications for those Fries addresses in *Helrunar* (for the Aurignacian e.g. Dowson & Porr 2001; for the Upper Palaeolithic e.g. Clottes & Lewis-Williams 1998; for the Neolithic and Bronze Age e.g. Bradley 2000; and for the Vikings e.g. Price 2001b).

It might once have been said that where academics and practitioners are concerned, 'never the twain shall meet', but current research on Paganisms is a reflexive affair (e.g. papers in Blain *et al* in prep). Not only are academic studies of Pagans by Pagans having an impact on Pagan communities themselves (e.g. Wallis 2003; in prep.), but non-academic Pagan books themselves make bold, new approaches to 'old' evidence which may contribute to academic discourse. Most notably, Fries approaches the northern 'witchcraft' of *seidr* as an ecstatic, shamanic technique from which the modern term 'seething' derives. This is an idiosyncratic move, unprecedented and in contrast to both academic and practitioner approaches to seidr which tend to focus on the negative aspects of the practice in the myths and sagas (e.g. Sørensen 1983), or the detailed description of the seiðkona in Eiríks Saga as the primary, detailed source on seidr (e.g. Lindquist 1997) from which a community-orientated oracular technique may be reconstructed for today (see especially Blain 2002). Such instances mark *Helrunar* out as an example of how contemporary practitioner insights may be of value to academics (and reflexive practitioners), though as a scholar I can not help but call for more detailed argument and referencing (but see Fries 1996). In the final analysis, Fries may (implausibly for academics) propose unifying cultural similarities across vast regions and time periods, but he also offers fascinating material which has implications for scholarly thought, as well as, perhaps most importantly, a plain-speaking, non-dogmatic and practical – 'freestyle' – approach for potential *Helrunars*. In being a book for practitioners, *Helrunar* may not be appropriately compared with Stutley's *Shamanism*; it stands out nonetheless as offering a more in-depth and thoughtful analysis than that of the academician's. For this reason at least, among others I have highlighted, scholars should not exclude such volumes as *Helrunar* from their review and analysis. Scholars of shamanisms and other 'magics' must take seriously and respond dialogically to such 'alternative' interventions.

Robert J Wallis

References

Aswynn, F. 1994. *Leaves of Yggdrasil*. Minnesota: Llewellyn.

Atkinson, J. M. 1989. *The Art and Politics of Wana Shamanship*. California: University of California Press.

Bates, B. 1996. *The Wisdom of the Wyrd: Teachings for Today from Our Ancient Past*. London: Rider.

Blain, J. 2002. *Nine Worlds of Seid-Magic: Ecstasy and Neo-Shamanism in North European Paganism*. London: Routledge.

Blain, J.; D. Ezzy and G. Harvey (eds) In preparation. *Researching Paganisms: Religious Experiences and Academic Methodologies*. Walnut Creek, California: AltaMira.

Bradley, R. 2000. *An Archaeology of Natural Places*. London: Routledge.

Castaneda, C. 1968. *The Teachings of Don Juan: A Yaqui Way of Knowledge*. California: University of California Press.

Clottes, J. and J.D. Lewis-Williams 1998. *The Shamans of Prehistory: Trance and Magic in the Painted Caves*. New York: Harry N. Abrams, Inc.

Crawford, O.G.S. 1957. *The Eye Goddess*. London: Phoenix House.

Diderot, D. et al 2001 [1765]. Shamans Are Imposters Who Claim They Consult the Devil–And Who Are Sometimes Close to the Mark. In: J. Narby and F. Huxley (eds) *Shamans Through Time: 500 Years on the Path to Knowledge*: 32-35. London: Thames & Hudson.

Dowson, T.A. 1999. Rock Art and Shamanism: A Methodological Impasse. In: A. Rozwadowski; M.M. Kocęko and T.A. Dowson (eds) *Rock Art, Shamanism and Central Asia: Discussions of Relations*: 39-56. Warsaw: Wydawnictwo Academickie (in Polish).

Dowson, T.A. and M. Porr 2001. Special Objects – Special Creatures: Shamanistic Imagery and the Aurignacian Art of South-west Germany. In: N. Price (ed.) *The Archaeology of Shamanism*: 165-177. London: Routledge.

Eliade, M. 1989 [1964]. *Shamanism: Archaic Techniques of Ecstasy*. London: Penguin Arkana.

Elliott, R.W.V. 1989 [1959]. *Runes: An Introduction*. Manchester: Manchester University Press.

Fries, J. 1992. *Visual Magick: A Manual of Freestyle Shamanism*. Oxford: Mandrake

Fries, J. 1996. *Seidways: Shaking, Swaying and Serpent Mysteries*. Oxford: Mandrake.

Gimbutas, M. 1974. *The goddesses and gods of Old Europe: Myths and Cult Images.* London: Thames and Hudson.

Gmelin, J.G. 2001 [1751]. Shamans Deserve Perpetual Labor for Their Hocus-Pocus. In: J. Narby and F. Huxley (eds) *Shamans Through Time: 500 Years on the Path to Knowledge*: 27-28. London: Thames & Hudson.

Gundarsson, K. 1990. *Teutonic Magic: The Magical and Spiritual Practices of The Germanic Peoples*. Minnesota: Llewellyn.

Harner, M. 1990 [1980]. *The Way of the Shaman*. London: Harper Collins.

Harvey, G. 2003. *Shamanism: A Reader*. London: Routledge.

Humphrey, C. 1996. *Shamans and Elders: Experience, Knowledge, and Power among the Daur Mongols*. Oxford: Clarendon Press.

Hutton, R. 2001. *Shamans: Siberian Spirituality and the Western Imagination*. London and New York: Hambledon & London.

Lewis-Williams, J.D. and T.A. Dowson. 1988. The signs of all times: entoptic phenomena in Upper Paleolithic art. *Current Anthropology* 29(2): 201-245.

Lindquist, G. 1997. *Shamanic Performance on the Urban Scene: Neo-Shamanism in Contemporary Sweden*. Stockholm Studies in Social Anthropology 39. Stockholm, Sweden: University of Stockholm.

Linsell, T. 1992. *Anglo-Saxon Runes*. Middlesex: Anglo-Saxon Books (Revised and reprinted as *Anglo-Saxon Mythology, Migration and Magic*, by Anglo-Saxon Books, 1994).

Mattingly, H. (Translator) 1948. *Tacitus on Britain and Germany*. London: Penguin.

Meskell, L. 1995. Goddesses, Gimbutas and 'New Age' Archaeology. *Antiquity* 69: 74-86.

Narby, J. and F. Huxley 2001. *Shamans Through Time: 500 Hundred Years on the Shamans Path*. London: Thames & Hudson.

Page, R.I. 1995. *Runes and Runic Inscriptions: Collected Essays on Anglo-Saxon and Viking Runes*. Woodbridge, Suffolk: The Boydell Press.

Pennick, N. 1992. *Rune Magic: The History and Practice of Ancient Runic Traditions*. London: Thorsons.

Pennick, N. 1999. *The Complete Illustrated Guide to Runes*. Shaftesbury, Dorset: Element.

Petrovich, A. 2001 [1672]. The Shaman: "A Villain of a Magician Who Calls Demons". In: J. Narby and F. Huxley (eds) *Shamans Through Time: 500 Years on the Path to Knowledge*: 18-20. London: Thames & Hudson.

Pollington, S. 1995. *Rudiments of Runelore*. Frithgarth, Norfolk: Anglo-Saxon Books.

Price, N. 2001a. *The Archaeology of Shamanism*. London: Routledge.

Price, N. 2001b. *The Viking Way: Religion and War in Late Iron Age Scandinavia*. Uppsala: Uppsala University Press.

Roscoe, W. 1998. *Changing Ones: Third and Fourth Genders In North America*. London: Macmillan.

Simek, R. 1993. *A Dictionary of Northern Mythology*. Bury St. Edmunds, Suffolk: St. Edmundsbury Press.

Sørensen, P.M. 1983. *The Unmanly Man: Concepts of Sexual Defamation in Early Northern Society*. Odense, Denmark: Odense University Press.

Taussig, M. 1987. *Shamanism, Colonialism and the Wild Man: A Study in Terror and Healing*. Chicago: The University of Chicago Press.

Thomas, N. and C. Humphrey (eds) 1994. *Shamanism, History, and the State*. Ann Arbor: University of Michigan Press.

Thorsson, E. 1984. *Futhark: A Handbook of Rune Magic*. York Beach, Maine: Samuel Weiser.

Wallis, R.J. 2002. The *Bwili* or 'Flying Tricksters' of Malakula: A Critical Discussion of Recent Debates on Rock Art, Ethnography and Shamanisms. *Journal of The Royal Anthropological Institute* 8(4): 735-760.

Wallis, R.J. 2003. *Shamans / neo-Shamans: Ecstasy, Alternative Archaeologies and Contemporary Pagans*. London: Routledge.

Wallis, R.J. In preparation. Between the Worlds: Autoarchaeology and neo-Shamans. In: J. Blain, D. Ezzy and G. Harvey (eds) *Researching Paganisms: Religious Experiences and Academic Methodologies*. Walnut Creek, California: AltaMira.

David Lewis-Williams, *The Mind in the Cave: Consciousness and the Origins of Art*. London: Thames & Hudson 2002. 320 pages. ISBN 0-500-05117-8 hardback. With 94 illustrations, 27 in colour, £18.95 US$29.95

The proposal that the origins of European cave art might lie in the experiences of shamans is not new, but the theorising of 'shamanism' and deployment of complex neuropsychological analyses in a sophisticated methodology for interpreting cave art is an innovative and important development. Among the off-the-cuff remarks linking cave art to shamans in the first half of the twentieth century, Horst Kirchner suggested the 'wounded man' in the Lascaux shaft scene might depict a shaman in trance (Kirchner 1952). In the 1960s, Andreas Lommel (1967) went further to suggest that the advent of shamanism marked 'the beginning of art'. More recently, Davenport and Jochim (1988) proposed a shamanic link between the apparent avian characteristics shared by the 'wounded man' and the bird-topped staff with which he is juxtaposed. Where Kirchner and Lommel's remarks are now best regarded as slight and generalist, Davenport and Jochim's more considered suggestion is intriguing, particularly in view of an article published in the same year, by David Lewis-Williams and Thomas Dowson: *The Signs of All Times: entoptic phenomena in Upper Palaeolithic art* (1988) now ranks as one of the most controversial papers in rock art research. Lewis-Williams's most recent book provides a timely introduction to the shamanistic interpretation of European cave art, argues a convincing case for the origins of image making in shamanism and offers a new argument concerning early modern human contact with Neanderthals.

The Mind in the Cave begins with a concise section on method and points out the misconception popular in rock art studies that more data is required before interpretation can begin, as if the data itself will 'implode' and reveal 'the answer'. But interpretation is a challenge: the inadequacies of art-for-art's-sake, totemism, sympathetic magic and structuralism are set-out, and as with all Lewis-Williams's work the writing style and argument here and throughout the volume are eloquent and engaging. In place of earlier interpretations, *The Mind in the Cave* introduces a 'neuropsychological model' (proposed in the collaborative 1988 article) for approaching cave art, which suggests three loosely defined and fluid stages in the progression of trance. In the first 'entoptics' stage, subjects spontaneously perceive 'entoptic visual phenomena' (from the Greek meaning 'within vision', also known as 'phosphenes'), specific complex and diverse luminous geometric imagery derived from the human central nervous system, produced specifically within the optic cortex, and characteristic of certain altered conscious states, which are classified into six principle types, including grids, zigzags and filigrees. In the second, 'construal' stage, subjects attempt to make sense of these geometric shapes and construe them into culturally recognisable forms: a Western subject may construe an entoptic grid into the string-grid of a tennis racket, while a cave artist may have construed an entoptic filigree into the horns of a reindeer. In the third 'entoptics and iconics' stage, subjects may perceive both entoptic and culturally derived iconic imagery: trance is at its most intense and subjects may feel they are a part of their imagery – therianthropes (composite human-animal images) in cave art may be associated with such experiences. In all three stages, imagery is subject to seven kaleidoscopic principles of visual transformation, including fragmentation, superpositioning and rotation. Once the neuropsychological origins of a specific rock art tradition are confirmed, the context-specific social, shamanistic expression may be explored. Lewis-Williams's examination of specific caves and their art in terms of shamanism is the most compelling component of *The Mind in the Cave*.

The application of this shamanistic interpretation to a variety of rock art traditions including cave art has been accused of metanarrative. Critics question the value of a model which can interpret all visual culture containing geometric images according to shamanistic trances (e.g. Francfort et al 2000). Proponents of the model contest its indiscriminate use also, arguing that it has been applied uncritically in a search for entoptics (Dowson 1999) with the misleading premise *entoptics*=shamanism, aptly termed 'a steamroller approach' (Garlake 1995). Since the publication of *The Signs of All Times*, proponents have refined their understanding of entoptics (e.g. Dronfield 1996), developed a more rigorous approach to shamanism (e.g. Dowson 1999; Wallis 2003 and forthcoming), and reiterated that critical application of the neuropsychological model requires utilising the model in its entirety, thereby dismissing the overtly simplistic *entoptics*=shamanism equation and embracing the heterogeneity of rock art (and other visual cultures) and shamanisms. Unfortunately, *The Mind in the Cave* side steps these issues so readers new to this research will be unaware of the vociferous debates surrounding them (for a critical review, see Wallis 2002). Layton (2003) points out that Lewis-Williams also omits discussion of counter-arguments from cave art specialists (e.g. Bahn 1997); short-sighted as this is, the counter-case argument (specifically regarding ethnographic analogies) has been set out elsewhere, concluding in support of the shamanistic approach (e.g. Dronfield 1993).

Critics argue that the shamanistic interpretation of rock art is stuck in its 'drug culture phase' (e.g. Bahn 1998); Lewis-Williams more thoughtfully remarks on the importance of examining the full range of human consciousness. He suggests image making (a less loaded term that 'art') was made possible with the evolution of 'higher' consciousness over 'primary' consciousness, by which he distinguishes between modern humans and Neanderthals (and makes an interesting distinction between the role of 'consciousness' rather than 'intelligence' in the process). Image making was part of a 'package deal' comprising art, religion and social differentiation which gave modern humans the edge over Neanderthals, and 'shamanism' was an underlying constituent of the social fabric which steered image production and consumption among modern human Palaeolithic communities. Here, Lewis-Williams (somewhat reluctantly) subscribes to the un-nuanced idea in evolutionary psychology that similarities between modern humans and Neanderthals are less significant than their differences, and I have remarked elsewhere on the shortcomings of his definition of shamanism (Wallis 2002). But importantly, image making was not an inevitable 'by-product' of the 'package deal': following Dowson (1998), Lewis-Williams challenges the role afforded cave art as 'the origins of art' ('art' being an eighteenth century construct) and passive handmaiden to cognitive evolution. In a dual achievement he successfully repositions shamanism as social and agentic in the origins of image making, and interprets cave art and associated archaeological data more fully and persuasively than any current or previous academic approach. It has been argued that the shamanistic approach is doomed to die out like many a bandwagon before it. To the contrary, *The Mind in the Cave* indicates that while an obsession with 'entoptics' has passed, the shamanistic interpretation remains at the forefront of rock art research. The book ends on a strange note, however, recommending that while this shamanistic cave art is awe-inspiring, people today should not themselves want to be shamans. Perhaps Lewis-Williams is concerned that his work will inspire neo-Shamanism rather than rational materialism. In some ways it might – and it would be none the worse for that.

Robert J. Wallis

References:

Bahn, P.G. 1997. Membrane and numb brain: a close look at a recent claim for shamanism in Palaeolithic art. *Rock Art Research* 14(1):62-68.

Bahn, P.G. 1998. Stumbling in the footsteps of St Thomas. *British Archaeology* (February): 18.

Davenport, D. and M.A. Jochim 1988. The scene in the shaft at Lascaux. *Antiquity* 62:559-562.

Dowson, T.A. 1998. Rock Art: handmaiden to studies of cognitive evolution. In: C. Renfrew & C. Scarre (eds) *Cognition and Material Culture: The Archaeology of Symbolic Storage*:67-76. Cambridge: McDonald Institute Monographs.

Dowson, T.A. 1999. Rock art and shamanism: a methodological impasse. In: A. Rozwadowski, M.M. Koœko and T.A. Dowson (eds) *Rock Art, Shamanism and Central Asia: Discussions of Relations*: 39-56. Warsaw: Wydawnictwo Academickie (in Polish).

Dronfield, J. 1993. Ways of seeing, ways of telling: Irish passage tomb art, style and the universality of vision. In: M. Lorblanchet and P.G. Bahn (eds) *Rock Art Studies: The Post-Stylistic Era, Or Where Do We Go From Here?*: 179-193. Oxbow Monograph 35. Oxford: Oxbow Books.

Dronfield, J. 1996. Entering alternative realities: cognition, art and architecture in Irish passage-tombs. *Cambridge Archaeological Journal* 6(1): 37-72.

Francfort, H-P., R.N. Hamayon and P.G. Bahn 2000. *The Concept of Shamanism: Uses and Abuses*. Budapest: Akadémiai Kiadó.

Garlake 1995. *The Hunter's Vision: The Prehistoric Rock Art of Zimbabwe*. London: British Museum Press.

Kirchner, H. 1952. Ein archäologischer Beitrag zur Urgeschichte des Schamanismus. *Anthropos* 47:244-286.

Layton, R. 2003. Review of David Lewis-Williams. 2002. The Mind in the Cave: Consciousness and the Origins of Art. London: Thames & Hudson. *Antiquity* 77(296):422-3.

Lewis-Williams, J.D. and T.A. Dowson. 1988. The signs of all times: entoptic phenomena in Upper Paleolithic art. *Current Anthropology* 29(2):201-245.

Lommel, A. 1967. *Shamanism: The Beginnings of Art*. New York: McGraw-Hill.

Wallis, R.J. Forthcoming. Shamanism and art. In: M. Walter and E. Fridman (eds) *Shamanism: An Encyclopedia of World Beliefs, Practices, and Culture*: in press. Santa Barbara, California: ABC-CLIO.

Wallis, R.J. 2003. *Shamans / neo-Shamans: Ecstasy, Alternative Archaeologies and Contemporary Pagans*. London: Routledge.

Wallis, R.J. 2002. The *Bwili* or 'Flying Tricksters' of Malakula: a critical discussion of recent debates on rock art, ethnography and shamanisms. *Journal of The Royal Anthropological Institute* 8(4): 735-760.

Book Reviews

Reprint: (original 1975, Frederick Muller Ltd, London) Images and Oracles of Austin Osman Spare, edited and compiled by Kenneth Grant, London, Fulgur, 2003, ISBN 0 9531016 2 2, 104 pages, 60 illustrations, Paperback (£19.50).

As Admin editor for this journal I am often frustrated by seeing numerous lovely books go across my desk on their way to reviewers. Usually I only have time to glance through them and become interested before bidding them farewell. Not in this case… having owned the original and marvellous version for some time I was simply not going to allow this copy to leave my sight! This unusual 'landscape' format large book is a delight. It is certainly not a 'cash-in' reprint of the original title from the mid-1970s, with which Kenneth Grant helped to launch the compelling art and highly individual magick of Austin Osman Spare onto the occult world (along with the works of Lionel Snell, Frank Letchford, Gavin Semple *et al*), and it has since become much sought-after by artists, magicians and researchers alike. Spare's influence on modern magic and art is highly significant and so this new book is to be welcomed, as it allows for wider circulation of the material. Instead of merely reprinting the book the publishers have taken the much harder road of locating and re-photographing the images using modern cameras (a work which itself could be the subject of a book, one suspects, since the pictures are widely scattered across private collections and museums), and completely resetting the book using 21st Century technology. The original was a stunning book, and regularly fetches over £250 UK on the second-hand market. This new edition is simply breathtaking, there is a new preface by Kenneth Grant, and a page-by-page comparison of the 1975 and 2003 versions is a fabulous exercise in itself; the new photography allows Spare's disturbingly beautiful, otherworldly and erotic images to take life and *sing* from the page in a way that the original book, great as it is, simply does not. It allows for the first time in several decades a detailed glimpse of the intricacies of Spare's art and philosophy at a manageable price.

The publishers are rightly known for their high quality output on 'all matters Spare', and yet this is even more than could have been hoped for, a stunning visual piece, and a challenge to all other publishers' standards of production; demonstrating just what can be achieved with the necessary application and will. A triumph, an epic and an epiphany.

Dave Evans

Giordano Bruno: philosopher of the renaissance, Ed. Hilary Gatti, Ashgate 2002; pp424, ISBN 0754605620 £50 hardback, £15.50 paperback

This book consists of a collection of essays derived from the papers presented to a conference held in University College London in June 2000, hosted by the British Society for the History of Philosophy. The 18 essays are split into four sections dealing with Bruno in Italy, Bruno in England, philosophical themes and 'influences and tradition', prefaced by an introductory essay by the late Giovanni Aquilecchia, a prominent Bruno scholar from Italy. Together they form a formidable and varied scholarly account of the life and work of Giordano Bruno, the 16th century monk and philosopher who Frances Yates claimed as a key figure within the Hermetic tradition. They represent a continuing reassessment of Bruno as a philosophical figure and form part of a body of work which has gradually begun to establish a different account of Bruno from that given by Yates. Hermetic philosophy is no longer seen as the key to Bruno's work by philosophical scholars and instead the Nolan is gradually being placed back within a more mainstream philosophical lineage. Whilst this may disappoint some who would hold to Yates' account as a key piece of evidence for a more prominent role for Hermetic thought, it promises a more rigorous and fascinating story of the birth of modern thought, formed as it was from both the heat of the new scientific thought and the passion of Renaissance religiosity.

The essays are inevitably surrounded by a large layer of scholarly apparatus, bringing with it a level of Latin and Italian that makes the work both rigorous as well as, at times, difficult to enter, particularly in terms of the references.

The bulk of the essays, however, are clearly written and do not presume too much of the reader, making it more than possible for those outside of Bruno scholarship to benefit from the historical research. At times the focus of the essays is on the minutiae of Bruno's work – such as the relations between Bruno and the printer in England who first published a number of his key essays – but they also range across issues which will have much broader interest, as in the comparison by Maurice Finocchario of the trials of Bruno and Galileo. Finocchario argues that Bruno was burnt as a philosopher who was unwilling to submit to what he saw as the essentially contingent power of the Inquisition rather than as the organiser of a magical Hermetic order or magician. He contrasts this with the relative ease with which Galileo was capable of coming to some sort of arrangement with the Church and perhaps most clearly amongst these essays paints Bruno as a Socratic figure literally willing to die for his principles. Whilst Finocchario's story is both fascinating and moving it also points to the essentially mytho-poetic status of a number of the pieces in the collection, in which the move to reassess Bruno as a philosopher rather than a Hermeticist underlies much of the impetus behind the research. There is clearly a scholarly dynamic at work here which, it must be said, is not hidden in any way but which itself may lead to over-determined readings of the life and death of Bruno. Whilst it may seem increasingly clear that Yates misread the work of Bruno in order to fit it into the Hermetic tradition it is not clear that Bruno fits any the more easily into the history of philosophy. There is still some work to be done to show the philosophical arguments and positions developed by Bruno and their relevance as anything other than a historical curiosity. The danger, albeit a limited one, is that the readings developed in this collection tend towards placing Bruno back within not a philosophical history but a theological one. The strangeness of Bruno's work to a modern philosopher cannot simply be accounted for by brief references to the holistic nature of the Renaissance scholar nor to the difference between modern philosophy and a practice that was still entwined with poetic and artistic production and there is a pressing need to establish more clearly what, if any, are the relations between the Hermetic tradition and the birth of modern philosophy.

Some of this philosophical work needed to reassess Bruno is contained in the essays by Mendoza, Schettino, Brown and Blum. Mendoza, for example, points to the radical monism at the heart of Bruno's work, with its implication of a materialist or immanent ontology that ran radically counter to the Church's spiritual transcendence. Schettino indicates, along with Brown, the way Bruno might be placed within a philosophical thread which stretches from Pythagoras, through Plato and Plotinus into the modern world and Blum points to the questioning of the role of philosophy that can be found – and found useful to the modern philosopher. In doing so it might be thought that the philosophers are bringing Bruno closer to the philosophy underlying the works of the Hermetic tradition even whilst the historians attempt to separate him from them. More important than any debate about the relations of Bruno to the Hermetic tradition, however, is the life and thought of Bruno himself and whether it is something worth studying and keeping alive. This collection is evidence that more than 400 years after the Church burnt him at the stake he is increasingly alive and provocative for a modern audience.

Matt Lee

Helen Parish and William G. Naphy (eds). *Religion and superstition in Reformation Europe.* **Manchester: Manchester University Press. 2002. 239 pages. ISBN 0719061571 (hardback). ISBN 071906158X (paperback). Paperback £14.99 Hardback £49.99**

This publication is a fine addition to MUP's impressive range of edited volumes. The book consists of nine essays grouped under two sections, 'Superstition, tradition and this world' and 'Superstition, tradition and the otherworld'. The contributions provide good geographical range, although more coverage of Protestant Scandinavia would have been welcome. The concept of 'superstition' is rarely tackled at length in studies of early modern religion, although most historians are now sensitive to its usage and context. The editors' introduction provides an excellent overview of the problems of defining superstition, the ways in which it has been employed in a derogatory sense at different periods, and how it became an important weapon in the conflict both between Catholicism and Protestantism and within each religion.

The first section focuses on aspects of religious devotion, identity and Reformation propaganda. Bridget Heal's contribution is an insightful examination of the fate of the cult of the Virgin in Protestant Nuremberg. For the reformers Marian devotion was superstitious and idolatrous. Some attempt was made to remove statutes and paintings of the Virgin but the city council was reluctant to act. While the reformers failed to suppress the Marian cult, Heal believes they eventually succeeded in downgrading her influence, steering the people towards more 'legitimate' forms of devotion. The tables are neatly turned in the following chapter, in which Jason K. Nye examines a German Catholic city's response to the spread of Protestantism. Nye discusses the ways in which the authorities in Rottweil sought to ward off the influence of the reformers by reinforcing the population's Catholic identity. Maria Craèiun's study of the impact of the Jesuits in Transylvania provides a useful addition to Graeme Murdock's recent book on Protestantism in the region, *Calvinism on the Frontier* (Oxford, 2000). The Jesuits are also the subject of Eric Nelson's contribution. He explores the negative myth-making surrounding the Jesuits generated by both Protestant and Catholic critics of the movement.

The essays in the second section will, perhaps, be of more direct interest to readers of this journal. The contributions by Ute Lotz-Heumann and Dale Johnson examine the role of religious prophecy, the former with regard to the Archbishop of Armagh James Ussher (1581-1656), and the latter with regard to the Scots Calvinist John Knox. As Lotz-Heumann explains, Ussher never claimed have a prophetic gift. It was his former chaplain and biographer, Nicholas Bernard, who created Ussher's posthumous reputation as a prophet. 'His' prophecies were reprinted several times for a popular audience during the second half of the seventeenth and early eighteenth century, whenever concern over a Catholic threat emerged. Unlike Ussher, Knox publicly declared that God had revealed to him 'secrets unknown to the world'. Johnson explains clearly how Knox accommodated his belief in his own prophetic communications with the view that only Scripture was the true word of God.

Astrology directly contravened both Protestant and Catholic doctrine, and was denounced as superstitious, but was nevertheless employed by both sides when it suited their purposes. Luc Racaut discusses its role in the propaganda battles during the French Wars of Religion, and how Catholics and Protestants accused each other of practising astrology while at the same time counting on the support of astrologers. P.G. Maxwell-Stuart's contribution builds upon the same theme by examining how both sides viewed the broader category of magic. He focuses on the demonological treatises written be two French pastors, François Perreaud and Lambert Daneau. Their views, argues Maxwell-Stuart, were essentially little different from those of their Catholic counterparts. The idea that the Protestant interpretation of magic was more rational is merely an aspect of later religious propaganda. The final chapter by Peter Marshall examines English Protestant explanations for ghosts. Theologians and preachers were quite clear that they could not be returning souls of the dead. As Marshall, points out though, there was less consensus about what they were other than papist falsehoods. Some considered them to be devils while others believed them to be the product of mental illness or over-active imaginations.

This absorbing collection of essays is required reading for students of the Reformation, and contains much of interest for those interested in attitudes towards magic in early modern Europe.

Owen Davies

A *Popular Dictionary of Paganism*, compiled by Joanne Pearson, RoutledgeCurzon, 2002, £15.99 ISBN 0700715916, 176 pages
Given the individualistic and iconoclastic nature of the 'average Pagan' (if 'average Pagan' is not too much of a contradiction in terms), one might have thought that Joanne Pearson was setting herself a quite Sisyphean task in setting out to compile *A Popular Dictionary of Paganism*. After all, the commonplace quip "ask two of us the same question and you'll get three different answers" or King Arthur Pendragon's claim that "we dance to our own tune, and we're all tone deaf" do not suggest that consistency or general agreement abound within the Pagan subculture.

However, nine times out of ten, Pearson succeeds splendidly in the endeavour she has undertaken, and her ability to crystallise and make lucid a complex, messy and multiple social reality is indicative of both experience in and insight into the world of Paganism. In these days in which neatly-classed phenomena are almost expected to overflow their supposed essential limits and definitive boundaries, it would seem churlish to quibble with the small minority of seemingly partial or debatable definitions supplied in the *Dictionary*. Likewise, it would seem unfair to explicitly pick out certain omissions, given the fact that no such reference book could claim to be totally comprehensive, or to point out certain anachronisms, for we know that groups come and go with a relatively high velocity in the structurally ephemeral realms of this particular subculture. Perhaps more serious would be the criticism that while some individuals on the Pagan 'scene' are mentioned in the *Dictionary*, the names of others whose contributions might seem no less significant do not appear, and there is moreover a lingering doubt in my mind as to whether commercial outlets ought to be mentioned at all in such a volume. That said, I have no doubt whatsoever that this book will prove an invaluable aid to both the relative newcomer to Paganism, and indeed to more experienced scholars. On the whole, the information supplied in the book more than withstands close scrutiny, and I have no doubt that *A Popular Dictionary of Paganism* will live up to its title and prove to be just that.

William Redwood

Wolfgang Behringer. *Witchcraft Persecutions in Bavaria: Popular Magic, Religious Zealotry and Reason of State in Early Modern Europe*. **Cambridge: Cambridge University Press. 2002. 476 pages. ISBN 0521525101 (paperback). £31**

The release of a paperback edition of Behringer's highly acclaimed book is good news for all of us who cannot afford academic hardback prices. *Witchcraft Persecutions in Bavaria* was first published in Germany back in 1987, and while in the years since German witchcraft historians have been very busy and numerous regional studies have appeared, Behringer's book remains one of the very few available in English. For this reason many readers may not fully appreciate how influential this book has been on German witchcraft studies, and rightly so. It is a meticulously researched regional study, which has important ramifications for understanding the dynamics of witch prosecutions in Europe more generally.

The book begins with a thoughtful consideration of witchcraft historiography and methodology, and then sets out on a chronologically survey of the witch trials in southeastern Germany, an area covering not just the old duchy of Bavaria but also present day parts of Central Franconia and the Upper Palatinate. Chapter 3 considers the first peak of prosecutions during the 1590s, the next chapter then examines the reasons for the comparative restraint of the early seventeenth century and why the trials peaked once again during the 1630s. Chapter 5 takes us through the relatively quiet period of the middle decades, the significant increase in executions during the 1670s and the slow decline in trials from then onwards.

One of the major strengths of *Witchcraft Persecutions in Bavaria* is the considerable attention Behringer gives to the eighteenth century. The last execution in the region was in Kempten in 1775, ninety years after the last witch was executed in England. Behringer's discussion and analysis of the drawn out religious and political debates regarding the crime of witchcraft, and the reasons for the continued prosecution and execution of witchcrafts during the mid-eighteenth century is a model of historical synthesis. Such a short review cannot do justice to such a *tour de force* of historical research and writing, but fortunately a wider readership can now afford to appreciate it. Finally, the translators J.C. Grayson and David Lederer must also be congratulated for doing such an excellent job.

Owen Davies

Witches, Druids and King Arthur by Ronald Hutton. Hambledon & London, 2003, pp. 365, ISBN: 1852853972, £25 in hardback, paperback to follow

It is hard to overestimate the influence that Ronald Hutton has had on contemporary Paganisms in the UK. His work, whilst scholarly and precise, is always illuminated by his sly sense of humour, and enlivened by minutiae and asides that never fail to capture the imagination of non-historians. Above all, Hutton is a great story-teller. Anyone familiar with Hutton's *oeuvre* might expect his new book to follow in the footsteps of its illustrious predecessors – for example, *The Pagan Religions of the Ancient British Isles, Stations of the Sun, The Triumph of the Moon* – 'thick' (in every sense of the word) chronological accounts of the history of Pagan folklore, ritual and practices. *Witches, Druids and King Arthur* is in some ways a departure for Hutton as it is a collection of essays clustered around the three themes of the title. So does this collection of Ronald's essays measure up to his more 'blockbusting' histories? The answer is undoubtedly 'yes'.

A power of Hutton's work has been its ability to question received wisdoms about the history of Pagan religions and rituals in Britain, not only changing the way that historians approach Paganisms, but also, perhaps more importantly, changing the direction that contemporary Pagan practices are taking. The structure of this book allows Hutton more of a free rein to pursue his passions without the strictures of assembling a more chronologically coherent history of Paganisms. Not that this book lacks coherence. The three sections are carefully chosen to reveal 'the interplay between fact and fiction in the making and analysis of history' (p. XI). However, Ronald is being modest when observing that this just is 'a perennial concern for historians' (*ibid.*), for the examples chosen are important ones for debates concerning notions such as the 'real', the 'inauthentic', and the 'hyperreal' across a whole range of social science and humanities disciplines. Hutton examines this notion of authenticity using three main heuristics – myth, Pagan history, and magic.

The first notional section encompassing 'myth' is divided into 3 chapters. The first is an essay entitled 'How Myths are Made'. In this chapter Hutton seeks to recover 'the meaning of the original Greek word *muthos*, which signified a story told to entertain or to play upon emotion rather than a logical discourse.' (p. 1). And entertain Hutton does as he touches upon, for example, the sociology of tradition, Celticity, the authenticity of oral history, and the witch hunt historiography during the course of this essay. Hutton's rationale is twofold: firstly, to argue for pluralism in historical research; and, secondly, to argue that history needs to be crafted in such a way to make it a mythic and transformative experience – something Hutton accomplishes here with ease. The second chapter examines the relationships between King Arthur and the Academy and shares some of the same concerns as the previous chapter. Indeed, reading though the rest of the book, one is tempted to ask, who is the 'real' Arthur – The legendary king, or his contemporary incarnation, the 'real life' druid and activist who has taken the name Arthur Uther Pendragon, and is living the myth on his own terms? (1). The final chapter of this section explores the mythic role that Glastonbury has played in the spiritual imagination. I saw the chapter as an important companion piece to the much more detailed exploration of the Glastonbury as myth and space in Adrian Ivakhiv's excellent book *Claiming Sacred Ground* (2). Like Ivakhiv, Hutton explores the complex intertwining of Christian, New Age, Pagan and esoteric discourses, which contribute to make the monuments of Glastonbury so enigmatic. Hutton rightly concludes by arguing that the power of Glastonbury is this enigma, citing that 'the intangible nature of its medieval and modern traditions, represent the greatest gifts which it makes to modern religion.' (p. 85)

The second notional section of the book retreads a more familiar Hutton terrain with its focus on the complex relationships between contemporary Pagan practices and ancient European paganisms. The first chapter 'The New Old Paganism' clarifies some of Ronald's earlier work by arguing that although many contemporary Paganisms have little in common with the polytheistic ancient paganisms, that Wicca, in particular, has more in common with the rites of the Greek magical papyri of Hellenised Egypt than other ancient traditions. Interestingly, despite the links that many academics have made between contemporary magical philosophies and Gnostic, Hermetic, and Neoplatonic thought, Hutton sees them as fundamentally opposed in the sense that these philosophies of late antiquity seek transcendence from the early realm to a spiritual one, Paganisms stress the immanence of spirit. The next chapter examines paganisms in late antiquity and after, stressing the ways in which Pagan deities (and associated traditions) were accommodated by, and in some ways survived, Christian belief. In particular Hutton argues that the survival of three main traditions have directly impacted upon contemporary Paganisms: Firstly, the notion of the divinity of the planets and the fact that their spiritual force could be harnessed by earthly magicians; secondly, that there exists a feminine form of the divine which mediates the power of the supreme deity; finally, that there is a system of hidden magical correspondences and spirits which may be used by magicians to harness divine power.

The final notional section of the book on 'magic' is arguably more diverse than the former two sections, but the essays are linked in that each takes a different approach to the general theme of re-enchantment. The first of these chapters – a revision of an article previously published in *The Pomegranate* in 2000 - comparatively examines ritual nudity, looking at key influences on 'skyclad' practices within Wicca. The next chapter examines the use of pagan images, symbols, and themes within the work of two influential fantasy writers – C.S. Lewis and J.R.R. Tolkien, both avowed Christians. Hutton argues that this tension between pagan and Christian motifs in their work contribute to their success. The third chapter examines the rise of contemporary Pagan Druidry in England, that is the land that lays the least claim of all the British Isles to having Celtic roots, taking in the rise of Goddess spirituality, The Loyal Arthurian Warband, and eco-Paganisms along the way. As such the chapter is a fine complement to, for example, Philip Carr-Gomm's *Druid Renaissance* (3). Finally, in perhaps the most important chapter for academics engaged in the nuts and bolts of empirical research, Hutton examines the problems and privileges of academic research into contemporary Paganisms, specifically Pagan witchcraft. Methodological issues pertaining to reactivity, reflexivity, auto-ethnography, and the insider/outsider debates are accessibly outlined. In particular, researchers into this area have to contend with the messy rationalist legacy left by the research of Tanya Luhrmann (4). Given this, Ronald details the ways in which academics – often Pagan practitioners themselves – have had to build bridges with Pagan communities as part of a dialogical research process, and, at the same time, have had to distance themselves from colonialist and orientalist assumptions about the nature of magical practices.

In many ways trying to review and précis a volume of collected essays is more difficult than reviewing a more monolithic work. Whilst some of this material is a reworking of earlier published papers, the cumulative power of these essays is undeniable: the whole is much more than the sum of the parts. The collection, like Hutton's other books, transcends the field of academic history and will be indispensable addition to the bookshelves of academics of contemporary magic and Paganisms, and practitioners alike.

Dave Green

Notes
1. For further explanation see www.warband.org/
2. Ivakhiv, A. (2001) *Claiming Sacred Ground.* Indiana: Indiana University Press.
3. Carr-Gomm, P. (ed.) (1996) *The Druid Renaissance.* London : HarperCollins.
4. Luhrmann, T. (1989) *Persuasions of the Witch's Craft.* Oxford: Blackwell.

Robert Poole (Ed.) *The Lancashire Witches: Histories and Stories,* **Manchester University Press, 2002, ISBN 0-7190-6204-7, 226 pages, paperback, £14.99**

This impressive volume was inspired by, and for the most part derives from, papers delivered at a conference held in Lancaster in 1999, with some additional materials and papers and a wealth of introductory and clarifying comment, but although some of the research is thus now a few years old it is far from dated or irrelevant. It presents eleven articles on a dizzingly broad spectrum of approaches to the academic study of witchcraft, written by those who already are, or certainly will be soon, highly regarded and influential scholars in the field. The initial thrust of the book is to provide a multidisciplinary coverage of the historical witch trials in the area in the 1600s, but it is far from a book limited to one time-slice and of interest only to those researching his particular locale. Instead the events are examined in contexts ranging across sociology, politics, economics, religion, psychology, gender issues, the theatrical depiction of witchcraft and many more- all areas that are relevant to the witch craze anywhere. It is unfair to select only some articles from such a high-quality collection, but James Sharpe provides a broad-brush introductory perspective on the witch trials in general, and current academic attitudes and methods with which they are approached- that allows the reader to engage even more so with the particular records examined herein, and would be a useful primer before opening *any* book on this subject. Marion Gibson's essay continues her most valuable and compelling analyses of the opinions expressed in witch trial pamphlets, often the 'gutter tabloid press' of the day (see her *Reading Witchcraft* and *Early Modern Witches* for more of this excellent and diligent research), the piece on sexual and spiritual roles of women by Alison Findlay is very thought-provoking and a well-crafted postscript article is provided by Joanne Pearson, whose insightful overview of modern Lancashire Wiccans (and local fundamentalists) and their varying attitudes to, and willingness to engage with, the local history will be of relevance to anyone researching modern paganisms, and, equally, to those practising them. A splendid detailed bibliography and extensive endnotes to the papers add to the usefulness of this work to those wishing to pursue further studies. In a similar way to *Witchcraft in Early Modern Scotland* by Roberts and Normand (see review in JSM 1) this book will be of multiple use to various researchers- a vital source for this County's historians certainly, but of thematic and methodological import to anyone working with witchcraft history, and written in a scholarly but far from dull tone that will engage all readers with an interest in this field. Another high quality title from MUP, and to be warmly recommended.

Dave Evans

Jason Semmens, *The Witch of the West: Or, The Strange and Wonderful History of Thomasine Blight*. Plymouth: privately printed. 2004. 52 pages, £3.99 UK plus £1 post and packing. ISBN 0-9546839-0-0 Paperback. Available from the author at www.cornishconjuror.com Please enquire there for shipping costs if ordering from outside the UK.

There are few well-researched, biographical accounts of cunning-folk, partly because of the paucity of sources and partly because of the lack of serious scholarly interest. Semmens' history of the famed nineteenth-century cunning-woman Thomasine Blight is, therefore, most welcome. This small book is fluently written and presented in an attractive style for the local interest market, but the content is the result of impressively meticulous research and is referenced to academic standards. Using the censuses, parish records and folklore sources Semmens pieces together Blight's life from her birth at Gwennap in 1793, through her two marriages - the second to the notorious cunning-man James Thomas, to her death at Helston in 1856. On the way he provides accounts of her and Thomas's magical activities including the embarrassing events of 1850/51 when Thomas fled from Cornwall after a couple complained to their local magistrate about his highly unusual suggestion for countering witchcraft. Thomas said he could cure the wife by sleeping with her husband. His marriage to Blight was another casualty of the scandal. *The Witch of the West* is well worth the price and will be of great interest to anyone interested in cunning-folk and the folklore of Cornwall.

Owen Davies

Alison Rowlands. *Witchcraft narratives in Germany: Rothenburg, 1561-1652*. Manchester: Manchester University Press. 2003. 239 pages. ISBN 0719052599 Hardback £45.

This book has been long awaited by historians interested in the German witch persecutions. German scholars are currently amongst the most active researchers on the early modern witch-trials, but few of the published results of their impressive output are available in the English language. Therefore any new contributions in English are welcome, doubly so when they provide such fascinating and thoughtful insights as Rowlands' work.

Germany is sometimes, and with reason, called the heartland of the witch-hunts. It is where the majority of the worst 'panics' and largest mass prosecutions took place. Towns such as Ellwangen tried and executed some 260 accused witches in 1611-12 alone. But Germany was not one political and legal entity. It was made up of hundreds of self-governing states, principalities and free cities under the broad umbrella of the Holy Roman Empire and its laws, as embodied in the Carolina Code. Consequently it is misleading to generalise about the German 'experience' of witch-hunts. It is becoming increasingly clear how uneven patterns of prosecution were between the myriad different states. Rowlands' book makes an important contribution to this process of reversing the usual focus of witchcraft research by examining why witch-hunts *failed* to occur, despite widespread popular fears.

Her study concerns the Lutheran imperial city of Rothenburg, a middle-sized town situated on the banks of the Tauber, in an area now encompassed by the state of Bavaria. In the early modern period its imperial status allowed this middle-sized town to govern its own affairs, and as Rowland makes clear the lack of serious witch-hunts there can largely be explained by the social, religious and political make-up of the ruling city council. Rowlands bases her findings on the thirty or so trials that she found in the voluminous town archives for the period 1549-1709. Such a low rate of prosecution was partly due to the council's sparing sanction of torture. In Rothenburg, legal procedure was adhered to with a scrupulousness not mirrored in some neighbouring states. Successive councils were also guided by the recognition that large-scale witch-hunts might have a potentially deleterious effect on the economy and social stability of a town the size of Rothenburg and its rural hinterland. The brake on witch-hunting was not entirely controlled from above. It would seem from Rowland's research that the general populous were also cautious about making witchcraft allegations. This, she believes, was in part due to the strong emphasis communities placed on the value of social harmony and individual honour, and in part a popular recognition that the local authorities were reluctant witch-hunters and tough on slanderous accusations.

Rowland's book is not only concerned with the important question of the pattern of prosecution. As the title indicates, it also provides a valuable textual reading of the detailed trial depositions and confessions in the Rothenburg archives. These are revealing about gender relations both between women and between men and women, and domestic and neighbourly tensions surrounding domestic authority and social space. Issues regarding the role of children in witchcraft accusations, which have been the subject of increased scholarly attention recently, are also well illustrated and thoughtfully analysed in chapter three concerning the story of a flight to a witches' gathering, as told by a six-year-old boy named Hans Gackstatt. His attention-seeking tale-telling ultimately led to the torture of both himself and his mother, though they were both eventually released. Rowlands sensitive reading of such cases adds to our understanding of the complex interaction of social relations, personal motivations, and collective and individual fantasies that shaped the content and expression of witchcraft accusations. One hopes the publishers will see fit to publish a paperback version so that readers beyond academia can appreciate this excellent study.

Owen Davies

***British Folk-Tales and Legends**: a Sampler*. **By Katharine Briggs. London: Routledge, 2002 (original edition, 1977). Pp. 373. ISBN 0-415-28602-6 Paperback edition £9.99 UK, $14.95 USA, $22.95 Canada.**

One of the most important contributions of the eminent, late folklorist Katharine Briggs (1898-1980) was the massive two-volume *Dictionary of British Folk-Tales* (1970-71), a collection of folk narrative materials from all regions of the British Isles. I remember poring over these tomes (2558 pages in all) in the library as an undergraduate, my head swimming with details of fairy and witch lore, magical cats and devil dogs, furiously taking notes and wishing there were some way I could capture the best of these stories for future reference. Now there is. Before her death, Briggs published a collection of narratives culled from the *Dictionary*, and Routledge has now re-issued it in its paperback "Classics" series.

British Folk-Tales and Legends: a Sampler contains one hundred and seventy-four of the folk narratives that first appeared in Briggs's *Dictionary*. They run the gamut of genres from animal tales and classic Märchen, to a rich collection of legends on everything from ghosts to witches and fairies, to exquisitely local historical traditions. Briggs has organized them according to Stith Thompson's categories in *The Types of the Folktale* (Helsinki: Academia Scientiarum Fennica, 1961), divided into eighteen separate sections, from "Fables and Exempla" (Part 1) to "Miscellaneous legends" (Part 18). Readers can easily find the sections that most interest them by looking them up in the Table of Contents. Here, they will find old favorites such as "Mr. Fox" (Reynardine), "Tom Tit Tot," "Cap o' Rushes," "The Green Children," "The Midwife," and "Dando and his Dogs," as well as less well-known local material and even some examples of what are popularly called urban legends, such as "The Stolen Corpse." As in the *Dictionary*, the stories are collected from a variety of sources: some field and archival collections, and some literary. Briggs gives the source after every text, and this edition has preserved the notes original to the *Dictionary* as well. Some material is cross-referenced within the text, and readers can also find references to tales in the *Dictionary* that did not make it into this anthology.

Of greatest interest to scholars of magical traditions are the bountiful sections on legends. From bogies and black dogs to devils and witches, the British corpus has always been especially rich in supernatural lore; but readers interested in folk magic should not confine themselves to the likely-looking sections. Genre is, after all, an invention of folklorists, and only approximate; moreover, motifs migrate easily from one genre to another. Thus stories in the "Fairy" section sometimes contain material about witches, and vice versa; and a prose text based on the ballad "Alison Gross," "the ugliest witch in the north country," appears, oddly enough, in the section on Märchen. Altogether these legends and Märchen preserve a range of British vernacular discourses on magic from about the 16th to the mid-20th centuries.

An introduction dating from the 1977 edition presents a sketch of contemporary folklore studies, including the range of subjects investigated by folklorists, issues of authenticity in folkloristics, and the categorization of narrative material into different genres. Readers should bear in mind that this section has not been updated, and those who wish to know more about folkloristic approaches in the 21st century need look elsewhere for enlightenment. Other shortcomings include the lack of bibliography and index, and the fact that for some reason Briggs gives motif numbers for only some of the material in the notes. Still, this is a delightful collection, and presents a feast of folklore for the reader in much more manageable form than the cumbersome *Dictionary*. It is indeed a classic.

Sabina Magliocco

Kathryn A Edwards (ed.). ***Werewolves, Witches, and Wandering Spirits: Traditional Belief & Folklore in Early Modern Europe.***

Kirksville: Truman State University Press. 2002. 226 pages. ISBN 1931112088 Paperback £22

This book is a real pleasure to read. It consists of ten essays covering a wide range of topics including ghosts, shape-shifting, possession, the Devil, magical treasure-hunters and diviners, as well as the werewolves and witches of the book's title. The editor provides a skilful introduction that helps contextualise and draw out the common themes emerging from such a diverse range of essays. As with most such collections on the cultures of 'early modern Europe', there is a significant bias towards certain countries and regions. Four of the essays concern France and two concern German lands. There is one essay a piece covering Spain and Italy, but no contributions from Scandinavia. This is not really a criticism, but it does highlight the difficulties of putting together collections of essays fully representative of European traditions and cultures.

The book begins with Robin Briggs' 'Shapeshifting, Apparitions, and Fantasy in Lorraine Witchcraft Trials'. This builds upon his detailed and insightful reading of the rich trial depositions from the Lorraine region of eastern France, on which he has published widely, most notably in his book *Witches & Neighbours* (1996). In this essay he approaches the material from a psychological perspective, applying the concepts of narcissism and emotional repression as a means of understanding people's fantasies and experiences of supernatural assault. The book ends quite neatly by returning to the psychological dimension, with Eric Midelfort's useful study of the development of psychiatric interpretations of demonic assault and possession during the late nineteenth and early twentieth centuries, particularly in the work of Jean-Martin Charcot and Sigmund Freud. Another of the contributors, Sarah Ferber, has also written on this subject, but here she concentrates on the tensions generated between laity and clergy in the contested world of exorcism in Catholic France. Ferber considers, in particular, the way in which theologians applied the term 'vulgar' as a means of demarcating sacramental boundaries of belief and devotion relating to possession. Dean Phillip Bell also deals with the way in which magic was an important component of broader tensions within communities. His subtle study of Jewish society in early modern Germany focuses as much on how

Jewish communities used tales of magic within their culture as on how Jews were victims of Christian fears of a satanic fifth column.

Several contributors consider the learned conceptions of the Devil and his realm. Sara T. Nalle examines the intriguing story of El Encubierto, a messianic, charismatic mystic who briefly rose to prominence in 1522 during a period of general unrest in the kingdom of Valencia. In Bruce Gordon's paper we switch to the intellectual world of sixteenth century Protestant Zurich and the writings of the head of the Zurich church Heinrich Bullinger and his contemporary the medical doctor and dramatist Jacob Ruef. Gordon takes us through Bullinger's views on ghosts (he believed they existed but forbade communications with them), fortune-tellers (they did the Devil's work by sowing discord in communities), and witches and cunning-folk (both were equally guilty of diabolic conspiracy). Ruef, like many medical men at the time, was fascinated by the sexual activities of incubi and succubi. In his book on childbirth and pregnancy he laid forth the case that although the Devil certainly had intercourse with humans no offspring had ever been produced. One example of such satanic copulation is recounted in the beginning of Anne Jacobson Schutte's essay. In 1594, a sixty-year-old healer named Gostanza da Libbiano confessed to the Inquisition under torture that she had participated in enjoyable orgies with the Devil. She later retracted her confession and was subsequently released. This case forms the backdrop to Schutte's main discussion concerning the Inquisition's investigation into the alleged diabolic relations of a Tuscan nun during the early 1720s. The eventual fate of the accused woman, Maria Fabri, is unknown but Schutte provides an instructive account of the motivations of both Fabri and her persecutors.

Nicole Jacques-Lefèvre's contribution tackles the subject of the werewolf, but instead of looking at the trial material she concentrates on the intellectual conception of lycanthropy. She looks at the subject from a literary and philosophical perspective, which makes for some hard reading, but the effort is worth it, as she constructs an insightful argument regarding the symbolism of the werewolf figure. In his discussion of apparitions in early modern Bavaria, David Lederer reminds us that it was not just witches and werewolves that were causing concern at the time. There was a general feeling that there were more ghosts around, particularly during the seventeenth century. Some of this anxiety may have been due to the impact of the Thirty Years' War, but it was also tied in with the problem of suicides and their troubled spirits. A third area of concern related to the magical invocation of ghosts by treasure-seekers. Such people, along with cunning-folk and other types of diviners, were also a cause of serious concern to the Paris police during the late seventeenth and early eighteenth centuries. Based on 300 practitioners named in police reports between 1700 and 1760, Ulrike Krampl's contribution provides a thoughtful consideration not so much of the diviners themselves but on the way in which such people were increasingly being labelled and treated as swindlers and 'false witches' rather than as the diabolic figures conceived by Bullinger.

Owen Davies

Abusch, Tzvi: *Mesopotamian Witchcraft: Toward a History and Understanding of Babylonian Witchcraft Beliefs and Literature.* **Ancient Magic and Divination V, General editors** Idem **and Ann K. Guinan. Leiden: Brill·Styx. 2002. xvi, 314 pages, Hardback. ISBN 90 04 1287 3   EUR 81 US$ 101**

This volume collects Abusch's important articles on Mesopotamian witchcraft.[1] The individual papers have been reprinted in general without alteration (except for the insertion of internal references), but are presented in a thematic order, along with a comprehensive bibliography, list of abbreviations, and indices of Akkadian and Sumerian words, gods and demons, and passages. The chapters are arranged into three parts: (1-5) a description of Mesopotamian witchcraft per se, (6-10) a characterization of the Mesopotamian exorcistic (anti-witchcraft) series Maqlû, and (10-13) a positioning of Maqlû within Mesopotamian intellectual and religious life. The fourteenth chapter gives a summary overview.

Despite much material that will interest specialists in the cuneiform languages (esp. chs. 7-9), Abusch is conscientious in presenting his arguments with sufficient clarity to make them generally accessible. I suspect the readers of this journal will be most interested in what Abusch's specific researches contribute to a general understanding of magic, and how he uses theoretical formulation of the nature of magic developed by scholars in other fields, and so will concentrate on this aspects of his work here.

The series Maqlû is a bilingual text (Akkadian with some Sumerian, already in the first millenium BC a scholarly language) of nine tablets, governing a ritual performed annually by a priestly exorcist (âðipû) to protect the king from any curses of any witch (kaððâpu). The canonical form of the series dates from the Neo-Assyrian period (early to mid-first millennium BC), but derives from much older tradition. Developed for the king, it is clear exorcists would perform this rite also for private clients, and that even poor private individuals used some form of it to protect themselves from witchcraft (8). Maqlû constitutes for Abusch a system of priestly magic which is used in distinction to witchcraft. In this formulation Abusch follows the scheme of the anthropologist Mischa Titiev,[2] which runs in Abusch's paraphrase: "religious rites are calendrical and communal, whereas magical rites deal with emergencies and often treat the crises of an individual" (3), rejecting the old Frazerian dichotomy between religion and magic. While this terminology nicely deals with Akkadian terms, it fails to address the historical use of the term 'magic' in Greek and Latin as well as English as a polemical term in distinction to 'religion'; indeed it seems to make magic merely an operative part of religion, insofar as this 'magic' is carried out by the priests most central to Mesopotamian society. Because of these usages, care would have to be taken to employ the results of Abusch's work in any theoretical or comparative study.

Abusch finds in Maqlû two conceptions of witchcraft: a standard or popular view according to which priests including exorcists themselves and other ritualists were believed to make curses (7-10), in other words human beings living in the community were believed to act as witches, as opposed to the scholarly elaborations of learned exorcists in whose view the witch was either a demonic agency, or at least a super-human sorcerer living in the uninhabited desert or mountains (10-63). Abusch sees this situation as parallel to the case of Medieval witchcraft, where peasant belief tended to attribute curses to marginal members of the community, while learned inquisitors created the myth of the Sabbath with its wild-hunt of demonic beings and inhuman witches (15).[3] Inasmuch as the exorcist in the Maqlû ritual takes on the form of a star and travels to the underworld and to heaven in the course of the rite (Abusch thinks this refers partly at least to a rite of incubation within Maqlû), Abusch is coming to believe that Maqlû developed from the same kind of archaic shamanistic practice that is now recognized as underlying the mythology of the Sabbath (285-86).[4]

The operative part of the ritual of Maqlû mainly consisted of making small images of the witches out of various materials and destroying them to render the witches powerless by magical analogy. This technique later became a mainstay of Greek cursing magic, only reinterpreted so that the curse was directed in that case not against witches, but by magicians against victims.[5] These cursing figurines (rather than 'voodoo dolls') are thus a very ancient part of Western magical tradition and have nothing to do with Afro-Caribbean religion beyond the usual phenomenon of projecting 'magic' onto alien cultures.

Abusch's work on Maqlû is indispensable for a historically grounded understanding of magic, not merely because it concerns some of the oldest magical tradition in the world, but because it deals with the first attempts of priestly scholars—the exorcists who created and used Maqlû—to come to terms with archaic and popular traditions of magic and witchcraft. Maqlû employed enduring paradigms of magic that are still widely recognized even in contemporary popular culture.

Bradley A. Skeen

Notes

1 1 Readers should also note Abusch's earlier monograph on the subject: Babylonian Witchcraft Literature: Case Studies Brown Judaic Studies 132 (Atlanta: Scholars Press, 1987). Both of these works are prolegomena to Abusch's promised new edition of Maqlû. The only prior edition (long since out-dated by new finds) is G. Meir, Die Assyrische Beschwörngssammlung Maqlû Archiv für Orientforschung, Beiheft 2 (Berlin, 1937).

2 M. Titiev, "A Fresh Approach to the Problem of Magic and Religion." In Reader in Comparative Religion: An Anthropological Approach, Second Edition, edited by W. Lessa and E. Vogt. New York, 1965.

3 Cf. R. Kiechhefer, European Witch Trials: Their Foundation in Popular and Learned Culture, 1300-1500 (Brussels, 1976).

4 Abusch cites on this: Carlo Ginzburg, Night Battles: Witchcraft & Agrarian Cults in the Sixteenth & Seventeenth Centuries trans. by John and Anne Tadeschi (Baltimore, 1983), as well as Ginzburg's copious later work on the same subject.

5 Christopher A. Faraone, "Binding and Burying the Forces of Evil: The Defensive Use of 'Voodoo Dolls' in Ancient Greece," Classical Antiquity 10 (1991): 165-220.

Obituaries

Tim Maroney, occultist and author, (1962 – 2003)
In July 2003 we were saddened to hear of the sudden passing at 41 of Tim Maroney. Tim was known as a passionate practitioner and theorist of Thelema, who was involved in print publishing and on many websites and online forums, often causing great arguments and heated debate in the forthright way in which he championed his beliefs. In person he was renowned in his home area of California as a great public speaker, wise, knowledgeable, humorous and informative. His early death is a great loss to the occult world; characters such as Tim are few and far between and he will be much missed. Ironically his last entry in his online journal mentioned how stressful his day job was becoming at that moment, and it seems that his famous 'big heart' gave out suddenly. Personally I survived a major attack by Tim for (what he saw as) 'my heresy' in a publication about Aleister Crowley a few years back, but since then we had patched up our differences and were engaged in useful and much more friendly conversation by email. He approved of the aims of this journal and was intending to submit an article; which we will sadly now never see.

Some of Tim's work from his website is preserved here: http://larabell.org/mirrors/maroney.org/

Dave Evans

Professor Gerald Hawkins
Gerald Hawkins, who died in May 2003 aged 75, if not known by name to many, will be known for his controversial scientific claims. The first 'orthodox' scientist to examine the Stonehenge ancient monument from the perspective of astronomy (a detailed study using early computers), his findings, published first in the prestigious journal *Nature*, and later, more fully in his book *Stonehenge Decoded* were remarkable, if hotly disputed. It is largely from Hawkins that 'stone circles as ancient observatories' has become a standard

topic of discussion (and argument) among generations of archaeologists, astronomers and pagans. Although his findings were often controversial and more 'grounded' researchers disputed his methods, his contribution to widening debate about the function of ancient sites has been priceless; he also did extensive work on the Nazca Lines in Peru, and developed some interesting mathematical models of crop circle geometry. It has been said about Carlos Castaneda that his books may be largely false, but his writings have induced many students to enrol in anthropology classes; the same may be true to some extent for Hawkins, whose fascinating writings, regardless of their accuracy may have increased the numbers of archaeology students; which seems be a fitting legacy.

Gerald Stanley Hawkins, Physicist and Archaeo-astronomer, April 20th 1928- May 26th 2003

Dave Evans

Professor Gerhard D. Wassermann (1919-2004)

Born in Leipzig, his family came to Britain in 1936. A Biologist and Philosopher, he graduated from Queen Mary College, University of London with first class Honours in Mathematics, and then obtained a Ph.D. in Quantum Mechanics from the University of London. After working for a while in Theoretical Acoustics (horn design) with Tannoy Products, he was invited by (the later) Nobel Laureate Sir Neville Mott to join his department at Bristol as Research Assistant to Prof. Herbert Fröhlich FRS.

In his career the author did research in Quantum Mechanics, Theoretical Optics, Theoretical Developmental Biology, Theory of Evolution. Biophilosophy, Philosophy of Science and Philosophy of Mind. He published many papers in prestigious journals (subject to peer review) and seven books. A Fellow of the Institute of Mathematics and its Applications and was elected in 1989 as a Fellow of the Institute of Biology and awarded a DSc from the University of London.

Professor Wasserman developed a major theory of paranormal phenomena which was published in the journal *Nature*, and later in book form as *Shadow Matter And Psychic Phenomena* and the sequel *Consciousness & Near Death Experiences.*

Mogg Morgan

Obituary-Postcript
Robert Lenkiewicz, 1941-2002
Further to the obituary printed in JSM1 we subsequently learned with great sadness that Robert's immense and important library of occult and other titles is likely to be broken up and sold off, due to post-mortem debt, and the remainder of the collection is not now likely to be made available to scholars for this reason. Many of his rare antiquarian magic, witch trial and alchemical titles were sold by auction at Sotheby's in London during the autumn of 2003.

Dave Evans

ALSO AVAILABLE ONLINE

Free TOC alerting service & Free online Sample Issue available - go to www.brill.nl/ejournals/Ejournals.html and select ARIES online version.

ARIES

Journal for the Study of Western Esotericism

EDITED BY ROLAND EDIGHOFFER (UNIVERSITY OF THE SORBONNE, PARIS), ANTOINE FAIVRE (ÉCOLE PRATIQUE DES HAUTES ÉTUDES, SORBONNE, PARIS) AND WOUTER J. HANEGRAAFF (UNIVERSITY OF AMSTERDAM)

VOLUME 3 (2003)
2 ISSUES PER YEAR
ISSN 1567-9896
LIST PRICE INSTITUTIONS EUR 80.- / US$ 93.-
LIST PRICE INDIVIDUALS EUR 42.- / US$ 46.-
PRICE INCLUDES ONLINE SUBSCRIPTION

Aries is the first professional academic journal specifically devoted to a long-neglected but now rapidly developing new domain of research in the humanities, usually referred to as "Western Esotericism". This field covers a variety of "alternative" currents in western religious history, including the so-called "hermetic philosophy" and related currents in the early modern period; alchemy, paracelsianism and rosicrucianism; christian kabbalah and its later developments; theosophical and illuminist currents; and various occultist and related developments during the 19th and 20th centuries, up to and including popular contemporary currents such as the New Age movement. *Aries* is a peer-reviewed journal publishing articles and book reviews in English, French, German and Italian.

Academic Publishers

www.brill.nl

♛ B R I L L

P.O. BOX 9000	TEL +31 (0)71 53 53 566	112, WATERSTREET	TEL 1-617-263-2323
2300 PA LEIDEN	FAX +31 (0)71 53 17 532	SUITE 601,	FAX 1-617-263-2324
THE NETHERLANDS	E-MAIL cs@brill.nl	BOSTON, MA 02109 USA	E-MAIL cs@brillusa.com

All prices are valid until 31 December 2003. Thereafter prices may be subject to change without prior notice. Prices do not include VAT (applicable only to residents of the Netherlands and residents of other EU member states without a VAT registration number). Prices do not inlcude shipping & handling except for journals where shipping and handling is included in the price (applicable to all customers worldwide). US dollar prices are valid only for customers in Canada, USA and Mexico. Please note that due to fluctuations in the exchange rate, the US dollar amounts charged to credit card holders may vary slightly from the prices advertised.

Mandrake

'Books you don't see everyday'

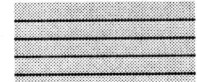

Jan Fries/Cauldron of the Gods: a Manual of Celtic Magick
552pp, Royal Octavo, 186992861x
£24.99/$40 uk pounds (includes postage)
172 illustrations, 230,000 words

S u r r e a l i s m & the Occult
by Nadia Choucha
£8.99/$14 paperback
ISBN 1869928164

Tankhem:Meditations on Seth magick
by Mogg Morgan
isbn 1869928555, 184pp, £10.99

History of Fun ('arouse & enlighten')
By Mary Hedger
ISBN 1869928636
£7.99/$14 paper

The Qabalah of 50 Gates
by Steven Ashe
1869928237 128pp, £10.99$15

Siddha Quest for Immortality
by Kamil V Zvelebil.
ISBN 1 869928 431. £13.99/$19.99

Hippalos: the conquest of the Indian Ocean by Kamil Zvelebil
272pp, 3 maps ISBN 1869928-415,
£9.99

Order direct from
Mandrake of Oxford
PO Box 250, Oxford, OX1 1AP (UK)
Phone: 01865 243671 for free catalogue
& credit card sales

Prices include economy postage
online at - www.mandrake.uk.net
Email: mandrake@mandrake.uk.net

The Journal for the Academic Study of Magic (JSM)

Issue 1
ISBN 1869928 679, ISSN 1479-0750
•23 /£13.99 /$25 (airmail) postpaid
Academic libraries & departments request proforma invoice

A multidisciplinary, peer-reviewed print publication, covering all areas of magic, witchcraft, paganism etc; all geographical regions and all historical periods.

Beyond Attribution: The Importance of Barrett's Magus/Alison Butler
Shadow over Philistia: A review of the Cult of Dagon/John C. Day
A History of Otherness: Tarot and Playing Cards from Early Modern Europe/Joyce Goggin
Opposites Attract: magical identity and social uncertainty/Dave Green
Memories of a sorcerer: notes on Gilles Deleuze-Felix Guattari, Austin Osman Spare and Anomalous Sorceries./Matt Lee
Le Streghe Son Tornate: The Reappearance of Streghe in Italian American Queer Writings/Ilaria Serra
Controlling Chance, Creating Chance: Magical Thinking in Religious Pilgrimage/Deana Weibel

Orders to: Mandrake, PO Box 250, Oxford, OX1 1AP (UK)
Tel +44 (01865) 243671
email Mandrake@mandrake.uk.net
secure online ordering:
www.mandrake.uk.net/books.htm

Advertisements

Information and Advertisements

Please refer to our website regularly for updated information, we intend to maintain a collection of useful links for researchers, covering resources, jobs, academic courses on magic, libraries, museums, special interest groups, publications, events, conferences, specialist book suppliers etc. A small selection appears below:

Advertisers for Issue 3: please contact Mandrake (address on back cover) for details, deadlines and rates.

**111 Magdalen Rd
Oxford OX4 1RQ
Tel 01865 245301
Fax 01865 245521**

**Thousands of titles
(new, secondhand & bargains)
search & orderable on our website**

mail@innerbookshop.com

www.innerbookshop.com

Open 10-5.45 - **Mon-Sat**

Books for mind, body and spirit

*Alchemy & Chaos Magick
to Wicca & Zoroastrianism*

Visit us (and the Magic Café next door) and see our **Noticeboards** for Oxford and National events or use our **Mail-Order Service** via telephone or fax as well

Printed in the United States
41255LVS00005B/1-24